FIGHTING TECHNIQUES
OF THE ANCIENT WORLD

3000 BC ~ 500 AD

EQUIPMENT, COMBAT SKILLS, AND TACTICS

FIGHTING TECHNIQUES
OF THE ANCIENT WORLD

3000 BC ~ 500 AD

EQUIPMENT, COMBAT SKILLS, AND TACTICS

SIMON ANGLIM   PHYLLIS G. JESTICE   ROB S. RICE   SCOTT M. RUSCH   JOHN SERRATI

THOMAS DUNNE BOOKS
ST. MARTIN'S PRESS ≋ NEW YORK

2200761

*Fighting Techniques of the Ancient World 3000 BC – AD 500:
Equipment, Combat Skills and Tactics*

Copyright © Amber Books Ltd 2002

THOMAS DUNNE BOOKS
An imprint of St. Martin's Press.

ISBN: 0-312-30932-5

First U.S. Edition June 2002

Editorial and design by
Amber Books Ltd
Bradley's Close
74–77 White Lion Street
London N1 9PF

Project editor: Charles Catton
Editor: Vanessa Unwin
Design: Floyd Sayers/Mark Batley
Picture Research: Lisa Wren

Printed in Singapore

10 9 8 7 6 5 4 3 2 1

CONTENTS

THE ROLE OF INFANTRY

Foot soldiers were the essential component of most ancient armies: the best known were the Hellenic phalanx and Roman legion, but others were just as important.

Infantry is the backbone of any army, being the one unit that can attack or defend equally effectively. The majority of battles have turned on the infantry's ability to close with the enemy and kill him (or force him to surrender) or to hold their position under attack.

The infantryman has two broad means of pursuing these ends, and from ancient times until the nineteenth century, most infantry units specialized in one of these – but not both – being trained, organized and armed accordingly. Method one is shock action, wherein attackers close aggressively with the enemy, smashing through weak spots or driving in flanks through mass, momentum and aggression. Shock troops tend to

THE MIGHT OF THE LEGIONS *is demonstrated here as these legionaries of Trajan's army throw their* pila *to parry a Dacian attack. The thin point of a* pilum *was designed to stick in an enemy shield and then bend. The legionary's opponent would either have to discard his shield or be hampered by the* pilum*'s weight.*

use concentrated formations, focusing maximum force against a narrow front. They will be armoured to protect them from defensive fire, and specialize in hand-to-hand fighting or short-range firepower; they will often be deeply indoctrinated – religiously or politically or with a code of manly conduct – maximizing their aggression and confidence. Method two is to shoot down the enemy with longer-ranged missile weapons; missile troops are usually lightly equipped and move in a looser formation than shock troops, using mobility to take up good shooting positions and to avoid counter-attacks by shock troops. They are often called 'skirmishers' and may have a secondary role as scouts and raiders.

Most armies contain both types of infantry. A combination of shock and missiles not only increases a commander's options, but also presents the enemy with a dilemma: if he masses his forces for shock action, he presents a concentrated missile target, but if he disperses

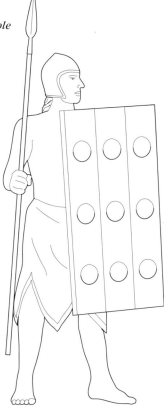

A SUMERIAN WARRIOR *armed with a bronze-headed spear and simple wooden shield made from planks. A bronze helmet was his only other protection.*

them to minimize damage from missiles, they become vulnerable to shock.

This chapter examines the evolution of both types of infantry between 3000 BC and AD 500. The most successful infantry armies of this period, the Greek and the Roman, centred on shock formations, and because this chapter examines infantry, it centres upon these two armies. However, they must be analyzed in the context of infantry forces throughout this entire period, and even they needed support from skirmish or missile troops, whose development must also be examined to understand fully the infantryman's role at this time.

Primitive Infantry

A tribe is a society tracing its origin back to a single ancestor, who may be a real person, a mythical hero or even a god: they usually view outsiders as dangerous and conflict against them as normal. This provides the crudest form of indoctrination for shock action: in tribes, all men are hunters and warriors, often going through rituals to mark their passage from boyhood, and a man's standing is established by closing with the enemy and killing him in large numbers. Warfare is often treated as a form of hunting, and the raid – for livestock or women or simply for the sake of fighting – is the commonest type of tribal warfare, although conquering or exterminating enemy tribes is not unknown. Tribal culture and the accompanying warrior ethic survived through Classical times to the present, playing a vital role in societies of this period – and not necessarily those designated as 'barbarians', as we shall see. However, from around 9000 BC onwards, with the coming of settled agricultural states, warfare metamorphosed, as disciplined, hierarchichal states raised disciplined, hierarchical armies. Moreover, the possession of permanent territories to defend or conquer brought the need for large-scale battle in which the losing army would be destroyed, the better to secure the disputed territory. The coming of 'civilization' therefore brought the need for organized bodies of shock troops.

The phalanx, a body of infantry fighting in close order with pikes or thrusting spears, is one

BRONZE ARMOUR *from the mid-second millennium BC. Found at Dendra, it almost certainly belonged to a Mycenean chieftain. The helmet was made from boars' tusks.*

of the oldest formations in warfare. The word is Greek, meaning 'roller', and the phalanx is associated closely with the armies of Classical Greece and Alexander the Great. However, phalanxes were used 2000 years before, in the armies of the city-states of southern Mesopotamia, established around 3000 BC.

The 'Vulture Stele' – named because it depicts bodies of the vanquished being eaten by vultures, a common motif of the time – records a victory of King Eannatum of Lagash between 2500 and 2400 BC. It depicts two types of infantry, the first clearly being a phalanx. We cannot see whether the troops in this phalanx are wearing armour because they are hidden behind large, oblong shields stretching from shoulder to ankle, but they wear bronze helmets covering the head down to the neck, with noseguards, similar to the

Corinthian style worn by Greek hoplites 2000 years later. Their shields overlap into a wall, and with spears couched underarm, they present a dense thicket of bronze spearpoints, suggesting a reliance on mass and forward momentum. The sound-box of a lyre from Ur, dating from around the same time, depicts phalanx troops wearing helmets similar to those on the Vulture Stele, as well as what appear to be ankle-length, leather cloaks reinforced with bronze studs. They also carry two-handed pikes, possibly foreshortened for artistic licence. The other type of infantry depicted on the Vulture Stele are unarmoured, except for helmets similar to the phalangites', and carry spears and round-bladed axes.

Most weapons were made of bronze, much of it of poor quality due to the rarity of its constituent tin in the Middle East. However, many of the weapons discovered by archaeologists are of silver or gold and buried with kings or nobles as a mark of status. These are possibly superior versions of standard battlefield weapons, which consisted of the spear, the axe and the dagger. Spears were clearly designed for thrusting at close quarters rather than throwing; early examples attach head to shaft with long or hooked tangs to ensure they stay in place when thrust into the body of an enemy or against a shield. Axes had rounded edges designed to shatter helmets and the skulls inside them. While elaborate ceremonial or ornamental daggers have been found, they were clearly intended as back-up weapons of last resort. Interestingly, in the light of the importance of fortification in Sumerian warfare, missile weapons are largely absent from both the archeological record and from contemporary illustration, although their use was not entirely unknown.

Chariots were used in Sumerian armies, but they do not appear to have been the main strike arm. It is likely that they were transport for commanders or for champions who dismounted to fight other champions or lead assaults. The ultimate expression of the warrior ethic, the champion was an important part of many armies in the earlier part of this period, often being mythologized to indoctrinate later generations. However, the phalanx depicted on the Stele and elsewhere must have played a key role in Sumerian warfare, perhaps forming the centre of the line, with light troops carrying spears and axes operating on the flanks. The phalanx was used possibly in a similar manner to its Macedonian counterpart, pinning the enemy centre while a charge by chariots or light troops settled matters on one or both flanks. Alternatively, the light-armed troops may have been phalangites re-arrayed in 'light order' for sieges or operations in rough country.

Egyptian Infantry

Old Kingdom Egypt (c. 2650–2150 BC) had a militia army based on a levy of adult males, which could number several tens of thousands, supplemented by mercenary tribal warriors from Nubia, to the south. A policy of fortifying the borders was sufficient to secure Egypt from her main threat – raids from tribal peoples of Libya and Nubia – although punitive expeditions into Nubia were sometimes launched. The Old Kingdom collapsed around 2150 BC, ravaged by natural disasters and civil wars until the rise of the Middle Kingdom (2050–1640 BC). The Middle Kingdom army was based on a levy of one adult male in a hundred, and was commanded by professional senior officers selected by the Pharaoh himself. One is recorded as 'the commander of the shock troops', implying the existence of a body of heavy infantry for shock action.

From 1720 BC onwards, Egypt was invaded by the Hyksos, a Semitic people entering across Sinai, who exploited political divisions within Egypt as well as their own technological superiority in order to subjugate Egypt by around 1674 BC. The Hyksos transformed Egyptian military culture by introducing the technology of the Middle East. Firstly, they taught the Egyptians how to build chariots fast and strong enough for decisive mobile action. Secondly, they showed them how to manufacture high-quality bronze weapons. Thirdly, they brought the composite bow. Previously, the

'Whoever wants to see his own people again must remember to be a brave soldier....Whoever wants to keep alive must aim at victory. It is the winners who do the killing and the losers who get killed.' – XENOPHON

Egyptians had used simple bows of wood or cane, with a range of around 100m (33ft). The composite bow was of Asiatic origin and consisted of a wooden core strengthened on the inside of the curve with glued-on strips of horn and on the outside with sinew; it would be recurved, or bent backwards, before stringing, resulting in a bow requiring considerable strength to draw, but capable of delivering a mighty blow out to 200m (656ft), particularly with the new bronze arrowheads, which improved both accuracy and stopping power. Later models would almost triple this range and be capable of penetrating metal armour at 200m (656ft). Armed with the composite bow, armies of the ancient Near East relied increasingly on massed archery, although shock remained important.

The army of the New Kingdom (1565–1085 BC) combined Egyptian organization with Hyksos technology and a new doctrine based on aggressive manoeuvre. At its core was a professional force motivated by promises of booty, slaves and land, which developed into a distinct 'military caste' as sons followed fathers into the army. In time of national emergency, this was supplemented by a levy, at first of 1 man in 100 (as under the Middle Kingdom), but expanding to 1 in 10 by the time of the invasion of the Sea Peoples in 1200 BC. This was not a tribal society, but a semi-urbanized one in which not every man was a warrior. Consequently, soldiers underwent basic training before being allowed near the enemy. One drawing depicts archers undergoing range practice supervised by what are, apparently, specialist instructors.

Unfortunately, the two battle accounts available, of Megiddo (1482 BC) and Kadesh (1300 BC), are more concerned to extol the genius of the Pharaohs concerned, Thutmosis III and Rameses II respectively, than with describing the fighting. However, there is much pictorial and documentary evidence for how the infantry of New Kingdom armies fought. Egyptian regular infantry were organized into companies of 250, subdivided into 'platoons' of 50, and divided into 2 broad types: archers, who by the time of Kadesh were equipped entirely with the composite bow, and the *Nakhtu-aa* (shock troops). Throughout this period, archers usually wore just loincloths or kilts and so were, apparently, not intended to close with the enemy. The equipment of the *Nakhtu-aa*, however, underwent a degree of evolution. A relief from the time of Queen Hatshepsut (1503–1482 BC) shows troops carrying broad-headed spears and short axes with small bronze heads, and short, round-topped wooden shields. From 1500 BC, armour was worn – usually stiffened cloth wrapped around the torso but also including leather or bronze helmets – and some troops were carrying short stabbing spears not unlike the Zulu *iklwa*. By Kadesh, *Nakhtu-aa* wore cloth armour as standard and carried shields which, while having the same round-topped design as before, were large enough to be formed into a phalanx-like shield wall. The bronze hand-axe had given way to the *khopesh*, a one-handed bronze chopper with a highly curved edge but no point – not quite a sword, not quite an axe – while some carried two-handed mace-axes combining a heavy rounded head with a semicircular blade.

Infantry tactics were built around mass bowshot, which could prove decisive, given the power and accuracy of the composite bow, the degree of training of Egyptian archers, and the rarity of effective armour at this time. Archers were evidently deployed in lines and trained to shoot in

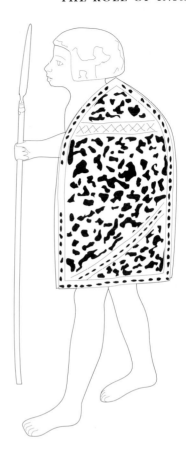

AN EGYPTIAN MODEL SOLDIER *dating from around 2000 BC, which formed part of a 'private army' found in Prince Emsah's grave at Asyut. Note the lack of armour, and the simple hide-covered wooden shield.*

volleys, supporting an advance by chariots or the *Nakhtu-aa*, who would throw spears before closing with the *khopesh* or axes against an enemy line disrupted by the barrage of missiles.

Egyptian infantry also included mercenaries. The Medjay were Nubian tribesmen used in the early part of the New Kingdom as skirmishers; they carried simple wooden stave bows and were held in such regard that they later guarded the tombs of the Pharaohs in the Valley of the Kings. From around 1200 BC, the Middle East was invaded by several waves of 'Sea Peoples', Indo-European tribal peoples originating from Asia Minor and the Aegean. Of these, the best-known were the Philistines, who settled in Canaan along the Palestinian coast. The Sea Peoples began to

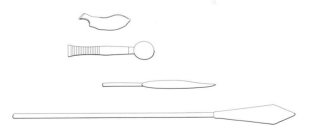

AN ASSORTMENT OF EGYPTIAN WEAPONRY, *from the top down, a knife; a club or mace made from stone and wood; a sword; and a spear. All the blades were made from copper or bronze.*

penetrate Egyptian society several generations before the main invasion, as traders, settlers and mercenaries: Rameses II had a bodyguard from the Sherden tribe at Kadesh. The Sherden were history's first specialist sword-fighters, the metal sword originating as a distinctly Indo-European weapon. Contemporary illustration shows Sherden and Philistines wearing bronze corselets and bronze helmets, horned for the Sherden, with wrap-around feather crests for the Philistines; both are depicted holding round shields, around 1m (3ft) across, by a single hand-strap, making them handier than Egyptian shields for the violent footwork of sword-fighting. Their main weapon is a slashing sword, around 1m (3ft) long, with a tapered point; the hilt and blade appear to be a single casting, as with bronze knives of the time now displayed in the British Museum. Swords were probably also of bronze initially, but from 1200 BC onwards, there was increasing use of iron, a new metal providing a superior cutting edge. Our knowledge of the Philistine champion, Goliath of Gath, indicates that single combat between champions formed an important part of Sea People warfare.

Men of Iron: the Assyrians

While historians tend to shy away from analogies, it is tempting to see the Assyrian Empire, which dominated the Middle East from 900–612 BC, as a historical forebear of Nazi Germany: an aggressive, murderously vindictive regime supported by a magnificent and successful war machine. As with the German army of World War II, the Assyrian army was the most technologically and doctrinally advanced of its day and was a model for others for generations afterwards.

The Assyrians were the first to make extensive use of iron weaponry. Unlike the tin necessary for smelting bronze, iron is common in the Middle East, so not only were iron weapons superior to bronze, but could be mass-produced, allowing the equipping of very large armies indeed. The Assyrian King, Shalmaneser III, marched into Syria in 845 BC with an army of 120,000; the Egyptians had armies of 20,000 each at Megiddo and Kadesh. The Assyrians needed large armies because they were in an almost constant state of war, conquering the

A STATUE OF TUTENKHAMUN *found in his tomb showing the Pharaoh ready for battle, his spear raised to strike down his enemies.*

largest empire yet seen in history and using coercion – and sometimes outright terror – to keep it in line. Contemporary accounts dwell less upon the military details of campaigns than upon gleeful descriptions of the skinning alive of captured enemy leaders and the extermination or forced deportation of their subjects; illustrations depict thickets of impaled bodies decorating the ramparts of fallen cities and Assyrian soldiers saluting their king with the heads of their enemies. The Assyrian heartland was the fertile territory of northern Iraq, and their conquests began around 1100 BC, when tribal conflicts escalated against Aramean raiders to the west. It was under King Ashurnasipal II (883–859 BC) that Assyria began to follow a coherent strategy, conquering Syria and the Levant and reaching the Mediterranean in 877 BC.

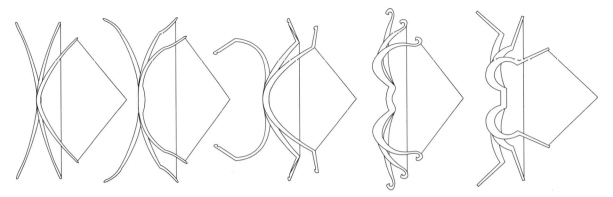

Ashurnasipal's son, Shalmaneser II, was at war for 31 of his 35 years on the throne, culminating in the largest field battle fought by the Assyrian army, against a Syrian-led coalition at Karkar in 853 BC. There are frustratingly few records of this, but we do know that it was a costly victory which saw the Assyrians temporarily abandon attempts to subjugate Syria.

DIFFERENT ANCIENT BOWS, *from the simplest on the left to the most advanced composite on the right. The diagram shows the bows in three positions: before stringing, at rest when strung, and when fully drawn, ready to release an arrow.*

The Assyrian Army of this expansionist phase was a combined arms force comprising a strike arm of chariots and a large cavalry force, but its backbone was its infantry . The army was manned through a form of part-time conscription, with Assyrian peasants called up during the summer months but released for the harvest so as not to disrupt the agricultural timetable. We are fortunate that the Assyrians left many realistic illustrations of their army in action and, unlike the Egyptians, depicted all arms and all ranks! The Balawat Gates come from one of the palaces of Shalmaneser II, and their 16 bronze reinforcing strips are now displayed in the British Museum. Each strip depicts events from a single campaign, one of them perhaps showing action from Karkar, with archers supporting a chariot attack, shooting from behind small oblong shields held by spearmen. Both troop types wear the distinctive Assyrian conical helmet and sleeveless, ankle-length hauberks – apparently of leather with vertical bronze strips sewn on, a style confirmed by archeological finds. Massed archers are also shown barraging walled towns. The Gates provide early evidence for the practice of accompanying each archer with a shieldbearer, mainly to protect him from enemy missiles.

A PERSIAN ARCHER AND SPEARMAN *drawn from a contemporary carving. The spearman's shield is substantial, and provides good protection for much of his torso. Both figures have short swords.*

Decline and Revival
Shalmaneser's succession by a line of weak kings saw Assyria suffer an 80-year decline, culminating

in vassaldom to their hated rival, Babylon. Assyria then underwent a revival under Tiglath Pileser III (745–727 BC). He carried out extensive reforms of the army, reasserted central control over the empire, reconquered the Mediterranean seaboard, and even subjugated Babylon. Under Sargon II and his descendants (721–627 BC), the empire reached its greatest extent: Sennacherib conquered the Philistines and besieged Jerusalem – unsuccessfully – in 701 BC, then in 693 BC flattened Babylon in reprisal for a rebellion. However, by the reign of Ashurbanipal (668–627 BC), Assyria was

severely overstretched. The northern borders were under constant threat from the Kingdom of the Medes and a nomadic steppe people, the Scythians, while the eastern frontiers were pressured by a revived Babylon. In 615 BC, the Medes invaded and ravaged Assyria, and in 612 BC a combined Medean and Babylonian army sacked the Assyrian capital, Nineveh, bringing the empire to an end.

Tiglath Pileser III replaced conscription with a manpower levy imposed on each province, and also demanded contingents from vassal states. Illustrations from Tiglath Pileser's time indicate that the archer-shieldbearer pairing was retained, but now shields were often replaced by tall, portable reed screens, covered with metal or oiled skins, and curved at the top to protect the pair from plunging shot. It may be that shields were carried in field battle while screens were used for assaults on fortified positions. Different formations were used by 700 BC. The British Museum displays sculpted panels from Nineveh from between 700 and 692 BC, depicting scenes from the campaigns of Sennacherib: one shows the assault on the Jewish city of Lachish in 701 BC. In front is a phalanx-like formation of shock troops, six to seven ranks deep, carrying circular shields and 2m (6ft) long thrusting spears, used overhand. They wear a shortened version of the scaled hauberk and a new style of helmet with a forward-sloping horsehair crest – they may be from the *Kisir Sharruti* (Royal Guard). Behind them come between six and seven ranks of archers, some unarmoured, some wearing armour similar to their ancestors' on the Balawat Gates, and behind these are three ranks of armoured slingers. The missile power supporting the shock troops is formidable; archaeological evidence shows that the Assyrian composite bow shot iron-headed arrows, made in state workshops, to a possible range of 650m (2132ft), while slingers used pointed bullets with a possible range of 100m (33ft) and capable of inflicting serious wounds through armour. It may be that the slingers are 'sniping' at individual targets on the battlements, while the archers are laying down a more general barrage supporting the assault troops. Each troop type seems to form a separate unit or sub-unit. Yet another screen from

AN ASSYRIAN ARCHER *prepares to shoot his bow. He carries a sword for self defence, but Assyrian archers were often accompanied by dedicated shield bearers, who protected them from the enemy's arrows.*

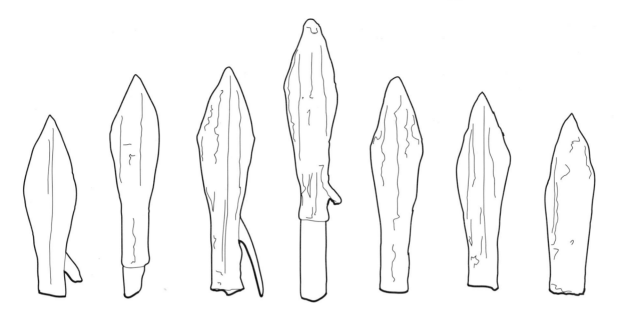

SCYTHIAN ARROWHEADS *from a 4th-century BC grave near Kiev in the Ukraine. The arrowheads were all made from bronze. Three have a long single barb to prevent their easy removal from a victim's body.*

the same site and period depicts troops guarding slaves in a mine, and they are clearly paired into archers and spearmen, while another shows an archer shooting from behind a screen as in Tiglath Pileser III's time – although these may be historical or schematic illustrations. Another panel, dated from around 620 BC, less than a decade before the end of the empire, again shows archers and spearmen forming separately. Regardless of formation, Assyrian infantry were equally capable of siege, field-battle and counter-guerilla operations, and were clearly trained to cooperate with other infantry types and other arms.

Rise of the Persians
In 550 BC, the Persian prince Cyrus overthrew the last King of the Medes and launched a series of campaigns to conquer Babylon and Anatolia. Cyrus' successors added Egypt, northern India and a section of south-eastern Europe. The Persian army of this period was based on levies of each *satrapy* (province) of the empire, and was enormous even by the standards of 2000 years later. The Greek historian Herodotus of

Halicarnassus, who is admittedly a source given to hyperbole, estimated the Great King Xerxes' army in 480 BC at 2.4 million, including 1.7 million infantry. The Roman historian, Arrian, estimated that Alexander faced a Persian army of 600,000 at Issos (333 BC), and one comprising a million

A SCYTHIAN ARCHER *from the 6th or 5th century BC. His* gorytos, *a combined bowcase and quiver, hangs behind his left thigh. He carries a composite bow.*

infantry alone at Gaugamela (331 BC); another Roman historian, Quintus Curtius Rufus, estimated Persian strength at Issos to be a more conservative 119,000 and at Gaugamela to be 245,000, of which 200,000 were infantry. We cannot verify these figures, but most accounts suggest a significant proportion of these armies was of low quality and dubious commitment; hence their repeated losses to smaller but better indoctrinated and commanded Greek and Macedonian forces.

Troops were organized into *hazarabam* ('thousands'), divided into *sataba* ('hundreds'), then into *dathabam* ('tens'). The backbone of early Persian armies was a regular infantry force that relied upon massed bowshot, and that continued the Assyrian practice of matching bowmen with shield-bearers. The front line of infantry formations consisted of *sparabara* (pavise bearers), the *spara* being a rectangle of leather interweaved with osiers, extending from shoulder to ankle. Each *dathabam* would deploy in a file of 10, with the *dathapatis* (section commander) holding the *spara* in front and nine archers lining up behind. The *dathapatis* carried a 2m (6ft) long thrusting spear to defend the rest of his section; should he fall, then the archers defended themselves as best as they could with falchions – short, curved swords with an edge but no point. Interestingly, the Persians did not initially use composite bows, but simple cane bows, with an effective range of around 150m (492ft); Persian archery was adequate for supporting cavalry charges but, for all its weight of shot, lacked the power to break a determined charge, as the disasters at Marathon and Plataea demonstrated. Once engaged hand-to-hand by Greeks or Macedonians, the Persians were disadvantaged by their lack of body armour; a glazed brick relief from the Persian Royal Palace at Susa shows members of the Royal Bodyguard, the Immortals, wearing ankle-length robes bearing appliqué

> *'the Athenians... charged the invaders at a run...When the Persians saw the Athenians running towards them... they thought [they] must be mad... because they could see how few of them there were'* – HERODOTUS

regimental badges but no armour, and we can assume that line infantry units were not any better equipped. In a rare Greek tribute to Persian courage, Herodotus notes that at Plataea (479 BC), once the line of sparabara was smashed in by the Spartan phalanx, the Persian archers behind fought bravely, but were beaten due to lack of armour and of training in hand-to-hand combat. It is unsurprising, therefore, that wherever possible, Persian troops tried to shoot from prepared positions or from behind natural obstacles.

Persians and Medes aside, the bulk of Persian infantry was levied from subject peoples, each contingent using their own national weaponry, organization and tactics. Herodotus recorded 35 different nationalities in Xerxes' army in 480 BC. Many of these tribal contingents seem to have been archers like the Persians themselves, but the Arab contingent carried composite bows, the Lydians' 'equipment was not very different from Greek' (implying that Xerxes may have had a small hoplite force) and the Thracians carried 'javelins, bucklers and small daggers' (suggesting these formed a large body of skirmishers).

Persian armies evolved over the next 150 years, partially as a result of their experience in Greece in 490–479 BC. Attempts were made to rectify the lack of heavy infantry through re-equipping Kurdish, Mysian and other mercenaries as *takabara*, fighting with thrusting spears and the *taka*, a large, leather shield. When possible, the Persians hired Greek mercenaries, mainly hoplites fighting in phalanx formation, but also peltasts and other skirmishers. Of these, the best-known was Xenophon's 'Ten Thousand', whose retreat from the heart of the Persian empire after the battle of Cunaxa (401 BC) is recounted in his *Anabasis*, a detailed, first-hand account of warfare of this period. Alexander faced 30,000 Greek mercenary hoplites at Issos and also some 60,000 troops from the *Kardaka*, young Persian noblemen described by Arrian – quoting one of Alexander's subordinate commanders, Ptolemy – as 'heavy infantry'. However, Xenophon describes them as accompanying the Great King on hunts carrying two javelins, a bow and a bronze picklike battleaxe. It may be that some were converted to hoplites by the Athenian mercenary commander, Timotheos, in the 370s BC, while others re-trained as peltasts. This is suggested by their deployment at Issos, 30,000 covering each flank of the Greek mercenary phalanx. The *Kardaka* were apparently not at Gaugamela, but the Persian Royal Guard were present, known as the 'Apple Bearers' after the apple-shaped counterweight at the butt of their 2m (6ft) long thrusting spears. Two are depicted in the famous mosaic found at Pompeii showing Alexander attacking Darius III's chariot; one of them carries a spear, the other a bow, hinting that *sparabara*-type organization may have been retained. The spearman carries a hoplon-type shield, while the bowman wears a cuirass apparently made of leather strips reinforced with bronze studs.

The Hoplite

Compared with those of the Middle Eastern empires, the armies of Classical Greece seemed small, technologically backward and tactically unsophisticated. Nevertheless, the Greeks inflicted crushing defeats upon the Persians at Marathon (490 BC) and Plataea (479 BC); and in 480 BC, as few as 7000 Spartans and allies pinned down at least 10 times their number of Persians at Thermopylae. Greek military culture was very different from that of the Middle East: the warrior ethic remained strong, resulting in armies based upon shock action by hoplites, heavy infantry fighting in phalanx formation. Hoplites came from a militia of propertied citizens, with a personal stake in the outcome of most battles, and intensely indoctrinated through nationalist propaganda and heroic myth. Therefore, the Greek national epic, the *Iliad*, with its detailed accounts of heroic single combat, is of less use as a record of military history than as an insight into the Classical Greek military mind.

The *Iliad* was composed by Homer around 800 BC, and describes a period during the Trojan War (c. 1000 BC), centring on the feud between the Greek hero, Achilles, and the Trojan, Hector. Other episodes are also woven into the narrative. The 'Greeks' of the Trojan War were from the pre-Classical, bronze age civilization of Mycenae, dating from c. 1400 BC to c.1000 BC. It is difficult to know whether Homer is describing warfare of the Mycenaean period or his own, two centuries later, or an artistic blend of both. Archaeological evidence indicates that Mycenaean armies may have been influenced by those of the Middle East, and consisted of a chariot arm supported by formations of infantry. Weapons discovered include bronze slashing swords not dissimilar to those of the Sea Peoples, and the broad bronze heads of heavy thrusting spears. The so-called 'warrior vase' from Mycenae shows a warrior carrying a thrusting spear and a crescent-shaped shield, wearing a horned helmet, possibly of bronze or studded leather, and a cuirass and greaves of an unidentifiable material. There is no evidence to refute the Homeric notion of single combat between champions – the story of David and Goliath indicates that this was practised among the Sea Peoples, who were contemporary and culturally similar to the Mycenaeans. However, many historians argue this was more part of Homer's own time, the so-called Greek 'Dark Age'. Battles of this period were undisciplined mêlées in which the warrior ethic reigned supreme, with aristocrats and champions duelling for prestige.

A radically different form of warfare emerged after 700 BC, as Corinth, Sparta and Argos developed the hoplite phalanx. There appear to have been two factors in this development, one economic, the other political. Economically, the re-opening of trade routes and the establishment of colonies in Italy, Anatolia and the Aegean islands increased prosperity, as well as the number of men able to afford armour and weapons, previously the mark of a small aristocracy. The politico-cultural roots of the phalanx lay in the emergence, also around this time, of the *polis*. A *polis* was, Aristotle argued, a self-sufficient and autonomous state, united by a sense of community and a common sense of purpose, expressed in a set of laws and civic obligations that bound all citizens equally. In Athens, all free men were obliged to vote on

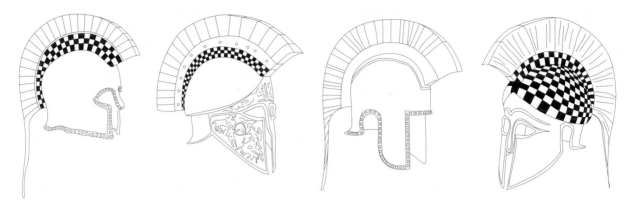

GREEK HOPLITE HELMETS, *from left to right: a simple Corinthian helmet; the classic Corinthian design with long cheek pieces; a later Illyrian helmet; and a late Corinthian design with a space for the wearer's ears cut out to improve their hearing.*

decisions of state, being literally 'roped in' to the Acropolis by slaves to do so, and all senior officials, including military commanders, were elected for fixed annual terms. In Sparta, male citizens were subject to a rigid, lifelong programme of military training and a code of conduct binding on every man from the two kings downwards, devised in the eighth century BC by the legendary lawgiver, Lycurgus.

The main obligation of the *polis* was to defend it in time of war. This was taken to the extreme in Sparta, where all men were lifelong conscripts forbidden to engage in any other profession than soldiering. However, even 'democratic' Athens required all male citizens between the ages of 17 and 59 to serve in war. It might be argued, therefore, that the phalanx was the *polis* in arms, a collective, egalitarian body of citizen-warriors, patriotically motivated in a way that no levy, mercenary or professional, could ever be, a physical symbol of the frontier. Add the almost complete homogeneity of weaponry within the phalanx and we find a formation completely alien to those found in the armies of the Middle Eastern Empires.

Basic Equipment
The essential piece of hoplite equipment was the *hoplon* or Argive shield from which he took his name. The *hoplon* was a shallow bowl, initially of wood edged with bronze, but later covered completely with bronze, and around 80–100cm (31–39in) across. It had a double grip, consisting of a leather or metal strap across its centre, through which the left arm was inserted to the

elbow, with a cord or leather grip for the hand on the outer rim. It could, therefore, be locked onto the forearm and its concavity meant it could be rested on the shoulder, making it easier to carry, but less wieldy than a shield with a single grip. The *hoplon* would invariably be painted with a blazon – faces of gorgons, minotaurs and other monsters being particularly popular – but the Spartans enforced strict uniformity, their shields bearing the letter *lambda*, for *Lakedaimonoi*, the name by which they are more correctly known.

The other distinctive piece of hoplite equipment was the helmet, which also varied in style. The commonest type was the Corinthian, which covered the entire head and face, with a T-shaped slit for the eyes and mouth, and later with a noseguard. This evolved into the Attic, which did not cover the face and had hinged cheekguards. The earliest type, however, was the Illyrian, which covered the skull and cheeks but not the face, and had a distinct metallic ridge on the crown. The later Thracian type was based on the Thracian pointed foxskin cap, with a peak protecting the face and long cheekguards, sometimes joined at the chin and sculpted to resemble a beard.

There is some debate over the remainder of hoplite armour. Some historians take Greek art literally, and argue that hoplites fought naked; however, other works of art and archeological finds do not support this theory. Bronze cuirasses and greaves have been found in large amounts, and there are many works of art depicting armoured hoplites. One of the earliest, the Chigi Vase, dating from around 650 BC, shows hoplites wearing 'muscled' bronze cuirasses, sculpted to resemble the torso musculature of the wearer. Muscled cuirasses have been found dating from the seventh century BC, but despite their regular depiction in Greek art, they were too expensive to be common items of equipment, and indeed, some are themselves works of art; they consisted of breast- and backplate fixed to each other by hinges, sometimes with a semicircular plate hanging from the breastplate to protect the groin. From the sixth century BC, cuirasses made of layers of linen, glued together to form a layer around 5cm (2in) thick, were more common. These consisted of a corselet covering the torso and shoulders, with a skirt covering the lower abdomen, usually split into *pteryges* ('wings') for ease of movement. Bronze greaves, sprung onto the calves and often sculpted to simulate their musculature, completed the hoplite panoply.

The main weapon of the hoplite was a thrusting spear, wielded overarm, 1.5–2.5m (4.9–8.2ft) long, with an ash shaft, a leaf-shaped iron head, and a bronze butt-spike. A number of sword types have been found, but from the fifth century BC, two types were common: one had a leaf-shaped iron blade around 60cm (24in) long, intended as a slashing weapon; the other was the *kopis*, which may have been of either Etruscan or Macedonian origin, and had a 65cm (26in) single edged, dogleg-shaped blade resembling that of the Gurkha kukri, of which it may be an ancestor. Swords were used purely as back-up weapons, the spear being the principal weapon for shock action.

Xenophon records the only detailed organization for a hoplite phalanx which, being Spartan, was probably not typical. The Spartan phalanx was divided into 6 *morai*, each *mora* being commanded by a *polemarch*; below him were 4 *lochagai*, 8 *pentecosters* and 16 *enomotarchs*, each commanding an *enomotia* (platoon) of 36 men. The *enomotia* was divided into 3 files of 12, with the *enomotarch* leading the right-hand file and his *ouragos* (second in command) at the rear. The Athenian army consisted of 10 *taxeis* (regiments), one drawn from each of the tribes of Athens and commanded by a *taxiarch*; the *taxeis* may have been of variable size, and, despite references to *lochagoi* in some battle accounts, it is unlikely that organization below *taxeis* level was as intricate as the Spartan.

VARIOUS DRILL POSITIONS *used by hoplites around 400 BC. From left to right: the hoplite standing at ease; at attention awaiting orders; the position adopted when advancing into battle; and when thrusting his spear overarm.*

As to how these units formed up for battle, the *hoplon*'s design meant that it could cover only the left side of the body, with a substantial slice protruding to the left; the phalanx formed in close order with shields overlapping, each man covering the unshielded right of the man to his left. This produced a phenomenon recorded by Thucydides:

'It is true of all armies that, when they are moving into action, the right wing tends to get unduly extended and each side overlaps the enemy's with its own right. This is because fear makes every man want to do his best to find protection for his unarmed side in the shield of the man next to him on the right, thinking that the more closely the shields are locked together, the safer he will be. The fault comes from the man on the extreme right of the front line, who is always trying to keep his own unarmed side away from the enemy, and his fear spreads to the others who follow his example' (Thucydides V.71).

Even the disciplined Spartans were not immune: at the battle of Mantinea in the Peloponnesian War (418 BC), which Thucydides describes in this passage, it resulted in the Spartan right wing gradually extending beyond the Athenian left, while the Athenian right extended beyond the Spartan left!

Thucydides notes that in the Spartan phalanx at Mantinea, there was some variation in number of ranks, but 'on the whole, they were drawn up eight deep' (Thucydides V.68). Xenophon hints that the Spartans varied the depth of their phalanx according to tactical circumstance; sometimes an *enomotia* formed up 3 abreast and 12 deep, sometimes 6 abreast and 6 deep. Thucydides relates that at Delium (424 BC), the Athenian phalanx was 8 deep, whilst their Theban opponents were 25 deep. Eight ranks seems to have been standard Athenian practice, as they are recorded as using it again outside Syracuse in 415 BC. The heaviest phalanxes were those of Thebes: at Leuctra (371 BC), the Spartans deployed 12 deep, only to be crushed on their right flank by a huge battering-ram of a phalanx, 80 men wide and 50 deep, purpose-formed by King Epaminondas of Thebes.

The phalanx was more than just a tactical steam-roller, however. In particular, Spartan hoplites, with a lifetime of intense drill, were capable of surprising maneouvrability for a shock formation. Xenophon describes how their training in countermarching allowed them to quickly re-orient their phalanx in any direction; Herodotus recounts that at Thermopylae, Spartan hoplites, perhaps using this method, successfully carried out feigned retreats, a tactic more usually associated with light troops. At Cunaxa, the Ten Thousand, trained by the Spartan Clearchus, smashed through the Persian left flank, opened ranks to allow Persian scythed chariots to pass through harmlessly, pursued their enemies 4.8km (3 miles) off the battlefield, about-turned to march back, and then stood their ground to repel a cavalry charge, suggesting a formation powerful, flexible and agile.

Common Tactics

However, the commonest phalanx tactic was a simple advance to contact. Thucydides described the advance of the two armies at Mantinea:

'[T]he Argives and their allies advanced with great violence and fury, while the Spartans came on slowly and to the music of many flute-players in their ranks. This custom of theirs has nothing to do with religion: it is designed to make them keep in step and move forward steadily without breaking their ranks' (Thucydides V.70).

Spartan and later other armies advanced singing the national battle hymn or paean, inspiring them to live up to their intrepid ancestors. It was generally agreed that an advancing phalanx was a terrifying sight: according to Xenophon, even seeing the Ten Thousand carry out a mock attack to entertain the Queen of Cilicia threw their Persian allies into a panic; later, at Cunaxa:

'[T]he Greeks sang the paean and began to move forward against the enemy. As they advanced, part of the phalanx surged forward in front of the rest and the part that was left behind began to advance at the double. At the same time they all raised a shout like the shout of 'Eleleu' which people make to the War God [Ares] and then they were all running forward. Some say to scare the horses they clashed their spears and shields together. But the Persians, even before they were in range of the arrows, wavered and ran away' (Xenophon, *Anabasis*).

It is unclear what happened when the enemy did not run. Contemporary evidence indicates that phalanx versus phalanx encounters were resolved by a mixture of pushing, shield to shield – the *othismos* ('shoving') – and stabbing with spears, until one side gave way. The Nereid Monument from Lydia, c. 500 BC, depicts two hoplites leaning into each other, shield to shield, each trying to stab the other with his spear; Thucydides' account of Delium (423 BC) speaks of stubborn fighting on the Boetian left, 'with shield pressed against shield', until certain troops 'give way', creating gaps in the Boetian line into which the Athenians charge; on the other flank, the Thebans 'got the better of the Athenians, pushing them back step by step at first and keeping up their pressure' until they break through the Athenian flank (Thucydides IV.96). Further evidence for the importance of mass pressure is the growing depth of the phalanx, culminating in the 50-deep Theban phalanx at Leuctra, where Epaminondas' exhortation of 'one more step to please me' suggests an almighty shoving match in

which the Spartans may have been literally run over. Given the length of the hoplite spear, in close formation the men at least four ranks back would have been able to stab at the enemy front rank, aiding their comrades' shoving and stabbing in the front rank by confronting their opposites with a multiple threat. As they would also have moved forward to replace fallen comrades in the ranks ahead of them, the deeper the phalanx, the more effective it would be in wearing down the enemy in a prolonged fight. Therefore, even if the phalanx did not smash the enemy at first contact, it could defeat them through attrition; in each case, depth of formation, combined with the determination of the individuals within it, was of paramount importance.

Marathon: 490 BC

In 490 BC, Persia invaded Greece, intent on destroying Athens before she became a major threat to her security. The result was Marathon, the

A FRONTAL VIEW *of a Macedonian* speira, *the basic unit of a phalanx. Apart from the front four or five ranks, their spears were held in the air to disrupt any missile fire directed against the phalanx.*

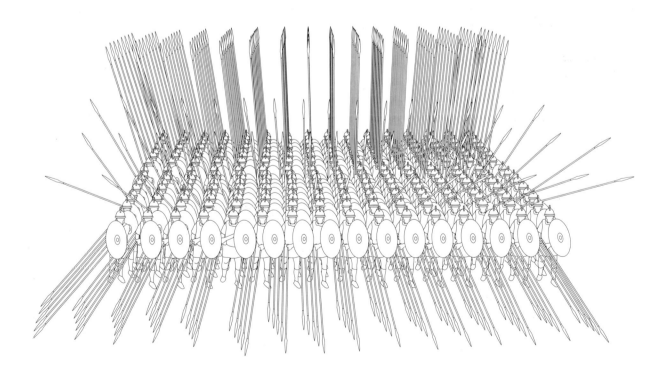

first of a series of battles in which Greek phalanxes defeated far larger Persian forces. Unfortunately, our main source for Marathon is Herodotus, who mixes history, myth and propaganda into a single, seamless narrative. His account of Marathon is unsensational by his usual standards, however, and is accepted as sound by most modern historians.

Marathon was the culmination of a lengthy 'cold war' between Persia and Athens. The conquest of Asia Minor by Cyrus the Great brought the Greek colonies of Ionia under Persian rule. Cyrus, a humane and tolerant conqueror, allowed the Ionians to retain much of their independence, provided they submitted to the authority of his *satrap* (governor) at Sardis, the old capital of Lydia in western Anatolia. However, they revolted in 499 BC, and were joined by 25 ships from Athens and Eretria. The Athenians and Eretrians disembarked at Ephesus, joined the Ionians in burning Sardis, then withdrew. Darius I had crushed the revolt by 494 BC, but never forgot or forgave the Athenians, who had supposedly sworn fealty to him in 507 BC: each night, he had a slave whisper to him 'Remember Athens!' while serving his evening meal. In 491 BC, Darius sent envoys to each Greek *polis*, demanding submission. Among the first to submit was the island *polis* of Aegina, which dominated the sea approaches to Athens. Athens responded by accusing the Aeginetans of planning to join Persia in a war against fellow Greeks; they were soon at war for real, with Sparta as Athens' allies. Darius used this hostility against a 'vassal' as pretext for an invasion of Greece.

Darius appointed two commanders, Datis, a Mede, and his own great nephew, Artaphrenes. Herodotus says they commanded 'a huge army', needing 600 *triremes* to transport it. Datis took Eretria by treachery, sacking the city and enslaving its population in revenge for the burning of Sardis.

Confident of overwhelming Athens, he then sailed to Marathon on the coast of Attica, choosing to give battle here because the open country suited his large cavalry force.

Athens mustered its hoplite class, which marched out to meet the Persians at Marathon. The Athenians had ten commanders, one elected from each of the tribes of Athens, who held overall command of the army for a day each in rotation. The most prominent was Miltiades, an ambitious, Machiavellian character who had been tyrant, or absolute ruler, in the Chersonese in northern Asia Minor before being evicted by Darius' vassals, the Phoenicians. Upon marching out of Athens, the commanders sent Philippides, a professional courier (called Pheidippides in some translations) to Sparta to request assistance. En route, Herodotus recounts, Philippides had a vision of the god Pan, a terrifying nature deity who infected his followers with frenzied rage and his enemies with equally frenzied 'Panic' fear. Pan promised his support to Athens and, given the role that Greek aggressiveness did play at Marathon, Herodotus' artistic licence is forgivable. Phillippides' actual mission was unsuccessful; the Spartans had a law that they would not fight during the period of the waxing moon, and the moon was not yet full.

Herodotus does not give details of the forces assembled at Marathon, but modern historians estimate the size of Datis' force at 19,000 infantry and 1000 cavalry. The Greek force consisted of around 10,000 Athenian hoplites and another 400 from Athens' ally, Plataea. The size of the Persian Army was a factor in the debate among the Athenian commanders about what to do next. Athens put even important military decisions to a vote, and the 10 commanders were split evenly, between those advocating retreat in the face of this bigger Persian force, presumably until the Spartans were able to join them, and those arguing

> *'[the Greeks] all raised a shout... then they were all running forward... clash[ing] their spears and shields together. But the Persians, even before they were in range of the arrows, wavered and ran away'* – XENOPHON

Hoplite c. 500 BC

A typical hoplite of the Persian Wars era. His primary weapon was a long iron-headed spear, which could be between 2–3m (6–10ft) in length. It was usually held overarm in combat, and underarm when manoeuvring. A bronze buttspike helped balance the weapon. He also carries a short sword about 60cm (2ft) in length, made of iron with bronze fittings. The sword was used in both a cutting and thrusting motion. It was carried in a scabbard hung from his shoulder. For protection he carries a hoplon *(shield) made of wood with a bronze face and leather inner lining. The* hoplon *was secured to the hoplite's forearm by a band, and he held a grip in his left fist. His Corinthian helmet is topped with a plume of horsehair, which could be dyed for effect. His torso is protected by a linen cuirass with metal scales added for greater effect. At the base of the cuirass were the* pteruges *or 'feathers', the linen strips which gave a measure of protection while allowing the hoplite to charge the enemy at a run. On his shins are moulded bronze greaves, while simple leather sandals are worn on his feet.*

GREEK BATTLE TACTICS
The phalanx as seen at Marathon, some four or more ranks deep.

Later, cavalry were introduced to protect the vulnerable flanks, while light troops (peltasts) harassed the enemy with javelins.

The Thebans used their peltasts and cavalry to pin one of the enemy's flanks while advancing in an oblique formation, with the lead unit heavily reinforced, to attack the other flank.

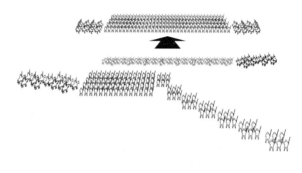

The Macedonian approach was for a deepened phalanx to advance to contact, with a unit of heavy cavalry breaking through a flank and hitting the enemy in the rear.

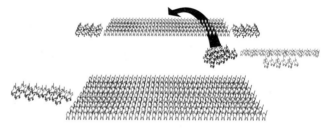

By the time of the Successors, elephants had been introduced onto the battlefield. The key was still an attack on the enemy's rear by heavy cavalry, but the elephants were used to disrupt the enemy line and discourage their cavalry.

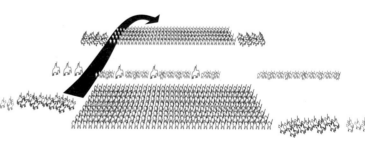

for an immediate attack, the most vocal of whom was Miltiades. The decision eventually fell upon Callimachus, the War Archon. Callimachus held this ancient, by now largely ceremonial, office which traditionally commanded the right wing of the army – the 'place of honour' in Greek and Hellenic armies – but more importantly now, held the casting vote if the 10 commanders could not agree. Miltiades approached Callimachus – apparently away from the others – and told him that it was his decision whether Athens would be the leading *polis* in Greece, or a Persian vassal, or would sink into civil war. Faced with such stark logic, Callimachus voted to fight. When next it was Militiades' turn to lead the army, he attacked.

Militiades extended the Athenian line to match the length of the Persian, this being key to what happened subsequently. The phalanx was weaker in the centre, which Herodotus says was 'only a few ranks deep', but each of the two wings was at full strength, presumably eight ranks deep. Callimachus commanded the right wing, as was his entitlement, with each of the tribes of Athens under their own commanders across the right and centre, and the Plataeans holding the left wing. The Greek commanders stationed themselves in the front line of the phalanx, their job now being to lead their fellow citizens into the attack.

Herodotus' description of the Athenian advance has caused heated debate among historians:

'When their battle lines were drawn up and the omens from the sacrifices were favourable, the Athenians were released, and charged the invaders at a run. The distance between the two armies was no less than eight stades. When the Persians saw the Athenians running towards them ... they thought the Athenians must be mad – mad enough to bring about their utter destruction – because they could see how few of them there were, and they were unsupported by cavalry or archers' (Herodotus VI.112).

Eight stades is about 1.7km (1 mile). Reconstructions of the battle, with re-enactors using authentic hoplite equipment, have shown that a close-order formation of armoured infantry could not have run flat-out for that distance under a hot Mediterranean sun and maintained any cohesion, particularly if under bowshot for the last 200–300m (656–984ft). The most convincing interpretation of Herodotus' account is that the Athenians advanced to contact like the modern British Army, advancing steadily until coming under effective fire and only then going into the attack. The Athenian version has the phalanx advancing at a steady trot, a pace at which close formation could be maintained, then accelerating into the charge when the first Persian arrows fell among them.

Despite Herodotus' claim that 'the fighting at Marathon was long and drawn out', it is likely that the Persian flanks crumpled on first contact, particularly if a single line of *sparabara* was struck by an eight-deep phalanx going at full speed. Behind them were archers with no armour or shields, just a falchion with which to defend themselves. Their formation broken, and with no hand-to-hand combat training, they were, unsurprisingly, soon running for the ships.

In the centre, the Athenians did less well. Not only was their line thinner, but they had to cross an area of scrub on the plain between the two lines, disrupting their formation, slowing their advance and exposing them to Persian archery for longer than their comrades on the flanks. Moreover, they faced élite Persian units as well as a large contingent from the Saka, tribal vassals of the Persians armed with a picklike battle-axe, particularly effective against armoured troops and later adopted by the Persian infantry as a whole. The Persians and Saka countercharged, broke through the Athenian centre and routed it.

It is unclear whether what happened next was planned or spontaneous. The Athenians and Plataeans on the wings gave up their pursuit and simultaneously attacked the flanks and rear of the Persian force that had broken through the Greek centre. In Herodotus' words, 'The two wings combined into a single fighting unit – and the Athenians won (Herodotus VI.113).' This hints at the double envelopment of a force pushing back the enveloping force's centre, as Hannibal did at Cannae 274 years later. However, the Persian centre must have escaped before it could be surrounded completely, as Herodotus notes that the Athenians also chased them back to the coast. There followed a desperate fight on the beach as the Persians tried to re-embark under Athenian attack; the Athenians captured seven Persian ships, but Callimachus and two other Athenian commanders were killed. The remainder of the Persian fleet escaped; however, Greece was safe for another 10 years. Popular myth has it that Philippides, having already run 225km (140 miles) in two days, then fought in the battle, ran the 42km (26 miles) back to the Acropolis in Athens, proclaimed, 'Hail, we are victorious', then dropped dead of exhaustion, the Athenians then instituting the 'Marathon' road race in his honour. However, as

Marathon

490 BC

The Athenian phalanx was weaker in the centre but each wing was at full strength, presumably eight ranks deep. The Athenians advanced steadily, charging when the first Persian arrows fell among them. The Persian flanks crumpled and ran for their ships. However the Athenian centre was disrupted by scrub, exposing them to Persian archery. Moreover, they faced élite Persian units and their well-armed Saka allies, who were particularly effective against armoured troops. The Persian line countercharged, broke through the Athenian centre and routed it. The Athenians and Plataeans on the wings gave up their pursuit and simultaneously attacked the flanks and rear of the victorious Persians. However, the Persians escaped before they could be surrounded. There followed a desperate fight on the beach as the Persians tried to re-embark under Athenian attack. According to Herodotus, the Athenians captured seven Persian ships and killed 6400 Persians for the loss of only 192 men.

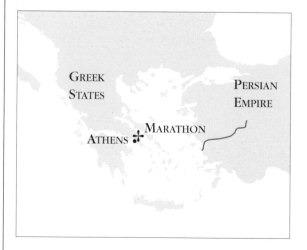

Myth has it that Philippides ran the 42km (26 miles) back to Athens to proclaim the victory before dying of exhaustion, the Athenians instituting the 'Marathon' road race in his honour.

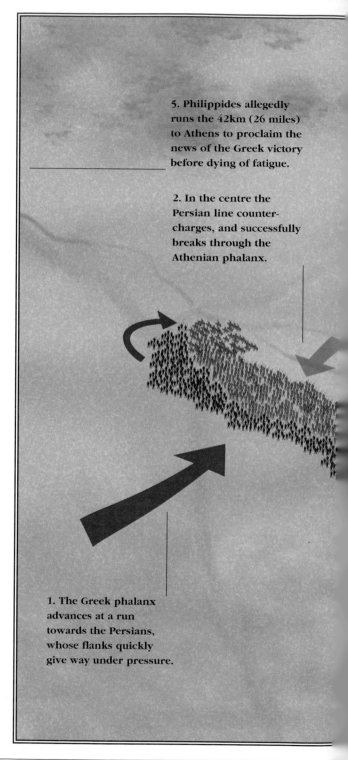

5. Philippides allegedly runs the 42km (26 miles) to Athens to proclaim the news of the Greek victory before dying of fatigue.

2. In the centre the Persian line counter-charges, and successfully breaks through the Athenian phalanx.

1. The Greek phalanx advances at a run towards the Persians, whose flanks quickly give way under pressure.

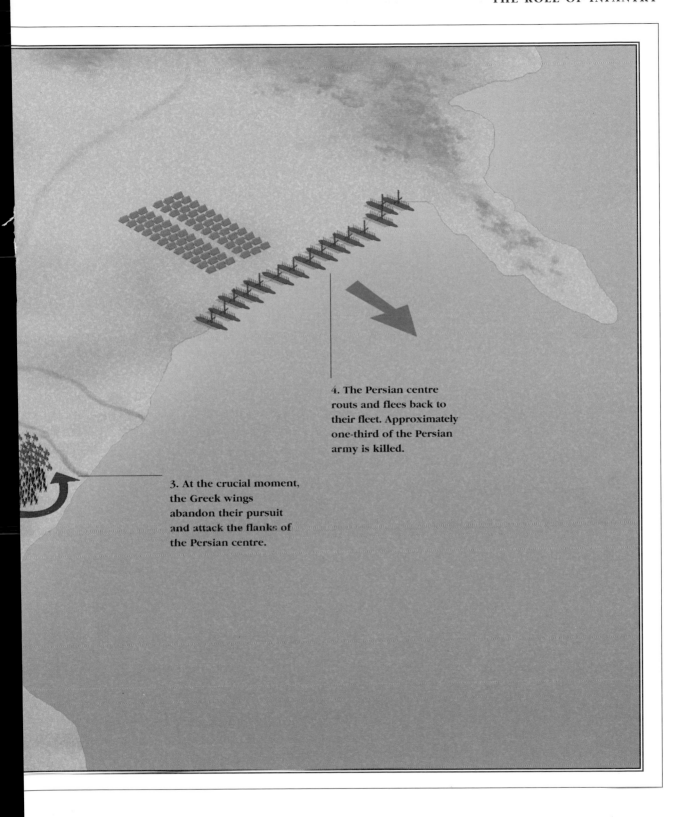

4. The Persian centre routs and flees back to their fleet. Approximately one-third of the Persian army is killed.

3. At the crucial moment, the Greek wings abandon their pursuit and attack the flanks of the Persian centre.

Herodotus – who could not have resisted such a tale – cites Philippides as a source for events leading to the battle, we can assume that this is a romantic myth. Herodotus remarks that 2000 Spartans arrived a few days later, and upon viewing the battlefield 'expressed their admiration for the Athenians and their achievement, and then returned home' (Herodotus VI.120).

Herodotus records that 192 Greeks were killed, but that Persian casualties were 6400, almost one-third of their army. Most of these casualties were probably inflicted in the initial fight on the wings and then as the Greeks pursued the beaten Persians to the beach. The deciding factors at Marathon were, firstly, the dissimilarities between the Athenian hoplites and their opponents, a Persian infantry who were not trained or organized for shock action but facing opponents who specialized in it; secondly, the superior will to win of the Greeks, born of a combination of their political and military culture and, if Herodotus is to be believed, from their belief that the gods were with them. This enabled them to charge a larger enemy force, successfully, under far from ideal conditions, and to turn the potential disaster of the Persian breakthrough of their centre into an opportunity for further aggressive action. The Athenians had little doubt from whom this came, building a shrine to Pan under the Acropolis and beginning an annual festival in his name.

Peltasts and Other Light Troops

Like the hoplite, the peltast was named for the shield he carried. The *pelta* was a crescent-shaped wicker shield covered with goat or sheepskin, carried by a central handgrip. Although common in the Mycenaean period, by the fifth century BC, the *pelta* was identified explicitly with skirmishers, referred to generically as 'peltasts'. However, the term was applied most correctly to the originals, the hill tribesmen of Thrace (modern north-eastern Greece and southern Bulgaria), where the pelta may have originated. The hilly, heavily forested areas over which the Thracian tribes fought produced warfare based on raids, ambushes and skirmishing, making the Thracians the most renowned light infantry in the Classical world. Contemporary illustrations of Thracian warriors show them wearing either foxskin caps and simple tunics, or stripped for speed, and carrying pelta and javelins. Most also carried the traditional Balkan weapon, the *rhomphaia* or *falx*, a one- or two-handed scythe with a curved, iron blade, 39cm (15in) long, which, according to contemporary evidence, could behead a man or hamstring a horse with a single blow.

Thracian peltasts served as levies in the Persian army that invaded Greece in 490 BC, and as mercenaries in Greek armies from the Peloponnesian war onwards. The Peloponnesian war saw most Greek armies supplement their phalanx with skirmishers and missile troops, and tactics become more sophisticated as the phalanx was required to counter these troops or cooperate with them. Some historians see this as a 'revolution in military affairs', when Greek armies, modelling themselves directly on the Middle Eastern example, turned rapidly into combined arms forces like those of Assyria and Persia. Modern military historians see

A THRACIAN PELTAST throws his javelin. A leather loop on the javelin gave him much greater accuracy and power.

such 'revolutions', wherein new technology or doctrine changes war beyond recognition almost overnight, as the key episodes in military history. The incorporation of light infantry into Greek armies does not conform with this model, however: skirmishing was traditional in Thrace and northern Greece, where terrain made the use of hoplites impractical, and it took 150 years to see skirmishers fully consolidated, with the phalanx, into the all-arms forces of Philip and Alexander.

The Importance of Light Troops

Greek armies included light troops as early as Xerxes' invasion in 490 BC, and Herodotus recorded that the Athenians had 800 archers at Plataea. They learned the value of combined arms early – note Thucydides' account of the Athenians pursuing the Corinthians from Megara in 459 BC:

'As the defeated Corinthians were retreating, quite a large section of their army…being uncertain of their route, plunged into an enclosure on someone's estate which had a deep ditch all around it so that there was no way out. Seeing what had happened, the Athenians closed up the main entrance with their hoplites and, surrounding the rest of the enclosure with light-armed troops, stoned to death all who were inside' (Thucydides I.106).

The composition of these 'light troops' is uncertain, as is whether the stones were thrown by hand or shot from slings, but their lack of real weaponry hints that they may have been the hoplites' slaves or servants, as light troops were not a regular part of Athenian armies.

Their absence was felt when the Athenian commander, Demosthenes, led a force of hoplites and a small number of archers into the hills of Aetolia in central Greece in the Peloponnesian War. Like the Thracians, the Aetolians lived in rough country and had developed a style of war exploiting this terrain, defeating Demosthenes' hoplites through what would later be called guerilla warfare:

'They came running down from the hills on all sides, hurling their javelins, falling back whenever the Athenian army advanced, and came on again as soon as it retired. So for some time the fighting went on this way, with alternate advances and retreats, in both of which the Athenians had the worse of it. Nevertheless they managed to hold out so long as the the archers still had arrows and were able to use them, as the light-armed Aetolians fell back before the volleys. But once the captain of the archers was killed, his men scattered.…the soldiers had become tired out with having to make constantly the same wearisome manoeuvres …Many were killed after rushing down into dried-up water-courses from which there was no road up or in other parts of the battlefield where they lost their way. …The main body…took the wrong road and rushed into the forest, where there were no paths by which they could escape and which was set on fire by the enemy so that it burned all around them' (Thucydides III.98).

Demosthenes learned his lesson. Sent to destroy a Spartan force on the island of Pylos in 425 BC, he engaged 800 mercenary Thracian peltasts and 800 archers to support his 840 hoplites and 8000 armed sailors. His experience in Aetolia taught Demosthenes how to use them to best effect:

'Under the direction of Demosthenes this force was divided into companies of roughly 200 men … who occupied the highest points of ground, with the object of causing the enemy the greatest possible embarassment; for he would be surrounded on all sides and have no single point

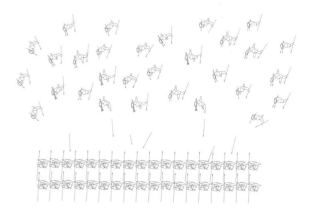

PELTASTS VERSUS A PHALANX: *the peltasts throw their javelins into the phalanx, but their lack of armour means that they can evade any attempt by the hoplites to bring them to battle. They can continue to wear down the phalanx with impunity.*

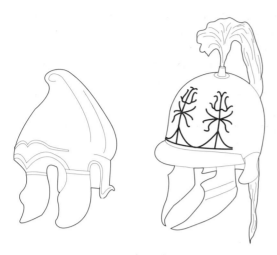

against which to counterattack; instead he would always be exposed to great numbers in every direction, and if he attacked those in front he would be shot at from the rear, if he attacked those on one flank, he would be shot at by those on the other. Wherever he went he would have enemies behind him, lightly armed and the hardest of all to deal with, since with their arrows, javelins, stones and slings they were effective at long range and it was impossible to come to close quarters with them; for in running away they had the advantage in speed' (Thucydides IV.32).

When the Spartans tried to give battle, the Athenian phalanx stood firm while the skirmishers on its wings wore the Spartans down. The Spartans retreated to a fort, with the peltasts picking off stragglers; the Athenians tried and failed to storm the fort, then settled down to a siege. This ended when a subordinate Athenian commander took a picked force of peltasts and archers along an 'impassable' hill path which the Spartans had left unguarded 'and suddenly appeared on the high ground in their rear, striking panic into the Spartans by the unexpectedness of the thing' (Thucydides IV.36).

Twelve years later, Demosthenes invaded Sicily, intending to capture Syracuse, the largest Greek colony on the island. A key factor in the ensuing disaster was that the lessons of Aetolia and Pylos had been forgotten or disregarded, even by Demosthenes. His attack on Syracuse failed, and he was forced to strike out for Catana, a friendly town in Sicily. This meant retreating through the hills of

A SELECTION OF LATER GREEK HELMETS, *showing from left to right: a 'Thraco-Attic' style with curved top; a Thracian type with plume, long cheek pieces and a protective peak; a Chalcidian helmet which retained the nasal protector; and another Thracian design with a cranial ridge for extra strength.*

southern Sicily, and a running battle with the Syracusans, supported by local tribesmen. At one point, the Syracusans blocked a pass across the Athenian route. While the Athenians tried to force the block, skirmishers, who were defended by Syracusan hoplites, hailed arrows, javelins and slingshot on them from the hills on either side, the phalanx providing a concentrated target. The attack was repulsed with heavy losses, but the Athenians were allowed to proceed, undergoing constant harassment by skirmishers, some of it at night. Demosthenes and 6000 hoplites were hemmed into a wood; experiencing a day-long hail of missiles, they surrendered. His co-commander, Nicias, refused terms initially, but two days later his thirsty and starving troops were ambushed as they tried to cross the River Assinarus, and he too gave in.

This was hardly a 'revolution in military affairs', but a demonstration of agrarian peoples exploiting rough terrain and traditional tactics to defeat larger and superficially more 'advanced' forces in a manner not dissimilar to twentieth-century Vietnamese defeating Americans or Chechens defeating Russians. Shrewd commanders engaged similar troops to either counter them or to exploit the advantages of such forces in appropriate country.

However, from the Corinthian War of 395-387 BC onwards, light troops became an integral part of Greek armies, the main inspiration for this being a gifted military innovator, Iphicrates of Athens. The early stages of the war saw Iphicrates, supporting Corinth, launch several raids into Arcadia in the central Peloponnese, using large forces of mercenary peltasts, including Thracians. These operations consisted of raiding villages for plunder, burning crops and ambushing forces of Arcadian hoplites as they tried to catch them. The Arcadians soon refused to venture outside their walled towns, and their Spartan allies jibed that they were as afraid of peltasts as children were of the bogey-man. They were to learn why outside Corinth in 390 BC, where the unnamed commander of a Spartan *mora*, which was escorting a group of pilgrims, was now marching back to his base at Lechaeum, leaving his cavalry to escort the pilgrims the rest of the way. Without cavalry or light troops of their own, and crassly overconfident, the Spartans were slaughtered by Iphicrates' peltasts: 'If they marched along the road, they could be shot at with javelins on their unprotected side and mowed down; if they tried to pursue their attackers, it would be perfectly easy for peltasts, light and fast on their feet, to keep out of the way of hoplites' (Xenophon, *Historia* IV.V.11).

The Spartan commander tried to counter the peltasts by detailing younger hoplites to break formation and chase them off. This failed, the hoplites being unable to catch the peltasts and making easy targets as they tried to fall back on the phalanx. The Spartans were soon joined by their cavalry, which was badly misused, being ordered not to charge and scatter the peltasts, but to keep a continuous front with the phalanx as it advanced. Taking steady losses, the Spartans eventually took refuge on a small hill outside Lechaeum, where a charge by Athenian hoplites finished them off. The use of younger hoplites for

'The main body...rushed into the forest, where there were no paths by which they could escape and which was set on fire by the enemy so that it burned all around them.' – THUCYDIDES

anti-peltast duties was originated by the Spartan commander Brasidas around 424 BC, and often worked; for instance, a year after the distaster at Corinth, King Agesilaus routed Acarnanian peltasts using this tactic; however, a crucial difference was that he supported his young hoplites with a cavalry charge.

After the Corinthian War, Athens contracted out Iphicrates and his peltasts to a number of customers, including King Artaxerxes of Persia. A total of 12,000 of Iphicrates' light troops fought in the Persian army in the Egyptian revolt of 376-373 BC, where Iphicrates made a number of innovations to make his troops more capable of holding their own in shock combat. Diodorus Siculus records that Iphicrates equipped his peltasts with 3m (10ft) long pikes, larger swords and possibly the *taka*. He intended them to form phalanx formation against hoplites or cavalry with the pike, giving them a reach advantage. Unfortunately, there are no accounts of this light pike phalanx in battle, but their influence on the Macedonian phalanx cannot be discounted.

Philip II and the Macedonian Phalanx

Philip II became King of Macedon in 359 BC, and began a series of military reforms, turning an ill-disciplined feudal levy into one of the most formidable armies of the Classical era, in what is frequently described by historians as another 'military revolution'. Philip professionalized the Macedonian army by introducing peacetime training and regular, structured pay for his men, as well as grants of land upon completion of service. Troops underwent regular drill and route marches in full kit, aimed at instilling physical fitness and instinctive obedience in his soldiers. Alongside these institutional innovations went a series of organizational reforms, the most important of which was the introduction of a new type of phalanx.

Iphicratid Hoplite

The success of his peltasts against Spartan hoplites in numerous battles, such as Lechaeum in 390BC, persuaded the Athenian general Iphicrates to reform his hoplites to give them a better chance against more mobile and lighter-armed troops. The traditional basic equipment of a hoplite was lightened. The classic metal greaves of the hoplite were replaced by boots called Iphicratids in the general's honour. The large hoplon *shield is also gone, a small shield with a painted leather front in its place. He wears the latest Thracian-style helmet, combining good vision with protection for the cheek bones. His cuirass is now made of quilted linen rather than stiff layers, common in the fourth century BC. To compensate for his overall lack of protection compared to a traditional hoplite, this soldier has been given a longer spear of 3.6m (12ft) in length, which would allow him to contact his traditionally dressed and equipped opponent first. Ironically, peltasts at the same time began to wear more armour and carried heavier equipment.*

Although contemporary descriptions of the Macedonian phalanx are fairly consistent, terminology varies. The principal unit of Macedonian or Hellenistic heavy infantry was the *taxis* or 'company' of around 120–130 men, paired into *speira* (later known as *syntigmata*, according to the commentator Asklepiodotos) of 256 men each; in the Hellenistic armies which faced the Romans in the second century BC, four *speiriai* were formed into a *chiliarchia*, approximately 1000 men commanded by an officer known variously as a *chiliarch* or *hegemon*, which were, in turn, grouped into 4000-man *strategiai*, commanded by a *strategos*. These arrangements do not match exactly the strengths given for the phalanx given at any battle and so it may be that the size of units varied over time or that – contrary to ancient sources – the perfectionist Asklepiodotos in particular – their organization was dependent on numbers of men available. Asklepiodotos was a philosopher, not a soldier, and so he may be describing the Platonic 'ideal form' of the phalanx; or he may be no less accurate than the tables of organization and equipment found in modern military manuals.

Philip's restructuring of the Macedonian army seems to have been inspired by a range of sources. Philip was a hostage in Thebes between 368 and 365 BC, and seems to have learned a great deal from Epaminondas. His phalanx may have been a hybrid of that used by Epaminondas at Leuctra, and that developed by Iphicrates in Egypt at the same time. At Leuctra, Epaminondas responded to his Spartan foes, who placed their main phalanx against his left flank, by placing his own directly opposite, increasing the number of its ranks from the traditional 8 to 48 or 50, according to the source. Advancing in oblique order, his troops smashed the Spartan right flank before the rest of his army was engaged. The phalanx described by Asklepiodotos, 200 years later, appears to have been based on similar principles. Multiples of 8 or 16 seem to have been common in Hellenistic military organization, and Asklepiodotos described the 'ideal' Macedonian phalanx as having 16 ranks; the phalanx would then be symmetrical and could be doubled in depth to 32 ranks to give it extra weight for the assault. Asklepiodotos describes

three orders for the phalanx; open order, in which phalangites had 1.96m (6ft) of space on either side;'locked shields' (*synaspismos*) with each man and rank separated by 30cm (1ft); and 'intermediate' (*pyknosis*), in which men and ranks were separated by 1m (3ft). Open order was used when advancing, locked shields to meet an attack. On whether spacings are measured head-to-head or shoulder-to-shoulder, Asklepiodotos is unclear.

Philip's most radical innovation was in weaponry. The principal weapon of the Macedonian and Hellenistic phalangite was the *sarissa*, a two-handed pike, couched underhand and not dissimilar to those introduced by Iphicrates, although some scholars have suggested that Epaminondas used it also at Leuctra. It may be that Philip adopted the *sarissa* firstly to increase the reach advantage of his phalangites over the spears of other Greek armies, secondly because a two-handed weapon is harder to parry. According to Polybius, the Greek historian of the second century BC, the *sarissa* was 6–7m (19.4–23ft) long, 4m (13ft) of which projected in front of the phalangite when couched for the charge:

'The consequence is that while the pikes of the second, third, and fourth ranks extend farther than those of the fifth rank, those of that rank extend beyond the bodies of the men in the first rank, when the phalanx has its characteristic close order as regards both depth and breadth…. [I]t is evident that each man of the first rank must have the points of five pikes extending beyond him, each at a distance of [1m (3ft)] from the next…. From this we can easily conceive what is the nature and force of a charge by the whole phalanx when it is sixteen deep. In this case those further back than the fifth rank cannot use their pikes so as to take any active part in the battle. They therefore do not severally level their pikes, but hold them slanting up in the air over the shoulders of those in front of them, so as to protect the whole formation from above, keeping off by this serried mass of pikes all missiles which, passing over the heads of the first ranks, might fall on those immediately in front of and behind them. But these men by sheer pressure of their bodily weight in the charge add to its force' (Polybius XVIII.29–30).

Hydaspes
326 BC

When the two sides finally met, Porus placed his elephants across his front to screen his infantry and frighten Alexander's cavalry. Alexander sent the Companions supported by horse-archers to attack the Indian left while it was still deploying. The Indian cavalry on Porus' right moved to counter the attack, but Alexander's left moved across the rear of the Indian line and trapped the Indian cavalry in a pincer movement. Then Alexander sent light troops with javelins against the elephants, some of which went berserk. Simultaneously, the phalanx advanced on the elephants. The elephants were herded back upon their own line, mowing them down. The Indian infantry were crowded into a disorganized, useless mass. Seeing the disorder in the Indian line, Alexander ordered the phalanx to lock shields and charge home, the cavalry attacking on the wings. The Indian line was smashed. The Indians lost 20,000 infantry, 3000 cavalry and all their chariots; most of the surviving elephants were captured.

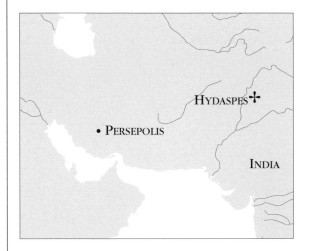

The Hydaspes was fought at the eastern extreme of Alexander's great empire. After the battle, he turned homewards, planning to sail around Arabia, but died in Babylon after a brief illness.

1. Alexander reaches the swollen Jhelum and decides not to cross. He leaves a force and decoy to feint a crossing.

5. Porus leaves part of his army as a screening force for the men Alexander left on the other bank of the Jhelum.

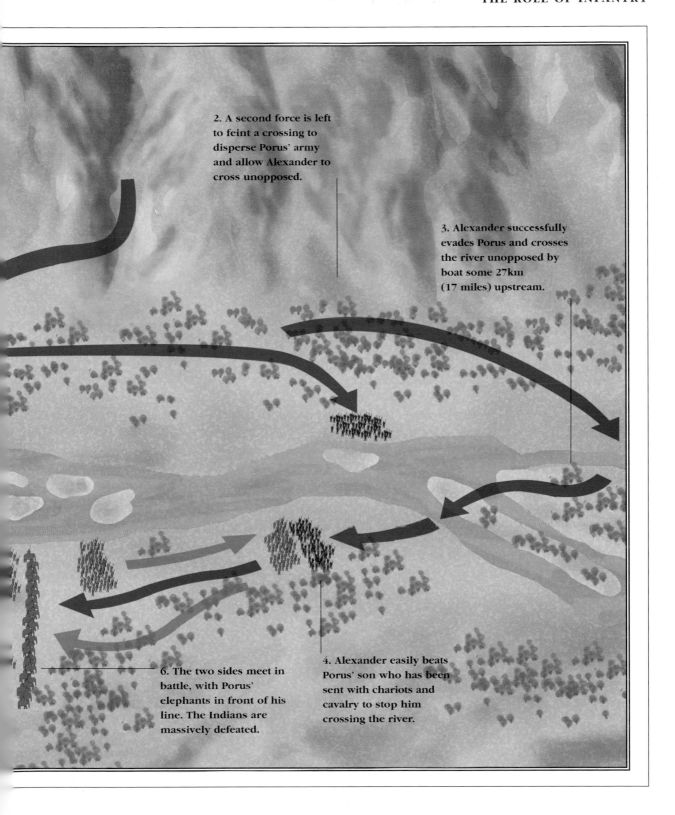

2. A second force is left to feint a crossing to disperse Porus' army and allow Alexander to cross unopposed.

3. Alexander successfully evades Porus and crosses the river unopposed by boat some 27km (17 miles) upstream.

6. The two sides meet in battle, with Porus' elephants in front of his line. The Indians are massively defeated.

4. Alexander easily beats Porus' son who has been sent with chariots and cavalry to stop him crossing the river.

The Macedonian phalanx took the *othismos* to its logical extreme, advancing at the double, presenting a dense hedge of spearpoints with a great block of men behind it, giving opponents the options of scattering, impalement or being run over. This suggests another factor in Philip's reasoning: by adopting a formation based on mass, rather than individual skill, it would be possible for his Macedonian peasant soldiers to beat Greek hoplites in a frontal assault. Moreover, as he would not have to armour the rearmost ranks, he could make a financial saving as well!

The first few ranks of the phalanx appear to have been armoured similarly to Greek hoplites. A seal of the fourth century BC shows a Macedonian *pezhetaroi* wearing what appears to be a linen cuirass with *pteryges*. Two helmet types, the *pilos* and the Thracian, seem to have been most popular, and muscled greaves were also common. The rear ranks apparently wore a simple tunic with a helmet or the *kausia*, a broad-brimmed straw hat similar to a sombrero. All phalangites carried the Macedonian shield, the *aspis,* which, according to Asklepiodotos, was a flattish bowl 60cm (24in) across, made of bronze – which is confirmed by archeological finds. The *aspis* was carried by an elbow grip like the *hoplon*, combined with a baldric slung over the shoulder, and was rimless in order to allow the left hand to grip the *sarissa*. Interestingly, no supplementary weaponry is mentioned in any account, although it is likely that knives or short swords would have been carried.

The Macedonian phalanx was powerful, but brittle. Its effectiveness was based on troops being indoctrinated to maintain the ranks under all circumstances. At the very least, it would have been difficult to maintain such a dense formation without training to march in step, and to respond instinctively to pre-set words of command or bugle calls. The Roman historian, Arrian, records that Philip's son, Alexander the Great, overawed the forces of Glaucias and Cleitus with a display of phalanx-drill, and later, at Gaugamela, the phalanx broke ranks smoothly in order to nullify the charge of Darius' scythed chariots. This 'collective action' had little place for individual initiative; Asklepiodotos gives the titles of officers in the phalanx, but does not describe their roles in any detail, apart from file leaders, who were tasked with maintaining proper formation and drill.

Hypaspists

There were other infantry types in the Macedonian army, the most mysterious being the 3000-strong crack corps known as the Hypaspists. Ancient sources do not describe them in any detail, and many historians presume that they simply formed an élite unit within the phalanx, while others see them as commando-type light infantry. That they fought at the right of the main line indicates they were heavy infantry, but perhaps of a different type to phalangites. The so-called Alexander sarcophagus shows Alexander accompanied by troops wearing leather or linen armour with *pteryges*, Thracian helmets and greaves, and carrying *hopla* – which suggests that, if these are indeed Hypaspists, they fought as hoplites. This would make tactical sense because the hoplite phalanx, while lacking the hitting power of the Macedonian version, was faster and more flexible. Large numbers of skirmishers and light troops, mainly mercenaries, were also used – Alexander's favourites were Thracian peltasts from the Agriane tribe, renowned for their skill with the *rhomphaia*. Phalangites and Hypaspists were also trained to fight in light order with short spears and javelins, for operations in rough country.

As to how Philip and Alexander used their infantry, Macedonian and Successor armies were combined arms forces. The phalanx hit the enemy's centre in oblique order, pinning and crumbling it from the flank inwards, allowing the main strike force – a body of heavy cavalry usually led by the commander-in-chief in person – to attack through or around one or both flanks. This is a pattern that can be seen in Alexander's battles and is still observable in Pyrrhos of Epeiros' defeats of the Romans 150 years later. There were variations on this theme, mainly involving the infantry. At the Hydaspes (326 BC) the phalanx was used as the main arm of decision, a role which became increasingly common after Alexander's death in 323 BC.

After his death, Alexander's empire was carved up into separate kingdoms by his generals, who became known as the *Diadochoi* (Successors).

The armies of the Successor Kingdoms were based on the Macedonian template, but with local variations, the one constant being the central role of the phalanx. Indeed, there was a notable decline in the cavalry strength of some of the Successor kingdoms, particularly Macedon itself, and the phalanx underwent a renaissance as the main shock arm, forming a notably higher proportion of the army than under Alexander. At the Hydaspes, Alexander had 5 *chiliarchi* (around 15,000 phalangites) out of a total strength of 40,000–50,000, as opposed to a possible 16,000–18,000 phalangites out of a claimed total strength of 70,000 under Pyrrhos at Ausculum (279 BC), and to Livy's report that at Kynoskephalai (197 BC) Philip V of Macedon's phalanx consisted of 16,000 men out of 23,000–24,000 and that Perseus' army at Pydna had a strength of 21,000 out of 43,000. These figures are conjectural, and may include other infantry. However, it can be deduced from classical accounts of battles between Roman and Successor armies that as this period progressed, Hellenistic commanders – like their classical Greek ancestors – relied increasingly upon phalanx assaults. In all of these accounts, the defeat of the phalanx leads invariably to the collapse of the entire army.

The principal drawbacks of the Macedonian phalanx were that it required flat, unbroken country in which to function properly and, because it was essentially a one-way, linear formation, it was extremely vulnerable to attacks on its flanks or rear. Philip and Alexander were always careful to use their phalanx in combined arms attacks in which cavalry or light troops operated on its wings, but the decline of cavalry in the third century BC meant that the phalanx's vulnerability to flanking attacks became acute. To counter this, a second phalanx would often form up behind the first, also giving the option of linking the two to form a single, 32-deep phalanx

'those further back than the fifth rank [in a phalanx] cannot use their pikes [in a charge]....But these men by sheer pressure of their bodily weight in the charge add to its force' – POLYBIUS

for added weight. To deal with problems of terrain, commanders formed 'articulated' phalanxes in which *taxeis* were interspersed with other troops; in his campaigns against the Romans between 281 and 275 BC, Pyrrhos divided his line evenly between phalangites and Italian light infantry; at Magnesia in 190 BC, Antiochos III drew up his phalanx in blocks 50 men wide, with 2 war elephants in each gap. Hoplite-type troops also featured in most Successor armies, as mercenaries or élite units such as the Argyraspides (Silver Shields), a 3000-strong unit in the army of Successor Macedon. This was made up initially of veterans of Alexander's campaigns but evolved into the royal guard unit which faced the Romans at Pydna. Large numbers of mercenary light troops were also used.

The Hydaspes: 326 BC

In early 326 BC, having destroyed the Persian Empire, Alexander crossed the Hindu Kush into India. He subjugated several northern Indian states bloodlessly, through exploiting the Indian tradition of weaker states offering homage to stronger ones in return for protection and proper treatment. Alexander greatly admired the dignified, soldierly bearing of the Indian princes and, in contrast to his policy against the Persians, was keen to win their friendship as well as their loyalty. However, one not prepared to submit was the most powerful ruler in north-western India, Parvataka, the Rajah of Paurava, who was called Porus by the Greeks. When Alexander reached the river Hydaspes, now called the Jhelum, he found Porus waiting with an army.

In the Classical world, Alexander was regarded as the perfect ruler and commander and a role-model for all who followed; consequently, there were no end of literary studies of his life and times, and we have no less than four classical accounts of the resulting battle. The earliest of these is from Diodorus Siculus, who wrote his

Universal History probably between 25 and 21 BC; Book 17 provides an account of Alexander's reign. Note that Diodorus can be as sensationalist as Herodotus. Quintus Curtius Rufus, a senator under Tiberius Caesar, wrote his *History of Alexander* during the period between 31 and 41 AD, when out of Tiberius' favour; his work is tinged with bitterness against 'great men'. Plutarch was a Greek essayist, who produced his *Lives*, a series of paired character studies juxtaposing famous Greeks with famous Romans, in the late first century AD; his *Life of Alexander* (paired with Julius Caesar) contains a brief account of the Hydaspes. The fullest and most authoritative account is that of Arrian (Lucius Flavius Arrianus), an experienced Roman general, who served in the

eastern wars of the Emperor Trajan and then defeated an Alan invasion of Asia Minor in 135 AD. He wrote using memoirs of some of Alexander's officers, which are now lost.

These authors differ on the strength of Porus' army. Curtius estimates 30,000 foot and 300 chariots; Plutarch, 20,000 infantry and 2000 cavalry; and Arrian, 4000 cavalry, 30,000 infantry

and 300 chariots. However, they agree that Porus commanded a powerful all-arms force, made up of the best soldiers Alexander ever faced, also including probably the most awesome weapon on the ancient battlefield, for Porus also had up to 200 war elephants.

Indian war elephants were large bulls, possibly gelded, 3.5m (11.5ft) at the shoulder and weighing up to 5 tonnes (5 tons). Each wore a caparison of ox or buffalo hide, and its harness would have been hung with bells to increase the noise the elephant made when it moved. The crew consisted of a mahout and up to four warriors, carrying bows or javelins, riding astride the elephant's back. But the main weapon was the elephant himself, trampling the enemy, clubbing with the trunk, and goring with the tusks, which may have been covered with sharp, iron sheaths.

Porus' infantry were also formidable. Like the elephant riders, they were drawn from the Kshatrya (warrior caste), and were full-time soldiers like the Macedonians. They were divided into two types. Firstly, archers with 1.4m (4.6ft) cane longbows shot arrows with iron or bone heads; although these were powerful, they were not accurate, and it is likely that the Indians relied on weight of shot, rather than precision. Secondly, there were javelin- and spearmen with shields made of skin stretched over cane. All save the richest were unarmoured, wearing the standard dress of a long kilt, and all carried slashing swords with iron, spoon-shaped blades.

Prelude to the Battle

Alexander's army consisted of 7000 cavalry, 40,000 infantry of all types and 5000 Indian allies. The Jhelum was swollen and Alexander decided against a resisted crossing against the elephants. He brought up his camp and proclaimed he would wait for the Jhelum to subside, but in actuality he was seeking alternative crossings. The Indians were kept guessing by nighttime feints and sham preparations to cross at various points. After several days, Alexander crossed the Jhelum 27km

THE BATTLE OF HYDASPES 326 BC *was a classic victory for Alexander, involving deception, a rapid night march and envelopment. Here the phalanx is being attacked by elephants and Indian infantry.*

(17 miles) upstream, wrong-footing Porus with a series of brilliant manoeuvres. This suggests he understood what would later be known as the operational level of war, that level above the tactics of the battlefield but below the strategy of the entire war. His general, Krateros, was ordered to remain near the camp with two *taxeis* of the phalanx and a mounted force, and to sham crossings, only crossing for real once Porus was engaged upriver against Alexander. To compound the deception, Attalos, an Alexander lookalike, was dressed in a suit of Alexander's armour and instructed to show himself at regular intervals where the Indians could see him. Another commander, Meleager (or Ptolemy, according to the source) was instructed to manoeuvre up and down the river with a force of cavalry and light infantry between the camp and the crossing point, launching regular feints to confuse Porus further; they too were to cross once Alexander was across. Alexander's own force consisted of his favourite troops, the infantry being made up of the Hypaspists, two *taxeis* of the phalanx, Cretan archers and Thracian peltasts. Porus sent his son with 120 chariots and around 4000 cavalry to resist Alexander's crossing. However, Alexander was across by the time he arrived, and in a short cavalry fight he scattered the Indians. Leaving a small force of infantry and elephants to screen Krateros' crossing, Porus then marched to meet Alexander.

Diodorus describes the Indian army that eventually faced Alexander as resembling a walled city, the infantry being the walls and the elephants the towers. Arrian details Porus' deployment:

'In the van he stationed his elephants at intervals of about 100 feet [30m], on a broad front, to form a screen for the whole body of the infantry and to spread terror among the cavalry of Alexander. He did not expect that any enemy unit would venture to force a way through the gaps in the line of elephants. ...terror would make the horses uncontrollable, and infantry units would be even less likely to make the attempt, as they would be met and checked by his own heavy infantry and then destroyed by the elephants turning upon them and trampling them down' (Arrian V.16).

The first stage of the battle can be passed over, as it was largely a cavalry action. Porus was correct in his assumption that Alexander's horses, unused to elephants, would go nowhere near them and Alexander was forced to carry out wide-sweeping manoeuvres, avoiding the Indian centre. He opened the battle by holding most of his infantry back and launching an attack with the Companion heavy cavalry – supported by Dahae horse-archers – against the cavalry on the Indian left, catching it as it was still deploying. Koinos, with a detachment of Companions, was deployed on Alexander's own left, with orders to shadow the Indian cavalry on Porus' right when Porus moved them to counter Alexander's attack on his left. This is exactly what happened, Koinos carrying out a bold move across the rear of the Indian line and the Indian cavalry finding themselves trapped in a pincer movement from which they escaped to the sanctuary of the elephant line.

The second stage centred on Alexander's infantry. Curtius tells us that before the battle, Alexander had been dismissive of the elephants:

'Our spears are long and sturdy; they can never serve us better than against these elephants and their drivers. Dislodge the riders and stab the beasts. They are a military force of dubious value, and their ferocity is greater towards their own side; for they are driven by command against the enemy, but by fear against their own men' (Curtius VIII.14.16).

This assumption shaped his tactics against the elephants. 'Then Alexander sent the Agrianes and the Thracian light-armed against the elephants, for they were better at skirmishing than fighting at

'But the bravest are surely those who have the clearest vision of what is before them, glory and danger alike, and yet notwithstanding go out to meet it' – THUCYDIDES

close-quarters. They released a thick barrage of missiles on both elephants and drivers' (Curtius VIII.14.24–25). The javelin barrage soon told, a number of elephants going berserk and charging about aimlessly. The Thracians alternately chased and fled from the elephants, using typical skirmish tactics, but sometimes moved in to attack an elephant at close quarters, perhaps when it became isolated from the rest. Curtius recounts that they used axes to hack off the elephant's feet, but is probably referring to the Thracian *rhomphaia*.

Simultaneously, the phalanx advanced on the elephants with the intention of restricting the space they had to fight. The elephants broke the phalanx at one point, as Arrian refers to them 'dealing destruction in the solid mass of the Macedonian phalanx' (Arrian V.17) but it would appear that elsewhere, the elephants were intelligent enough to realize that this relentlessly advancing mass of sharp points meant danger. They were literally herded back upon their own line, Curtius noting that 'They charged into their own men, mowing them down; their riders were flung to the ground and trampled to death. More terrified than menacing, the beasts were being driven like cattle from the battlefield' (Curtius VIII.14.30). As well as being trampled, the Indian infantry were crowded into a disorganized, useless mass. Moreover, it appears that many Indian archers arrived on the battlefield with their bows unstrung; they had to brace them on the floor to do this, and due to the muddy ground – no doubt churned up further by the elephants – many could not string their bows.

Seeing the disorder in the Indian line, Alexander ordered the phalanx to form *synaspismos* – locked shield formation – and charge home, the cavalry attacking on the wings. The Indian line was smashed. Arrian estimates that the Indians lost 20,000 infantry, 3000 cavalry and all their chariots; most of the surviving elephants were captured and absorbed into the Macedonian army. Alexander's infantry losses were 80, most of them to the elephants, and his cavalry lost 230. Porus was captured after being gravely wounded and his elephant killed under him. He recovered from his wounds, and Alexander was so impressed by his dignified bearing and courage in adversity that he restored him to his throne and made him an ally.

The Republican Roman Legion

Until the sixth century BC, the tribes of mainland Italy were influenced more by the Celtic Halstatt culture to the north than by the Greeks to the south, and Celtic influence is observable throughout Roman military history. Warfare conformed closely with the tribal model, and there is evidence of an élite order of champions and warrior-priests dedicated to the war god, Mars, the father of Romulus and Remus, who were the mythical founders of Rome. Archaeological finds from this period indicate that the Romans were sword-fighters from the earliest; blades up to 70cm (27.5in) long, some of iron, have been found, along with bronze spearheads. Helmets were bronze and of the Calotte type, essentially a simple pot-shape worn like a hat. Armour consisted mainly of pectorals, bronze plates designed to cover the heart and also (with larger examples) the abdomen, which were held in place by leather straps. Two types of shield have been found; one is large and round, and possibly of Etruscan origin, while the other is the oval *ancile*. How these were carried is unclear from surviving examples.

Around 600 BC, Rome was subjugated by the Etruscans, a non Indo-European people of obscure origin whose culture centred on several large towns to the north. The Etruscans had contact with the Greek colonies in Sicily and southern Italy and adopted the hoplite phalanx shortly before establishing this hegemony, imposing its organization on Rome and other vassals.

The Etrusco-Roman army was formed from a levy of all adult male citizens. Livy relates that the second Etruscan king of Rome, Servius Tullius, organized Roman society into classes based on wealth and social standing, divided into voting groups known as centuries ('hundreds'), with each class equipping itself for war according to a scale based on financial means. The richest formed eighty centuries of the First Class, equipped with full hoplite armour and weaponry. The 20 centuries of the Second Class had similar equipment, except that they did not wear body armour (perhaps wearing pectorals instead) and carried the oval 'long' shield (*scutum*), instead of the *hoplon*. The Third Class consisted of another 20 centuries, armed in the same manner, but without greaves. The Fourth and Fifth Class were skirmishers and light troops, the Fourth consisting of 20 centuries of javelinmen and the Fifth of 30 of slingers. Assuming that each century consisted of 80 men, as later, and including the 2 centuries of musicians and 18 of cavalry, this gives a total infantry strength for Servius' army of 14,400, comparable with Greek armies of the time.

Rome ejected the Etruscans in the late sixth and early fifth centuries BC, but apparently retained the Servian-type phalanx. Like many military reforms, the evolution of the phalanx into the legion described by Polybius originated in defeat, beginning with that inflicted by the Gauls at the River Allia in 390 BC. The Samnite wars of 343–290 BC brought further catastrophes at the Caudine Forks in 321 BC and Terracina in 316 BC. Samnium was rugged, hilly country; this and contemporary representations depicting Samnite warriors carrying spears and javelins but never swords, suggest a style of warfare based on skirmishing, in which dense, tightly controlled formations would be at a severe disadvantage. Indeed, the Caudine Forks was essentially a giant ambush of a Roman army in a valley in the Apennine mountains. The Romans may therefore have opened up their battlefield formations following their humiliations in the hills of south-central Italy.

Livy's account of the Roman army of the mid-fourth century BC borrows heavily from Polybius. However, it includes sufficient points of departure to suggest a different formation and may, therefore,

be our best account of the armies that faced Pyrrhos in the early third century BC and Hannibal 170 years later. The phalanx was now re-organized into legions, divided into maniples made up of two centuries each, but the old division according to status was retained, in modified form:

'The first line, the *hastati* [spearmen] consisted of fifteen maniples stationed with short gaps between them; each maniple included twenty light-armed soldiers, the rest of its number being men with oblong shields: 'light-armed' was applied to those carrying only a spear and javelins. This front line contained the pick of the young men who were just reaching the age for service. Behind them came the same number of maniples formed from men who were stronger and more mature; these were called the *principes* and all carried oblong shields and had especially fine arms' (Livy VIII.8.8).

These first two lines were known collectively as *antepilani* ('before the columns[?]').Those who formed up behind the *antepilani* differed in both organization and equipment:

'[I]mmediately behind the standards were placed another fifteen companies, each one of which was divided into three sections.... a company consisted of three sections or *vexilla*, and a single *vexillum* comprised sixty soldiers, two centurions and one vexillarius or standard bearer, so that altogether there were 186 men. The first standard led the *triarii* [third rankers], veteran soldiers of proven courage, the second *rorarii*, younger and less experienced men, the third the *accensi*, who were the least reliable group' (Livy VIII.8.8).

This presented the enemy with a chequerboard pattern resembling a series of flattened wedges:

'When an army had been drawn up in this order, the *hastati* were the first to open the battle. If they failed to dispatch the enemy, they slowly withdrew and were received through the gaps between the *principes*. Then the fighting was taken up by the *principes*, with the *hastati* behind them, and the *triarii* knelt under their standards, with their left legs stretched forward and shields resting against their shoulders, holding their spears fixed to the ground and pointing forwards

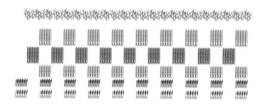

THE EARLY REPUBLICAN LEGION *of the mid-4th century BC with light troops in front, followed by the hastati, principes, triarii, rorarii and accensii.*

so that the line seemed to bristle with a protective palisade. If the *principes* too fought with no success, they gradually fell back from the front line to the *triarii* ... Once the *triarii* had allowed the *principes* and *hastati* through the gaps in their line they rose up and quickly closed their ranks, blocking the lanes, so to speak, and then, with no reserves to rely on behind them, fell upon the enemy in one unbroken force' (Livy VIII.8.8).

Concentrated Actions

It would appear that the legion was, effectively, a collection of smaller units, fighting not one linear battle but a pattern of concentrated actions under local command. The wedge arrangement would thus be eminently suitable for creating and exploiting breaches in the enemy line. Livy omits the functions of the *rorarii* or *accensii*, who appear to have been either camp guards or armed servants, although he does once refer to the *rorarii* breaking ranks and joining the *antepilani* at the height of a battle. Nor does he say much about weaponry; the title *hastati* suggests that these troops, at least, might have used the *hasta*, a single-handed thrusting spear, up to a certain date, but Livy's and Plutarch's (heavily anachronistic) accounts imply that swords were being used extensively by the late fourth century BC, while Livy refers to Gauls in a battle in 351 BC being 'weighted down by the missiles which…stuck in their shields and made them very heavy to carry', suggesting that the the heavy throwing spear, the *pilum*, might have been in use by this date.

Further Reforms

The legion underwent further reform following encounters with mobile, deftly handled Carthaginian armies in the Punic Wars. Our most detailed description of the Legion of the Macedonian Wars comes from Polybius, the organization he describes possibly emerging during the Second Punic War. The army was still a middle- and upper-class citizen militia, each free man of the legionary class being expected to perform 16 years' military service before the age of 46 (20 years in emergencies) with musters held annually in time of war. However, the nature of Roman soldiery had changed: since 392 BC they

had been paid regularly and so resembled modern conscripts more than a citizen levy, and the obligation to serve throughout the long wars of the fourth and third centuries BC led to many legionaries becoming, effectively, career soldiers. There were increasingly frequent relaxations of property requirements, and peasants and even slaves were called up after the catastrophic defeat at Cannae (216 BC).

The 'Polybian' legion was 4200 strong, although it could be expanded to 5000. It was organized into centuries of 80–100 men each, 2 centuries being paired into a maniple, the main tactical unit of the Roman army of this time. The legion also included javelin-armed skirmishers (*velites*), consisting of 'the youngest and poorest', and cavalry for scouting. The legion retained a version of the chequerboard formation, Polybius relating that it marched in this formation when in hostile territory.

It is likely that the practice of relieving lines by maniples continued, although by now this was just one tactical option amongst several. The first and second lines consisted of 10 maniples each of *hastati* and *principes* ('those in the prime of life'). According to Polybius, these carried the *scutum* and two *pila*:

'The *pila* are of two sorts – stout and fine. Of the stout ones, some are round and a palm's length in diameter and others are a palm square. The fine *pila*, which they carry in addition to the stout ones, are like moderate-sized hunting-spears.…Each is fitted with a barbed iron head of the same length as the haft. This they attach so securely to the haft, carrying the attachment halfway up the latter and fixing it with numerous rivets, that in action the iron will break sooner than become detached, although its thickness at

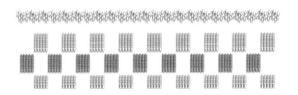

POLYBIAN LEGION *in marching formation, with the* velites *in the front rank, and the* hastati, principes *and* triarii *following in that order.*

the bottom where it comes in contact with the wood is a finger's breadth and a half; such great care do they take about attaching it firmly' (Polybius VI.23).

Finds from Numantia and Telamon confirm the existence of two types of *pilum*, both comprising a barbed head on the end of a long, iron shank, attached to a wooden shaft. One has the shank attached by a socket, the other has a flattened iron tang riveted into a cleft in a thickened end of the shaft. These might correspond to Polybius' 'thin' and 'thick' spears respectively. The *pilum* was, perhaps, the deadliest throwing spear ever, capable of piercing armour and shield, and sometimes pinning shields together. The spear's own weight would bend the iron shank and the barbed head was impossible to remove from a shield in a hurry, and a *pilum*-struck shield would be weighed down severely.

The principal weapon of the *hastati* and *principes*, however, was the Spanish sword (*gladius hispaniensis*), which Polybius describes as 'excellent for thrusting, and both of its edges cut effectually, as the blade is very strong and firm' (VI.23). The *gladius* was, apparently, adopted from the Celtiberian tribes of Spain after the Second Punic War, and was certainly in use by Kynoskephalai in 197 BC. (The *hastati* retained their title, despite the change in weaponry, just as some regiments of the modern British Infantry are still known as 'Fusiliers'.) The *gladius* was forged from iron (examples made of Toledo steel have been found) with a blade around 50cm (20in) long: contradicting Polybius, the blade's centre of gravity was close to the hilt which, combined with its long point, suggest that it was optimized for stabbing rather than cutting. Indeed, the late Roman military critic and polemicist, Flavius

ROMAN LEGIONARY HELMETS AND AUXILARY HELMETS. *Top row, left to right: a bronze Coolus type made in Gaul, c. 50 BC–AD 100, with a horsehair crest and feathers; an Imperial Gallic iron helmet c. 15 BC with prominent 'eyebrows'; an iron helmet from the second half of the 1st century AD, with bronze decoration and cheekpieces turned outwards at the rear to deflect blows. Bottom row, left to right: a bronze auxiliary helmet dating from the middle of the first century AD; an Eastern archer auxiliary's helmet made of iron or bronze in a metal frame, c. AD 100; a legionary's iron helmet from the early 4th century AD, made in two halves and joined in the middle for simplicity and mass production.*

Vegetius, insisted that recruits should be taught to strike with the *gladius* 'not with the edge, but with the point', as one swift stab to the guts will drop an opponent quicker than a multitude of cuts (a doctrine the Romans applied to battlefield tactics as well). Vegetius tells us 'the ancients' made swordplay a central part of their training:

'They wove shields from withies, of hurdle-like construction…such that the hurdle has twice the weight that an official shield normally has. They also gave recruits wooden foils likewise of double weight, instead of swords….Each recruit would plant a single post in the ground so they could not move and protruded 6ft [1.96m]….Against the post as if against an adversary the recruit trained himself with the foil and hurdle as if with sword and shield, so that now he aimed at as it were the head and face, now threatened the flanks, then tried to cut the hamstrings and legs, backed off, came on, sprang, and aimed at the post with every method of attack and art of combat, as if it were an actual opponent' (Vegetius I.11).

Each rank of *hastati* or *principes* deployed with each man displaced from the one in front, forming up 1m (3ft) from shoulder to shoulder to give room for throwing *pila*. Each rank closed up on the one in front as *pila* were thrown, until the whole maniple was in close order. Then, with the enemy disrupted by the initial volleys of spears, the forward ranks charged home with the sword, with those behind throwing spears overhead. In contrast to the massed anonymity of a phalanx attack, the resulting fight would consist of a patchwork of single combats, the Romans seeking victory through the individual prowess of highly trained swordsmen. The Greek historian Dionysius of Halicarnassus described Roman swordsmanship in battle against Gauls in the fourth century BC. His account may be anachronistic, as he wrote it 300 years later, but it might also give a graphic description of Roman swordsmen in action at any time between the Punic Wars and the middle period of the Empire:

'Now the barbarians' manner of fighting, being in large measure that of wild beasts and frenzied, was an erratic procedure, quite lacking in military science. Thus, at one moment, they would raise their swords aloft and smite after the manner of wild boars, throwing the whole weight of their bodies into the blow like hewers of wood…and again they would deliver crosswise blows aimed at no target, as if they intended to cut to pieces the entire bodies of their adversaries, protective armour and all; then they would turn the edges of their swords away from the foe. On the other hand, the Romans' defence and counter manoeuvring against the barbarians was steadfast and afforded great safety. For while their foes were still raising their swords aloft, they would duck under their arms, holding up their shields, and then stooping and crouching low, they would render vain and useless the blows of the others, which were aimed too high, while for their own part, holding their swords straight out, they would strike their opponents in the groin, pierce their sides, and drive their blows through their breasts into their vitals. And if they saw any of them keeping these parts of their bodies protected, they would cut the tendons of their knees or ankles and topple them to the ground roaring and biting their shields and uttering cries resembling the howling of wild beasts' (Dionysius XIV.10.17).

Militia Army

The army described by Livy and Polybius was still a militia in which each man provided his own equipment, and so complete uniformity in armour or weaponry was unlikely. The shield (*scutum*) appears to have been of Celtic origin and was made of plywood covered with canvas and then leather, with iron trim on the upper and lower edges for protection. It was held by a simple handgrip behind the boss, making it less likely to restrict the carrier's movement than the *hoplon*, handier for spear-throwing and sword fighting, and capable of being used offensively, either punching with the boss or hacking with the edge. Polybius records that all legionaries wore pectorals, except for those rated above a certain property qualification, who wore chainmail hauberks; and a monument that was raised to mark Aemilius Paulus' victory at Pydna shows Roman infantry wearing muscled cuirasses. Three types of helmet were popular: the Etrusco-Corinthian or Italo-Corinthian was essentially a bronze hat, sculpted to resemble a miniature Corinthian helmet; the

Pydna

168 BC

Perseus seized the initiative and crossed the river
with his phalanx. Paulus sent his elephants against
the Macedonian left wing, which soon scattered.
However, the battle resolved into a desperate
infantry fight in the centre, pitting the Roman
legions against the Macedonian phalanx. Each
legionary had to fight 10 pikes with just his sword,
once his *pila* were thrown, and the Romans could
not break through to fight at close quarters. The
Romans' Pelignian allies were forced to retire, but
the front ranks of the phalanx became uneven as
they moved onto rough ground and their formation
began to break up. Paulus sent his cohorts into the
spaces in the enemy's line to come to close
quarters; as soon as they got between the ranks of
the enemy and separated them, they attacked the
Macedonians' flanks and rear. The phalanx was cut
to pieces, and apart from an élite unit who held
their ground, they broke and ran. Plutarch estimates
Macedonian deaths at 25,000, Roman at 80–100.

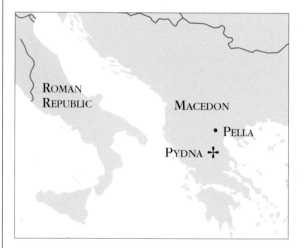

*Pydna marked the end of Macedonian power in
the Eastern Mediterranean, and the beginning of
Roman hegemony. Macedonia was divided into
four republics under Roman protection.*

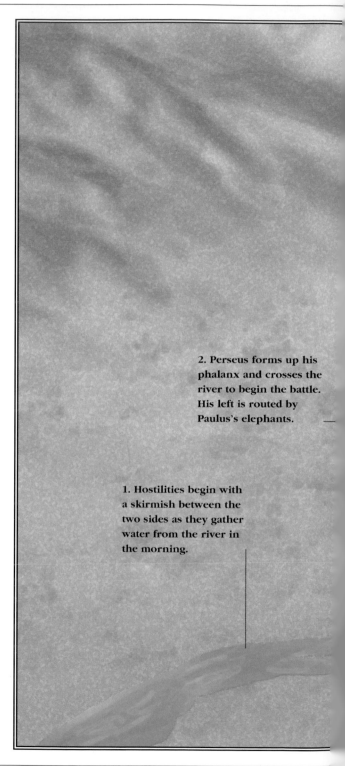

**2. Perseus forms up his
phalanx and crosses the
river to begin the battle.
His left is routed by
Paulus's elephants.**

**1. Hostilities begin with
a skirmish between the
two sides as they gather
water from the river in
the morning.**

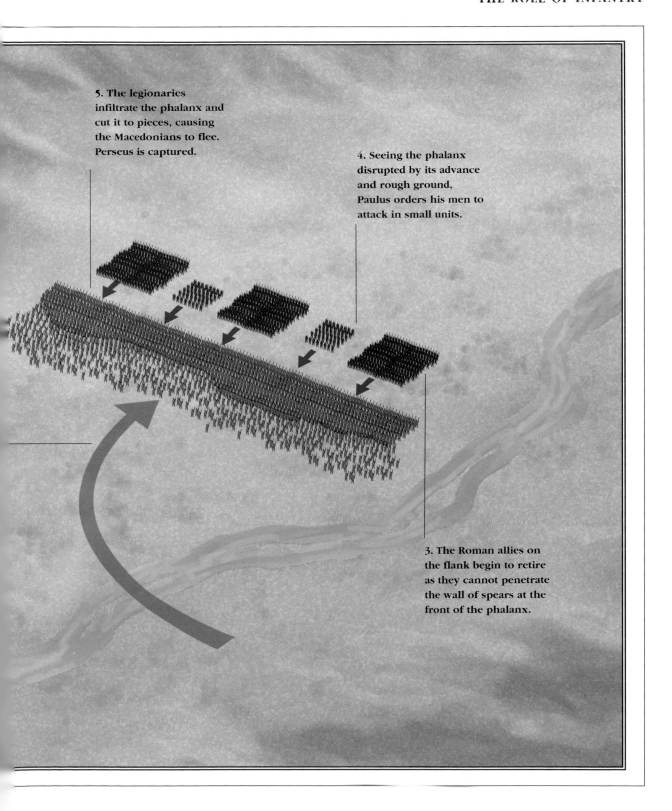

5. The legionaries infiltrate the phalanx and cut it to pieces, causing the Macedonians to flee. Perseus is captured.

4. Seeing the phalanx disrupted by its advance and rough ground, Paulus orders his men to attack in small units.

3. The Roman allies on the flank begin to retire as they cannot penetrate the wall of spears at the front of the phalanx.

Attic was another Greek style popular in Italy. The most distinctly 'Roman' helmet was the Montefortino, which seems, like the *scutum*, to have been of Celtic design and is named after the cemetery in Ancona where a large number were found. In its simplest form, the Montefortino consisted of a bronze bowl with a short, horizontal peak extending over the back of the neck, with broad cheekpieces, which also covered the ears and extended below the jawline. It was traditional among the Latin tribes to wear a single greave on the left, or leading, leg, although greaves seem to have been abandoned altogether by the end of the Second Punic War.

The Romans were clearly heavily indoctrinated for sword-fighting. While the emphasis on swordsmanship has Homeric overtones, it may also reflect a persistence of the tribal approach to war and a national character more individualistic and macho than the Greek. There was a cult of single combat in Rome dating from the earliest times. According to Livy, a Roman–Etruscan dispute was settled by the combat of six champions from each side in 670 BC, and the epochal episode of Horatius Cocles and his two companions defending the Tiber bridge against the entire Etruscan army dates from 508 BC, at least 100 years before Rome first heard the *Iliad*.

The antediluvian Roman phalanx survived with the third line of the legion, the *triarii*: 10 centuries of experienced, older men armed with thrusting spears (*hasta*) and kept as a rearguard, 'the battle coming to the *triarii*' being a traditional Latin metaphor for a tight situation. By Polybius' time it would appear that the *rorarii* and *accensii* had been disbanded and the *triarii* expanded; this is possibly due to the almost incessant wars of the third and second centuries BC increasing the number of veterans entitled to triarius status.

The Republican Roman army underwent two further phases of reform. Scipio Africanus converted the *triarii* and *principes* into a mobile reserve, using them to envelop the flanks of the Carthaginian army at the Great Plains and to extend the Roman line to match the Carthaginian at Zama. In the late third to early first centuries BC, increasing use was made of the *cohors* (cohort), a formation made up of a maniple each of *hastati*, *principes* and *triarii*; indeed, from the late second century BC, it was the cohort, not the legion, that was the main unit of manoeuvre in Roman armies.

The growing tactical agility of the legion suggests that, in addition to individual weapons handling, soldiers must have drilled as units, perhaps up to legion level. Moreover, the dispersed manipular formation necessitated some devolution of command and the Romans

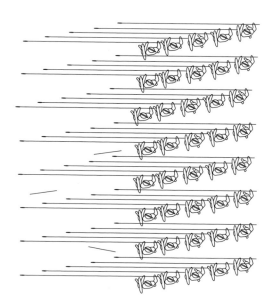

possessed a sophisticated system of 'officers' and 'other ranks'. Polybius records that each maniple was commanded by a senior centurion elected by the soldiers. Above these were tribunes, elected magistrates whose military service formed part of their civic function; each legion was commanded jointly by six tribunes. These reported to the consul, one of the two joint chief magistrates of Rome, who commanded the army. A typical Roman army of the Punic or Macedonian Wars consisted of two to four legions forming the centre, with *alae* (wings) of troops from Roman tributaries armed and organized in the legionary manner, on either flank. Legionary troops made up the bulk of these armies, forming 20,000–30,000 soldiers out of an estimated 40,000 at Heraclea; 20,000 out of 40,000 at Ausculum; 18,000 of 26,000 at Kynoskephalai; and 10,000 out of 37,000 at Pydna.

The standard Roman 'tactic' – at least prior to the shock of defeat at the hands of Hannibal – was straightforward shock action aimed at the enemy centre. The Romans expected the superior training, aggression and bravery of their soldiers to be the decisive factors – far more so, in fact, than any contribution from the tribunes, who would often be too busy fighting hand-to-hand in the front line or even duelling enemy champions to exert much supervision. The headlong charge into the sword-fight was the standard Gallic approach

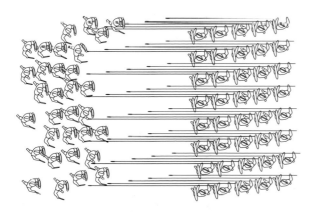

A ROMAN LEGION VERSUS A PHALANX: *the legionaries throw their* pila *in an attempt to disrupt the phalanx. They then close with the formation, trying to get into hand-to-hand combat range, where the superior sword-fighting skills of the Romans will tell.*

to battle, another possible influence on the Romans, but the Romans differed from the Gauls in their intensive training, organization and battle drills, which gave the legion a flexibility and speed of response that was perhaps unmatched in any other army of the time.

The reforms detailed above were matched by a shift in style of command away from heroic leadership from the front. As early as 340 BC, Livy reports, the Consul Manlius Torquatus sentenced his own son, a cavalry commander, to death for accepting a challenge to single combat contrary to orders, and from this time there is a shift away from leaders expressing their machismo through single combat towards leading their troops in heroic charges or last stands or in daring, battle-winning maneouvres. Note also Polybius' description of the ideal centurion: 'They do not desire them so much to be men who will initiate attacks and open the battle, but men who will hold their ground when worsted and hard-pressed and be ready to die at their posts (VI.24).' It would be difficult indeed to manage maniples or cohorts without some commanders standing back and observing the fight, and adjusting the formation as the situation developed.

Pydna: 168 BC

The Macedonian phalanx depended on cohesion: if this were lost through the 'friction' of battle, its effectiveness was compromised severely, if not lost altogether. Hence the preference of Hellenistic commanders for battles in level, open country and their recurrence on the same sites, such as Kynoskephalai, Magnesia and Koronaea.

Nowhere was this fatal weakness demonstrated more graphically than at the battle fought at Pydna in northern Greece in 168 BC, between the armies of King Perseus of Macedon and the Roman Consul, Lucius Aemilius Paulus. Pydna resulted from the power struggle between Rome and the Macedonian and Seleucid Successor kingdoms almost immediately following Rome's victory in the Second Punic War. In 197 BC, a Roman army had defeated a Macedonian at Kynoskephalai. Roman elephants broke the Macedonian left wing, encouraging a tribune to take 20 maniples from this wing and lead them on a downhill charge against the rear of the Macedonian phalanx, which had been previously pushing back the Roman left. War broke out again in 171 BC, and when Paulus was elected a consul in 168 BC, the Senate instructed him to bring matters to an end.

His father had been killed at Cannae, and Paulus was the brother-in-law of Scipio Africanus, who finally defeated Hannibal at Zama in 202 BC. While still in his twenties, he had won two victories over the Celtiberians and, when first elected a consul in 182 BC, won a campaign against the Celtic Ligurians of north-western Italy. Paulus was about 60 in 168 BC when he was pressed to run for a second consulship, specifically to deal with Perseus, who had inflicted a series of humiliating defeats upon the Romans. At the time, Perseus was camped in a strong, prepared position near Mount Olympus, from which the Romans were having difficulty shifting him.

There are two sources for the ensuing battle. One is Plutarch's *Life of Paulus*; the other is *The History of Rome* by Livy (Titus Livius). Little is known about Livy, who seems to have been a professional writer and produced his *History* between 30 BC and AD 17. While a magnificent writer, Livy must be approached with caution; he was a believer in Rome's heroic progress towards her 'preordained destiny', and his narrative is coloured by this throughout. Although what he wrote on Pydna has not survived, much relevant technical information can also be gleaned from the most respected historian of these times, Polybius. Polybius was not only interested in military affairs, but spent many years after Pydna within Paulus' household as a Greek hostage; accompanied Paulus' son, Scipio Aemilianus, during the Third Punic War; and was at the destruction of Carthage in 146 BC.

Upon confronting Perseus' position, Paulus sent a force of *extraordinarii*, cavalry and light infantry from Rome's Italian allies, to sever its lines of supply. Perseus retreated to Pydna,

choosing to give battle here because, Plutarch tells us, '[t]he place afforded a plain for his phalanx, which required firm standing and smooth ground' (Plutarch, Aemilius Paulus, XVI), yet it was also surrounded by hills, providing his

A RECONSTRUCTION OF THE BATTLE OF PYDNA
demonstrating how the broken ground disrupted the Macedonian phalanx, allowing the Romans to close with the phalangites and use their superior swordsmanship to good effect.

skirmishers with plentiful opportunities to harass the pursuing Romans.

Paulus caught up and halted his army overnight while devising a plan of attack. He had with him 2 Roman legions, another 2 of Italian allies and a force of Numidian cavalry for a total strength of 37,000 men, plus 34 war elephants. Perseus' phalanx numbered 21,000, and he had 17,000 other infantry and 4000 cavalry. The next morning, fighting broke out between Rome's Pelignian allies

ROMAN BATTLE TACTICS

The velites (V) are in skirmish order in front of the hastati (H), who are formed up in open order in front of the principes (P) and triarii (T); the latter are in close order. When the legion is ready to advance, the velites are recalled to regroup.

The front centuries of the hastati move to the right, while the rear centuries move forward to fill the gap and present a solid line to the enemy. They then throw their pila and charge on the run.

After a period of time, the hastati are recalled, reversing their earlier movement, and withdraw in close order to reform behind the triarii. Meanwhile the principes advance, filling the gaps left by the hastati and maintaining a solid line.

The principes manoeuvre so as to present a full line before charging their opponents again.

If the enemy has still not broken after the efforts of the principes, the triarii, armed with spears, move up to replace them. The principes then reform.

The commander is now left with the choice of either starting the process again, or withdrawing.

NOTE: IN ALL THE DIAGRAMS THE ENEMY IS APPROACHING FROM THE BASE OF THE PAGE.

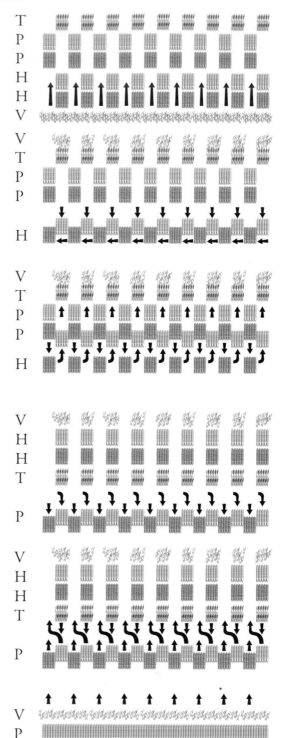

and Thracian peltasts as they drew water from a stream between the armies, and Perseus marched out his entire army.

Paulus reacted by forming up his own forces and charging his elephants against the Macedonian left wing, which soon scattered. However, the battle resolved itself into a desperate infantry fight in the centre, pitting the Roman legions against the phalangites of the Macedonian Chalkaspides (Bronze Shields) Corps. Plutarch notes that Paulus himself feared for the outcome of this clash:

'Aemilius came up and found that the Macedonian battalions had already planted the tips of their long spears [*sarissas*] in the shields of the Romans, who were thus prevented from reaching them with their swords. And when he saw that the rest of Macedonian troops were drawing their targets from their shoulders round in front of them, and with long spears set at one level were withstanding his shield-bearing troops, and saw too the strength of their interlocked shields... amazement and fear took possession of him' (Plutarch, Paulus, XIX).

When legion engaged phalanx frontally on level ground, Polybius tells us, spacings meant each Roman had to fight 10 pikes with just his sword, once his *pila* were thrown. If fighting on the phalanx's terms, the legion could face bloody defeat, as happened to the Pelignians – troops armed in the legionary manner – on Paulus' flank:

'The Romans [*sic*], when they attacked the Macedonian phalanx, were unable to force a passage....For the Romans tried to thrust aside the long spears of their enemies with their swords, or to crowd them back with their shields, or to seize and put them by with their very hands; while the Macedonians, holding them firmly advanced with both hands, and piercing those who fell upon them, armour and all, since neither shield nor breastplate could resist the force of the Macedonian long spear, hurled headlong back the Pelignians...who, with no consideration but with animal fury rushed upon the strokes that met them, and a certain death. When the first line had thus been cut to pieces, those arrayed behind them were beaten back; and though there was no flight, still they retired...so that even Aemilius, as

Poseidonius tells us, when he saw it, rent his garments. For this part of his army was retreating, and the rest of the Romans were turning aside from the phalanx, which gave them no access to it, but confronted them as it were with a dense barricade of long spears, and was everywhere unassailable' (Plutarch, *Paulus*, XX).

It is likely that the front ranks of the phalanx became uneven as individuals or groups either resisted or gave way, and as they pushed the Romans back, they moved onto rough ground and their formation began to break up. The looser manipular formation was now at an advantage and, Plutarch tells us, the Romans now fought a junior commander's battle:

'[T]he ground was uneven, and the line of battle so long that shields could not be kept continuously locked together, and Aemilius therefore saw that the Macedonian phalanx was getting many clefts and intervals in it, as is natural when armies are large and the efforts of the combatants are diversified; portions of it were hard pressed, and other portions were pressing forward. Thereupon he came up swiftly, and dividing up his cohorts, ordered them to plunge quickly into the interstices and empty spaces in the enemy's line and thus come to close quarters, not fighting a single battle against them all, but many separate and successive battles. These instructions being given by Aemilius to his officers, and by his officers to the soldiers, as soon as they got between the ranks of the enemy and separated them, they attacked some of them in the flank where their armour did not shield them and cut off others by falling upon their rear' (Plutarch, *Paulus*, XX).

Livy corroborates this:

'The most manifest cause of the victory was the fact that there were many scattered engagements....The strength of the phalanx is irresistible when it is close-packed and bristling with extended spears; but if, by attacks at different points, you force the troops to swing round their spears, unwieldy as they are by reason of their length and weight, they become entangled in a disorderly mass; and further, the noise of any commotion on the flank or rear throws them into confusion, and then the whole formation

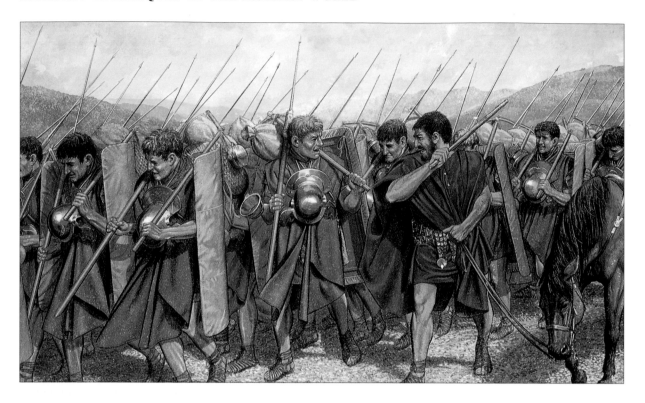

LEGIONARIES ON THE MARCH *encouraged by one of their officers. Under Marius a legion was expected to perform frequent route marches to keep the men fit and ready for battle.*

collapses. That is what happened in this battle, when the phalanx was forced to meet the Romans who were attacking in small groups, with the Macedonian line broken at many points. The Romans kept infiltrating their files at every place where a gap offered' (Livy, XLIV.42).

Once the phalanx broke up, the Roman *hastatus,* or *principe*, had an almost unbeatable advantage over the the individual phalangite. He was trained to fight in a looser, more flexible formation and with the *gladius* – a shorter, handier weapon than the *sarissa*.Moreover, Plutarch claims that the phalangites threw away the *sarissa,* leaving them to defend themselves against these well-trained swordsmen with only a dagger and a small wicker shield.The phalanx was cut to pieces, and apart from 3000 men from an élite unit who held their ground and were killed almost to a man, they broke and ran, the Romans

slaughtering so many of them in the pursuit that the River Leucus, near the battlefield, ran red with their blood a day later. Plutarch estimates Macedonian deaths at 25,000, Roman at 80–100.

The kingdom of Philip and Alexander was humbled in one morning. The most important factor in this was the organization of the Roman legions, combined with a system of battle drills that enabled rapid response of orders and the exploitation of situations as they developed. Add to this a style of command that did not attempt to impose control from the centre and that was tolerant of initiative and therefore less prone to problems posed by terrain or enemy action, which enabled commanders at all levels to exploit opportunities for aggressive action.This dovetailed nicely with the ethos and weaponry of the individual legionary who, unlike the phalangite, was capable of fighting effectively in small groups or even singly if the situation demanded.

Gaius Marius and the 'New' Legion

By 100 BC, the cohort was a permanent formation within the legion, the citizen levy had been supplanted by professional soldiers, and the legions were converted into permanent, numbered formations akin to the divisions of modern armies. Although the legion was still divided into three lines called *hastati*, *principes* and *triarii*, distinctions of armour and weaponry were abolished, the entire legion now fighting with the sword and *pila* combination. These were the legions of Pompey, Caesar and the Civil Wars, and this organization was retained, with some evolution, into the second century AD.

These changes have been seen as another 'revolution in military affairs', attributed to one man, Gaius (or Caius) Marius, six times consul of Rome, victor in the war against King Jugurtha of Numidia (110–105 BC) and saviour of Italy from a massive barbarian invasion that took place between 102 and 101 BC. Marius changed Roman political culture, using the army as a power base and military success to build a political reputation, setting the pattern for all Roman politicians after him, Julius Caesar especially. Whether Marius changed Roman military practice to the same extent is more problematical, as many of the innovations credited to him can actually be seen as the culmination of a lengthy period of evolution.

The army of Marius' time was still based on a levy of property-owning Roman citizens, serving for a term of six years; indeed, the Senate ordered a muster in 52 BC, 50 years after Marius led his 'new' legions against the Cimbri. However, as mentioned already, the almost incessant wars of the third and second centuries brought changes in the personnel of the Roman army. The restriction of service to certain citizens was relaxed when Rome needed more soldiers, and the length of some conflicts meant that there were many soldiers with nothing to go back to; they were allowed to re-enlist voluntarily at the end of their six years, effectively becoming long-service career soldiers. This transition gathered pace due to the type of campaign Rome fought increasingly from 200 BC onwards. The wars against Pyrrhos and Hannibal had been wars of national survival, in which every citizen was expected to defend the homeland; after Zama, Rome fought wars of expansion or imperial defence, often far from Italy and lasting for many years. For these 'optional' conflicts, Rome tended to look to volunteers, offering donatives or plots of land as an incentive to re-enlist. Moreover, experienced soldiers had the prospect of promotion to the centurionate, bringing social prestige and monetary reward.

The Jugurthine War was one such 'optional' conflict. Marius, upon being elected Consul with a mandate to end the war, 'enlisted many a poor and insignificant man, although former commanders had not accepted such persons, but bestowed arms, just as they would any other honour, only on those whose property assessment made them worthy to receive these' (Plutarch, Gaius Marius, IX). These 'poor and insignificant men' were from the *capite censi*, the lowest class of Roman citizen, who owned no property at all and so had previously been disqualified from military service. Thanks to Marius, they were now levied in very large numbers indeed. Marius' reasoning seems to have been more political than military; he had become a consul despite humble origins and an unfortunate propensity to speak his mind, and was unlikely to enjoy further success unless he created a natural constituency for himself.

Marius' New Army

These new levies could not afford their own equipment. The state had already begun to provide weapons and equipment; in 122 BC, another populist politician, Gaius Gracchus, Tribune of the People, had passed a law requiring the state to provide a soldier's clothing. This may explain the growing standardization of weapons and equipment from the mid-second century BC onwards. Unfortunately, pictorial and archaeological evidence for what this new type of legionary looked like is sparse, the main source being the altar recording a levy of troops during the consulship of Domitius Ahenobarbus in 115 BC. The carvings on the altar show a senior officer, presumably a tribune, and four legionaries. The legionaries wear sleeveless mail hauberks cut to just above the knee, over simple tunics; one wears a Montefortino helmet, while the other three, and the tribune, wear Etrusco-Corinthian helmets, all with flowing horsehair crests. The legionaries carry oval *scuta* with a single, horizontal handgrip behind the boss, and the *gladius* in a scabbard slung below the right arm on a belt of indeterminate material. The *pilum* was still standard issue, and Marius is credited with an important technical innovation:

'Up to this time, it seems, that part of the shaft which was let into the iron head was fastened there by two iron nails; but now, leaving one of these as it was, Marius removed the other, and put in its place a wooden pin that could easily be broken. His design was that the [*pilum*], after striking the enemy's shield, should not stand straight out, but that the wooden peg should break, thus allowing the shaft to bend in the iron head and trail along the ground, being held fast by the twist at the point of the weapon' (Plutarch, *Marius*, XXV).

The objective again was to render a *pilum*-struck shield useless, and possibly even trip up the shield carrier!

Marius used cohorts skilfully, perhaps explaining why the creation of the cohort is sometimes attributed to him. Formalization of the cohort system may have been necessitated by the spread of the Empire, and the need to garrison large areas with semi-independent units. However, the growth in long-service soldiery meant that the legions themselves gradually became permanent formations indoctrinated with a corporate identity not dissimilar to that of the regiments of the modern British Army. The *genius* (guardian spirit) of each legion was solidified in the form of the eagle standard Marius issued to each one under his command. This was more than just a regimental colour, it was also a totem of awesome religious importance, and the loss of an eagle in battle was seen as a national disaster.

Unfortunately, we do not have a Polybius to detail the tactics of the 'new' Roman army, so we must reconstruct these from references in the works of Plutarch and Caesar. Caesar describes the legion as still fighting in three lines, and there are references in Tacitus to legions fighting in wedges in battles of the first century AD, so it is possible that manipular formation was still used occasionally. However, there is strong evidence for the use of the cohort, rather than the legion, as the main tactical unit, the larger number of smaller units increasing the flexibility of Roman armies and leading to greater tactical sophistication. At Koronea (90 BC), Marius' detested rival, Lucius Cornelius Sulla, moved a force of four cohorts to meet a Pontic attempt to stretch his left flank while personally leading a fifth to meet an attack on his right. At Pharsalus (48 BC) Caesar used a special force of six cohorts, drawn from the *triarii* of each legion, to counter an attempt by Pompey's cavalry to turn his flank. Pharsalus is also interesting in indicating that, under some circumstances, the loose, sword-fighting formation of the manipular legion was abandoned in favour of a denser formation, in which legionaries would fight shield to shield, retaining their *pila* as thrusting spears. Marius adopted such a formation against the Teutones between 102 and 101 BC, and this is how Caesar's reserve cohorts met Pompey's cavalry at Pharsalus. Describing Roman tactics against the Alans in AD 135, Arrian recommends that such a formation should be used against heavy cavalry. It would appear that, when facing cavalry or infantry in dense formation, the legion stood on the defensive in this formation, usually on high ground, until the enemy attack was spent, then opened ranks, drew swords and counterattacked, as at Aquae Sextae and Caesar's XII Legion's battle against the Belgae in 57 BC. Alternatively, against lighter troops, they would immediately throw *pila* and countercharge, as seen in Tacitus' accounts of battles between Romans and Britons.

Another development was a steady increase in the missile power supporting the legion. In addition to auxiliary archers and slingers, each legion had a detachment of artillery, intended to support a siege or defend the legion's camp, but sometimes used in field battle. Vegetius records that each legion had 55 bolt throwers (*ballistae*) and 10 catapults. In some battles, missile power was used as the main killing instrument, with the legions exploiting the situations it created. At Koronea, Sulla used firebolts from his artillery and volleys of *pila* from his rear ranks to shatter the Pontic phalanx. His legionaries cut into the breaches created by this missile power to destroy the phalanx in a near-repeat of Pydna.

Roman Legionary 168 BC

This is a fairly typical legionary of Marius' time, forced to carry his equipment with him on the march. He is armed with a single pilum, *although most legionaries would carry two into battle. Also visible is his* gladius *in a scabbard hung from his left shoulder. On the other hip is a small dagger for emergencies. His shield is a wooden* scutum, *built from cross-laid planks bound with iron, and with an iron boss that could be used to punch opponents. The outside of the scutum was covered in leather For protection, this legionary wears a bronze helmet with flexible cheek pieces. He wears a mail cuirass with leather trimming to protect his neck. His sandals are made of leather and have hob nails on their soles. Amongst the equipment carried would be entrenching tools, a bedroll, a cloak, and cooking implements, plus rations for several days in the field.*

Aquae Sextae

102 BC

Marius ordered Claudius Marcellus to hide 3000 men in the hills. Marius then instructed his legionaries to allow the Germans to charge uphill; they were to throw *pila* once the Germans were in range. The Germans charged up the hill, where their formation was disrupted by the slope, the rocky terrain, and the volleys of *pila* from the Romans above, which inflicted heavier casualties than usual, due to the Germans' dense formation and lack of armour. A shoving and stabbing match then ensued, in which the Romans, with the *gladius*, better training and uphill position, had a decisive advantage. The Germans were pushed back down onto the plain, where they tried to form a shield wall. It was now that Marcellus' cohorts charged down from the hills behind the Teutones and hit them in the rear, just as Marius attacked their front. The German rear routed, scattering the front ranks, and the entire army fell apart. Plutarch estimates that 100,000 Germans were killed.

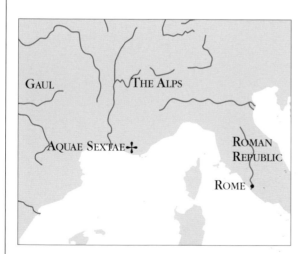

Aquae Sextae and the later battle of Vercellae sealed Marius' military reputation, and put an end to the danger to the Roman Republic from the migrant German horde.

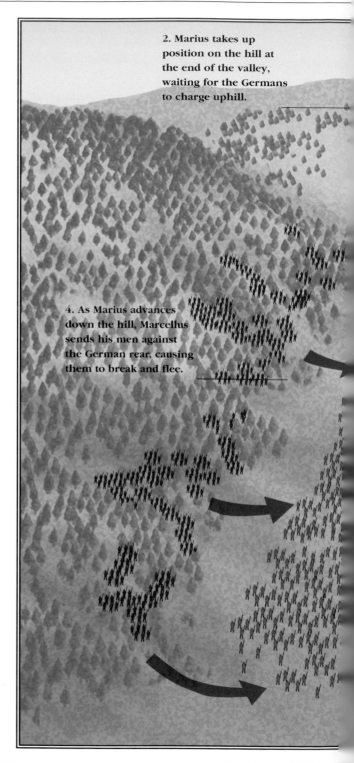

2. Marius takes up position on the hill at the end of the valley, waiting for the Germans to charge uphill.

4. As Marius advances down the hill, Marcellus sends his men against the German rear, causing them to break and flee.

1. Before the battle Marius places Marcellus with 3000 men ready to launch an ambush against the Germans.

3. The Germans, disrupted by the Roman *pila*, the slope and the rough ground, fall back to the plain.

A CELTIC SHIELD *from the 1st century BC. Such shields were similar in size to the Roman* scutum, *but were made of wooden planks covered with a stretched piece of hide, which was usually decorated.*

Aquae Sextae: 102 BC

In 105 BC, the Roman provinces of Cisalpine and Transalpine Gaul underwent a massive invasion by tribal peoples from the north. A total of 300,000 warriors – and larger numbers of old people, women and children – arrived in a huge wagon train, probably driven west by pressures of land and population. This horde was a multitribal coalition centred on two Germanic tribes, the Teutones and the Ambrones, and also including

Scythians and a mysterious people called the Cimbri: 'The most prevalent conjecture was that they were some of the German peoples which extended as far as the northern ocean, a conjecture based on their great stature, their light-blue eyes, and the fact that the Germans call robbers Cimbri' (Plutarch, Marius, XI). Having said this, Plutarch speculated that the Cimbri were Cimmerians, northern Gauls, and his (possibly anachronistic) description of their weapons and fighting style strengthens this view.

Rome had unpleasant memories of the Gauls. One of the pivotal events in Roman history was the Gallic invasion of 390 BC, when the High King, Bran (Brennus), annihilated a Roman hoplite army and then sacked Rome herself. The Gauls beat the Romans again in 285 BC and invaded Italy again in 225 BC; they were also enthusiastic allies of Rome's enemies, including Hannibal. Consequently, Roman campaigns against the Gauls were often genocidal, even by their standards.

It is unsurprising, therefore, that the Romans saw the invasion as a threat to national survival. When an army under Quintus Servilius Caepio was defeated by the barbarians in mid-104 BC, and the horde then veered towards Italy, the Senate had no option but to swallow its pride and summon its bitterest critic, Marius, who returned from Numidia with his army and took up his second consulship on 1 January 104 BC. This indicates the depth of the emergency, as Roman law previously stipulated that no consul could be re-elected within 10 years of his first term, and Marius had been a consul just three years before. Marius celebrated his triumph over Jugurtha and baited the Senate by appearing in front of it still dressed for the parade, before setting out with his army.

Speed was of the essence, and Marius dispensed with a large, slow baggage train by ordering his soldiers to carry their own baggage, an expedient that earned them the nickname of 'Marius' Mules'. Fortunately, the barbarians veered off into Spain, giving Marius more time to train his force. For all his ferocity of manner, Marius was popular with his troops. He was what later generations would call a 'soldier's soldier', immensely tough, speaking the same language as the ordinary soldier, eating the same food and sharing his work. As a disciplinarian, Marius was hard but fair, and his acquittal of a tribune who had killed Marius' nephew in defence against an attempted homosexual rape was key in winning his soldiers' trust.

That summer, the Teutones and Ambrones split from the main horde and made for Italy. In their way was Marius' army, which occupied a fortified position on the River Rhone. Marius kept his troops confined within the fort, but ensured that they had regular sightings of the barbarians to inure them to their appearance. The Romans' fear soon turned to contempt. Considering the barbarians as loud-mouthed braggarts, good only for robbing unarmed civilians, they began to demand that Marius bring matters to a conclusion. The Teutones attacked the fort, but were beaten back by volleys of *pila* and firebolts. Bypassing the fort, they made for Italy.

Marius broke camp and followed, intercepting them at Aquae Sextae (Aix-en-Provence). While the Romans were building another camp, servants went forward to collect water from a river that ran near the barbarian camp. A major fight broke out here between Ligurian auxiliaries and Ambrone warriors, in which the Ligurians, joined by Roman legionaries, inflicted heavy casualties on the Ambrones.

The main battle took place next day, and involved an excellent example of manoeuvre by cohorts. It took place in a valley dominated by steep, heavily wooded hills. Marius ordered Claudius Marcellus, a tribune, to take 3000 men – around 6 cohorts – to hide in the hills until battle was joined, then charge downhill against the enemy rear. Marcellus' force was clearly infantry, as Plutarch records that Marius kept his cavalry under his own direct command, using them to screen the deployment of the remainder of his legions around his hilltop camp.

Belying their 'barbaric' image, Germanic tribesmen were a semi-disciplined force whom

> *'[Marius] enlisted many a poor and insignificant man, although former commanders had not accepted such persons, but bestowed arms…only on those whose property assessment made them worthy'* – PLUTARCH

Caesar reported as fighting in a solid, phalanx-like formation. However, any advantages derived from this formation, and the aggression of the warriors, was undone by their crude weaponry. Apart from stolen items, or those recovered from the battlefield, swords were not carried and the main German weapon was the *framea*, a thrusting spear with a head of poor-quality iron, almost useless against armoured troops. Moreover, the Germans fought semi-naked and so were especially vulnerable to missiles.

Marius instructed his legionaries accordingly, ordering them to stand firm and allow the Germans to charge uphill; they were to throw *pila* once the Germans were in range, then draw swords, lock shields, and push the Germans back down the slopes. To set an example, Marius, who was then 56 years old, would fight in the front line!

Roman Success

Everything went according to plan. The Teutones obligingly charged up the hill, and their formation was disrupted by the slope, the rocky terrain, and the volleys of *pila* from the Romans above, which no doubt inflicted heavier casualties than usual, due to the Germans' dense formation and lack of armour. An *othismos*-like shoving and stabbing match then ensued, in which the Romans, with the *gladius*, better training and uphill position, had a decisive advantage. The Teutones were pushed back down onto the plain, where they tried to form a shield wall. It was now that Marcellus' cohorts charged down from the hills behind the Teutones and hit them in the rear, just as Marius attacked their front. The German rear routed, scattering the front ranks, and the entire army fell apart. Plutarch estimates that 100,000 Germans were killed, and if we include non-combatants in the German camp, which the Romans then torched, this figure may not be too great an exaggeration. A number of Teutonic chieftains were captured and taken to Rome in chains to march in another triumphal parade before being whipped to the Forum and publicly garrotted. However, upon arrival in Rome, Marius learned that the Cimbri had broken through the Alpine passes and were now threatening Italy herself.

Marius summoned his army from Gaul. It is interesting that, rather than raise another levy, as might be justified by the situation, Marius chose instead to rely on long-service veterans who had been with him in Numidia and Gaul. While such troops had formed the hard core of Roman armies for generations, Marius' campaigns mark a change in military culture, as professional soldiers were now clearly preferred. Boeorix, the King of the Cimbri, challenged the Romans to fight

on the plain of Vercellae, agreeable to both sides as it suited the Cimbri's vast numbers and manoeuvre by the Roman cavalry.

Marius' force numbered around 35,000, which he drew up with his veterans on the wings and the less-experienced forces of his fellow consul, Quintus Lutitius Catullus, in the centre. The Cimbri had 15,000 cavalry and enough infantry to cover a square 6km (3.7 miles) on each side!

A LATE 1ST CENTURY AD LEGION *shown in full. It was divided into ten cohorts. The first cohort had five centuries of about 160 men each, the remainder had six centuries of about 80 men. Each legion had an attachment of about 120 horsemen to act as scouts and despatch riders. The legion was commanded by a legate, a senator appointed by the emperor.*

The Cimbric cavalry deployed on their right, and tried to use feigned retreats to draw the Romans to their left, to give the infantry on the Cimbric left an opportunity to outflank them. However, the Romans did not fall for this, and the battle turned on a dour infantry fight in the centre, in which a key factor was an enormous dust storm. Sulla, who fought in this battle, later claimed it was sent by the gods in retribution for Marius' presumption that they were with him – it is more likely to have been whipped up by the Cimbric cavalry. The heat and the dust favoured the Romans, who were used to such conditions, but the volleys of *pila* that met the Cimbric charge, and the superior swordsmanship of the Romans, must have told as well; Dionysius' description of Romans fighting Gauls hints at what the battle in the dust might have been like. Eventually, the Cimbri broke, and were pursued back to their camp by the Romans, who were greeted with horrific scenes as the Cimbri women murdered their men and children, before killing themselves, rather than be taken prisoner.

Rome was saved, and Marius was hailed a third founder of Rome after Romulus and Camillus. In a rare gesture of magnanimity, he shared a joint triumph with Catullus. More than any tactical brilliance, Marius owed his success to the superior training and technology of his legions, which enabled them at Aquae Sextae to defeat a larger number of poorly armed Germans. At Vercellae, the Gauls were probably as well armed as the Romans, and Plutarch emphazises that the better training and superior physical fitness of the Romans decided the battle.

Legions of the Empire, 14 BC to AD 200

Recognizing, like his great uncle Caesar, that military success was a good basis for political popularity, the first Roman Emperor, Augustus, followed a policy of cautious expansion, alternated with consolidation of the Empire's defences. This was halted after three legions were destroyed, and their eagles captured, by the German chieftain, Hermann (Arminius) in the Teutoberg Forest in AD 9. Augustus advised his successor, Tiberius, against further conquests. Nonetheless, there were two later bursts of expansion: in AD 43, the

Plutarch's description of their armour and weapons conforms with that carried by Gauls in other sources: they wore 'helmets made to resemble the maws of frightful wild beasts or the heads of strange animals...[and] breastplates of iron, and carried gleaming white shields. For hurling, each man had two lances; and at close quarters they used large, heavy swords.' The latter was a distinctly Gallic weapon.

Emperor Claudius ordered the invasion of Britain and between AD 101 and 115, Trajan conquered Dacia (modern Romania) and Mesopotamia. Trajan's successor, Hadrian, adopted a passive-defensive policy based on fortifying the frontiers.

Imperial strategy demanded a small, professional army. In 31 BC, there were 60 legions, but Augustus cut their number to 28, made up of long-service volunteers. The traditional 16 years of wartime service was restored as the minimum enlistment period, later expanded to 20. Property qualifications were dissolved completely, entry now being open to all Roman citizens who could pass selection. Each legion was commanded by a legate (a senator appointed directly by the Emperor), and six tribunes. The senior tribune was a candidate for the Senate, the others followed a career path alternating between service in public life, the legions and the auxiliaries.

Organization remained similar to under Marius, with 10 cohorts consisting of 6 centuries of 80 men each, formed into maniples. However, some time after AD 50, the first cohort was expanded to 5 double-sized centuries for a strength of 800 men. According to Vegetius, the first cohort was an élite consisting of the best soldiers in the legion, and it guarded the Eagle and the images of the Emperor that it carried into battle.

While the legate and the tribunes commanded the legion, it was the 59 centurions who formed its professional cadre. While most centurions were promoted legionaries, men from the Praetorian

ROMAN LEGIONARY SHIELDS *from left to right: a scutum used from the 7th century BC to around AD 50; a 'squared-off' scutum, c. 10 BC, used until c. AD 175; a shield with a circular boss to save weight, c. AD 20; a rectangular shield from c. AD 40 used until after AD 200; an oval shield used from c. AD 150 to Rome's fall.*

Guard or from the equestrian class, directly below the senatorial, could also apply. Vegetius relates that centurions were promoted on a circular system, beginning with a legionary promoted from the first cohort to become junior centurion in the legion, commanding the second century of the third maniple of the tenth cohort, then progressing onwards and upwards towards *primus pilus*, commanding the first maniple of the first cohort. Whether a cohort was commanded by a tribune or its senior centurion is unclear; Vegetius says they were commanded by tribunes, although how 6 tribunes were divided among 10 cohorts is problematical, and Vegetius does sometimes use the word 'tribune' as a generic term for 'officer'. At the pinnacle of the centurionate was the senior centurion of the first cohort, the *primus pilus*, a post that could take between 30 and 40 years to reach and that, because this was the first cohort, would require education and experience beyond that of other senior centurions. This post could be held only for a year, after which the holder would either retire, usually to a senior post within the Imperial administration, or be promoted to *praefectus castrorum* (prefect of the camp). *Praefectus castrorum* was a new post created by

Augustus; he oversaw supplies, including armour and weaponry, and the construction of the fortified camp that the legion built each night while on the march in hostile territory; he commanded the legion in the absence of the legate and senior tribune and, until the second century AD, supervised training and disciplinary procedures. He was the legion's senior professional officer, and it is likely that a prudent legate would have sought his advice on many matters, including tactics.

Officers commanded through example and fear: while Caesar and Josephus provide numerous anecdotes of centurions inspiring their men through personal bravery and upright character, Tacitus tells of Centurion Lucilius, nicknamed 'Fetch Me Another' by his men because every time he broke a cane over a legionary's back, he would call for another. Lucilius and several other centurions were lynched during a mutiny on the German frontiers in AD 14, when it was also revealed that his legate had a private bodyguard of ex-gladiators to protect him from his own men.

'the barbarians…quite lacking in military science…would raise their swords aloft and smite after the manner of wild boars, throwing the whole weight of their bodies into the blow like hewers of wood' – DIONYSIUS

Legionary equipment underwent a limited degree of evolution. The *pilum* was used at least until AD 200, in a form similar to that of the Republic, but getting progressively lighter; pictorial evidence from a relief in the Vatican indicates that some *pila* may have been steadied by round lead weights at the junction of the head and the shaft. The sword shortened, the blade being typically around 50cm (20in) long, but it had a relatively longer point, indicating that it had become purely a stabbing weapon. Legionaries continued to wear chainmail hauberks until the late first century AD, when these were slowly supplanted by that most distinctly 'Roman' piece of equipment, the *lorica segmentata* (segmented cuirass). Legionaries are depicted wearing the *lorica segmentata* in numerous carved illustrations and figurines, most notably on the column Trajan raised in Rome to mark his victory in Dacia. Because these are uncoloured, it was assumed for many years that the *lorica segmentata* was made strips of hardened leather, this influencing a number of Hollywood reconstructions of Roman soldiers. Then, in 1964, two complete sets were discovered at a site near Hadrian's Wall, and accurate reconstructions were possible. In actuality, the armour was made of iron strips held together with hooks, straps or thongs; it covered just the upper body and shoulders, but was lighter and easier to mass-produce than mail. At around the same time it was being introduced, the oval *scutum* was replaced by a rectangular shield made of layers of plywood covered with leather, and edged with bronze, still carried by a horizontal handgrip behind the boss. There appears to have been little uniformity in helmets: some legions continued with the Monte-fortino well into the first century AD, but increasing use was made of the Gallic, so named because it was first produced at armouries in Gaul and perhaps based on a type worn by Gauls. The Gallic helmet bore a superficial resemblance to the Montefortino, but the neck guard was lengthened and lowered to protect the nape of the neck, and many examples have a reinforcing strip across the front of the cap to protect the face from plunging missiles or a downward sword-slash.

The Auxiliaries

The legions formed the main strike arm of the Roman army, tending to be called out to deal with major threats. Garrison work and 'optional' operations fell upon the *auxilia*, units made up of non-Roman citizens and subject peoples of the Empire, which would also support the legions in larger conflicts. *Auxilia* could consist of tribal levies, mercenaries or allies, but from Augustus onwards, there were at least 70 cohorts of auxiliary infantry made up of long-service professionals and organized similarly to the legionary cohort.

Each auxiliary cohort was recruited from a specific province of the Empire, its title indicating its province of origin. From the late first century AD, though, cohorts would frequently be posted elsewhere and recruitment from their new area could produce some strange ethnic mixes. The main incentive for enlisting was that, upon completing 25 years of service, the auxiliary and his descendants would be granted Roman citizenship, with all its entitlements. Cohorts could be of archers, slingers or heavy infantry – all are depicted on Trajan's column – but all seem to have followed a similar basic organization. The cohort was commanded by a tribune or a prefect from the equestrian class; it consisted of 6 centuries until the mid-first century AD, when the number of centuries was increased to 10 for a full strength of about 800.

As befits their 'second class' status, auxiliary equipment was at least a generation behind that of the legions. On Trajan's column, auxiliary heavy infantry are depicted wearing chainmail hauberks and carrying oval *scuta*, but also wear Gallic helmets and use the *gladius*. Interestingly, archers are depicted wearing similar hauberks to the heavies and also carry the *gladius*; pictorial and archaeological evidence shows that they carried composite bows with a range of around 600m (1970ft). Slingers are shown on Trajan's column wearing just tunics, implying they were used as skirmishers; their slings are shorter than earlier models and shot tennis-ball sized stones on the first spin.

Tactics of the Imperial Army

Battle accounts of this time are frustratingly vague, and reconstructing the tactics of the Imperial Army involves a degree of conjecture. For the climactic battle with Queen Boudicca (Boadicea) in AD 70, Tacitus relates that the Roman Governor of Britain, Suetonius Paulinus, adopted a similar defensive-offensive doctrine to that of Marius at Aquae Sextae. Choosing a good defensive position – a narrow valley with woods behind it and with open country in front – he ordered his legions to stand their ground until the Britons were in range, then throw *pila* and countercharge with the *gladius*, routing them easily.

However, large field battles were uncommon in this period. More frequently, campaigns centred on counter-guerilla operations, usually concluded by the legions storming the insurgent's strongholds. Campaigning therefore became more often a logistical and engineering problem than a tactical one, and apparently became formulaic: while he may be exaggerating, the historian Josephus – who fought the Romans in the Jewish Revolt of AD 66–73 before defecting to them – dwells on the Romans' intense rehearsal of every aspect of a campaign, their tight central control of battles and the excessively deliberate nature of their tactics, contrasting with the artfulness of Pydna or Kynoskephalai and suggesting an increasingly drilled and stereotyped approach. Josephus' accounts of the storming of fortresses in Judea and Tactitus' reconstructions of attacks on British hill forts corroborate each other on this, but if Roman tactics were stereotyped, so were those of their enemies, and set practices were probably essential in an army with often amateur commanders.

The doctrine of relying on massive missile power may also be a symptom of this. When the future Emperor, Vespasianus, besieged the Jewish town of Jotapata in AD 68, he began each day's

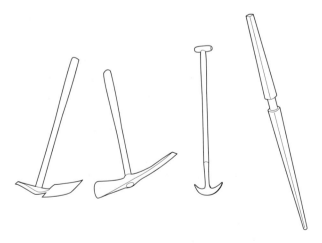

A LEGIONARY'S TOOLS *and a palisade stake from examples found at Hadrian's wall. The tools are, from left to right, an entrenching tool, a pickaxe and a turf cutter, all reconstructed from archaeological finds.*

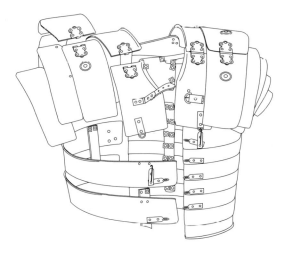

A RECONSTRUCTION OF THE *LORICA SEGMENTATA showing how the iron segments are held together with hooks and riveted leather straps to produce a flexible yet effective armour.*

assault with a bombardment by at least 350 artillery pieces and 7000 auxiliary archers; when his son, Titus, stormed Jerusalem two years later, he may have had some 700 artillery pieces in support. Missile power was also increasingly important in field battle: against the Alans in AD 135, Arrian deployed his two legions in a tight shield wall, behind which were two lines of archers and artillery, shooting down the Alan cavalry from behind the protective barricade of the legions.

Covered by this missile power, legions assaulted fortified positions, sometimes using special formations. The best known of these was the *testudo* (tortoise), wherein the front rank crouched behind the shields of the second rank, which were held out between each man in the front rank. The men on each end held their shields outwards and those in the middle held their shields above their heads; the following ranks locked onto these, the outer men holding their shields out to the side, the middle above them, forming a roof of overlapping shields. This is an indicator of the level of training of the Imperial Army, as it required intense drilling and rehearsal to form properly. A well-formed *testudo* was impenetrable to missiles, but Josephus includes a horrific description of the defenders of Jotapata

breaking one with boiling fat, the one weapon that could penetrate the shield-roof.

The Legion Loses its Tactical Edge

From the mid-second century AD, the main external threat to the Roman Empire came from 'barbarians', Germanic tribal peoples living beyond the frontiers. In the early second century, barbarian tribes coalesced into two confederations, the Franks on the lower Rhine and the Alamanni on the frontier linking the Rhine to the Danube. Behind these were Goths and Vandals, Nordic peoples migrating from the Baltic, pressing the western tribes against the Roman frontier and posing a direct threat to the eastern provinces. From the fourth century, these were themselves pressured from the east by the Huns, nomads who were migrating to eastern Europe from Central Asia. In the east, Persia revived under the Sassanid emperors, who coveted Roman Mesopotamia and Syria, which had been been part of the sphere of influence established by Cyrus.

These pressures resulted in a series of irruptions into Imperial territory. Combined with chronic civil unrest, these led to the fall of the Roman Empire in the west. The Roman army, the Empire's ultimate guarantor of security, could not halt this; throughout this period it suffered a series of reverses at the hands of barbarians, of which Hadrianopolis (AD 378) was the biggest and best known. A common theme of literature of these times was that Rome was being punished for abandoning traditional institutions, religious and military ones in particular. Roman politics of the fourth and fifth centuries AD were marked by frequent reassertions of 'traditional values', of which attempts by the Emperors Julianus (AD 361–363) and Eugenius (AD 392–394) to restore paganism are the best known. Although a Christian, Vegetius is part of this trend: his *De Re Militarii* is addressed to an unnamed emperor, perhaps Theodosius I (AD 379–395), and is a polemic calling for a return to the military practices of the Republic and early Empire.

Initially, barbarian incursions consisted of short, shallow raids, which led to Roman punitive expeditions into the barbarian hinterland. With the coming of the Huns, incursions became larger, aiming at conquest and settlement, and often resulted in large battles. Independent of lines of supply, barbarian forces were highly mobile and, once they had breached the Empire's outer defences, could be difficult to catch. This required a response: under Marcus Aurelius (AD 161–180), whose Danubian campaigns showed up the inadequacy of Rome's defensive system, the Roman Army restructured to meet the threat. Septimius Severus (AD 193–211) created a mobile central reserve, made up of a specially formed legion and a reformed Praetorian Guard, to reinforce beleaguered provinces in time of crisis. Gallienus (AD 254–268) created independent cavalry armies under their own commanders. Thanks to a manpower levy, Diocletian (AD 284–305) expanded the army to a strength of around 500,000, doubled the number of legions, and posted them along the frontiers alongside *vexillationes* (detachments) of cavalry, attempting a return to the preclusiveness of the pre-Severan era. Constantine (AD 306–337) reduced the strength of a legion from 5000–6000 to 1000, and built up mobile forces by stripping

detachments from the frontier legions, which were now of limited use.

Constantine intended the screen of garrisons – *limitanei* – in the frontier zone to check minor incursions and hinder larger invasions by holding fortified towns and strongpoints along lines of communication, giving the mobile forces (*comitatenses*) time to concentrate. If the barbarians dispersed to forage, they could be hunted down piecemeal by small detachments or, if these massed together, could be brought to battle by the mobile army. The late Roman historian, Ammianus Marcellinus, tells us that these armies incorporated a substantial mounted arm, including horse archers and *clibanarii*, heavily armoured cavalry possibly based on the Persian *cataphractus*. However, like its predecessors, the mobile army centred on heavy infantry. Ammianus reported that infantry were 'the main strength' of the force that Julianus took into Persia in AD 361,

A RECONSTRUCTION OF THE *TESTUDO from a relief, showing various objects hurled at the legionaries in an attempt to disrupt their formation. Boiling fat proved successful for the defenders of Jotapata.*

while the *Notitia Dignitatum*, a formal 'order of battle' for the western and eastern armies dating from the 390s, lists 13 'legiones' alongside 6 *vexillationes* of cavalry for the main western field army based in Italy.

It is mainly with the 'legion' that Vegetius concerns himself, beginning by discussing recruitment. The massive increase in the size of the army created manning problems: service in the legions was traditionally restricted to Roman citizens, so Caracalla (AD 211–217) increased the recruiting base by extending Roman citizenship to all free men within the Empire. Perhaps the most sweeping change in Roman military practice since Marius came when Diocletian abandoned the small professional army for a larger conscript one, levying recruits compulsorily from cities and landowners, and obliging sons of soldiers to follow their fathers into the army. This was deeply unpopular as, for nearly 400 years, Rome had been an urbanized society in which only a tiny minority had any enthusiasm for soldiering. Ammianus implied that severing the thumb to avoid the levy was a common practice in his day, while Valentinian I (AD 364–375) discovered that his own soldiers were harbouring men liable for service by disguising them as 'servants'. That the avoidance of call-up was causing serious problems is indicated by Valentinian I's edict that self-mutilators should be burned at the stake; Theodosius I (AD 379–395) made them serve, but required that groups should send two fit men for every one mutilated. The most serious consequence of this was the decline of the intense indoctrination and discipline that had given the professional legion its tactical edge. Ammianus relates numerous accounts of indiscipline, and of Roman soldiers fleeing the battlefield, and it may be that Vegetius' reference to the 'military mark', which was branded on the hand, served as a precaution against desertion. Indeed, Vegetius gives over the whole of the first section of his work to arguing for greater selectivity in recruiting and a return to previous training methods.

According to Ammianus, Gauls had few qualms about serving in the Roman army, and it is probable that the great majority of the army of his period consisted of men from the provinces, rather than Italy itself. Caracalla's and Diocletian's innovations resulted in the intake of large numbers of men of non-Latin stock and, in some provinces, only 'semi-Romanized' in language and culture. There were certainly sizeable numbers of barbarians in Ammianus' army, the result of a deliberate policy by several Emperors, who saw them as a means of increasing the army's strength while reducing pressure on the borders. The historian Zosimus reports that many of the Goths who invaded Thrace in AD 270 eventually enlisted in the Roman army; that following a victory over the Franks in AD 278, Probus sent many of his prisoners to Britain, 'where they proved very useful to the emperor in subsequent revolts'; and that a substantial part of Constantine's army at the Milvian Bridge (AD 312) was made up of 'troops from the barbarians he had conquered and the Germans and the other Gauls…together with those collected from Britain'. Whether these

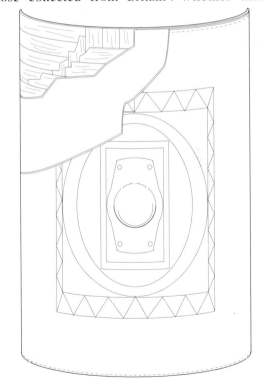

ROMAN SHIELD CONSTRUCTION *showing a* scutum *from the 3rd century AD. Laminated strips of wood were laid across each other and covered with linen and hide. The hemispherical boss was made from iron.*

intakes were incorporated into the regular army or served as federates, seperate contingents under their own tribal chieftains, is unclear. However, it is notable that Goths and Germans, bound by a warrior's code and admiring of strong leaders, tended not to panic, mutiny or disobey orders, unlike Romans.

Information on the organization of the late Roman legion is vague. The *Notitia Dignitatum* suggests that legions of the *comitatenses* had a strength of 1000, but could be broken down into 'detachments' of 500 men; it may be that

Constantine reduced the strength of the legions to produce a larger number of more mobile units. Ammianus and Vegetius both mention *auxilia* of 500; some of these bear the names of German tribes, and at Strasbourg one of these gave the German war-cry, the *barritus*, indicating recruitment mainly or perhaps exclusively from these groups. From the early fifth century, there are references to forces of 6000, broken down into 5 units, and 6 units of infantry totalling 4000. It would appear, therefore, that the strength of infantry units varied.

LEGIONARY TRAINING *using a wicker shield and wooden sword. A variety of strokes are practised against the wooden post, but the short, thick* gladius *was primarily used as a stabbing weapon in battle.*

cavalry from the Augustan period. It is unclear whether Vegetius' *spatha* is the same weapon, although a painting from the third century AD, in the Church of Dura Europos in Syria, shows foot soldiers (or perhaps dismounted cavalry) fighting with long, slashing swords. The possibility that by the fourth century infantry were using the sword mainly as a slashing weapon is implied by Vegetius in his plea that soldiers 'be taught to strike not with the edge, but with the point' of the sword. Vegetius was also of the opinion that the legionary spears were inferior to the Frankish *angon*, which he mistakenly believed was the same weapon as the *pilum*. He also tells us that many infantrymen had given up wearing armour, even helmets – surely a disadvantage when facing the Goths, who accompanied their charges with hails of missiles and later used massed bowshot, or against Hunnic horse archers. Examples of both types of spear have been discovered; the *spiculum* had an iron head 22cm (8.6in) long and a shaft around 1.6m (5ft 2in) long, while the *vericulum* was a shorter weapon, 1.1m (3ft 7in) long.

Another missile weapon was the *plumbata*, a type of heavy dart, which has also been found in large numbers at third- and fourth-century sites. It has been reconstructed as a fleched weapon with a barbed head, resembling an arrow. Vegetius related that certain selected units carried five *plumbata* in the hollow of the shield. That armour surviving from this period consists almost entirely of helmets gives credence to Vegetius' lament; however, pictorial evidence indicates that mail hauberks and possibly leather, muscled cuirasses were worn at least until the mid-fourth century. Helmets bore the mark of unskilled mass-production to meet the needs of the new conscript army. The Intercisa helmet is named after the site at Hungary where the first examples were discovered: the cap is made of two iron pieces riveted to a crest, with an iron neckguard and cheekpieces stitched to the lining. Round or oval shields are depicted in several illustrations of the time, and flat, oval shields made of plywood

Equipment

Vegetius records that the principal weapons of the Roman infantry soldier of his time were a sword, which he calls the *spatha*; a dagger; a heavy spear called the *spiculum*, which could be thrown or retained for stabbing (Ammianus refers on one occasion to barbarians being 'run through with pikes'); and a lighter spear, the *vericulum*. All these show barbarian influence. The identity of Vegetius' *spatha* is problematic. The *spatha* was a slashing sword with a 70.5-cm (28-in) blade, possibly based on the Gallic longsword and used by Roman with rawhide stitched on have been found at Dura Europos.

The legion formation Vegetius describes is more reminiscent of the Persian *sparabara* line than the old legion, although Vegetius is ambiguous about whether his 'lines' consist of ranks of individual soldiers or blocks of units. The missile power of this formation is formidable, intended perhaps to prevent barbarians reaching hand-to-hand range, where their size and strength could prove decisive. The first two lines consisted of armoured infantry, the first being 'experienced and seasoned soldiers, formerly called *principes*', presumably carrying throwing spears and the *spatha;* and the second, archers and troops armed with the *spiculum*. These would have a frontage of 1m (3ft) per man and a depth of just under 2m (6ft), the spears needing a short run-up to be thrown effectively. These troops 'act like a wall', a sanctuary and pivot of manoeuvre for the third and fourth lines, which are of javelineers, light archers and dartmen. These go forward to skirmish with the enemy but, if driven back, retreat behind the first and second lines, adding to the weight of their missiles. The fifth line is made up of ordinary slingers as well as artillery, men carrying the 'hand ballista' – an early type of crossbow – and the sling-staff, a weapon purportedly invented by Philip II and made of a 1m (3ft) long wooden staff with a leather sling attached, discharged with an overarm action. Behind these is a sixth line of heavy infantry acting as a reserve, which Vegetius identifies with the ancient *triarii* (perhaps this term was still used). Vegetius implies that they were crack troops intended to act as a 'fire brigade' in tight situations.

Tacitus refers to the armies of first-century German armies being 'arranged in wedges'. Ammianus refers to Roman troops taking up a wedge formation (*cuneus*) at Strasbourg and again in a battle between Julian and the Persians, while Vegetius discusses ways in which such formations

'a wise general [stations] brothers in rank besides brothers, friends besides friends…for whenever [they] are in danger …the [soldier] necessarily fights more recklessly for the man beside him' – ONASANDER

could be countered. The nickname for this formation was the *caput porci* ('pig's head') and it was still used in the eighth century by the Goth's cousins, the Vikings, who claimed to have been taught it by the war-god Odin himself and who called it the *svynfylking* ('swine array'). The Romans had always been quick to borrow good ideas from their enemies, and Vegetius argues that the main advantage of the wedge is that it allows a concentration of missile power into one position. His counter to the wedge is the pincers, and is made up of a body of *triarii* formed into a 'V' shape to contain the wedge. The saw is less clearly described, but may involve *triarii* charging through a broken line ahead of them to repel the enemy and allow the line to be repaired. Several other formations were used, Ammianus relating that the *testudo* was still used in Julianus' army, and also referring to armies forming squares.

In conclusion, the decline in the effectiveness of the Roman Army arose from expansion to meet the barbarian threat. Military service became compulsory, an unpopular move that contributed to the Army's decline, but which was compensated for – ironically – by the recruitment of barbarians. This led in turn to a 'barbarization' of Roman weapons and tactics. The tactical edge earned by the professionalism, superior weaponry and tactics of the legions of the Republic and early Empire had been sacrificed to strategic ends.

Strasbourg: AD 357

The Alamanni were one of the confederations of German tribes menacing the western Roman Empire in the third and fourth centuries. They invaded the Empire four times before AD 356, and had twice threatened Italy herself. In AD 356, an Alamann army under King Chnodomar invaded Gaul: the ensuing battle at Strasbourg was key in breaking the Alamann threat permanently and in establishing the reputation of the Emperor

Julianus, better remembered as Julian the Apostate. Julianus was a nephew of Constantine, and was appointed Caesar (co-regent) by his cousin, Constantius II in 355, when he was still a student, studying philosophy in Greece. Constantius' choice was controversial, for the Roman Empire had been a Christian state since Constantine, and Julianus was an openly practising pagan. His heroes were Plato, Aristotle, Lycurgus of Sparta and Marcus Aurelius, the Roman philosopher-emperor of the second century AD who had also been a formidable soldier. Ammianus Marcellinus relates an anecdote of an blind old woman, possibly a soothsayer, predicting Julianus would be 'the man who will restore the temples of the gods', and his reign was marked by measures to restore paganism as the state religion and a subtle persecution of Christians. Julianus was a gentle character, so there was no return to the extermination of Christians by earlier Emperors, but they were excluded by law from many professions, including the army.

This was in the future, however, as Constantius sent Julianus to Gaul to deal with the Alamanni. Constantius' reasoning is unclear: Julianus had no military experience, but he was a prince of the blood and popular with the citizenry. Perhaps Constantius hoped that the Alamanni might rid him of a dangerous rival. In Ammianus' view, Julianus' virtues were so self-evident that greatness simply fell upon him. Ammianus was an officer in Julianus' army, serving alongside him until just before the Strasbourg campaign, when he was posted to the Eastern Empire; years later, he set out to write a history of the Roman Empire, continuing from where Tacitus had ended his coverage, in AD 96. Only the books covering the period between AD 354 and 378 have survived, but these cover events for which Ammianus, or people he knew, had first-hand experience. Ammianus seems an ideal source for this period, but must be read carefully: he was a pagan, hero-worshipped Julianus, and is at pains to contrast Julianus' virtues with the vices of Christian 'despots', such as Constantius. Moreover, despite his admiration for Tacitus, Ammianus seems to have borrowed his extravagant style from Livy, and his battle accounts are usually triumphs of style over substance.

By the time Julianus arrived in Vienna, Chnodomar had sacked Cologne and then invested Autun, which was being defended by a small body of veteran troops. Julianus reached Autun on 24 June in AD 356 to find the Alamanni ravaging the surrounding countryside. Determined to bring them to battle, he took a force of cavalry and artillery and marched ahead of his main army towards Troyes, arriving after a series of small battles with Alamanni raiding parties. He then ordered his army to concentrate at Reims, from which he marched on to Cologne, by-passing Alamann-occupied towns on the way. He fought two small battles: one when the Alamanni attacked his rearguard of two legions, with the rest of the army coming to the rescue; and the other at Brumath, when Julianus found his path blocked by a smaller body of barbarians, and so drew up his forces in crescent formation, threatening the Germans with double envelopment, who scattered before this could be achieved. Upon reaching Cologne, Julianus repaired its fortifications and concluded a separate treaty with the Franks, before wintering at Sens. With the Romans dispersed among several garrison towns, the Alamanni counterattacked and briefly besieged Sens. A stalemate ensued; the barbarians lacked

A SELECTION OF ROMAN PILA, *from left to right: a 5th-century BC Etruscan version; a 4th-century BC pilum with riveted tang; a light pilum of the 3rd century BC; a pilum of the 1st century AD; a pilum from c. AD 100 with an added bronze weight.*

Strasbourg

AD 357

The Germans formed into wedges, and seeing this, the Romans halted, while the Roman left wing probed their right. Julianus then ordered a general advance, and the Germans countercharged. The legions on the left soon drove the Germans back, but the Roman cavalry on the right panicked. The battle resolved into an infantry fight with the Romans raining arrows on the barbarians, whose formation may have been broken up by this barrage. The Romans formed a shield wall, and a shoving match ensued as the Alamanni tried to push them back. Some broke through the Roman line, only to be defeated by the Primani legion. Unable to break through the Roman shield-wall elsewhere, and taking massive casualties, they ran. The Romans broke formation and chased them to the Rhine, where Julianus rallied them and ordered that the Germans be bombarded with missiles as they swam across. The Alamanni lost 6000 men, the bulk probably dying during the pursuit or in the Rhine.

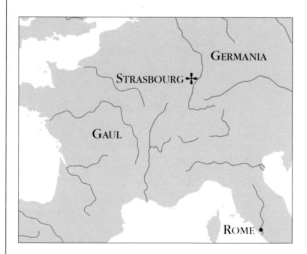

The battle of Strasbourg is unusual, for most actions fought against Germanic migrants were on a much smaller scale. By the end of AD 357, Julianus had cleared Gaul of all barbarians.

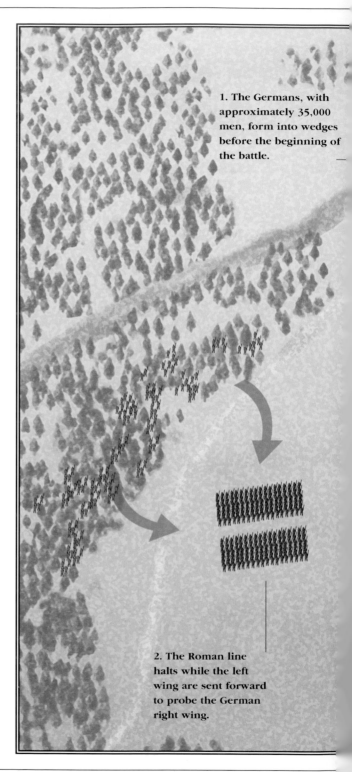

1. The Germans, with approximately 35,000 men, form into wedges before the beginning of the battle.

2. The Roman line halts while the left wing are sent forward to probe the German right wing.

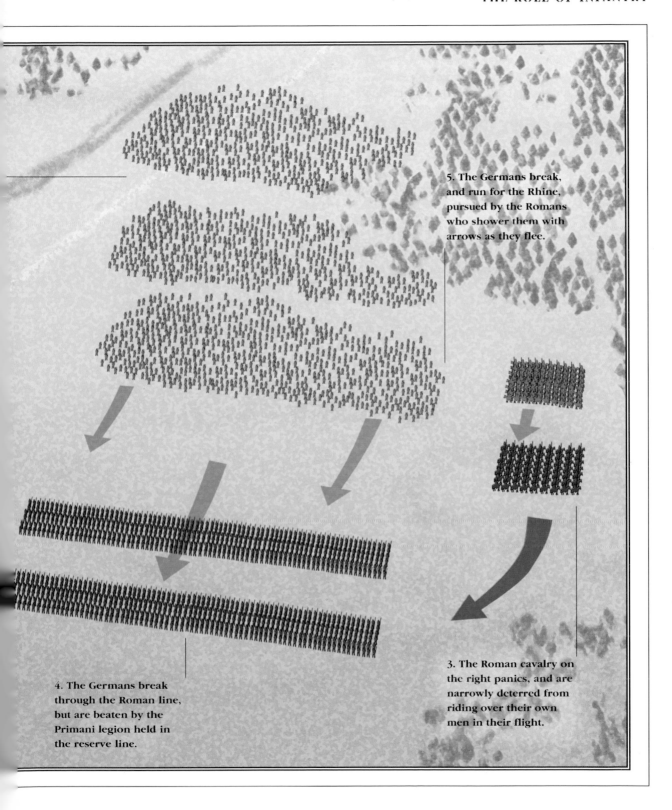

5. The Germans break, and run for the Rhine, pursued by the Romans who shower them with arrows as they flee.

4. The Germans break through the Roman line, but are beaten by the Primani legion held in the reserve line.

3. The Roman cavalry on the right panics, and are narrowly deterred from riding over their own men in their flight.

the equipment to storm the town, and Julianus lacked the numbers to sortie against them. Eventually, the besiegers withdrew.

Raids Renewed

In the spring of AD 357, the Alamanni renewed their raids, cutting deeper into Gaul than usual. While not a full-scale invasion, this was seen by Constantius as an opportunity to destroy the Alamanni once and for all. He sent 25,000 men from Italy under the command of Barbatio, the *Magister Militum* (Master of Infantry), one of the joint seconds in command of the army. Julianus devised a plan by which the Alamanni would be caught in a pincer movement between the two Roman armies, squeezed into a small space, and then destroyed.

Julianus was fortifying Saverne and sending auxilia to raid Alamann-held islands on the Rhine, when news arrived that the Alamanni had attacked Barbatio's force and routed it. Barbatio, '[W]ho was a coward and indefatigable in disparaging Julian's exploits' (Ammianus, II.6) retreated to winter quarters. This reduced Julianus' forces to 13,000 to face a barbarian army of 35,000. Despite this, when Chnodomar marched towards Strasbourg, Julianus, seeing a rare opportunity to bring the entire Alamann army to battle, marched out to meet him.

They met on the west bank of the Rhine, where the Alamanni were still bringing their force across. The Alamanni formed into wedges, and seeing this, the Roman Army halted, while Severus, commanding the Roman cavalry on the left wing, probed the Alamann right. Julianus then ordered a general advance along the entire line, and the Alamanni countercharged. The legions on the left soon drove the Germans back, but the Roman cavalry on the right panicked when a senior officer was wounded. Indeed, they would have ridden over their own line had the legions not stood firm and refused to let them pass, and had not Julianus himself cajoled them back into action.

The battle resolved into an infantry fight along the whole line. Given the weight of missile power that Vegetius ascribed to the late Roman legion, Ammianus' references to volleys of javelins hissing through the air, hails of darts, and volleys of iron-tipped arrows not slackening throughout the day may not be too much of an exaggeration, and the barbarian formation may have been broken up by this barrage. Consequently, the Alamanni had the worse of the hand-to-hand fighting (where it happened) – a fact which is interesting given that there was now very little difference in weaponry, discipline and training between Roman and barbarian. Indeed, German auxiliaries of the Cornuti and Bracchiati cohorts raised the German war-cry, the *barritus*, to let their opponents know who they were facing. The Romans formed a shield wall, and a shoving match ensued as the Alamanni tried to push them back with their shoulders and knees, and with frantic sword-strokes. Chnodomar himself led a force of tribal chiefs which broke through the Roman line, only to be defeated by the Primani legion. This was a well trained, possibly professional force of the type Vegetius recommended for reserve duties, Ammianus describing them fighting in the traditional legionary manner, ducking under their shields to avoid the wild sword-swings of the barbarians, and then stabbing them in their exposed sides.

This was the Alamanni's final success. Unable to break through the Roman shield-wall elsewhere, and taking massive casualties, they ran. Their bloodlust up, the Romans broke formation and chased them to the Rhine, where Julianus rallied them and ordered that the Germans be bombarded with missiles as they swam across. The Alamanni lost 6000 men, the bulk probably falling during the pursuit or drowning in the Rhine, and Chnodomar was captured and sent to Rome, where he died shortly afterwards. Roman losses were 243, including 2 tribunes.

Julianus was hailed as *Augustus* (Emperor) by his troops on the battlefield. He refused this title, and ordered that the cavalry unit which almost cost him the battle should parade the following day in women's clothing. He followed his victory with a series of large raids across the Rhine, and the following year concluded a peace treaty with the surviving Alamann kings. Despite being insanely jealous of Julianus, and bizarrely claiming that he had led the army at Strasbourg, Constantius named Julianus as successor when he was dying of malaria during a campaign against the Persians in AD 361.

Roman Auxiliary AD 350

By the time of the Battle of Strasbourg in AD 357 the appearance of the Roman soldier had changed dramatically from when the empire was at its peak. This figure is armed with a long spear and carries a long sword more suitable to the cutting strokes favoured by the Germanic auxiliaries in Rome's service than the gladius. His shield is oval, made of wood with a leather or linen covering and a metal rim and boss. He wears a simple iron helmet made in two halves and joined in a central ridge, with flexible cheek pieces. He wears no armour, relying on his shield for protection. Instead of the Roman sandal, he wears a hobnailed boot.

CHAPTER 2

MOUNTED WARFARE

Mounted soldiers brought a shock element to the ancient battlefield, but they were equally useful for scouting terrain or pursuing a broken enemy.

I n the late Neolithic period, peoples in Europe and Asia began domesticating animals capable of being ridden or used to pull vehicles. Men were riding horses in the North Pontic region by 4000 BC. At about the same time, donkeys were being domesticated in Egypt and southwestern Asia, with Bactrian camels in the Iranian plateau and Arabian camels in the southern Arabian peninsula becoming domesticated in the millennium that followed. The Indian elephant was tamed by the Indus Valley civilization (between 2500 and 1750 BC), while northern Africa tamed its African elephants only in the closing centuries of the first millennium BC. Of these animals, the donkey's military service – after an early moment of

HANNIBAL ENTERING CANNAE *on elephantback in triumph after his defeat of the mighty Rome. Elephants had helped Hannibal in his crossing of the Alps, but once the Roman troops and cavalry became inured to these strange beasts, they were relatively ineffective on the battlefield.*

glory – was almost wholly as a beast of burden, and camels saw only limited use in battle. Elephants had a notable combat role, however, and horses furnished the basis for chariotry and cavalry, two of the most important branches of, respectively, Bronze Age and Iron Age military forces.

While horses may have been ridden into battle from the earliest period, the first mounted military force that we know existed was chariotry. The first attested use of chariotry occurred in Mesopotamia, where Sumerian depictions from about 2500 BC show warriors riding in 'battle-cars' (as scholars call them), which were heavy vehicles

A SUMERIAN CHARIOT *or 'battle car' from c. 2500 BC. These vehicles were only one person wide, with tall fronts and a quiver of javelins attached to the side. The driver's reins were attached to nose rings on the onagers, which gave him the ability to stop the chariot, but little control over its direction.*

with narrow bodies and tall fronts. The driver of the cart sat ahead of the warrior, who threw javelins from quivers attached to its sides. There were four solid disk wheels, each made of three sections joined together, and probably held onto fixed axles by long cylinders (naves) so the wheels could rotate independently of each other. However, the lack of a swivelling front-axle would have made turning at high speed likely to upset the cart. There were two-wheeled vehicles as well, which were more manoeuvrable than the four-wheeled types, but they could carry only one man and were probably used to carry messages and transport officers.

The battle-cars were drawn by four equids, either donkeys or onager/donkey hybrids; horses were almost unknown in the Near East at this time. Control lines passed through metal rings (*terrets*) on the draught pole to nose rings on the animals. Pulling on the lines would allow the driver to stop the team, but exerting directional control required voice commands or the use of a goad or whip. The yoke extended over the two inner animals only. The outer two were attached by neckstraps, so their tractive power would have been small. Having less weight to pull, though, they would have been more willing to set a faster pace, stimulating the yoke animals to do the same. Tests show that the four-wheeled vehicle could attain speeds of 15–20km/h (9.3–12.5mph).

The carts were state-owned, issued to men before going into battle and returned afterwards. One Sumerian city-state, Umma, had a unit of 60 vehicles, and other cities doubtless fielded equivalent forces, manned in many cases by members of the royal household. The two-man carts are shown in pursuit, riding over fallen foes, a typical depiction of later chariots as well. We can only speculate on their other uses, but the reliance of their drivers on javelins means they had to come fairly close to enemy troops. A cart of such heavy weight, slow speed and poor manoeuvrability would have been at great risk when operating near enemy troops. Once soldiers became used to the battle-cars, it is probable that they soon developed ways of defeating them. No representations of carts in battle appear in the last three centuries of the third millennium BC; the idea must have been abandoned.

What was needed was a lighter cart, more tractable animals and better means of control. These factors first had an effect in the Near East in the first quarter of the second millennium BC. Firstly, the horse began reappearing in the region, after an initial presence in Anatolia around 3000 BC. Although small by modern standards, these horses equalled or exceeded the other equids in size and speed, and were more trainable and elegant. Their use in chariotry came quickly. By the twentieth century BC, light, open carts with spoked wheels, drawn by a pair of yoked horses, start appearing in Anatolian illustrations. The four-spoked wheels were far lighter than the solid wheels of the battle-cars. However, control was still effected by a single rein to a nose ring and therefore remained poor. By the eighteenth century BC, Syrian illustrations show a pair of reins running to each animal, clearly indicating the introduction of the bit and bridle. The 'riding over fallen enemies' motif reappears at the same time, showing that at least some kings had taken their chariots to the battlefield. By the mid-seventeenth century BC – if not before – two-man

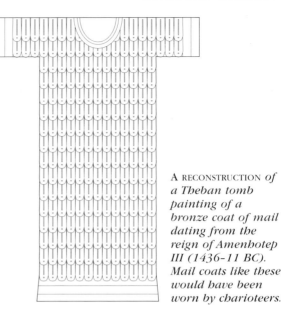

A RECONSTRUCTION *of a Theban tomb painting of a bronze coat of mail dating from the reign of Amenhotep III (1436–11 BC). Mail coats like these would have been worn by charioteers.*

chariots featuring driver and warrior, the latter armed with bow and quiver, are clearly in use, although at first they numbered only in the dozens. The chariot now became a weapon of war, one that dominated Late Bronze Age warfare in the Near East. During the course of the second millennium BC, chariots came into use throughout Europe, Asia and North Africa, as well as Central Asia, India and China.

New Kingdom Chariots

The nature and use of the chariot in the Near East are best illustrated by finds from New Kingdom Egypt, which include entire chariots placed in tombs. Chariots were of light construction, with specific woods carefully chosen for the various pieces and bent into shape. Wheels with four, and later six, spokes were set into naves on axles over 2m (6ft 6in) in length. The axle was at the rear of the car for increased stability; illustrations sometimes show the axle underneath it, but this was done by the artist to save space. The floor of the car consisted of intertwined leather strips for increased lightness. A wooden frame ran around the front and sides of the car, leaving the rear open for access. The result was a strong but light vehicle, weighing only 34kg (75lb). One man could pick it up and two bear it easily, allowing chariots to be carried through terrain in which

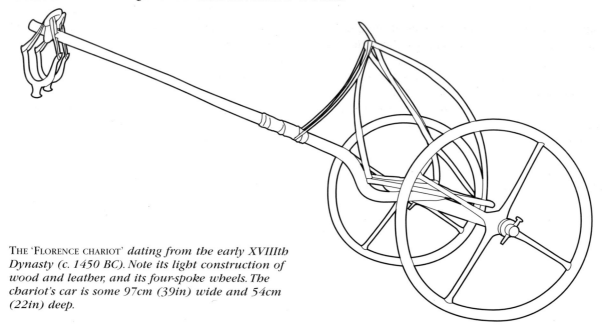

THE 'FLORENCE CHARIOT' *dating from the early XVIIIth Dynasty (c. 1450 BC). Note its light construction of wood and leather, and its four-spoke wheels. The chariot's car is some 97cm (39in) wide and 54cm (22in) deep.*

they could not be driven. In modern tests, a pair of ponies drew a replica chariot at speeds up to 38km/h (24mph). Being two-wheeled, the chariot could turn easily, but its wide body carried two combatants, a driver and a warrior.

In Egyptian illustrations we generally see a pharaoh riding alone in his chariot, reins wrapped around his waist, bow drawn to ear, slaughtering animals or the enemy. Driving a chariot in this manner is possible, at slow speeds and with no manoeuvring. It is therefore adequate for a carefully staged royal hunt, but in combat there would have been a driver who grasped the reins with his right hand while holding up a shield with his left to protect himself and the warrior. The latter had the reins looped around his body in the manner of a harness, so both hands remained free for the bow, otherwise he would have had to grab a handhold every time the chariot hit a bump. Away from combat, the driver used both hands on the reins. In addition to the driver's shield, Egyptian and Asian charioteers wore helmets and long coats of bronze scale armour. In these coats, several hundred overlapping scales 2mm (0.07in) thick were sewn onto a cloth garment. Curtains of scale armour or metal-studded leather were also added to cover the open sidings of the chariots.

Horses were protected by heavy cloth trappings or, less often, by scale armour.

Composite Bow

The bow the charioteers used was a powerful composite weapon, which pre-dated the chariot by some centuries, but now came into its own. It could shoot an arrow to a range of 175m (574ft), two to three times farther than the wooden self-bows used by most foot archers. The early composite bows were 90–120cm (35–47in) in length and had an angular or simple re-curved shape. More complex forms were to follow in the next two millennia, but the basic design remained the same: a wooden core with a horn-lined front and backed with sinew, all glued together. When drawn, the horn acted to resist compression, while the sinew stretched, only to pull back into shape when the bowstring was released. Although highly effective, composite bows were expensive, requiring specific types of wood, horn and tendons, and long construction times of at least 1 year for a good bow and 10 for a superb one. They required much skill, strength and practice. The Egyptians depict pharaohs in their chariots galloping past copper ingots set on posts as targets and shooting them full of arrows. It is very unlikely that even the most powerful composite bow could have penetrated ingots 'three fingers thick' (about 56mm/2.2in), let alone a 'handsbreath thick' (about 75mm/2.9in), as pharaohs are reported to have done, since an arrow can penetrate 2–3mm (0.07–0.11in) of metal at most. Still, there is no doubt that the weapons were very powerful.

Armed with bows able to outrange most infantry weapons, chariot archers could shoot up tight-packed infantry formations at will. Their swift steeds pulled their chariots faster than men could run, allowing them to escape footsoldiers' counter-attacks or to ride down fleeing enemies. Chariot forces could pass around infantry formations to attack them in the flank or rear. They also patrolled lines of investment during sieges, scouted, carried out raids and skirmished in advance of the main forces. Given these capabilities, it would have been difficult for any people dwelling in regions accessible to chariots to maintain their independence without having chariots of their own. In effect, this meant every civilized state in the Near East required them. Once everyone possessed them, of course, the only way to gain superiority was to build and maintain as many as possible.

Armour, composite bow, chariot and horses all required a good deal of wealth, manpower, skill and effort to procure and maintain. If noble charioteers did not provide animals, men and equipment from their own resources, as was the case in Vedic India, then the palace had to do so, or at least furnish charioteers with land allotments to support their operations. Most Near Eastern chariotries were organized and supported by the palace. A *maryannu* – as a chariot warrior was called in the Near East – was a valued professional, and necessarily strong, athletic and skilful. As for the horses, which were no bigger than large ponies, they began training in their first year and were pulling chariots by their third, becoming proper chariot animals in their fourth through to their ninth years. Painstaking horse-training efforts are detailed in Near Eastern texts. After months of careful exercising, feeding and grooming, the horses could trot long distances without tiring, easily covering 50–60km (31–37 miles) in a day's march, and could pull a chariot at top speed for a distance of almost 2km (1.2 miles). The Egyptians are known to have organized their chariots in troops of 10, led by a 'First Charioteer', with 5 troops forming a squadron under a 'Standard Bearer of Chariot Warriors', and several squadrons

PHARAOH'S CHARIOT IN BATTLE *as depicted in the tomb of Tutankhamun. The horses are as highly decorated as the chariot they pull. Note the large number of arrows carried in quivers on the chariot.*

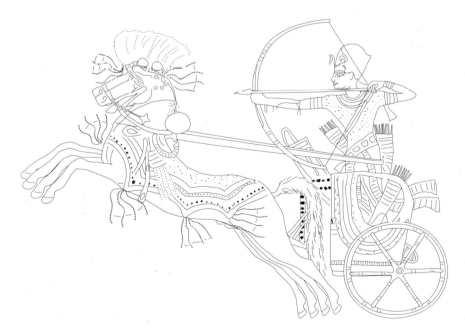

Egyptian Chariot

This late Bronze Age Egyptian chariot is typical of those used at Kadesh. The driver holds the reins of the horses, and in battle would carry a shield to protect the archer. The archer carried a powerful composite bow, and in battle would tie the reins around his waist, so that he could fire on the move. The chariot was extremely lightweight, only 35kg (77lb), and could travel up to 38km/h (24mph). It was capable of travelling up to 50-60km (31-37miles) a day. Chariots were used for patrol, raids and pursuit. When in battle, they gave harrassing fire from the front, attacked their opponents in the flank or rear, and would charge through a disordered enemy.

being combined to form a battalion (or *pedjet*) led by a 'Commander of a Chariotry Host'. A *peherer* ('Runner'), attached to each chariot, was a light-armed man who fought on foot in its support. Other states had similar organizations with troops of 5 or 10 chariots (and squadrons that were multiples of these troops), and also used runners.

Something of chariot tactics can be seen in the Battle of Kadesh. This was fought by the forces of New Kingdom Egypt under Rameses II against those of the Hittite king, Muwatallis, who ruled Anatolia and northern Syria. At stakes was control of what is today Lebanon and southern Syria. The battle occurred in the fifth year of Rameses' reign (1300, 1286 or 1275 BC). We know of it from a remarkable series of reliefs and inscriptions created at Rameses' orders in a number of Egyptian sites. The information provided is biased, contradictory and sometimes incredible, but it provides the most complete picture of a Late Bronze Age chariot action available.

In the first year of the war, Rameses had advanced suddenly and taken Amurru, the coastal region north of Byblos, returning home at the end of the campaigning season. Surprised, the Hittite king made no move at the time but, for the following year's campaign, gathered forces from all his subjects and allies throughout Anatolia and northern Syria, including at least 3500 chariots and perhaps 10 times that amount of infantry. Where to go next was obvious: the city of Kadesh on the Orontes, east of conquered Amurru and dominating the northern end of the Bekaa Valley.

Sure enough, May of next year found Rameses headed north through the Bekaa Valley to Kadesh. After camping in the hill country south of the town, Rameses forded the Orontes at the head of his army. It was composed of four divisions named after Egyptian gods – Amun, Re, Ptah and Sutekh – each raised from different regions of Egypt and including in their numbers chariots, foot archers and spearmen. How many of each marched with Rameses is not stated. While still south of Kadesh, Rameses encountered two Arabs from the Shosu tribe, who said they had been sent by their leaders to tell him that their tribe wanted to defect from the Hittites. When Rameses asked where they were located – presumably to see what use they could be – he was told that they were with the Hittite king, who was still far to the north. The Egyptian record says: 'But the two Shosu who said these words to His Majesty said them falsely, it being the Fallen one of Hatti [Muwatallis] who had sent them to spy out where his Majesty's army was in order to prevent His Majesty's army from making ready to fight with the Fallen one of Hatti.' Believing the false deserters, Rameses proceeded to a location northwest of Kadesh and encamped with Amun, the lead division of his army.

The other divisions were still on the march north when an Egyptian scout brought in two captured Hittite scouts. After being beaten, they were questioned by the Pharaoh, who asked where the Hittite king was located, only to be told that he and his massed army were standing ready to fight behind the Old City of Kadesh, just across the Orontes and a mere 4–5km (2.5–3 miles) from the Egyptian camp! Rameses called together his high officers, berated them for the failure of their intelligence efforts and ordered his remaining divisions to hurry north.

The Hittite Trap

It was already too late, for Muwatallis had sent 2500 of his chariots across the Orontes. The divison of Re was on the road west and south of Kadesh when some, or all, of the Hittite force attacked it. Caught in march order, the Egyptians were quickly put to flight and dispersed. The entire Hittite force then

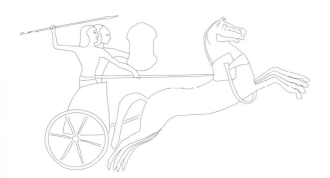

PART OF A RELIEF *showing Hittite chariots from the Battle of Kadesh, found in the temple at Abydos. The Hittites fought at Kadesh with three-man chariots: the other warrior is missing in this representation.*

Kadesh

1300, 1286 or 1275 BC

Believing the Hittites to be far off, Rameses encamped with Amun, the lead division of his army, north of Kadesh. Muwatallis then sent 2500 of his chariots across the Orontes. The divison of Re was caught in march order and routed. The entire Hittite force then attacked the Egyptian camp. Amun was being defeated when the *Ne'arin* ('Youths') arrived from Amurru. Meanwhile Rameses led a forlorn hope, carrying out successful attacks of his own, while the *Ne'arin* put the disordered Hittites to rout. Muwatallis sent 1000 chariots to the rescue, but between Rameses, the *Ne'arin* and the arrival of Ptah, they too were defeated, and with heavy losses. The Hittite king never committed his infantry forces. In fact, after the battle, it was Rameses who retreated. Muwatallis pushed onwards, reaching as far south as Damascus, before the campaign ended. After years of intermittent hostilities, the two powers made a peace that left both Amurru and Kadesh as Hittite possessions.

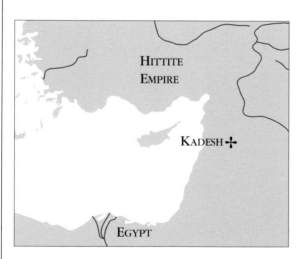

Rameses' campaign was an attempt to win back territory that had been Egypt's a few centuries before. Although he failed to regain all of the lost territory, he nonetheless secured a lasting peace.

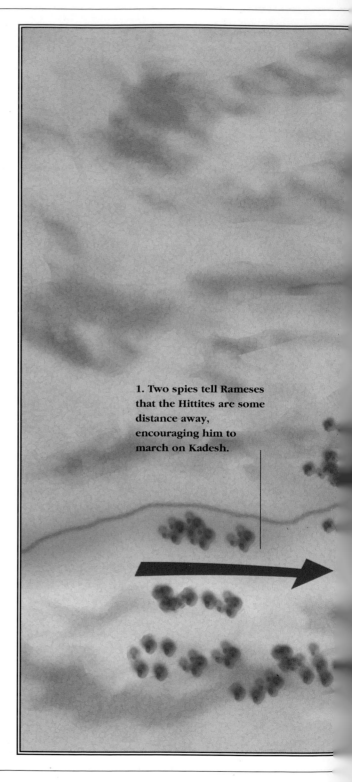

1. Two spies tell Rameses that the Hittites are some distance away, encouraging him to march on Kadesh.

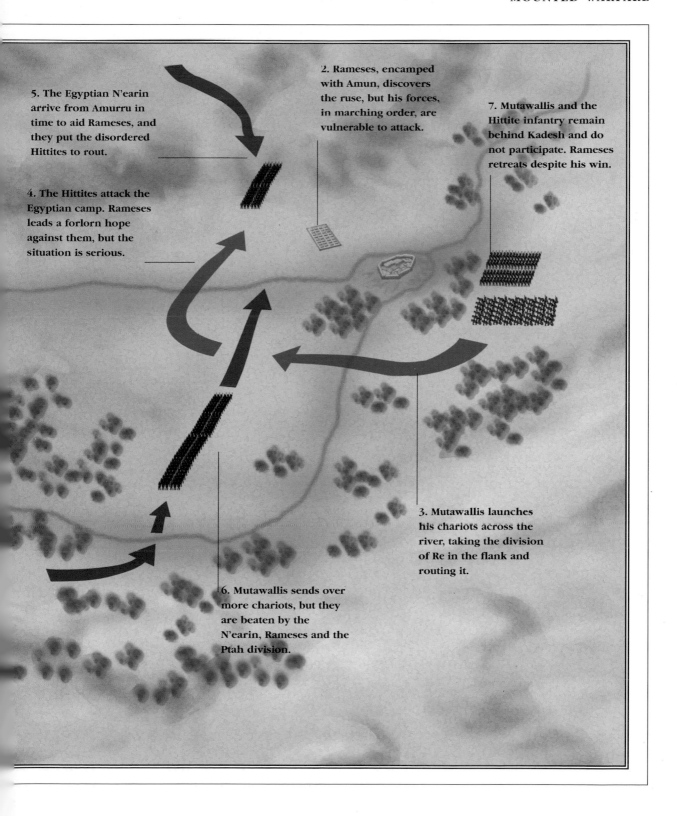

5. The Egyptian N'earin arrive from Amurru in time to aid Rameses, and they put the disordered Hittites to rout.

2. Rameses, encamped with Amun, discovers the ruse, but his forces, in marching order, are vulnerable to attack.

7. Mutawallis and the Hittite infantry remain behind Kadesh and do not participate. Rameses retreats despite his win.

4. The Hittites attack the Egyptian camp. Rameses leads a forlorn hope against them, but the situation is serious.

3. Mutawallis launches his chariots across the river, taking the division of Re in the flank and routing it.

6. Mutawallis sends over more chariots, but they are beaten by the N'earin, Rameses and the Ptah division.

turned north and attacked the Egyptian camp. At this point, the literary records of the Egyptians claim that Rameses rode out alone behind his horses, 'Victory-in-Thebes' and 'Mut-is-contented', and with the glory of Amun upon him, alone cut down the wretched enemy in their hundreds and thousands, routing also 1000 other chariots that had been sent to the aid of the first group by Muwatallis, who was cowering across the river with his infantry. Many of the fleeing Hittites were pushed into the Orontes and drowned. Despite being abandoned by his chariotry and infantry, about which he was explicitly bitter, Rameses won the day and the Hittite king sought peace. Or so it is claimed in the texts. In fact, after the battle, it was Rameses who retreated. Muwatallis pushed onwards, reaching as far south as Damascus, before the campaign ended. After years of intermittent hostilities, the two powers made a peace that left both Amurru and Kadesh as Hittite possessions.

When we look at the reliefs, we see Hittites in the Egyptian camp. True, they are shown being repulsed and killed, but they are in the camp nevertheless. A body of troops called *Ne'arin* ('Youths') appear on one side of any relief showing the camp. This term referred to picked troops, and they have been identified with Egyptians coming from the land of Amurru, who are mentioned in the literary sources, and were probably troops left there the previous year as a garrison, but who were now ordered to join Rameses at Kadesh. Also appearing on some reliefs are men from the Ptah division, which had been following Re in the march north. What seems to have happened was this: Amun was suddenly and massively attacked after the rout of Re (some of whose commanders are shown racing into the camp just ahead of the Hittites). He withered under the onslaught and was on the verge of being defeated when the *Ne'arin* arrived. Rameses, in the meantime, led a forlorn hope in one corner of the field, carrying out successful attacks of his own, while the *Ne'arin* put the disordered Hittites to rout. Muwatallis sent 1000 chariots to the rescue, but between Rameses, the *Ne'arin* and the arrival of Ptah, they too were defeated, and with heavy losses. The Hittite king never committed his infantry forces, probably seeing no point in feeding them piecemeal across a ford into a fast-changing situation best left to his chariots.

There is much about the battle that was out of the norm. For one thing, it was no set-piece action, in which the chariots would have been deployed

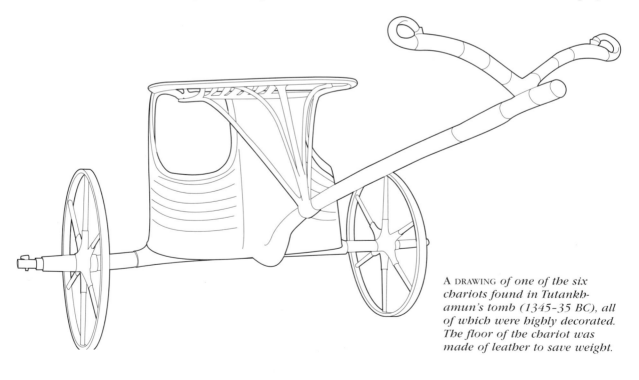

A DRAWING *of one of the six chariots found in Tutankh-amun's tomb (1345–35 BC), all of which were highly decorated. The floor of the chariot was made of leather to save weight.*

on the wings of their armies. Also, the Hittites are shown with three men in a chariot, something confirmed by the literary sources. One is a driver, who holds the reins, while a second holds up a shield. The third carries a spear, when he is shown with any weapon at all. Only the Hittite king has any quivers on his chariot, and only in one relief is a Hittite chariot archer otherwise shown. This has been interpreted to mean that Hittite charioteers were equipped to engage in close combat only, and so were easily shot up by the Egyptians in the counterattacks once the element of surprise had been lost. If so, this was a recently developed tactic, since a relief of Seti I, Rameses' father, shows Hittites in two-man chariots using bows. Since the Hittites are never depicted as killing, or even endangering, any Egyptian in the reliefs, it may be that the Egyptian artists felt they could omit Hittite archers and quivers, perhaps to help make clear in these highly detailed and visually confusing depictions who were the Egyptian slayers and who the Hittites about to be slain. As for the three-man team, it appeared later, but in chariots with three or four horses, and not two as shown here. Perhaps it was felt that the ability of each man to concentrate on his specific duties made him more efficient, and so compensated for the slower speed of the three-man chariot. It may also have been a tactic for this particular occasion. Muwatallis' plan to attack the Egyptians on the march and in camp meant his charioteers would be facing large numbers of infantry. The additional man in each chariot doubled the number that could dismount and fight, both in the attack on the camp and probably in other situations as well.

In the reliefs, the *Ne'arin* chariots are shown attacking line abreast, as are the Hittites in one relief. This presumably was the normal formation for combat. Assuming a chariot-length space between each vehicle to permit turning and prevent collisions, two lines of opposing chariots could be expected to penetrate each other in a charge, the archers firing as they went. Then the lines would reform and charge again and again, until one side or the other gave way. This is implied by the practice of firing at ingots while on the charge, since chariots would usually have avoided coming so close to enemy infantry. When moving across the battlefield, both sides are shown in column. The Hittite forces, raised from many different regions, were probably organized according to local custom, each force being led by a king, prince or other high nobleman. Rameses claims to have killed several such men, and others are shown being plucked from the Orontes.

Such was the greatest battle of the golden age of chariot warfare. With the collapse of the Bronze Age civilizations of the Near East in about 1200 BC, the expensive, palace-supported chariot forces began to give way to a new form of horsed unit, the cavalry. However, the process took centuries. Reliefs from the Neo-Assyrian Empire (934–609 BC) show the transition clearly. The earliest depictions of Assyrian cavalrymen come from the reign of Ashurnasirpal II (883–859 BC). They were essentially a chariot team on horseback, the archer firing his bow while his companion grasped the reins of both horses and raised a shield. The men sat back on the animals, holding on to them with raised knees, riding bareback and bare-legged, and wearing no armour besides helmets. Men in the Near East, either messengers or scouts, had ridden horses in this way during the Bronze Age, sitting back on the animal's loins or croup with their knees drawn up as though they were riding an ass or mule. This is unsuited to fast riding and can injure a horse's kidneys. Chariots continued in use in Assyria, but were now heavier in construction than before and drawn by three horses, only two being yoked.

> *'Those who face the dizzying heights and cross the dangerous defiles, who can shoot at a gallop as if in flight, who are in the vanguard when advancing...are called cavalry generals.'* – ZHUGE LIANG

By the reign of Shalmaneser III (858–824 BC), some horses were equipped with large riding cloths, which were held on by elaborate breastbands and collars. By the reign of Tiglath Pileser III (744–727 BC), horsemen were still riding in pairs, still bareback and bare-legged, but sitting more naturally, just behind the horses' withers. They also wore corselets and used spears, allowing each man to hold his own reins in his left hand. There was a new chariot design, with larger wheels (eight-spoked) and a rectangular car with higher sides, carrying three men – a driver, an archer and a shieldbearer. To pull this heavier load, there were three or four horses, which were all yoked. This made the chariot less manoeuvrable than the old, light, two-horse vehicles. By the reign of Ashurbanipal (681–631? BC), horse archers who also wielded spears are shown, wearing boots and leggings, and controlling their horses with single, looped reins weighed down by a tassel, allowing the rider to drop the reins and use his bow while still giving the horse the illusion of being under control. In addition, the horse now had a heavy cloth trapping for its protection. As for the chariots, they were even taller, their wheels even larger, their horses protected by trappings, and the number of men (all corseleted) had risen to four, with two being shieldbearers. The existence of enemy horse archers and lancers, and the lack of manoeuvrability of these large vehicles, brought about ever-increasing efforts to protect them and their riders.

It is therefore understandable that, with the fall of the Assyrian Empire, the chariot ended its days as a major weapon system in the Near East. It did live on in the form of the scythe-bearing chariot, a Persian invention first seen in use at the Battle of Cunaxa in 401 BC. Xenophon, a Greek historian who was present at the battle, reported them as being ineffective, but was impressed enough to describe them in his historical novel, the *Cyropaedia*. They were four-horse chariots of heavy construction, wheels widely separated, with armoured car bodies enclosed on all sides, there being a door in the rear. The driver rode alone, and was heavily armoured, his horses also being protected. There were scythes 1m (3ft) long set at the end of each axle, and other scythes placed underneath the axle to catch anyone who fell under there. The idea was to lash the horses into a frenzy and charge at enemy forces, cutting down unwary individuals and forcing gaps to open in enemy formations, which could be exploited by other forces. This proved effective against an unprepared foe, provided the chariots had cavalry support or were used in conjunction with other attacks. However, a prepared and experienced foe had little trouble dealing with them. If chariots attacked without support, the defenders would simply open ranks to let them through, then dispose of the unmanoeuvrable vehicles with infantry as they slowed and tried to turn. If the chariots had support, the defenders would join ranks, present a row of spearpoints and make an uproar, frightening off the horses, or would simply overwhelm the attackers with showers of javelins. Despite numerous failures, however, the scythed chariot continued in use in the Near East until the first century BC.

Chariot Transports

There was another way to use chariots, however: as transports for infantrymen, who could dismount, fight and then remount and escape easily. Such methods may have been used in Bronze Age Greece, where depictions of chariots almost never show them carrying bowmen. Homer's descriptions of chariot use suggest this as well, as do early Iron Age depictions on pottery, while the earliest cavalry in Greece are shown in pairs, sitting 'donkey seat', one man a mounted heavy infantryman instead of an archer. The parallels with Assyrian depictions suggest chariot use in combat down to the seventh century BC, but as conveyances for infantry, rather than chariot archers. The Greek colony of Cyrene in North Africa used four-horsed chariots into the closing centuries of the first millennium BC to transport heavy infantry to border areas so they could be fresh for battle. During that millennium, the Garamantes people of western North Africa also used chariots. Some of their four-horsed chariots had two draught poles, each with yokes for two horses, instead of the usual single pole, a feature also occasionally seen in Cyprus and other Near Eastern regions during the early first millennium

BC, as well as in the scythed chariots described by Xenophon. Carthage also employed chariots down to the end of the fourth century BC.

In Europe it was the Celtic peoples who employed the chariot the longest, using it in battle in Italy and Anatolia until the third century BC. As everywhere else, it was gradually replaced by cavalry, but when Julius Caesar invaded Britain in 55 and 54 BC, he encountered strong chariot forces. The chariots were lightly built, with open fronts and backs and double hoops on both sides, and were drawn by two horses. They were owned and driven by men of nobler birth than the chariot fighters. Caesar described their tactics:

'First of all they drive in all directions and hurl javelins, and so by the very terror of the horses and the noise of the wheels they generally throw ranks into confusion. When they have worked their way in between the troops of cavalry, they [i.e. the chariot fighters] jump down from the chariots and fight on foot. In the meantime, the charioteers gradually retire from the battle, deploying their chariots so that, if these [the fighters] are pressed by a multitude of the enemy, they may have a ready means of retiring to their own side. Thus they show the mobility of cavalry and the stability of infantry in battle, and by daily use and practice become so accomplished that they are ready to gallop their teams down the steepest of slopes without the loss of control, to stop and turn them in a moment, to run along the draught pole, stand on the yoke, and then most quickly dart back into the chariot.'

As long as they maintained a guerilla campaign against his forces, Caesar found them very difficult to combat. Only during his second invasion was he able to inflict heavy losses upon them, when they pushed a massed attack too close to his legionaries, who charged and repulsed them, after which they were pursued very closely by his cavalry. Chariots also met the Romans when they invaded a century later, but with less success; they are last heard of when Agricola defeated the Picts at Mons Graupius in AD 83.

The Role of Cavalry

It may seem surprising that, since cavalry was possible, chariots were ever employed. The Plains Indians of North America became good irregular light cavalry within a few centuries after first seeing horses, so the delay of cavalry development for 3000 years in Eurasia seems very strange. Why did chariots come into use, and why was cavalry so late to develop?

A CHARIOT WITH A STANDARD *from a drawing of the Assyrian monuments of Assurnasirpal II (884-859 BC). Assyrian chariots in this period had three horses, but only two were attached to the yoke, implying that the third was used as a spare, or to encourage the other horses to run faster.*

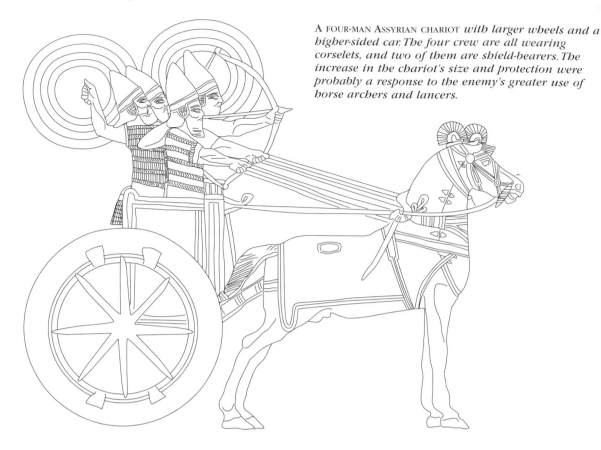

A FOUR-MAN ASSYRIAN CHARIOT with larger wheels and a higher-sided car. The four crew are all wearing corselets, and two of them are shield-bearers. The increase in the chariot's size and protection were probably a response to the enemy's greater use of horse archers and lancers.

One reason for this is the nature of the society that made the discovery. The Sredni Stog culture, located between the Dneipr and Don Rivers, was not a society of hunter/gatherers who hunted migrating herds – as did the Plains Indians – but a settled, agricultural people with domestic herd animals. They hunted horses and eventually came to domesticate them, finding riding a useful skill in both pursuits. Although efforts to exploit the steppe – the vast range of grasslands running across Eurasia from Hungary to Manchuria – followed soon after the domestication of the horse, the societies that made the attempt were still largely settled in nature. Full-scale nomadic pastoralism did not develop until late in the second millennium BC. It was not until between 3000 and 2500 BC that the domestic horse was fully established in the European steppe, and another millennium before it was commonplace throughout most of Eurasia and North Africa. By then, donkeys and carts had been

in use in the Near East and Mediterranean region for a very long time, and the horse was adopted in the light of this experience.

Another reason for the slow development of cavalry was the difficulty of riding a horse in antiquity. It was an athletic activity, for until the invention of the treed saddle near the end of the first millennium BC, men rode bareback or on saddle-cloths, gripping horses with their thighs. As we have seen, those living in areas where donkey travel had been known for millennia had to learn a new way of sitting on an animal. Moreover, until the invention of the stirrup, which did not become common until the Middle Ages, men had to vault onto the backs of their steeds, pulling themselves up with their left hands and keeping their right out straight to help bring themselves over. This was difficult enough to do for a lightly clothed man; for one wearing armour and carrying a shield, it was much more difficult.

Moreover, horses had to be broken from their wild state and taught to carry men, to stand still while they mounted, and to obey their commands. As herd animals, horses have a vocabulary of dominance and submission that humans can learn to exploit; this is how a horse can be ridden at all. In most cultures, domination came from controlling the horses' heads. For this task, the Sredni Stog developed the bit, a mouthpiece fitting into the gap between the horse's front incisors (and canine teeth in stallions) and its molars. Holding the mouthpiece in place are cheekpieces, one on each side, which attach to the headstall, a series of straps surrounding the head, while reins run from the bit to the rider's hands. The entire device, called a bridle, was clearly in existence, in a primitive form, by c. 4000 BC. Riders had to learn to use these devices and other means to command their steeds, and the horses learn to obey them. Finally, horse and rider together had to learn how to jump obstacles and ride over rough terrain without parting company. Developing the gear and training techniques required must have taken much time and effort.

Cavalry in Combat

Then there were the problems involved in taking horses into combat. Riders had to learn to handle swords, spears, lances and other hand-to-hand combat weapons while on horseback, how to throw javelins or shoot arrows accurately atop a moving horse, how to keep their seats while weighed down with body armour and shields, and how to ride with their fellows in formation, performing complicated manoeuvres. For the rider this was difficult enough. It was worse for the horse. Wild horses bear no burdens, travel in herds, shy from any unusual sight, smell or sound, and flee from danger at high speed. That is how they evolved to deal with predators. War horses must bear a man, armed and often armoured, obey his every command, operate away from other horses at times, endure strange and frightening things without shying, and move towards danger, not away from it. As a result, ancient warriors sought animals with 'spirit', and so often rode stallions, seldom gelding the animals. Of course, this meant problems with biting as well as

fighting amongst the animals as they sought to establish dominance in the 'herd' of the cavalry unit to which they belonged. Ancient riders responded by using muzzles and very harsh bits and nosebands, the bits often spiked so that a hard enough pull would result in physical damage. Without stirrups, riders had no purchase when trying to 'pull up' a horse, so they believed they needed something to show the horse who was in control with the least possible effort. When an ancient poet described bloody foam dripping from a horse's mouth, he was not speaking metaphorically. In addition, Asian horsemen used whips or goads, while spurs are known from Greece in the fifth century BC, and from Celtic lands soon afterwards.

There were other problems as well. Primitive horses stood at between 132cm (52in) and 140cm (55in) to the withers – the high point on

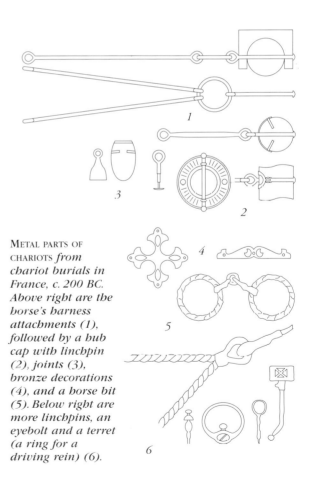

METAL PARTS OF CHARIOTS *from chariot burials in France, c. 200 BC. Above right are the horse's harness attachments (1), followed by a hub cap with linchpin (2), joints (3), bronze decorations (4), and a horse bit (5). Below right are more linchpins, an eyebolt and a terret (a ring for a driving rein) (6).*

the back near the base of the neck – and so today would be classed as ponies rather than horses. No ancient horses would be classified as large horses, like today's Clydesdales and Belgians, and it was not until the first millennium AD that the average size of horses in Europe or North Africa reached that of today's light horses, the standard riding animals. While the small horses of antiquity could be ridden, most could bear only lightly equipped cavalrymen. In addition, horses are primarily grass eaters and have small stomachs, grazing almost constantly in the wild. They need a good deal more food than humans do, and their constitution is more delicate. If adequate grazing is lacking, they must be kept in stables and fed grain. This was the norm in agricultural societies, making horses an expensive proposition. Either governmental services had to provide and maintain warhorses – as was the case in the Near Eastern chariotries and the cavalry of the Roman Empire – or members of the upper classes had to provide horses and horsemen, perhaps with governmental support.

Given all the difficulties, it is not difficult to understand why chariots preceded cavalry in the Ancient World. The small horses had an easier time when pulling a light cart, even with armoured men in it, than they had when carrying the men directly on their backs. Yokes attached to straps could not be tossed off, unlike riders, and additional gear was easily carried, something not true until the saddle was invented. Chariot warriors could fight standing up, not perched on horses' backs, and mount and dismount easily. With a driver to attend to the horses, a chariot warrior had only to concern himself with combat. If the Plains Indians had known of the wheel, perhaps they would have built chariots, too.

Once men learned to ride, of course, they had much to gain from the warhorse. The horse's speed comes from long legs and powerfully muscled shoulders, buttocks and thighs, the limbs being so levered to the muscles as to provide the most efficient use of energy. Moreover, each leg ends in a hoof, the expanded nail of a single toe, so that the animal is, as it were, permanently running on tiptoe, allowing for even fuller extension of the limbs. As a result, the horse is a swift runner, walking at a pace of 3–4km/h (1.8–2.4mph), trotting at 19km/h (11.8mph), cantering at 25km/h

THE EARLIEST DEPICTION *of cavalrymen in action comes from the reign of Assurnasirpal II (884–859 BC). Essentially, these are charioteers on horseback: one rider holds the reins of both horses while the other fires his bow at the enemy. However, they wear only helmets for protection, although one has a large shield on his back. They are both riding bareback, sitting upright on the horses and gripping with their raised legs.*

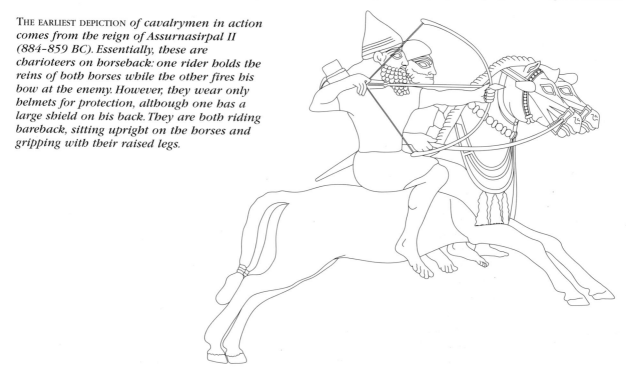

(15.5mph) and galloping at speeds of up to 70km/h (43.5mph). Once humans and horses learned to engage in combat, they had a range of strategic and tactical capabilities that no infantry army could dream of possessing, and were able to manoeuvre and operate in difficult terrain far better than a chariot team. In addition, horses do have a degree of aggression, as any animal must, and can become hardened, even enthusiastic, combatants. Some were even taught to attack foes with teeth and hooves. And there can be no doubt that men on horses are intrinsically impressive, and frightening, to opponents on foot.

At the beginning of the first millennium BC, as we have seen, cavalry began to replace chariotry in the Near East, and eventually everywhere else. Pressure from steppe nomad peoples may have been a large factor in this development. For instance, at the time when they were first adopting cavalry, the Assyrians were warring with the Medes, an Iranian people who apparently already fielded horse archers able to ride by themselves and fire arrows while riding away from an enemy – the famous 'Parthian shot'. At that time, domesticated horses had been present almost everywhere in Europe, Western Asia and North Africa for several centuries or even millennia, and many individual breeds of horse had been, or were being, developed. The ancient sources mention some 50 named breeds. We will discuss several of them in the following pages.

By the middle of the first millennium BC, the three most noteworthy horse-riding peoples were the Scythians, the Persians and the Greeks. The Scythians were steppe nomad horse archers. They are not the earliest known, these being the Cimmerians, who made the first known steppe nomad invasion of the Near East in the eighth century BC, when they crossed the Caucasus and wrecked kingdoms throughout Anatolia before finally being destroyed. Other Cimmerians seem to have scattered into Europe, to judge by finds made of their characteristic horse bits and harness along the Danube into Switzerland, southern France and even Britain. It was the Scythians who drove them out of the North Pontic region, and indeed followed them into the Near East, where they played a role in the

destruction of the Assyrian Empire. Scythians kings and nobles are depicted wearing highly decorated scale mail armour, with bronze or iron helmets, often Greek made or influenced, and rode steeds of 144–150cm (57–59in) to the withers. These horses, usually unarmoured, were relatively scarce. A pony about 140cm (55in) high, with a coarse neck, head and shoulders, but fine quarters and tail, was the usual mount.

The Scythians used their version of the composite bow, which became popular in the eastern Mediterranean and the Near East. It had a double-curved body with curved tips and was only 75–100cm (30–39in) long. It was extremely powerful; some graves yield human skeletons with arrowheads embedded in the skull or spine 2–3cm (0.7–1.1in) deep. The bow was extremely stiff, requiring great strength and skill to string. Arrowheads were bronze and usually had three blades; some were also barbed and many were poisoned. The bow was carried in a case to protect it against wet conditions that could easily ruin its glue and warp its wood. The case, called a *gorytos*, could carry 75 arrows. Besides the bow, Scythian horsemen often carried a straight sword or a war axe, spears with leaf-shaped heads, lances 3m (10ft) or more long, and darts – as javelins meant only for throwing are called – with barbed heads. Some Scythians carried shields, which were generally wooden with leather facings, and these

AN ASSYRIAN HORSE ARCHER. *Unlike the earlier illustration, this archer is both sitting correctly on the horse, and riding on a saddlecloth. As riders' horsemanship improved, so did their usefulness.*

could be slung across the rider's back, leaving both hands free for the bow.

Warlike People

Accustomed to a life of protecting their own herds and raiding those of others, the Scythians were a warlike people. Detailed descriptions of their battle tactics have not survived, but to judge from the actions of similar peoples, their battles probably opened with exchanges of arrow-fire at long range, feigned attacks and retreats being used to draw the foe into a vulnerable position. Once the arrows were expended, the survivors would close, exchange showers of darts and javelins, then fight hand-to-hand. The armoured nobles on the larger horses would have dominated that phase of combat. Against strong opponents the Scythians would retreat into the steppe, harass the invaders and pick their moment to counterattack. They employed these tactics against the Achaemenid Persian monarch Darius I when he invaded Scythia in 512 BC. They retreated as he advanced, then turned to harass him, attacking his foragers day and night, and constantly defeating his cavalry. The only things that saved Darius were his infantry, armed largely with composite bows, and his mules and donkeys, which upset the Scythian horses by their unusual sounds and appearance, for at that time they were not found that far north. Darius eventually had to beat an ignominious retreat before his army starved. The Scythians later destroyed a Macedonian army sent against them by Alexander the Great, although they had earlier been defeated in the Balkans by the Macedonians.

From the late fourth century BC, other steppe nomads, the Sarmatians, invaded from the east and finally overcame the Scythians. One reason for this may have been the Sarmatian nobles' horses. While the ordinary Sarmatian breed was small and swift, horse carcasses and skeletons excavated at Pazyryk in Central Asia reveal animals reaching 152cm (60in) or more in height. Typically chestnut or brown, sometimes bay, with dark hooves (known to be less prone to crack or wear away than light-coloured hooves), the males were gelded, a response to the breed's noted wilfulness, which was difficult to manage. With these animals, the Sarmatians could field heavy cavalry with both

man and horse in armour, though this was made not of metal but of scales of horses' hooves or light, tough rawhide. The men wielded long lances held in both hands and charged at a breakneck gallop. Supported by their own horse archers, they must have enjoyed a real advantage over the lighter Scythian cavalry.

Persian Cavalry

In the Near East and Iran, the Achaemenid Persians (560–330 BC) followed the Assyrians' example, using foot archers and spearmen in combination with bow- and spear-armed cavalry. This worked well locally and could defend against steppe nomads, but it failed in offensives against the Greeks, whose heavily armoured spearmen, called hoplites, wore body armour and carried shields designed to turn spearpoints, and which also worked well against arrowheads and javelin points. This is seen in fighting that occurred before the climactic Battle of Plataea in 479 BC, when the Persian commander Mardonius sent his cavalrymen against a portion of the Greek army. They attacked in squadrons, each firing arrows or throwing javelins, before wheeling and moving off. The Greeks suffered much injury, but still held on, and the lightly equipped Persian cavalrymen did not dare come to close quarters. Athens – one of the Greek states participating in the battle – had raised a small corps of archers before the campaign, and now sent it to the rescue. A long fight ensued, ending when a Greek arrow wounded the horse of Masistius, the Persian cavalry commander. The animal reared and threw

PERSIAN RELICS, *from left to right: arrowheads, a spear- or lancehead, a dagger, and two cavalry bits. Bits gave riders much greater control of their mounts.*

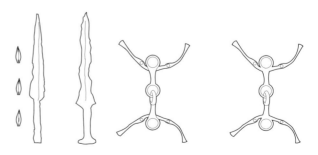

Scythian Horse Archer c. 450 BC

The Scythian archer was able to shoot arrows accurately at his enemy whilst riding on horseback – no mean feat without a saddle or stirrups. His primary weapon was his composite bow, which when not in use was stored in his gorytos, a bowcase that doubled as a quiver for his arrows. He also carried a sword, and evidence has been found of Scythian horsemen carrying spears or javelins, and small axes with a narrow head. Some archers also carried oblong shields of leather-covered wood or wicker, worn on their back while firing their bows. The rider shown here wears the characteristic peaked hat and a tunic covered by some scale armour and secured by a scale belt around his waist, but many Scythians fought without armour. They often wore colourful tunics and trousers. Note also the lack of protection for the horse.

him, and he was set upon by the Athenians. His corselet of golden scales warded off their spear thrusts at first, but eventually they killed him and secured his body, despite the massed attack of his infuriated troopers. In the later pitched battle that ended the campaign, the Persian cavalry played no known role and were perhaps dismounted to fight as infantry.

Masistius had been riding a Nisaean breed of horse, which was famous for its great size, 152cm (60in) to the withers. It had a hooked nose, a massive head, thick neck and a well-fleshed body quite capable of bearing an armoured man such as Masistius. Bred on the Nisaean Plains in Media, where the government kept 50,000 brood mares, they were distributed as the king wished. With such animals available, the Persians increased the amount of armour worn by their cavalrymen beyond the usual helmets and corselets, experimenting with an armoured apron that was fitted onto the horse to protect the rider's thighs. By the fourth century, they developed lamellar armour, made of metal bands, that covered the arms and legs. Horses were also sometimes

A THESSALIAN CAVALRYMAN *dating from around 400 BC. Although he has a saddlecloth, he is sat well back on the horse with his legs raised. He carries no shield, and has only an unusual helmet for protection.*

outfitted with headpieces and breastpieces. However, the cavalry still fought with bow, spear and javelin, as the Assyrians had, making no known use of the lance.

As for the Greeks, one might at first glance not expect a folk living in a mountainous, sea-girt series of peninsulas and islands to have had much to do with cavalry, and indeed the vast majority of their city-states never fielded any cavalry at all. Even major states such as Athens and Sparta did not do so until the last half of the fifth century BC. But Greece does have some good horse country, especially in Thessaly, Boeotia and Euboea, and many of the overseas colonies did as well. More importantly, Greek aristocrats liked to ride, and considered horse-owning as a sign of their status. Horse and chariot racing were very popular, and Greeks developed advanced techniques of high schooling. Many breeds of horse were developed in Greece, of which the biggest and fastest was the Thessalian, at least after Xerxes' army wintered in Thessaly in 479 BC; access to the Persian's Nisaean stallions almost certainly improved the stock. Greek horse breeds in general were showy in appearance, with a fine head and haughty carriage, but seem to have had poor quarters and staying power, and were eventually overbred into near uselessness as military mounts.

Supported by state funding, the enthusiastic aristocrats who comprised most Greek cavalry fought either as light cavalry armed with javelins and entirely unarmoured and unprotected, or as heavy cavalry equipped with spears, javelins, helmets and scale corselets or bronze cuirasses. The latter were shaped to reflect human musculature, and are called 'muscle cuirasses' by scholars. The Greek and Roman officer class often wore these expensive items. The Greeks, whose favourite weapon was the spear, outfitted it with a butt-spike that could be used in place of the point if the spear broke. They also utilized infantry 'runners' called *hamippoi*, to operate with their cavalry as the Egyptian runners had with their chariots. The Athenians experimented with Scythian-style horse archers during the fifth century BC.

In combat, Greek cavalry was typically deployed on the flanks of their predominantly

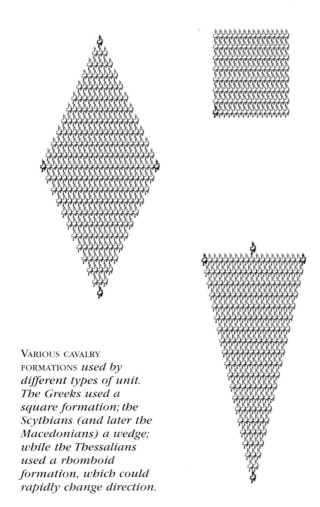

Various cavalry formations *used by different types of unit. The Greeks used a square formation; the Scythians (and later the Macedonians) a wedge; while the Thessalians used a rhomboid formation, which could rapidly change direction.*

hoplite armies. Except for Thessaly (and then only when it was united), no Greek state possessed more than 1000 cavalry, and usually less. It was difficult for such small numbers to have much of an impact, but in more than one battle, cavalry helped overcome an enemy flank or cover their side's retreat, and there were actions in which cavalry and light-armed missile troops surrounded and harried to destruction isolated bodies of hoplites. Cavalry was also very effective against light-armed troops and foragers, and could force enemy infantrymen marching through countryside the cavalry was protecting to stay in their ranks, limiting the amount of damage they could do.

Given the small number of cavalrymen available, Greek commanders realized they had to integrate their efforts with those of their infantry in order to get the most out of each body. As one

general, Iphicrates, is reported to have said, the hoplite formation was the torso; the light-armed troops, the hands; the cavalry, the feet; and the general, the head of the army. One who understood this fully was Philip II (359–336 BC), king of Macedon, the region lying north of Thessaly. Beset by northern tribes and feeling pressure from Greek states, Philip reorganized his people's army, creating a heavy infantry force equipped with pikes called *sarissas*, organizing effective bodies of light troops from tribesmen or mercenaries, and adding light cavalry from Thrace and Thessaly to his Macedonian aristocratic cavalry, which he organized and expanded under the title 'Companions'. They were armed with a lance 3m (10ft) long, with a leaf-shaped blade at its tip, a larger blade at the rear, and a strap at its balance point. Also known as a *sarissa*, it was made of cornel wood and weighed in at under 5kg (11lb), so light it could be thrown. In fighting at the River Granicus in 334 BC, Companion cavalrymen soundly defeated javelin-armed Persian horsemen in a fierce mêlée, due in large part to the greater length of their *sarissas*.

Philip adopted a variety of cavalry formations from various sources, including the square and oblong cavalry formations of the Greeks and Persians, the rhomboid formations used by Thessalian light cavalry, and the wedge formations used by the Scythians. In square and oblong formations, the horses and riders were organized by rank and file, with everyone in front reaching the enemy at the same time, maximizing the combat strength of the unit. In the rhomboid and wedge formations, the commander rode up at the tip, easily visible to everyone in the front of the formation, so he could guide it to weak spots in the enemy forces, or away from threats. The rhomboid, looking like a square tipped on edge, was defensible from any angle, and used for light cavalry, while the wedge was used by the Companions.

With the help of this army, Philip overcame every power in the region. He was starting to invade Persian territory when he was assassinated. His son, Alexander III, better known as Alexander the Great, took his army east and overcame the Persians in mighty battles, which are notable for the coordinated use of his forces to overcome numerically stronger, but less adept, opposition. An example of this is the Battle of Gaugamela (331 BC). Facing a Persian army whose infantry was a negligible factor, but whose cavalry was several times more numerous than his own, Alexander had to avoid letting his army be enveloped by the enemy's horse. He therefore advanced with his right wing ahead, his left refused (hanging back), infantry units supporting his cavalry units, and his phalanx of heavy infantry formed in two lines so the rear half could turn and defend against enemy cavalry coming from the rear. Advancing his right against the Persian left, Alexander caused the Persians there to charge and commit themselves to battle prematurely. Finding themselves unexpectedly up against infantry as well as cavalry, the Persians were held, and Alexander was able to lead his Companions and their supporting heavy and light foot in a charge that severed the Persian line and began rolling up the centre. In the meantime, the Persian right had charged against the Thessalian light cavalry and other forces on Alexander's left and engaged them heavily, some even breaking through to raid the Macedonian camp, but Alexander was able to aid his men on the left wing and complete the victory. Despite meeting a far more powerful cavalry on terrain ideally suited to its use, Alexander and his troops overcame it by careful coordination of their efforts as light and heavy infantrymen and cavalrymen.

> *'...meet the foe with two objects before you, either victory or death. For men animated by such a spirit must always overcome their adversaries, since they [are] ready to throw away their lives'* – SCIPIO

Shield Protection

During all these centuries, neither the Greeks nor the Macedonians seem to have made much, if any, use of shields on horseback, and the same may have been true of the Persians and, indeed, most other cavalrymen. Only occasionally do illustrations depict men who are clearly shield-bearing cavalrymen, not mounted infantry or chariot teams on horseback. The reasons are obvious enough: shields were a drag on the left arm, tending to unbalance the rider even more than a corselet and helmet did, and also made control of the reins much more difficult. However, as the numbers of cavalrymen increased in western Europe, the level of riding skill increased as well, and those peoples unable to equip their horsemen with body armour had to use shields, or abandon any idea of close combat. Too much of Europe was forested or otherwise difficult terrain, where a rider could not always avoid hand-to-hand combat. This is probably why the chariots of the Greeks and Celts fielded infantry fighters, not archers. By the fourth century BC, Celtic riders are depicted with shields, and other European peoples soon followed suit, including, within two centuries, the Greeks themselves.

One of the most notable battles in the west during this era, in which the shield-bearing cavalries of North Africa, Spain, Gaul and Italy all clashed, was that of Cannae in 216 BC, during Rome's Second Carthaginian War (218–202 BC). Hannibal, the great Carthaginian commander, had marched from Spain to Italy across the Alps and inflicted three major defeats upon the Romans in two years. For some time, the Romans had unwillingly contented themselves with dogging Hannibal's heels as he moved from place to place seeking supplies. But after spending the winter and spring of 216 BC in this fashion, Hannibal managed to break loose, leave his winter quarters in Gerunium in northern Apulia, and move south to take Cannae (modern Monte di Canne), whose citadel had been turned into a major Roman supply depot. This not only secured his position for a time, but left the Roman Army distressed for supplies. Its commanders repeatedly asked the government how they should act, since it seemed difficult to continue to refuse battle under the circumstances. Weary of the stalemate, the Senate and People of Rome ordered the consuls Lucius Aemilius Paulus and Gaius Terentius Varro to levy additional troops and lead a total of eight Roman legions and an equal number of allied Italian troops against Hannibal. They did so, and presently Hannibal, commanding 10,000 cavalry and slightly more than 40,000 infantry, found himself facing 80,000 infantry and more than 6000 cavalry, the largest army Rome had ever massed in one place.

We shall pass over the manoeuvrings of both sides prior to the battle, as well as many of the debates raised by the often-conflicting accounts of the sources. These place the battle south of the river Aufidius (modern Ofanto) near Cannae; the modern river runs along the northern edge of the range of hills where Cannae was located. It is likely that the river, which has often changed its bed, ran further to the north at this time. The Romans refused battle north of the river, but deployed south of it, hoping to retrict the operations of Hannibal's cavalry. Having to deploy so many men in a battlefield only some 3.5km (2 miles) wide, the Romans abandoned their normal open formation and massed their heavy infantry deep and close together. On their right flank, they posted the Roman cavalry (1600–2400 in number), placing them between the infantry and the river; on their left flank, the 3600–4800 allied Italian cavalry between the hills and the infantry. Stationed at some distance in front of the entire line were light-armed troops, who skirmished with those of the enemy. The Roman cavalry was composed of enthusiastic aristocratic amateurs as in the Greek city-states, lightly equipped, wearing helmets but no body armour, carrying a round ox-hide shield suitable for turning aside javelins but not for hand-to-hand combat, and wielding slender spears better for throwing than for close action; they wobbled and broke easily and lacked butt-spikes, so if the points broke off, they were of no further use. The men could mount and dismount easily, but were at risk in close combat. They were organized into squadrons (*turmae*) of 30 with three officers (*decuriones*) and three file closers (*optiones*) each, indicating troops of 10 men. In battle, they probably fought in 3 ranks of 12 men each. The Italian allies were presumably similarly equipped and organized, having been under Roman rule now for several decades. Their horses were like the Greek breeds, with those of the Veneti being particularly well known for their speed, if not beauty.

Hannibal's Deployment

Seeing the Romans deploy, Hannibal sent his slingers and spear-armed light troops to skirmish with the Roman light infantry while he deployed the rest of his army. On his left, close to the river, he placed his 6000–7000 Spanish and Celtic cavalry facing the Roman horse; then half of his African heavy infantry, by now armed with captured Roman equipment; then his Spanish and Celtic foot, more lightly armed than the Africans and Romans, and deployed in alternating companies of Celts and Spaniards. On the right of his infantry, he deployed the other half of the heavy African foot; and on his right wing, his 3000–4000 Numidian cavalry. After drawing up his army in a straight line, he took the central companies of the Celts and Spaniards and advanced them, keeping each unit in touch with

A NUMIDIAN LIGHT CAVALRYMAN *from around 200 BC. He is armed with a javelin and small shield. These horsemen were such good riders that they had no need of a bridle to control the horse.*

Cannae

216 BC

The Romans deployed in front of the river to reduce Hannibal's room to manoeuvre. Hannibal adopted a crescent-shaped formation, the middle towards the Romans. After skirmishing between the light troops, the Iberian and Celtic cavalry on the left dismounted to fight their Roman opponents, and soon got the upper hand. The Roman legions forced the Celtic and Spanish infantry in the crescent to give way, drawing in men from both wings of the Roman line towards the centre. The Africans on each end of Hannibal's infantry line wheeled and attacked while the Celts and Spaniards rallied. The Romans now found themselves surrounded on three sides. The Celtic and Spanish cavalry re-mounted and rode behind the Roman line to attack the Italian cavalry in the rear. Caught between them and the Numidians, the Italians fled. The Celtic and Spanish cavalry then attacked the rear of the Roman infantry, who were trapped and butchered. Some 50,000 Romans were killed, including Paulus.

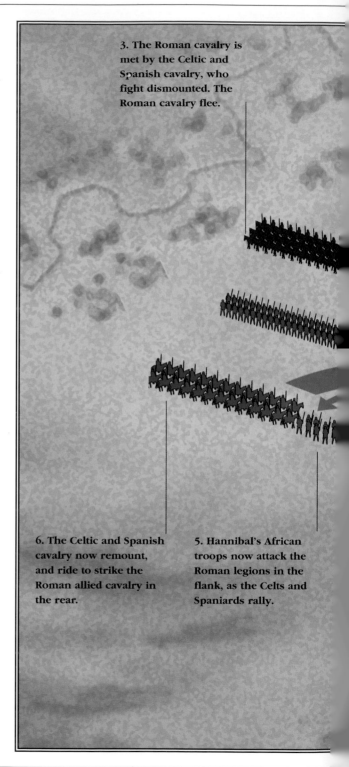

3. The Roman cavalry is met by the Celtic and Spanish cavalry, who fight dismounted. The Roman cavalry flee.

6. The Celtic and Spanish cavalry now remount, and ride to strike the Roman allied cavalry in the rear.

5. Hannibal's African troops now attack the Roman legions in the flank, as the Celts and Spaniards rally.

ROMAN
REPUBLIC

ROME•

CANNAE ✛

Cannae was perhaps Rome's greatest defeat, but typically she soon recovered, and Hannibal, neglecting to march on the capital, was effectively isolated in the south of Italy.

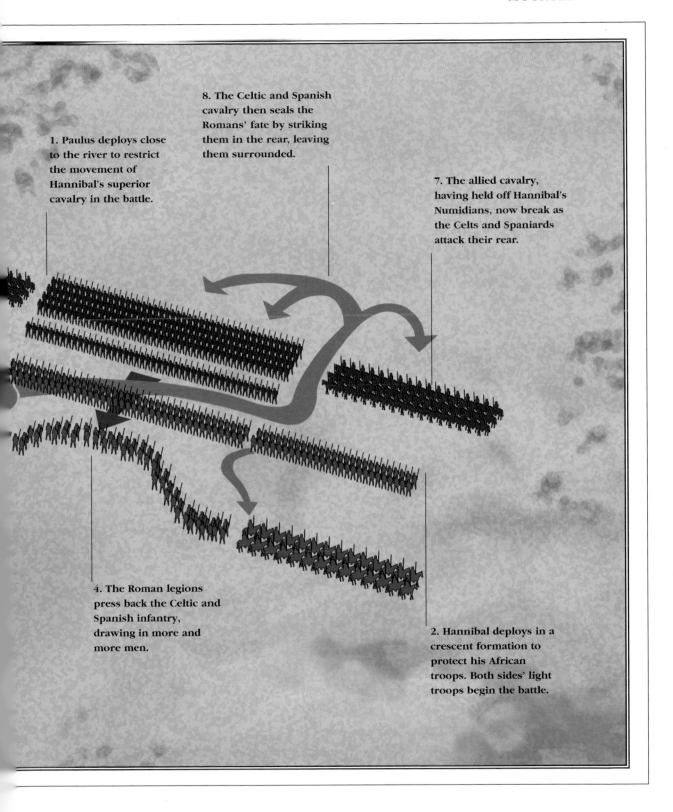

1. Paulus deploys close to the river to restrict the movement of Hannibal's superior cavalry in the battle.

8. The Celtic and Spanish cavalry then seals the Romans' fate by striking them in the rear, leaving them surrounded.

7. The allied cavalry, having held off Hannibal's Numidians, now break as the Celts and Spaniards attack their rear.

4. The Roman legions press back the Celtic and Spanish infantry, drawing in more and more men.

2. Hannibal deploys in a crescent formation to protect his African troops. Both sides' light troops begin the battle.

its neighbours; the result was a crescent-shaped formation. Hannibal wished to begin the heavy fighting with his Spaniards and Celts, keeping the Africans as a reserve.

As the armies advanced, at first only the light troops engaged, without advantage on either side. 'But at the same time,' says one source, Polybius, 'the Iberian and Celtic horse on the left, coming to blows with the Romans, fought a truly barbaric battle; for the action was not the customary turning about and wheeling, but at once falling upon one another they fought locked man to man, dismounting from their horses.' Another source, Livy, points out that both cavalries, squeezed between the river and the infantry, had no room to manoeuvre around each other, but had to charge front to front, and says that once the horses of both sides came to a standstill, the combatants began grappling and pulling each other off, until most were fighting on foot.

This may be so, but remember that by this time most western cavalrymen bore shields on horseback, and so could fight effectively in hand-to-hand combat on foot in a way that shieldless cavalry could not. This was certainly true of the Spaniards, who were armed like their infantry with spears, javelins (including the all-iron *soliferrum*) and forward-curving sabres called *falcata*. They wore helmets and various types of light body armour, and carried small, round bucklers known as *caetra*. Spanish horsemen often fought on foot, on occasion forming a ring, with their horses in the centre. Already displaying that advanced knowledge of horsemanship for which the Spanish are still famous, they trained their steeds to kneel and remain quiet on a specific signal, and had a kind of picket pin attached to the reins to allow them to tether their horses in battle. As for the Celts, who in this case came either from Spain or from Northern Italy, we do not know that they had such well-trained horses, but they made many equestrian innovations before, during and after this period. Their relatives, who invaded Greece in this same century, had their noble cavalry supported by mounted squires who could act as replacements. All the Gauls bore large oval or circular shields on horseback, even when they otherwise fought naked (which may have been

the case here), and used the same spears and long swords their infantry did, so they only needed to tell off one man in four to hold the horses while the rest fought on foot. The Romans who dismounted had to do this as well, or abandon their steeds entirely.

Hannibal probably had three times as many horsemen as the Romans on this wing, but these numbers would have done him no good bottled up by enemy cavalry. Human beings can mass together and push as a group, as the Roman infantry was now trying to do, but horses cannot. Hannibal may well have planned to have his horsemen dismount and attack on foot if the Romans did not immediately give way before the initial charge. If the Romans fell back, his men could remount and give chase. So what Livy believed was an accidental tactic may have been quite deliberate.

Success for Hannibal

Better-armed and more numerous than the Romans, the Celtic and Spanish cavalry soon got the upper hand, killing most of the enemy and driving the rest along the river. It was only then, Polybius says, that both sides' heavy infantry met in combat, which shows how quickly the Roman cavalry was defeated. The consul Paulus had been with the Roman horse at first, but was wounded by a slingstone and unable to respond for a time; he ended up in the centre of the Roman line, trying to bring about the breakthrough the Romans needed. The Roman infantry did force the Celtic and Spanish infantry in the crescent to give way. Drawn by the fighting, soldiers from both wings of the Roman line crowded towards the centre and moved forward, only to advance past the Africans on each end of Hannibal's infantry line. As planned, the Africans wheeled and attacked both flanks of the Roman formation, stopping it in its tracks. The Celts and Spaniards rallied, Hannibal and his brother Mago themselves fighting alongside them, and the Romans now found themselves surrounded on three sides.

In the meantime the Numidians had been fighting the Italian allied cavalry led by Varro on the Roman left. Neither side had gained any great advantage or suffered any great loss, due to the

Numidians' particular brand of tactics. These people, the nomadic Berbers of North Africa, literally grew up on horseback and were famous for riding without a bridle and bit, guiding their superbly trained horses by use of a stick, a neck-rope, and the shifting weight and movement of their bodies. They were classic light cavalry, superb for skirmishing, ambushes and pursuits, but not for pitched combat, being equipped only with javelins, knives and light shields, but no armour. They rode a breed of pony called Numidian or Libyan, known for its small size, remarkable endurance, swiftness and obedience. The Italians in squadron formations charged against the Numidians, who scattered individually out of the way. Having drawn off the enemy units, the Numidians then turned together and attacked from all sides at once, forcing them back. Given

their animals' stamina, the Numidians could have continued this game indefinitely.

Now Hasdrubal, commander of the Celtic and Spanish cavalry, intervened. Having re-mounted his men, he rode behind the entire Roman infantry line and deployed to attack the Italian cavalry. Caught between Hasdrubal and the Numidians, the Italians broke and fled. Leaving the Numidians to pursue them, Hasdrubal led his squadrons against the rear of the Roman infantry. While Hannibal had doubtless planned this, it is to the credit of Hasdrubal and his men that they resisted the natural impulse to chase a fleeing enemy and turned to harder labours. Their horses still scarcely exercised after a ride of only a few kilometres, Hasdrubal's Gauls and Spaniards attacked in support of the African infantry, simultaneously delivering successive charges at many points.

Until this moment, the Romans might still have been able to break through, despite the attack of the African foot, or at least fall back in order. Now they were trapped. Some 50,000 were killed, including Paulus. As many as 7000 Roman citizens and an unknown number of Italians were taken prisoner, most coming from the 10,000 infantry that Paulus had left in the main Roman camp with orders to attack Hannibal's camp during the battle. They had made the attack as ordered, but were defeated and trapped. As for the cavalry, most of the Roman horse was killed; Varro and 70 Italians got away to Venusia, and about 300 others escaped to various cities. The Numidians hunted down the rest. Hannibal lost 4000 Celts, 1500 Spaniards and Africans, and 200 cavalry.

Despite this terrible defeat, the Romans went on to win the war and eventually conquered all the lands on the shores of the Mediterranean, and as far north as Britain and the Rhine and Danube Rivers. In the second century BC, the Romans continued using citizen cavalrymen, albeit arming them with stronger Greek shields and spears, but in the first century they ceased fielding their own

A GALLIC CHIEFTAIN *from the time of Caesar's campaigns in Gaul. He wears an iron helmet and chailmail, and is armed with a 2.4m (8ft) long spear and a long Celtic sword. He carries a shield strapped to his back. Most Gallic cavalry had no armour or shield.*

cavalry and light infantry, relying instead upon units of *auxilia* (literally 'aids') raised from allied and subject peoples, especially the Gauls and Spaniards. After Augustus created the imperial state from the ruins of the republic, auxiliary units became professional military formations whose members served for 25 years, being granted Roman citizenship upon retirement.

Auxiliary cavalry took a variety of forms. The majority were organized into *alae* ('wings') of two types, the *ala quingenaria* with 16 *turmae* of 30 men each, for a total of 480 troopers, and the *ala milliaria* with 24 *turmae* for a total of 720. The larger formations were the élite cavalry of the regular army, with only one unit per province. *Alae* were commanded by a *praefectus alae*, each

ROMAN CAVALRY SHIELDS *clockwise from top left: a round, spined design from c. 200 BC; c. 1st century BC Celtic style; a typical c. 1st century AD oval design; c. AD 300, with a rounder, more dished shape.*

turma being commanded by a *decurio*. As with other Roman units, standards and horn calls were used to control the *ala*'s operations, allowing the members of a troop to follow their leader through all the manoeuvres required of them in battle. The unit standard was a small square flag called a *vexillum*, and an image of the emperor was also carried by the *ala*, with *signae* being carried by each *turma*. During the second century AD, the old standards began to be replaced by the *draco*, a Sarmatian device consisting of a hollow, open-mouthed bronze dragon head with a long tube of purple cloth attached behind it. When the standard was in motion, the tube billowed out and wiggled, hissing like a snake. The device looked impressive and could frighten enemy horses unused to its sound and appearance.

As well as the *alae*, there was a mixed infantry/cavalry formation called a *cohors equitata*. This could be made up from *quingenaria*, in which case it had 4 *turmae* of horse and 6 80-man centuries of foot; or from *milliaria,* with 8 *turmae* of horse and 10 centuries of foot. The cavalry of a *cohors equitata* was not expected to equal the level of drill of an *ala*, but was competent nevertheless. Its role was to provide the cohort with a mobile patrolling and striking force when garrisoning frontier fortifications. On campaign, the *turmae* would be detached and probably joined with others into an ersatz *ala*. In addition, the legions had bodies of cavalry, the *equites legionis*, attached to them, perhaps only 120 men for each legion until the third century AD. The emperors and provincial governors had horse guards, the *equites singulares*. Finally, the practice of enlisting barbarian and client-kingdom cavalrymen persisted, these being formed into units called *numeri* and, later, *cunei* ('numbers' and 'wedges' respectively).

Types of Roman Cavalry

The Romans raised many types of cavalry, including Numidian and Dalmatian light horse; other light horse equipped with the Spanish *caetra*; lancers wielding the two-handed Sarmatian lance; and, in the east, horse archers and eventually fully armoured lancers. But in the early Empire, the trooper armed with javelin, double-ended spear and a shield was the norm. In his style of equipment he followed Gallic models – and, of course, often was a Gaul. During the last four centuries BC, the Gauls had made many innovations in armament and riding. These included chain armour, made of iron or bronze rings (*lorica hamata* to the Romans); various helmet styles featuring prominent neckguards and cheekpieces; a long, slashing sword called the spatha, 64–90cm (25–35in) in length; and strong shields, typically oval in the case of Roman cavalry, although hexagonal, rectangular and round ones are known as well. These were over 1m (3ft) in length, flat, made of wood-ply covered with leather and painted with unit identification designs, having a metal rim and a central metal boss, where the handhold was located. The Gauls also introduced the snaffle bit; new styles of horse harness; the horseshoe (apparently a means of fixing nailheads in place for movement in snow, rather than for daily use); and, most importantly, the horned saddle. Unlike the earlier cloths and pads and the saddle cushions that appeared in Central Asia in the fourth century BC, this device had a wooden tree that was padded to meet the measurements of the specific horse, then covered with leather. In form it had four horns, one on each corner, protected by bronze horn plates. The horns were angled so as to hold the rider in his seat. While horse riding still required considerable athleticism, not least in mounting and dismounting, the saddle made this easier, and also gave the rider somewhere to hang his equipment. One result of the adoption of the saddle was that Roman cavalrymen began wearing leather breeches, which held them onto the saddle better than sweaty, bare flesh. Riding boots and spurs completed the trooper's equipment.

The Romans worked hard to maintain their cavalry's efficiency. Training of man and horse alike was long and rigorous, with troopers being given infantry as well as cavalry drill, since they could often find themselves fighting on foot. Units in garrison completed marches of 20 Roman miles three times a month, during which they practised their tactical evolutions, pursuits, retreats and countercharges, all on as varied a terrain as possible in order to accustom the horses and their

riders to working in both flat and rough country. Moreover, teams of horsemen would train for a mounted tournament display called the *hippika gymnasia*, in which they wore highly decorative sports equipment, performed complex manoeuvres and demonstrated they could throw javelins accurately, close in with a thrusting spear, remount at a full gallop if unhorsed, fight solo or as part of a group of lancers, use bows, slings and other weapons, and attack from any direction while using their shields to ward off missiles. As long as the Roman Army maintained this training regimen, it could be certain of possessing impressive and useful cavalry.

While western horsemen were becoming Imperial Roman cavalrymen, another line of development occurred in the Eurasian steppe and the Near East. As we have seen, the Sarmatians protected horse and rider alike with armour of rawhide or horses' hooves. Soon Iranian peoples were doing the same, using iron or bronze. The Greeks called these cavalrymen cataphracts (*kataphraktoi*, 'covered over'), the later Roman term being *clibanarii* (oven men), a comment on the experience of wearing full armour in the heat of a desert day. In fact, heat prostration was a genuine problem for man and mount under such conditions. The cataphract's weapon was a 3.5m (11ft 6in) lance called a *kontos* (bargepole) by the Greeks. The *kontos* was often held in both hands, Sarmatian style, but the later Sassanian Persians are attested as tying their lances to their saddles, so the horses could absorb the shock of the impact. Heavily armoured, cataphracts could attack horse archers even if these had not expended their arrows, and charge at a trot against the front ranks of formed infantry.

Information about the cataphract's equipment comes to us from many sources, especially graffiti and remains of armour from the Roman city of Dura Europos in Syria. The men wore metal helmets with chain or scale aventails to protect the neck, and metal face masks with human features. Besides its use as a defence, the sight of the unmoving metal face masks, to say nothing of the appearance of armoured horses themselves, could unnerve those horses unused to them. The riders' torsos were protected by scale or chain

Roman Cavalryman c. AD 100

This Roman auxiliary cavalryman was equally as capable of fighting dismounted as he was from the saddle. He is armed with a spear as his primary weapon, but if dismounted he fought with his spatha (long sword). The spear was mostly used overarm during battle. His oval shield allowed him to fight dismounted at no disadvantage when facing conventional infantry. It was made of wood with a leather covering, and a metal boss. His helmet is iron, but the cheek pieces and brow are made of bronze. He wears a chain mail cuirass, but no armour on his legs or feet, only the same leather sandals as a legionary would wear. He has a scarf around his neck to prevent his helmet from chafing. He sits on a saddle constructed from a wooden frame, with a leather covering stretched over it. A saddlecloth is worn under the saddle to prevent it from chafing the horse.

armour, lamellar plates, or a combination of these, while arms and legs were protected by segmented armour of the sort first developed by the Achaemenid Persians. Bronze and iron scale horse armours found at Dura Europos were designed to protect a horse's top and sides. Bronze armour was preferred, since horse sweat caused iron scales to rust. Each trapping had a hole left on the back for the saddle and a triangular piece to cover the horse's tail. *Peytrals* (chest coverings), *chamfrons* (head coverings) and *crinets* (neck coverings) were not found at Dura, but scale *peytrals* and *crinets* are easily imagined, and plate *chamfrons* with eyeguards have been excavated at Roman sites. Separate neck- and headpieces were needed, for the horse had to be able to move its neck, head and ears. Heavy cloth horse trappings with plate reinforcements are also depicted on reliefs.

Obviously the horses bearing these loads must have been large and strong, and indeed one of the Dura Europos pieces was clearly worn by a well-fleshed horse 152cm (60in) to the withers. Both the Sarmatians and the Achaemenid Persians bred horses of that description, and by the end of the first millennium BC, others were available in the Near East, including the Armenian, Cappadocian, Persian and Parthian. The latter had a fine, small head, without as hooked a nose as the Nisaean and was noted for its courage and speed. The Parthians trained their horses to run in a fast, short-stepping, high-actioned trot by exercising them frequently in a furrowed training field; after enough stumbles, the horses learned to make their steps very short in order to put their hooves in the furrows. This resulted in a surprisingly smooth ride, a great help for any horseman and especially one weighed down in heavy armour.

The Battle of Carrhae

These Parthians were in origin the Parni, a tribe of the semi-nomadic Dahae who lived north of Hyrcania and provided the Achaemenid Persians with horse archers. By the middle of the first century BC, they had taken control of Persia and Mesopotamia, establishing themselves as a land-owning military aristocracy. Its king, of the Arsacid line, was the feudal superior of his nobles, including the seven great Pahlavi families that

dominated entire regions. The Parthians developed an all-cavalry army, the nobles being cataphracts, their retainers horse archers. Having large grazing lands, the Parthians were able to adopt the steppe nomad practice of bringing along herds of horses as re-mounts, giving their armies excellent strategic mobility.

The Parthians had come into contact with the Romans during the latter's conquest of Anatolia and Armenia during the first half of the first century BC. Relations were at first good, but soon soured due to high-handed Roman behaviour. It was not long before the Romans were tempted to intervene in Parthian affairs, and in 54 BC Marcus Licinius Crassus took command of the province of Syria with the goal of invading Parthia. Crassus had no *casus belli*; he simply needed military victories to cement his family's political position in Rome. He was accompanied on the campaign by his son Publius, who had served with Caesar in Gaul, conquering Aquitania. He brought 1000 crack Gallic horse to Syria, where he was one of his father's chief officers.

By the autumn of 54 BC, Crassus was ready to lead his seven Roman legions on campaign. He crossed the Euphrates at Zeugma and conquered Parthian Mesopotamia as far as the river Balissos (modern Balikh), taking Carrhae (modern Harran), Zenodotium, Nicephorium, Ichnae and probably Batnae. The Parthians were currently distracted by a civil war, and the local *satrap*, Sillaces, was no opposition. Crassus left 7000 infantry and 1000 cavalry to garrison the cities and returned to Syria for the winter. The Parthians harassed the cities during the winter, but recaptured none of them. In the next year's campaign, Crassus aimed to drive into Mesopotamia. Artavasdes, king of Armenia, urged Crassus to invade Parthia through his territory, where he would enjoy the shelter of the hilly country against the Parthian cavalry, and have the assistance of 10,000 Armenian cataphracts. Because he had left garrisons in northwestern Mesopotamia, Crassus felt he had to return to relieve them. He nevertheless expected Artavasdes and his cavalry to join him there.

Gaius Cassius Longinus, another of Crassus' commanders (and one of the future assassins of Julius Caesar), advised him to proceed down the

AN EARLY CAVALRY HELMET *minus its cheek flaps.*

ROMAN CAVALRY EQUIPMENT. *On the left is an oval shield and its boss. The shield would usually carry a painted design on its front.*

SWORDS, LANCEHEADS, SPURS *and hooks for armour from a variety of archaeological digs in Europe and Syria.*

PART OF A SUIT OF RINGMAIL *showing individual links.*

A ROMAN CAVALRY HELMET *with flexible cheek flaps.*

A DECORATED CHEEK FLAP *complete with a moulded ear.*

A PLAIN CHEEK FLAP *to protect the side of the wearer's face.*

BRONZE ARMOUR *plates held together by leather straps.*

Euphrates, thus ensuring that he always had the river as a supply route and flank guard. Instead, Crassus crossed the Euphrates at Zeugma. He followed a caravan trail shown him by Abgar, the Roman client king of Edessa, and set out in pursuit of what he thought was a retreating Parthian army. He and his men came to, and crossed, the stream of the Balissos – not a strong current but still flowing in May. His army endured a forced march throughout the day and then had to prepare for an encounter with the Parthian army somewhere south of Carrhae.

The Parthian troops came from the personal following of the head of one of the seven great

AFTER THE BATTLE OF BEDRIACUM *in October AD 69, Vespasian's cavalry pursues the fleeing army of Vitellus. These cavalrymen are armed with a lance and shield, with a large sword in their scabbards.*

Pahlavi clans, the Surenas, who ruled Seistan as their fief. We do not know his name, the Greeks and Romans calling him Surena; we do know he was not yet 30 years old, but already the second most powerful man in the kingdom and a noted warrior. He was accompanied by a train of 10,000 people, including servants, concubines and the drivers of 1000 camels, but also, more importantly, 1000 cataphract lancers and a larger number of horse archers, perhaps as many as 6000. The local *satrap*, Sillaces, and his following were also present. Most of the Parthian Army had followed the king, Orodes, into Armenia instead; Crassus would receive no help from Artavasdes.

When word reached Crassus that the enemy was ahead, he first followed Cassius' advice and formed his army in one long, thin line with his cavalry stationed on both flanks, in order to keep

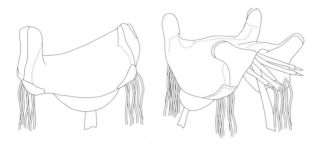

TWO VIEWS OF A ROMAN SADDLE *as reconstructed by the historian Peter Connolly. The saddle was essentially a wooden frame covered with leather and padded to fit the horse's dimensions.*

the Parthians from getting around him easily. But then he changed his mind, formed his army into a square and advanced. As the Greek biographer Plutarch describes it, the square had 12 cohorts of 500 legionaries on each side, each cohort having a squadron of cavalry stationed with it to aid in local counterattacks. Since Crassus had 7 legions, 4000 cavalry and 4000 light troops, there should have been 70 cohorts present, but 14 of them had probably been left in the Mesopotamian garrisons the year before, while the remaining 8 cohorts were probably kept within the square as a reserve, along with the light troops and Publius' 1000 Gallic horse. The other 3000 cavalry were divided into the support squadrons for the cohorts, and would have numbered about 60 men each.

Although Crassus had not led an army since 70 BC, when he played a major role in the defeat of Spartacus, he did have reason to feel confident. The Romans had encountered cataphracts and horse archers on a number of occasions in the past 150 years, and had emerged triumphant. That these victories had involved large infantry armies and particular terrains would not have seemed important to a Roman. Moreover, the oncoming Parthians appeared few and weak, for Surena had deployed his men in column so that only the head of the force showed, and ordered his cataphracts to cover their armour with skins and robes.

When they neared the Romans, however, Surena gave a signal. His musicians sounded their great kettle drums, and his cataphracts threw off their coverings to reveal gleaming bronze and steel. The Parthians then made to charge the

Romans, but seeing the surprise had not noticeably shaken the enemy's composure, they broke ranks and seemed to disperse. Before Crassus realized what was happening, they had ridden around and surrounded the legionary square. He ordered his light-armed troops to charge, only to see them driven back into the square by a shower of arrows. Plutarch wrote:

'The Parthians, taking position at a distance from each other, began to fire their arrows from all sides at once, not with accurate fire (for the close-packed ranks of the Romans would not allow even someone who wished to do so to miss his man), but giving strong and violent impacts from bows that were strong, large, and so very curved that they could send off missiles with great force.'

By this point composite bows had 'ear laths' – stiff, straight tips made of bone, which acted as levers to increase the force of the bow beyond that of the Scythian model. Plutarch says their arrows fractured armour and tore their way through every covering. If they kept their ranks, the Romans were wounded in great numbers, while if they charged and tried to come to close quarters, the Parthians rode away and turned in the saddle to shoot as they fled, making the proverbial 'Parthian shot'.

THE ROMAN SYSTEM *of harnessing a horse – not very dissimilar to how horses are harnessed today. Although the saddle is unusually shaped, it has a girth to stabilize it, and a bridle and metal bit.*

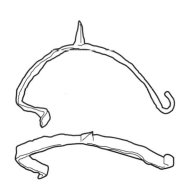
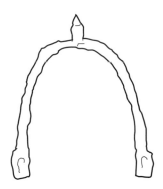
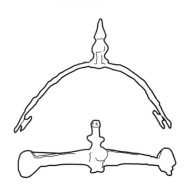

ROMAN SPURS, *known by how they were attached to the horseman's footwear. From left to right, an iron hook spur, an iron loop spur, and an iron rivet spur. Spurs could also be made from bronze, and elaborate decorated spurs have also been found.*

As long as they could hope the enemy would run out of arrows and then depart, or fight at close quarters, the Romans held out and made futile local counterattacks. But when they saw that many of Surena's camels were laden with arrows, from which the Parthians took a fresh supply, it became clear there would be no end to the ordeal. Crassus then sent messages to his son, in command of the right wing, and ordered him to force an engagement, since the enemy was especially numerous on that side and threatened an encirclement. Publius accordingly took his 1000 Gallic horse, 300 other cavalry, 500 archers and the 8 cohorts nearest him (their places presumably taken by the reserve cohorts) and led them all to the charge. This had worked for Alexander at Gaugamela, where the Persians had fought as a large, formed army. Here the Parthians wheeled about and rode off. Shouting that they did not stand their ground, Publius pursued. But after 'fleeing' for a long distance, the seeming fugitives wheeled back about and were joined by additional troops. The Romans halted, to find cataphracts in their front and horse archers riding around on all sides in loose formation, firing incessantly and raising so much dust that the Romans could barely see. Victims of the ancient steppe nomad tactic of the feigned retreat, many of the legionaries were killed and most of the rest incapacitated.

Publius then led his cavalry in a vigorous charge against the cataphracts. It was an unequal struggle, Publius' men 'striking with small, weak spears against breastplates of rawhide and steel, but the Gauls' lightly equipped and unprotected bodies being struck by *kontoi*', as Plutarch says. Nevertheless the Gauls worked wonders:

'…for they laid ahold of the *kontoi*, and grappling with the men pulled them from their horses, although it was hard to move them owing to the great weight of their armour. Many of them got off their own horses and, crawling under those of the enemy, stabbed them in the belly; these would rear up in their anguish and die trampling upon their riders and enemies mixed together. But the Gauls suffered most of all from the heat and thirst, to which they were unaccustomed, and most of their horses were destroyed by being driven against the *kontoi* of the enemy.'

The survivors were forced back upon the legionaries, taking with them a badly wounded Publius. They all retreated to a hillock, only to be shot up by the horse archers, then charged by the cataphracts. Only 500 men survived to be taken prisoner. Publius committed suicide, as did the other Roman notables present.

Meanwhile, Crassus had started to move forward, coming to his son's aid, but presently he and his army beheld Publius' head being carried forward on spearpoint by the Parthians. Although Crassus put on a brave front, his men lost heart. Now the Parthians returned to the attack, this time adding the charges of their cataphracts to the arrows of their horse archers. Some men dared to attack the cataphracts, but did little damage and were quickly killed, for the *kontoi* struck with

Carrhae

53 BC

The Parthians made to charge, but instead they surrounded the Roman square. Crassus ordered his light troops to attack, but the Parthians rode away, shooting arrows as they fled. Crassus ordered his son Publius to attack with a detachment. The Parthians wheeled about and rode off. Publius pursued, but after 'fleeing' for a distance, the 'fugitives' were joined by more troops. The Romans halted, to find cataphracts in their front and horse archers riding around on all sides. Publius then charged the cataphracts. It was an unequal struggle. The survivors retreated to a hillock, shot up by the horse archers, and then cut down by the cataphracts. Publius committed suicide. Seeing his head on a spearpoint, Crassus' men lost heart. The Parthians returned to the attack, this time adding charges by their cataphracts to the arrows of their horse archers. Fighting in this manner continued until nightfall, when the Romans were at last able to retreat, the Parthians being ill-equipped to fight at night.

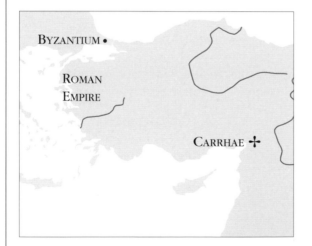

Carrhae was the result of the Roman's first campaign against the Parthians, who gave their name to the 'Parthian shot', an arrow delivered as the bowman fled on his horse.

2. The Romans launch local counterattacks, but the Parthians evade them easily, showering the Romans with arrows.

4. The 'fleeing' Parthians draw Publius away from the main Roman body before wheeling about and charging him.

1. The Parthians charge at the Roman square in a column to disguise their numbers, but break off and surround it instead.

3. Publius is sent with a detachment against some of the Parthians, who apparently flee. Publius gives chase.

5. Publius' detachment is cut down by Parthian arrows and cataphract charges. To avoid capture, Publius commits suicide.

6. The Roman square suffers further cataphract charges and showers of arrows. They finally escape after dark.

such force, Plutarch claims, that they could often penetrate two men's bodies at once. Fighting in this manner continued until nightfall.

Retreat and Slaughter

The rest of the story may be summed up quickly. The Romans retreated by night, when the Parthians were ill-equipped to fight, leaving behind some 4000 wounded to be slaughtered by the enemy. Most of the Roman survivors made it to Carrhae, although four cohorts lost their way and were destroyed. Surena moved up to blockade the city, and the Romans tried to withdraw, again by night. Many escaped, over 10,000 in all, but Crassus was intercepted and killed, his head being carried to Armenia by Sillaces as a present for the king, who had just reached an agreement with Artavasdes. The two monarchs, enjoying a production of Euripides' *Bacchae* at a banquet, saw Crassus' head used as a prop in the play. As many as 20,000 other Romans met their ends in the desert, with 10,000 others being captured and enslaved.

'The Parthians…began to fire their arrows from all sides at once…giving…violent impacts from bows that were strong, large, and so very curved that they could send off missiles with great force' – PLUTARCH

Fortunately for the Romans, the all-cavalry Parthian armies were poor at siege warfare, and had a difficult time operating in forests and mountainous terrain, so their counter-invasions of Syria were easily repulsed and the war petered out. Over the decades, the Romans learned to cope with the Parthians. Roman shield-bearing cavalry could harass cataphracts with javelins while using their greater speed and agility to evade a counter-charge, and chase away horse archers if there were not enough cataphracts to protect them. At short range, horse archers were at a disadvantage, lacking the shields western cavalrymen carried to protect themselves against missiles. A short, controlled charge could keep the horse archers out of effective range, but as the fate of Publius showed, it did not do to pursue the enemy too far. In addition, since a horse that has been ridden all day must rest and graze at night, Parthian camps were vulnerable to Roman night attacks, making close blockades of Roman cities dangerous for the Parthians and causing them to camp far from enemy forces. It was also useful to increase the number of missile-armed infantry in the army, particularly slingers, whose heavy stones and lead shot could injure even cataphracts. Crassus had too few light troops, and too many of them were javelin-throwers, to judge from the charge he ordered. The legionary square remained in use, with caltrops thrown down to maim the cataphracts' horses. Finally, the Romans raised their own *alae* of horse archers, adding cataphracts in the third century AD.

In AD 226 the Parthian state was overthrown by a Persian dynast named Ardashir, who founded the Sassanian Persian empire. Much better organized than the Parthians, the Sassanians fielded the same types of cavalry, but added large infantry armies capable of siege warfare. For the next four centuries, they pressed the Romans in the east, sometimes very hard. In the west, the Romans faced pressure from the Sarmatians, Dacians, Picts and especially the German tribes. The cavalry of the latter, provided as usual by their wealthier men, was mounted in the early centuries upon the local breed of horse, which was small, ugly and not very fast, but constantly exercised and well-trained; supposedly they were trained to stand and wait, even in the midst of battle, while their riders dismounted, fought and returned. They were the usual western shield-bearing, javelin-throwing cavalry, practising mainly simple forward movements with turns or wheels to the right, to keep the shields facing the enemy. However, some tribes were also practised in river crossings, swimming their horses over while still in formation. Picked light infantry with javelins and shields often accompanied the cavalry, adding their fire to the horsemen's missiles and passing

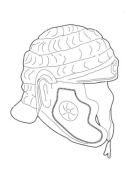

ROMAN CAVALRY HELMETS, *from left to right: an 'Attic' type c.AD 40, made of iron with bronze decoration; an officer's crested helmet from c.AD 75, again with bronze decoration; next is an iron or bronze helmet from c.AD 250, with a hinged mask attached by a leather strap; and the last is an iron helmet from c.AD 350, made in two halves and joined in the centre.*

through to attack the enemy's mounts. In the later period, from the third century AD onwards, German cavalry became more heavily armed, adding helmets and some body armour, and assistance from light infantry became less common. In most tribes the cavalry was never numerous, but the strong cavalry of the Ostrogoths, assisted by their foot archers, allowed them to form a kingdom in the North Pontic region. Later, the Vandals, after conquering North Africa, became essentially a mounted warrior aristocracy armed with sword and javelin.

During the first two centuries AD, the Romans held off barbarian attacks on the frontiers and occasionally carried out major offensives as well. However, in the third century a long series of civil wars, barbarian invasions and secessions created a crisis situation that looked to result in the collapse of the empire. One response was to greatly increase the number of cavalry – from around 80,000 in the early second century to about 200,000 in the early fourth century – and form many of them into a mobile cavalry reserve that could move quickly against threats on many fronts. After numerous reorganizations and mobilizations, there were many new formations, with some of the old *alae* still remaining, especially in the border troops. However, the cavalry of the new field armies was composed largely of units called *vexillationes*, after the *vexillum* standard. These may have had a 'paper strength' of 500 men, but 200–400 was the norm.

The majority were shield-armed cavalry as before, though in the east cataphracts made up about a quarter of the field army's cavalry, with horse archers at 15 per cent. Both types could be found elsewhere as well. Some of the cataphracts were armed with bow as well as lance, something that had become a regular feature of Sassanian cavalry. By the end of the fifth century AD, this type of trooper had become the standard in the east. By that time, of course, there was no longer a Roman empire in the west.

One reason for this was the Huns. Around AD 370, they gained sudden prominence in the North Pontic region, destroying the kingdom of

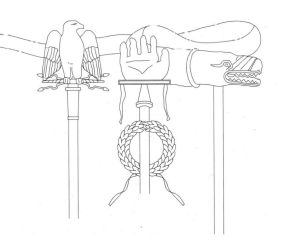

ROMAN STANDARDS, *including a* draco *on the right. This was effectively a windsock that produced a moaning sound when travelling at speed – for example, when charging into battle. Its purpose was to induce fear.*

the Ostrogoths and sending the survivors scurrying for the safety of the Roman border. The Romans, though, treated their guests badly. The result was a conflict that, on 9 August 378, saw the Goths destroy a Roman army at Adrianople, a Gothic cavalry charge turning a defeat into a disaster. The battle was the beginning of the end for the Roman empire in the west, for the Goths were never suppressed, and in 406 several other tribes crossed the Rhine and began occupying Roman territory in response to the westward movement of the Huns. For 80 years, the Huns varied between assisting the Romans against the other barbarians and making tremendously destructive raids into Roman territory.

Who were the Huns? Roman writers describe them as quintessential steppe nomads, ugly men who spent their lives on the backs of their ugly horses. They were lightly equipped horse archers, their powerful composite bows shooting arrows tipped with bone, which suggests they came from the deep steppe, where it was difficult to trade for metal. Bone strips reinforced the tips and handles of the bows, whose lower halves were shorter than their upper halves, a design adapted for horseback use. The Huns' accuracy with the weapon never failed to astonish the Romans. In battle they deployed in wedge-shaped masses, manoeuvred as though to charge, then divided suddenly into scattered bands and attacked, rushing about in seeming disorder, but moving so quickly their opponents had no time to respond. When their arrows were expended, they would gallop in and fight ferociously with sword and lasso, the latter weapon being one that Central Asian nomads had been using in battle for a

A ROMAN CAVALRY TROOP *attacking the rearguard of a Dacian army during Trajan's campaigns in the region. Note the ornamentation on the commander's helmet and fittings.*

KING DECEBALUS OF THE DACIANS *commits suicide rather than face capture by his Roman pursuers in AD 107. Light cavalry was ideally suited for such tasks as pursuing a defeated foe.*

millennium. Their horses were large, hooked-nose animals with long bodies, narrow faces, bent backs, long manes, scrawny muscles, skinny haunches and wide hooves, but they were also even-tempered, bore wounds well, were trainable and willing to work and capable of withstanding cold and hunger. Being steppe animals, they could find grazing on their own in situations where stable-reared animals would starve.

The Hun Homeland

Despite the Huns' reputation, the theory has arisen that once they occupied the Alföld, the great Hungarian Plain, they settled down and became a largely infantry army. It is calculated that the Alföld could provide grazing for only some 320,000 horses, assuming no herds of cattle, sheep, pigs or goats also occupied the plain – which is utterly improbable. That characteristic of steppe peoples – each nomad owning numerous horses – would have ceased to exist. Hun villages and a capital city, attested by the sources, argue that the Huns had

abandoned their nomadism for settled life. They imported Roman horses, animals fed with grain in stables and ill-suited for year-round foraging. In their campaigns, they engaged in siege warfare, fought carrying shields over 1m (3ft) high, and were defeated several times by ragged collections of tribesmen and the remaining Roman forces. Surely, proponents of this theory argue, the facts show the Huns had gone to ground.

Although seemingly plausible, these arguments falter at many points. While chroniclers may have considered the Huns an innumerable horde, there is no reason to believe they actually were very numerous; even a few tens of thousands of warriors would have been enough to make them a dangerous force, given the conditions of the period. Many steppe peoples had villages and cities, yet remained predominantly nomads. Hun siege engines were not complicated, and they had the assistance, we may be certain, of Roman deserters in building them. Many cities of the period were largely depopulated, so capturing them was not necessarily a difficult task for an experienced and well-organized attacker. As for shields, we have seen Roman cavalrymen operating with ones as big as the sources suggest the Huns carried, and Scythian horse archers slung shields across their backs, so the Hun use of shields is no surprise. They remained archers down to the Battle of the Nedao in AD 453, when the Hun kingdom was overthrown. And the Avars, who supplanted them in the Alföld, remained horse archers for centuries after their settlement, so why not the Huns?

As for rag-tag collections of tribesmen and Romans defeating the Huns, consider the Battle of the Catalaunian Plain in AD 451. This famous action occurred in north-western France in late June or early July, after Attila, the king of the Huns, had invaded with a large army and sacked numerous cities. There is a great deal we do not know with certainty about the action, including the numbers involved, the deployment of the various contingents or the location of the battle (in the vicinity of Châlons-en-Champagne, Troyes or Méry-sur-Seine, with the last being marginally the most favoured site). However, we do know Attila first gathered his subject allies, mostly German tribesmen, then proceeded from Hungary along the Danube and the Rhine, to destroy Metz on 7 April – a march of some 1100km (684 miles). This would be a remarkably fast movement for an infantry army. It is worth noting too that those tribes settled on the Hungarian plain typically launched their military campaigns in late winter or early spring, when forage for horses was in low supply in Hungary, and the invaders could exploit the accumulated winter forage of the peoples being attacked or the fresh spring grass. The timing of this campaign and the speed of the march, then, point to a cavalry army. While Attila's German subjects had never been steppe nomads, their nobility did fight from horseback; perhaps it was these people and their retainers who accompanied the Huns now. Later reports have Reims and Tongres (Tongeren) destroyed, along with at least a dozen other cities in what is today Belgium, Germany and northern France, as well as Paris being bypassed, Troyes

'Many [Gauls] got off their own horses and, crawling under those of the enemy, stabbed them in the belly; these would rear up in their anguish and die trampling upon their riders and enemies' – PLUTARCH

spared and Orléans besieged – from where Attila retreated on 14 June, when an army came to the city's rescue. Even assuming, as is likely, that Attila split his army into several detachments to carry out these attacks, this is very fast work, carried out in just two months. Again, it points to a predominantly cavalry army.

The retreating Huns were pursued by an army composed of the Visigothic tribe, then living in Aquitania under their King Theodorid, and a coalition of Roman allies led by Flavius Aëtius, the last great general of the western Roman Empire, who had brought a small Roman army from Italy. These allies included Germans, namely the Salian Franks (who were settled along the coast), Burgundians from Savoy and Saxons living in Normandy, as well as Celtic Bagaudae from Brittany and Roman military colonists from the region. Although the Visigoths and Romans had good cavalry, these were primarily infantry armies, so it may seem surprising that they caught the Huns at all. But in fact, even cavalry armies were tremendously slowed once they had plundered an enemy, since the train of prisoners, herds and other goods slowed them to a crawl. It was a military truism throughout antiquity that the best time to attack a raiding cavalry force was when it was on the march home, laden with loot.

Roman Allies

In addition, among the Roman allies were Alans from settlements in the Orléanais and elsewhere in northern France. These were descendants of Sarmatian steppe nomads and spoke an Iranian dialect. They are known to have retained their equestrian skills, and to have fought as heavily armoured cavalry. They were good allies, and doubtless well equipped. In the battle, they fought in the centre of the allied army, facing the Huns, a task for which they were perfectly suited. Our

Cataphract c. AD 200

These heavy cavalry were known to the Romans as clibanarii (literally 'oven men') after the temperatures endured by these riders when wearing their armour in Asia Minor. They became increasingly important on the ancient battlefield from the second century AD onwards. Their mounts were carefully bred to be strong enough to carry the weight of their armour and that of their rider. Most of the armour worn was scale mail, with some chain mail covering flexible joints. Leather was used to line the inside and edges of the armour. It was common for the rider to cover his face in either a mask or a veil of chainmail, leaving only his eyes showing. His main weapon was a lance of some considerable length, but a two-handed sword was also carried. With all his armoured protection, the rider had no need of a shield.

Catalaunian Field

AD 451

Attila, uncertain of the outcome of the battle, delayed beginning it until the afternoon, when a struggle to win the crest of the hill occurred. This was won by the Roman general Aëtius and the Visigothic prince Thorismund. The Visigoths, holding the right flank took the hill. They were then facing their relatives, Attila's Ostrogothic subjects. The Romans and their allies had the left flank, facing Attila's Gepid subjects. Of the general battle that followed, we are told few details, save that it was hard fought, very bloody and continued until nightfall. The Visigoths fought as hard as ever, despite the loss of their king, and are credited with the victory, separating from the Alans, falling upon the Huns and nearly killing Attila himself. Evidently they defeated the Ostrogoths, drove them back, then turned and attacked the Huns. Attila fled to his camp,.where the allies decided to lay siege to his position, but the Visigoths and the Salian Franks presently marched off, allowing Attila to escape.

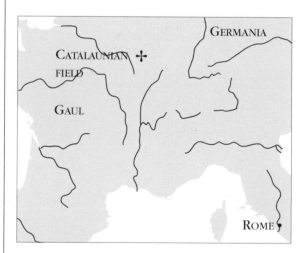

The location of the Catalaunian Field has never been conclusively determined, although sources agree that the battle took place in June or July in north-eastern France.

3. The Alans either break or desert, but the Romans and Visigoths stand firm and hold the Huns' attack.

5. Attila retreats to his camp, where he is besieged. However, the allied army breaks up, allowing him to retreat.

2. Attila launches a general attack, focusing on the Alans in the allied centre, and avoiding the Romans on the flank.

1. Thorismund, the Visigoth prince, wins control of a hill dominating one of the flanks of the two armies.

4. Thorismund then comes to Aetius' aid, threatening a double envelopment of the Huns, who break.

main source for the battle, a Gothic historian named Jordanes, reported that the loyalty of the Alans was suspect, and that Roman allied troops were lined up behind them. Since the Alans and Goths were old enemies, and the Alans held the Huns throughout the battle, it is likely the Goth's accusation is a canard, and that the allied troops were infantry operating in support of the Alans.

The battlefield rose on one side by a slope to a hill, with the Huns occupying the 'right side' of the hill, the allies the 'left side'. Attila, uncertain of the outcome of the battle, delayed beginning it until after the ninth hour of the day, about 1500 hours, when a struggle to win the crest of the hill occurred, won by Aëtius and the Visigothic prince Thorismund. The latter's presence suggests it was the Visigoths, holding the right flank of the army, who took the hill. They were facing their relatives, Attila's Ostrogothic subjects, in that part of the field. Since we know German cavalry could fight on foot as well as on horseback, there is nothing surprising about either Gothic force struggling to control a hill. The Romans and their allies had the left flank, facing Attila's Gepid subjects. Of the general battle that followed, we are told few details, save that it was hard fought, very bloody and continued until nightfall. The Visigothic king, Theodorid, was killed, either thrown from his horse and trampled by his own men, or slain by an Ostrogoth's spear. Despite this, the Visigoths fought as hard as ever, and are credited by Jordanes with the victory, separating from the Alans, falling upon the Huns and nearly killing Attila himself. Evidently they defeated the Ostrogoths, drove them back, then turned and attacked the Huns. Attila fled to his camp, which was fortified by a barrier of wagons (a standard nomad tactic). Prince Thorismund unwittingly came to this camp in the dark of the night, thinking he had reached his own lines, only to be attacked, wounded and dragged from his horse. He was rescued by his followers. Aëtius also became separated from his men in the darkness and wandered about, until he came upon the Visigothic camp and passed the night with his allies.

On the following day, the allies realized that Attila was still holed up in his camp. They decided not to attack him directly but to lay siege to his position, since the Huns had no supply of provisions and were hindered from approaching the Roman camp by showers of arrows from the archers inside. Attila was so desperate, it is said, that he ordered a funeral pyre of horse gear to be prepared, intending, if his enemies attacked, to throw himself onto it and so avoid capture. Fortunately for the King of the Huns, the Visigoths presently marched off, and the Salian Franks did so as well, their later historians blaming Aëtius for having tricked them into leaving. Be that as it may, the fact that the allies could plan to besiege Attila in his camp, aware that his only exit was through the Roman camp, indicates that the Huns had been manoeuvred into a cul-de-sac, probably with their backs against a river. This would explain why Attila could not simply ride away after the defeat. If true, it speaks extremely well for Aëtius' generalship that he, who would have had to coordinate the movements of the allied forces, had managed to trap Attila in this fashion.

There is, therefore, no reason to believe that the Huns had entirely given up their ancestral way of life in a matter of decades. However, even if that theory is mistaken, it is true that the limited

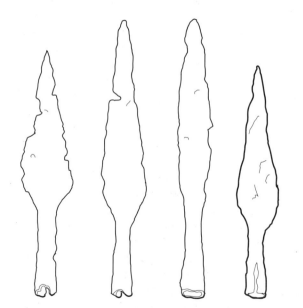

ROMAN LANCEHEADS *found in Germany. They had sockets to give them a secure fitting to their wooden handle. The lance could be used in a charge or hurled like a javelin.*

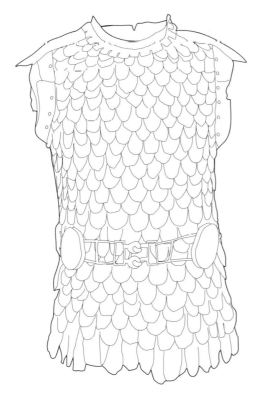

ROMAN LORICA SQUAMATA (scale mail) as worn by cataphracts. Most scales that have been found are bronze and are 20-29mm by 10-15mm (0.9-1.14in by 0.39-0.59in), but larger iron examples exist.

amount of grazing available in central and western Europe, as opposed to the steppes of Eurasia, acted to discourage the migration of steppe nomads. The wet climate of western Europe also played a role, stimulating the growth of forests, which hindered the movements of cavalry and made more difficult the use of the nomad's composite bow, a weapon whose susceptibility to damp conditions we have already noted. And so western Europe largely avoided the steppe nomad invasions that wreaked such havoc throughout history in other parts of the Eurasian continent. Attila the Hun was an exception that proved the rule.

Elephants

Horses were not the only animals used in combat in antiquity. Both elephant species, African and Indian, saw use in combat, as did both species of camels. Elephants are large herbivores that average 5.1 tonnes (5 tons) in weight and possess a long,

manoeuvrable trunk; a pair of tusks; broad, thin ears; wrinkled grey skin 2.5cm (1in) thick; four thick column-like legs; and a slender tail. There are two sub-species of African elephant, the Bush and the Forest, the former being the largest of all elephants, over 250cm (98in) high, with a very large, triangular ear. Forest elephants are smaller, under 250cm (98in), and have a more rounded ear. Both subspecies have two 'fingers' at the end of their trunks and concave backs. The Indian elephant has a smaller ear, a convex back, one 'finger' instead of two, and can grow larger than the African Forest elephant, but usually never as large as the Bush. Its tusks are smaller than an African's; indeed, female Indian elephants usually have very short tusks, if they have any at all. Elephants are herd animals, large-brained, with considerable intelligence and coordination. They cannot trot, gallop or jump, but can walk quickly – up to 16km/h (10mph) – and move through very rough terrain, descending slopes by breaking down steep banks and sliding down, and swimming across rivers using their trunks as snorkels. Anywhere a large army could go, they could go, as was shown by Hannibal's famous crossing of the Alps in 218 BC with 37 elephants. The animals bore up well under conditions of cold, snow, deprivation and difficult slopes. Their only failure came in the crossing of the Rhine, when the unaccustomed motion of the rafts beneath their feet panicked them. Several leapt into the river, carrying their mahouts (riders) along. The men drowned, but the elephants walked on the bottom and breathed through their trunks, reaching the shore safely.

The Indian and African Forest elephants can be tamed, trained and used in war; the larger Bush elephant cannot. Given the expense of supporting a herd, many of whose members would be juveniles unable to work, elephants were not bred in captivity. Instead, wild elephants were trapped, tamed and trained. In ancient times, taming required a hard and cruel week of 'breaking in', followed by several months of training the animal to bear a rider and carry out his commands. It still took two to three years to train them fully. Note too that the same riders, or mahouts, must always carry out the training and look after their animals;

an elephant is a wild creature that must consider a rider and his demands part of its life in order to perform its tasks.

The use of the elephant in warfare was largely confined to India until the fourth century BC, when Alexander the Great invaded India and fought King Porus in the Battle of the Hydaspes (328 BC). Porus' elephants proved the most difficult portion of his army for the Macedonians to defeat. Deeply impressed, the generals who formed the Successor kingdoms out of Alexander's empire (several of them veterans of the battle) eagerly sought to form elephant corps of their own. Initially, these utilized Indian elephants only. However, the Ptolemaic dynasty of Egypt, cut off from Indian sources by the rival Seleucid kingdom, which controlled most of the Near East, sent expeditions down to the Horn of Africa to collect African Forest elephants for training, and Carthage in turn employed Forest elephants from north-western Africa. The elephant corps was headed by an official called the *elephantarchos*, an important court official in the Hellenistic Macedonian kingdoms.

Each elephant had his or her own name (for example, Ajax, Patroclus, Nicon and the famous Surus, Hannibal's mount). The mahout sat on the elephant's neck, controlling his animal by voice, the pressure of his toes under the animal's ears and his *ankush* (*harpe*, *custis*), a rod with a hook projecting from the shaft a little way down from its point. Mahouts are usually portrayed helmeted but unarmoured, which is odd, since they were an obvious target for enemy arrows and javelins. Perhaps artists portrayed them as they usually saw them in parades, rather than as they actually appeared in battle. They were equipped with personal weapons for self-defence, but their real weapons were their elephants. Mahouts were often called *Indoi* (Indians) even though most would not have come from the subcontinent. Of course, Indians taught westerners the skills involved in elephant training, and many mahouts must have come west with their animals.

Elephants were often outfitted with elaborate trappings and bells, the better to awe the foe with their splendour. Headpieces and even body armour were sometimes employed, while tusks could be equipped with iron points or sword blades. In the early battles, the mahouts fought alone, or with a warrior sitting upon the elephant's back, but by the early third century BC, the Macedonian kingdoms began equipping elephants with thorakia, wooden towers protected by shields hung on their sides and held on the animal's back by chains passed around its belly, front or backsides. Two to four men armed with bows, javelins or long spears fought from the *thorakia*. The Carthaginians did not adopt the practice, however, perhaps because their African Forest animals were too small to bear such structures easily.

In battle, elephants were sometimes kept in reserve or placed in the main line of battle, but the usual tactic was to deploy them line abreast in front of the battle line, where they could disrupt enemy formations, then either trample down the enemy directly or render them vulnerable to follow-up attacks. A guard of light-armed troops was often deployed with each elephant to protect it from enemy missile fire and to exploit its successes. Horses unused to elephants were frightened by the sight and smell of the beasts, and inexperienced human enemies found them equally terrifying. Sixteen elephants were credited with the victory won in 275 BC by the Seleucid king Antiochus I against the Galatians – Celts who had recently invaded Anatolia. They sent the enemy cavalry and chariots reeling in panicked retreat through their own infantry, who fled in turn. Against individual human enemies, an elephant could use its natural combat moves, hurling an attacker into the air with its trunk, crushing him with its forehead and rolled-up trunk, goring him with its tusks, kneeling on him to crush him, or (if Indian) trampling him under the soles of its feet. Finally, elephants could be employed against fortifications, pulling down battlements with their trunks and breaking open gates.

The Drawbacks of Elephants

For all their potential effectiveness, elephants had serious drawbacks as well. The stress of captivity – and especially the brutal training necessary to accustom an essentially peaceable animal to the sights and sounds of battle, arousing its animal fury for the act of killing – must have reduced the average lifespan of the animals, as is true of captive circus or zoo elephants today. This in turn meant that war-elephants were a wasting asset, with perhaps a fifth of a herd dying of natural causes during the course of a decade. Constant replacement was needed if the herds were to be maintained, but India and eastern or north-western Africa were distant from the centres of Mediterranean civilization. There may have been some attempt at breeding; King Pyrrhus of Epirus took at least one calf into battle at Beneventum in 275 BC. But breeding elephants in captivity is a difficult and expensive matter even today, and probably would have been so in antiquity as well. Simply maintaining a herd of animals whose adults each eat some 160kg (353lb) of forage a day must have been difficult enough.

'the elephant...encircled the soldier with its trunk, and lifted him up in the air. The soldier ...hewed with his sword again and again at the encircling trunk [causing] the elephant to drop the soldier' – CAESAR

The biggest drawback to elephants in combat, however, was their tendency to stampede. When wounded, frightened or maddened by enemy attacks or stratagems, and especially when their mahouts were also wounded or dead, elephants would attempt to flee the battlefield, trampling over anything in their way, including friendly soldiers. More than one ancient battle was lost when a general's own elephants came reeling back through his formations. There are references to mahouts being equipped with mallets and chisels, or special knives, which they would use to kill their own elephants if this happened.

The Battle of Raphia

An excellent example of how elephants were used in battle, and the effect they could have on the course of action, is provided by the Battle of Raphia in 217 BC, fought by Seleucid king Antiochus III against Ptolemy IV of Egypt for control of the province of Coele Syria (essentially modern Lebanon, Palestine/Israel, Jordan and southern Syria). They met in battle on 22 June near the town of Raphia on the eastern edge of the Sinai peninsula, on a desert plain some 40km (25 miles) southwest of Gaza. Antiochus had 62,000 infantry, 6000 cavalry and 102 Indian elephants; Ptolemy 70,000 infantry, 5000 cavalry and 73 African Forest elephants. The centres of both armies were formed of heavy infantry phalanxes armed with the Macedonian *sarissa*, with lighter infantry on both flanks and cavalry on the wings. In front of the cavalry and some of the infantry on each wing, the kings deployed their elephants. No accompanying guard of light troops is mentioned; it was animal against animal, rider against rider, as Polybius reports:

'A few only of Ptolemy's elephants ventured to close with those of the enemy, and now the men in the towers on the back of these beasts made a gallant fight of it, striking with their *sarissas* at close quarters and wounding each other, while the elephants themselves fought still better, putting forth their whole strength and meeting forehead to forehead. The way in which these animals fight is as follows With their tusks firmly interlocked they shove with all their might, each trying to force the other to give ground, until the one who proves the strongest pushes aside the other's trunk; and then, when he has once made him turn and has him in the flank, he gores him with his tusks as a bull does with his horns. Most of Ptolemy's elephants, however, declined the combat, as is the habit of the Libyan [i.e. African] elephants; for unable to stand the smell and trumpeting of the Indian elephants, and terrified, I suppose, also by their great size and strength, they at once turn tail and take to flight before they get near them. This is what happened on the present occasion. When Ptolemy's elephants were thus thrown into confusion and driven back on their own lines,

War Elephant c. 275 BC

The animal shown here is an Indian elephant, but African Forest elephants were also used in ancient battles, although they were smaller in size. All elephants were controlled by a mahout, who was often, initially at least, an Indian. The figure in the artwork is unarmoured, but it is unlikely that mahouts would be completely unarmoured, as they were obvious targets for enemy missiles. If they were killed, their charges would usually run amok, causing chaos in their own lines. The elephants often had metal bands or caps on their tusks to improve their lethality. The tower carried on its back is secured by thick chains around the elephant's body and rests on a thick cloth protecting the elephant from missiles. The tower was of lightweight construction, leather stretched over a wooden framework, with shields hung over the side for added protection. The tower normally carried an archer and a pikeman.

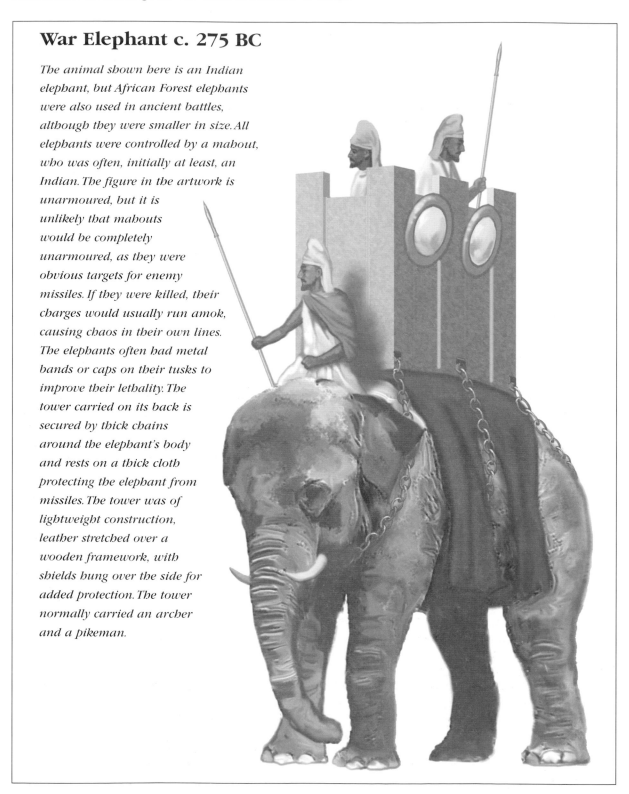

Ptolemy's Guard [infantry] gave way under pressure of the animals.'

With this assistance, Antiochus' right wing triumphed over its Ptolemaic opponents. But, despite similar success by the elephants on Antiochus' left, clever manoeuvring by Ptolemy's general there ended in the defeat of Antiochus' left flank. Then Ptolemy himself joined his phalanx in the centre and routed Antiochus' centre, which was heavily outnumbered. Defeated, Antiochus retreated, but the sources differ on who captured whose elephants. Antiochus sought peace and the war was ended. Peace held until Ptolemy IV died in 204; by 200 Coele Syria was in Antiochus' hands.

Defending against elephants required a good deal of courage and preparation. Defenders of fortifications could prepare spiked traps and hurl quantities of torches at them from the wall tops, frightening them into flight. Men facing them on foot tried to work their way around to the sides, rear and underbelly of the animals, then hurl javelins into them, hamstring them with axes or swords, or hack off their trunks. Mahouts were also choice targets for missiles. Heavy infantry sometimes tried to form deep and ward off their attacks, but Scipio at Zama in 202 BC showed it was better to leave gaps between units of infantry, so that charging elephants could be hustled down these paths by light-armed troops and then destroyed. Sometimes very ingenious methods were attempted: at Asculum in 279 BC the Romans fighting Pyrrhus employed heavy ox-carts outfitted with swivelling beams that had spiked or scythed tips and cranes that hurled heavy grappling irons wrapped in tow, daubed with pitch, and set alight. These impressive weapons failed, apparently because Pyrrhus was able to redeploy his elephants and avoid the carts. But the Romans persevered, and are supposed to have won a battle against his elephants, probably at Beneventum in 275 BC, by sending squealing pigs against them. Bizarre as it sounds, similar efforts occurred at other times in antiquity. The people of Megara, for instance, reportedly smeared pigs in fat and set them on fire before letting the unfortunate animals loose to frighten Macedonian elephants. While wild elephants are reasonably tolerant of other animals, the strain of captivity can breed a

neurotic fear of small animals, so that a dog barking or, yes, even a small mouse running across a floor can panic a circus elephant. The same could be true of war elephants.

We have a good example of the steps that could be taken to prepare for an elephant attack from Caesar's actions prior to the Battle of Thapsus in 46 BC. Caesar was in the Roman province of Africa, essentially modern Tunisia, to battle some remaining enemy forces from his civil war against Pompey. The client king of neighbouring Numidia, Juba, was allied with the Pompeians and, among other forces, had brought along 70 African elephants. The author of the pseudo-Caesarian *Bellum Africanum* writes: 'He [Caesar] had yet another cause for anxiety – the panic with which the size and number of the elephants gripped the minds of his soldiers. Here, however, was one problem to which he had found an answer; for he had ordered elephants to be brought across from Italy' [presumably circus animals]

'...to enable our troops not only to become familiar with them, but also to get to know both the appearance and capabilities of the beast, what part of its body was readily vulnerable to a missile and, when an elephant was accoutred and armoured, what part of its body was still left uncovered and unprotected, so that their missiles should be aimed at that spot. He had also this further object in mind, that his horses should learn by familiarity with these beasts not to be alarmed by their scent, trumpeting or appearance. From this experiment he had profited handsomely; for the troops handled the beasts and came to appreciate their sluggishness; the cavalry hurled dummy javelins at them; and the docility of the beasts had brought the horses to feel at home with them.'

In the event, it was Juba's elephants who proved to be poorly trained. Attacked by Caesar's slingers, they were frightened by the whizzing sound of the slings and by the stones and leaden bullets launched against them, and they panicked, turning swiftly and trampling under foot the supporting troops behind them in their haste to get away. But not all escaped:

'I ought not, I think, to omit to mention the gallantry of a veteran soldier of the Fifth Legion

Raphia

217 BC

The Seleucid king Antiochus met Ptolemy IV of
Egypt in battle near Raphia. Antiochus had
102 Indian elephants, Ptolemy 73 African Forest
elephants. Both armies' centres were formed of heavy
infantry phalanxes armed with the Macedonian
sarissa, with lighter infantry on both flanks and
cavalry on the wings. The elephants were in front of
the cavalry and some of the infantry on each wing. A
few of Ptolemy's elephants closed with those of the
enemy to fight, but most declined. Unable to stand
the smell and trumpeting of the Indian elephants,
they fled and were driven back on their own lines.
Ptolemy's infantry gave way under pressure of the
animals. As a result, Antiochus' right wing triumphed
but, despite similar success by the elephants on
Antiochus' left, clever manoeuvring by Ptolemy's
general there ended in the defeat of Antiochus' left
flank. Then Ptolemy himself joined his phalanx in the
centre and routed Antiochus' heavily outnumbered
centre. Defeated, Antiochus sought peace.

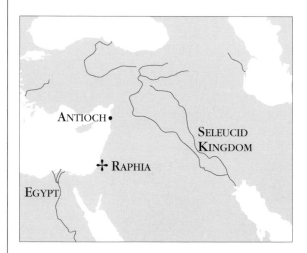

The Battle of Raphia was fought for control of
the Coele Syria region. Although Antiochus lost on
this occasion, he later conquered it after the
death of Ptolemy in 204 BC.

1. Ptolemy's African
elephants meet Antiochus'
Indian elephants; scared
by the latter's smell and
noise, most flee.

4. Ptolemy leads his
centre against Antiochus'
outnumbered phalanxes.
Ptolemy wins the day,
and Antiochus retreats.

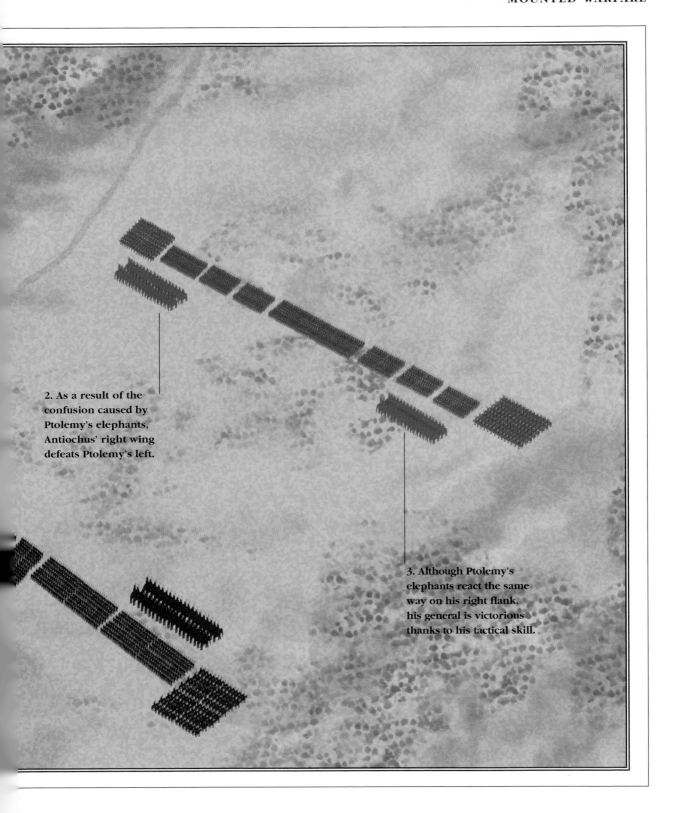

2. As a result of the confusion caused by Ptolemy's elephants, Antiochus' right wing defeats Ptolemy's left.

3. Although Ptolemy's elephants react the same way on his right flank, his general is victorious thanks to his tactical skill.

[of Caesar's army]. On the left wing an elephant, maddened by the pain of a wound it had received, had attacked an unarmed sutler, pinned him underfoot, and then knelt upon him; and now, with its trunk erect and swaying, and trumpeting loudly it was crushing him to death with its weight. This was more than the soldier could bear; he could not but confront the beast, fully armed as it was. When it observed him coming towards it with weapon poised to strike, the elephant abandoned the corpse, encircled the soldier with its trunk, and lifted him up in the air. The soldier, perceiving that a dangerous crisis of this sort demanded resolute action on his part, hewed with his sword again and again at the encircling trunk with all the strength he could muster. The resulting pain caused the elephant to drop the soldier, wheel round, and with shrill trumpetings make all speed to rejoin its fellows.'

Caesar took 64 elephants, equipped, armed and complete with towers and harness. They later participated in his triumph for his African victory and in an arena combat; he may even have intended to take some to the Near East for use against the Parthians. Properly trained, they might have proved useful.

After this, elephants saw little use in Roman warfare, most elephants ending up in the arena, the demands of which contributed greatly to the hunting out of the Forest animal in northwest Africa. However, the kingdom of Meroe in central Sudan had begun to tame and use Forest elephants during the Hellenistic period, eventually bequeathing the practice to the Ethiopians. In the third century AD, the Sassanian Persians began importing Indian animals for use against the Romans in the Near East. After passing three centuries without fighting elephants, the Romans found themselves facing the animals again. They resisted successfully enough, for the most part, but they were still impressed. A late Roman historian who had fought against Persian elephants, Ammianus Marcellinus, said 'the human mind can conceive nothing more terrible than their noise and huge bodies'.

Camels in Ancient Warfare

The two-humped, or Bactrian camel, was employed primarily as a transport animal by Iranian and Central Asian peoples, although the Achaemenid Persians did field Bactrian camel forces on occasion. The one-humped Arabian camel, or dromedary, was more often used in warfare. Originally a food animal, then used as a beast of burden, by the twelfth century BC it was being ridden by Midianite and Amalakite tribesmen in the northern Arabian peninsula. It took another millennium for the dromedary to become established throughout North Africa as well. Both species of camel are ruminating mammals, which store fat in the humps atop their bodies. Their feet are broad, flat, leathery pads, with two toes on each foot, designed to keep them from sinking in the sand. The Bactrian camel is adapted to cold, mountainous areas, with long, darker-coloured hair, shorter legs and a more massive body than the dromedary, which is adapted to hot, arid climates and a mainly flat terrain. Adult Bactrians stand 200cm (78in) to the top of their humps, Arabians to 215cm (85in). Weighing in at 300–600kg (661–1322lb), camels can bear loads of 130–200kg (287–441lb) at a walk for extended periods, dromedary caravans covering 40km (25 miles) a day, Bactrian ones 50km (31 miles) a day. However, a riding dromedary, a specialized breed, can maintain a speed of 13–16km/h (8.1–10mph) for up to 18 hours.

As a combat animal, the camel has some potentially strong advantages. Evolved to live in desert areas, it has few natural enemies, and is consequently much less skittish than a horse. Though notoriously ill-tempered, it is docile enough when properly trained and handled. It has better endurance than a horse, and can forage on practically any type of grass, leaf or twig. The camel's ability to go for a week without drinking is well-known. Combined with other adaptations to desert conditions, camels, especially dromedaries, offered their riders remarkable strategic mobility; raids made by North African nomads over 1000km (622 miles) of desert are attested. Moreover, horses unfamiliar with camels were likely to shy away from them. Cyrus the Great of Persia exploited this tendency at the Battle of Sardis in 546 BC. Faced by strong spear-armed Lydian cavalry forces, he assembled all the camels that followed his army bearing supplies and baggage, then removed their loads and set men upon them equipped like cavalrymen. He ordered them to advance against the Lydian horse, directing his infantry to follow the camels and his cavalry to follow the infantry. Unable to bear the sight or smell of these strange animals, the Lydian horses reacted as Cyrus had expected, and fled. The Lydians dismounted and fought on foot but despite their courage, were defeated. The camels in this instance were almost certainly Bactrian, but Arabians had the same effect.

The camel's advantages were largely outweighed by disadvantages that limited its range and importance as a beast of war. Evolved for desert conditions, camels do not prosper in wet climates, which interfere with their procreative cycle. Riding dromedaries efficiently was a difficulty, since the animal's hump, a store of fat, will break down and collapse under a burden. The first answers were to put a cushioned saddle atop the rump of the animal, or to surround the hump with cushions tied front and back. Reliefs of Ashurbanipal show raiding Arabs on camels, each with two naked riders, one of whom controls the animal with a long stick while the other fires a large self-bow. Perched uneasily atop cushions as they were, it is unlikely this poor man's imitation of a chariot team could have used any sort of mêlée weapon. The well-armed Assyrians had no problems defeating them.

Sometime after 500 BC, however, the North Arabian saddle was invented. It consisted of two large arches or saddle bows shaped like inverted Vs, connected by sticks, and resting on pads set in front of and behind the hump. A rider could sit firmly upon cushions placed on the saddle; hang equipment and supplies from it; and fight from it effectively, even using spears and long swords, as well as missile weapons. He would also have had an easier time controlling the animal, using a bridle and reins as well as a stick on occasion. Now better equipped, dromedary riders had more of a military impact, playing an important role in allowing first the Nabataean Arabs, then the city of Palmyra in Syria, to dominate desert trade routes. The Romans themselves raised units of *dromedarii* to patrol her desert frontiers. The

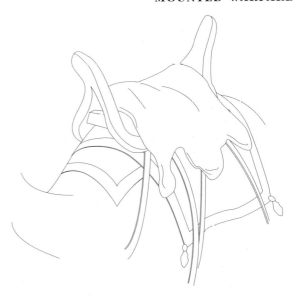

A RECONSTRUCTION OF A CAMEL SADDLE *as used in the Middle East around the 2nd and 3rd centuries AD. A wooden frame protects the camel's hump, while the rider sits on cushions and padding.*

Parthians and Sassanian Persians also made use of camel units; the Parthians even experimented (unsuccessfully) with cataphract camels.

Despite this, however, the camel could not compete with the horse as a war animal, since it lacked the horse's speed and manoeuvrability. Having no natural enemies in the desert, camels did not evolve the ability to move very fast. Riding camels can attain a pace of 25km/h (15.6mph), but only for an hour, after which they must rest and recuperate. A gallop is an unusual pace for them, demanding a well-trained animal and expert rider, and it can be maintained for only about 1km (0.6 miles). Nabataean forces were primarily camel-mounted infantry, and the chief military strength of the Palmyrans lay in their horse archers and cataphracts, not their camelry. Even desert Arabs preferred to dismount from their camels and fight on foot, or ride horses into battle. As a result, although camel portage came to replace the use of wheeled vehicles in the Near East and North Africa during the early Middle Ages, the dromedary as a beast of war had only limited regional importance, while the Bactrian, operating in territory friendlier to the horse, had even less.

CHAPTER 3

COMMAND AND CONTROL

For any ancient commander, control of an army in battle was a virtual impossibility. Once the fog of war had descended, most generals had little influence on the outcome.

A former Athenian cavalry commander tried to put the lessons of a lifetime of military service into words:

'For a general must also be capable of furnishing military equipment and providing supplies for the men; he must be resourceful, active, careful, hardy and quick-witted; he must be both gentle and brutal, at once straightforward and designing, capable of both caution and surprise, lavish and rapacious, generous and mean, skilful in defence and attack; and there are many other qualifications, some natural, some acquired, that are necessary to one who would succeed as a general.'

ROMAN LEGIONARIES *march onto the parade ground of Housesteads fortress in Britain, ready to receive training from their centurion. Note the various standards, including one showing the image of the Emperor in Rome. Constant training gave the imperial legions their discipline in battle.*

Xenophon had studied with Socrates and learned his soldiering in the saddle during one of the most militarized periods of Greek history. The old soldier understood well that a military force without a commander is like a man without a head. Whatever else their strengths and weaknesses, collected forces need competent leaders exercising command and control; without these, they are, and will always be, useless. Military forces need commanders to exist, let alone to function, and commanders throughout history to the present day face the absolute necessity of controlling whatever military assets they can garner if they are to conduct organized violence in pursuit of their desired goals.

So many analogies exist, but the term 'military machine' is useful, for it hints at both the complexity and the precision necessary for the operation of an armed force. In the hands of a master, its performance can astound; in the hands of an incompetent, the best and most skilful planning and construction can instantly come to ruin. The means by which ancient armies found and received direction in a battle are the subject of the current chapter.

Using some specific case studies of command and control (or generalship), taken from the ancient world, we will outline the challenges facing generals on the battlefield. Before we do so,

certain simple truths of mechanics, methodology and technology must be understood.

Structure

The military command structure is perhaps the most ancient form of truly mass cooperation known to man. Primal hunters and even modern primitive societies recognize, for the most part, that for any sort of group endeavour requiring immediate, violent action, the leadership of a single individual is to be preferred to a lack of direction or protracted argument. From that simple requirement, societies in the ancient world evolved around a single individual who directed events, the Greek term for this concept becoming the modern English term 'monarchy'. Societies with a king recognized that ruler's place at the ultimate head of any military endeavour. Albeit with notable exceptions, the decisions of a single human being would, in this period and in the centuries succeeding, direct the fate and actions of thousands upon thousands of other individuals in times of war and peace.

At the most basic level of technology, the individual ruler – whether by virtue of his (or her) superior strength, birth, or persuasiveness, or patronage by an even more powerful individual – could only direct subordinates within the actual sound of his voice, or within eyeshot of agreed-

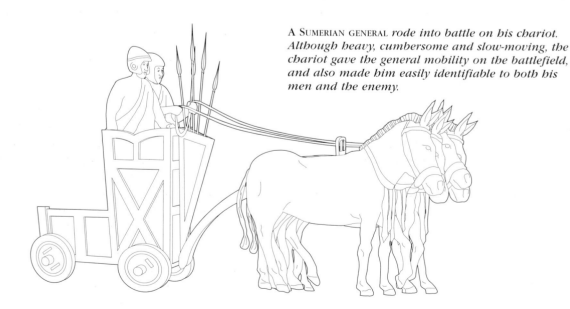

A SUMERIAN GENERAL *rode into battle on his chariot. Although heavy, cumbersome and slow-moving, the chariot gave the general mobility on the battlefield, and also made him easily identifiable to both his men and the enemy.*

upon signals. Eyeshot is an important thing to understand here, in the sense of what are now called 'line of sight' communications. Our references to the use of flags and flag signals in antiquity are restricted overwhelmingly to naval combat, where the flat calms necessary for the ancient vessels to fight also made an admiral's banner and signal pennants visible for miles. Before the age of the telescope, a flag was of no more use than a raised insignia on a pole, and a such a standard served to identify units from Artaxerxes' Persian cavalry to the last of the Roman Legions.

Personal qualities of persuasiveness, charisma and the ability to communicate orders clearly have always aided the commander. Communication was and is vital to command and control. A small group of hunters could do very well with one loud-voiced leader; the massive armies of Rameses the Great or Constantine needed, at the very least, other voices to pass the orders along. From so simple a need came the beginnings of the military chain of command, the one leader speaking his orders to others, who then passed the commands to still others, to yet others, down to the smallest units of any army. At the highest levels, the modern US armed forces might consist of Theatre or Army groups, of task forces or departments, but the actual function of these supra-units on the battlefield will depend upon units the size of a modern squad, seven or so men under a single non-commissioned officer's supervision. Such structures had their forebears in ancient armies.

In an age of general-kings and military emperors, one other problem faced ancient commanders, and the best of their subordinates. More than one king or emperor found himself overthrown by a general sufficiently competent or successful to secure more favour among the ranks of the army than enjoyed by the ruler himself. Kings needed and sought talented subordinates, but the reward for a general, loyal or not, who succeeded too well in the command and control of his forces might well be suspicion and death. A similar reward was often, naturally, granted for outright incompetence, failure or even bad luck. The pressures on a subordinate commander of an armed force to succeed without being too successful, posed an inevitable drag on the amount of military success any military unit could achieve on the ancient battlefield.

> *'... the general must neither be so undecided that he entirely distrusts himself, nor so obstinate as not to think that anyone can have a better idea ... for such a man ... is bound to make many costly mistakes'* — ONASANDER

Training

The commander's eternal need for suitable men to command men commanding still other men required competent subordinate officers. Such subordinates had to be capable of deciding when to implement or modify received orders, and when to transfer what information back up the chain of command to acquaint the higher levels with changes in the tactical situation. Regulation of the flow of data to and from the commander is vital to a force in battle. Experience is a harsh, if excellent, teacher, and units and officers of all ranks have lived or died depending on how quickly a given commander was able to benefit from what had been learned in the field. If it came to the commander's notice, a vital fact relayed or, alternatively, costly bewilderment or hesitation could prompt the heights of reward or the depths of censure.

Promotion from the very lowest ranks has provided armed forces with some of the most skilled commanders in history, but complications prevent and have prevented such means from supplying all an army's needs. The most skilled infantryman is quite unlikely to acquire the talents and knowledge required for the exacting and tremendously vital mission of supplying food and equipment to an army, a task infinitely more difficult in a world where the heaviest of freight transport available remained an oxcart or a train of capricious pack mules. The rough and exacting soldier from the front is likely to encounter opposition from parties with interests, social levels and traditions to be found in societies stratified by social conventions unrelated to military performance. Moreover, the knowledge of an individual soldier, however skilled, would live and die with that single human being, unless means could be found of preserving and nurturing such skills in his comrades.

Learning Through Observation

It is true that apt soldiers can learn from their commanders, and throughout history young officers have acquired their own skills by watching the techniques of their seniors. The young Alexander's career as commander of his father Philip's magnificent Macedonian army was virtually secured by the simple rule of heredity. His father nonetheless seasoned him in the field, culminating in the future conqueror's signal success against the combined forces of the Greek states at Chaeronea in 338. Philip's need for a skilled and subservient officer corps combined neatly with a need for political hostages and he collected the sons of powerful Macedonian families to be taught, trained and schooled at his court at Pella. The interests and authority of these young men could then be harnessed to the overriding goal of the Macedonian king.

The concept of a formal military academy was very long in creation, none such ever appearing within the timescale of our volume. The biographer Plutarch's *Life of Lycurgus* records that Greek Sparta remained the marvel of the Greek world for its peculiar and merciless system of training the combined youth of the city-state in the harshest skills of war. Greek and Roman male children received, under the rubric of athletic training, basic weapons instruction, which has been preserved in modern track and field events; but even Spartan females were trained in the military arts, and their sons pressed through the most exacting conditions of physical and mental discipline. The system was meant to keep the Spartans themselves supreme as an elite over large numbers of subject peoples and slaves. The 'Lycurgan Constitution' functioned for centuries,

and produced soldiers held in awe by all who encountered or fought them. Even a nation with such a regimen, however, could be beaten, and Sparta eventually collapsed under pressure from other states and the precarious nature of its own slave-supported system.

The concept of élite units of superior quality was known and applied with great success in the ancient world. The bodyguard of the king or emperor, such as the famous Roman Praetorian guard, were hand-selected from the entire force available by the ruler, who had an eye to the vital goal of self-preservation. These men could prove vital in battle, preventing the 'decapitation' of a force and often saving a state's cause on the battlefield by physically saving the commander from harm. Their own lives and preferment depended, after all, on their commander's.

Other élite units fought superlatively upon the main battlefield itself. Ten thousand selected Persian soldiers carried silver pomegranates on their spears, their superior equipment and morale marking them as 'The Immortals', whose numbers were replaced from the regular army as they fell or retired. The Theban 'Sacred Band' of 300 picked troops formed the core of the Greek line at Chaeronea in 338 BC, and a stone lion still stands over hundreds of grave sites, where the soldiers chose death over the possibility of retreat. Larger units could be 'élite' forces, such as Julius Caesar's favoured *Legio X Fretensis*, the legion that buoyed his fortunes over barbarian and Roman alike, while the crack navy of the island of Rhodes was routinely expected to engage and prevail over vastly superior numbers – and did.

Before actual combat, simple training of the body of recruited or intended soldiers did take place, certainly in the Greek and Roman world. Homer's heroes competed in feats of strength, agility and accuracy, and a run in full armour was a part of the earliest Olympic Games. By the Hellenistic era, the youth of the Greek city-states were receiving instruction in the operation of catapults, recently introduced, while future Roman officers competed in horsemanship and other exercises on the *Campus Martius* (the Field of Mars). Vegetius' surviving manual describes the means and exercises used to train the standing

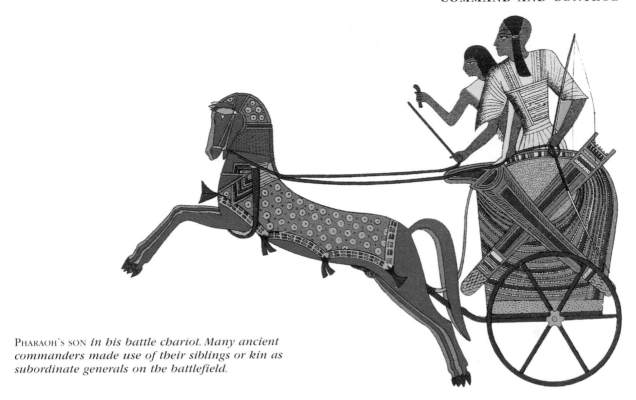

PHARAOH'S SON *in his battle chariot. Many ancient commanders made use of their siblings or kin as subordinate generals on the battlefield.*

army of the middle Roman Empire, in all-weather buildings specifically built for the purpose. All such drills and training cultivated a mindset of accepting orders and swiftly implementing them on the battlefield in the face of significant distractions and general confusion.

What might be called 'hereditary expertise' was a less distorting means of inculcating advanced military command skills within a society. Publius Cornelius Scipio and his brother Gnaeus did not teach formal classes to potential officers at some Roman equivalent of St Cyr, but they did pass on the lessons they learned at their grandfather's and father's knee to young family members eager to learn the means by which family heroes had kept troops motivated, outmanoeuvred opposing forces, and found supply and sustenance in the field. Scipio Africanus, the Roman general's son, defeated at length Hannibal Barca, another (Carthaginian) general's son, when traditions and skills clashed at Zama. Even failure could be instructive to a family disgraced by some legendary débâcle, its succeeding members acutely aware of what had gone wrong and

determined not to make the same mistakes. The risk of domestic censure was as lingering or damaging as a superior's wrath, and made brothers, nephews and grandsons potentially excellent subordinates to a commander of senior rank, particularly superior family rank. Under the conditions peculiar to the ancient world, one could do much worse than – and at times actually much better by – adopting a policy of nepotism in the selection of one's staff.

Supply

It is true that the ancient commander did not face the horrifying necessities required by modern mechanized warfare, when not only a spark plug, but the right spark plug is vital to the success of a modern attack. Still, as the saying has it, 'for the want of a nail, a kingdom was lost'. In antiquity, armies traditionally fed themselves from the enemy's territory or bought what food they needed from friendlier locals. The need for supply, however, restricted the campaigning seasons. Winters along the Mediterranean coast were a bad time to fight not because of the weather, so much as the fact that food and fodder were less readily available to armies in the field. A slinger equipped with lead missiles had greater range and power than if he used David's smooth stones from a brook, but they would either have to be transported or foregone by his commander. The same was even more true for archers and, eventually, artillerymen. Throughout most of the ancient world, roads were rutted and barely more passable than the surrounding countryside, although two of the very greatest ancient empires, that of the Persians and the Romans, moved armies and their supplies along excellent all-weather road networks. Wagons, pack trains and oxcarts could sustain the men and horses of an ancient army in bad weather and inhospitable territories, and successful generals, such as Alexander, found ways to secure and use them. Lines of supply were vulnerable, however, and required guarding, and an army without this drain on resources had an advantage. A supply of men is as vital as food to an army taking casualties, and the problem of securing reinforcements in hostile territory proved fatal to more than one ambitious general.

Communication

Communication is sufficiently vital in modern command and control for it to be grouped with them under the military abbreviation 'C³'. As noted, subordinates were a way of transmitting orders from the single commander to the smallest units of a force, but transmitting orders to subordinates and news of altered solutions to the commander is still a problem today and was a serious problem throughout our period. Cultures capable of mustering and feeding vast armies were necessarily literate; literacy allowed at the least a lack of distortion in the transmission of information throughout the host. However, a written message could also be intercepted by the foe. The speed of transmission of such messages was also limited by the speed and safety of those couriering the messages themselves. A runner on foot might survive where a horseman would fall to enemy missiles, a chariot might outrun pursuing spearmen, or might, after a crash, deliver vital information to the foe from a messenger's dead hand. The Spartans, for one example, recognized

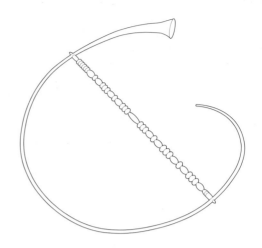

THE CORNU *was the curved war-horn of the Roman army, used to give signals and intimidate the enemy. The horn was wrapped around the musician's right shoulder.*

that possibility and used a system of encoding orders called the *scytale*, while various ancient writers describe other means of preventing a written message being detected or understood.

Some transmissions of information could be relatively instantaneous, under good conditions. A general-king could, at a glance, learn the location of units within his line of sight by their individual flags or standards. In fact, the Egyptian term of rank for a subordinate officer was 'standard bearer'; the term describes the origin. A commander could learn that combat had begun by the sound of the actual fighting. Likewise, the commander's own banner or distinctive insignia served to direct communication to a central point, once visible, at the cost of directing the enemy's activity towards the ever-vulnerable head of the army's 'body'. Very quickly, means of audio transmission of simple orders became established within the ancient armies. One of our oldest illustrations of Greek warriors in formation shows them keeping their step to the music of a flute player, cadence being necessary to regulate the speed of an advance and for the even more basic purpose of preventing massed formations from fouling each other.

A trumpet carried further, and had an association with army command going back to

Aesop's fable, from the sixth century BC, of the unarmed trumpeter executed by his captors for causing an entire army to fight. Trumpet players competed in judged competitions. By Alexander's time we have a specific reference to specific trumpet signals at a commander's discretion. By the time of Vegetius' writings in the fourth century AD, trumpet calls, at least, showed considerable sophistication, with one set of instruments used to signal the movements of standards, the other the troops and the third non-combat details. A flag's mere movement and position could signal the status of a given unit, but we do not find in antiquity any sort of visual signal more complex than the execution of a previously agreed-upon order, such as an attack, retreat or movement.

At sea, warships and merchant vessels could identify their natures by specified banners, or even by lantern signals at night over the flat surface of the sea. Admirals, then as now, flew their command pennants from their 'flag ships', and there are some tantalizing accounts of the gleaming surface of a shield sending signals to fleets at sea, as shall be seen in the account of Aegospotami; or to an invading army, as flashed to the Persians from behind the Greek lines at Marathon. However, the vagaries of nature, and specifically the wind and sun, did not prompt overwhelming reliance on such signals by most commanders.

All such means of data transmission faced grave, and at times even dire, complications. A flag could be dropped by a wounded bearer, captured by the enemy, and used deliberately or inadvertently to mislead. Darkness, confusion, dust or defeat could prevent messages from reaching their desired recipient, and the sound of a trumpet or flute could very easily be lost to the wind and the uproar of armed combat. Factors that exacerbated such difficulties were usually avoided by prudent commanders, hence the relative lack of night attacks in the ancient world, or battles fought in any but open territory in good weather conditions. A daring commander could profit from gambling that his own orders would not go awry under different circumstances, but such a gamble faced stakes of terrifying risk.

With such generalities in mind, the reader should recognize that this study uses a modern concept to describe ancient sources, events and data – an anachronism, but one designed to further an understanding of command and control in the ancient world. There now follows a series of battles that show the problems faced by the ancient commanders.

Kadesh

Rameses II's great battle of 1285 BC receives its due of coverage in another section of this volume, but an analysis of it from the prospective of problems of command control is most useful. It is redundant to remark upon how many of the

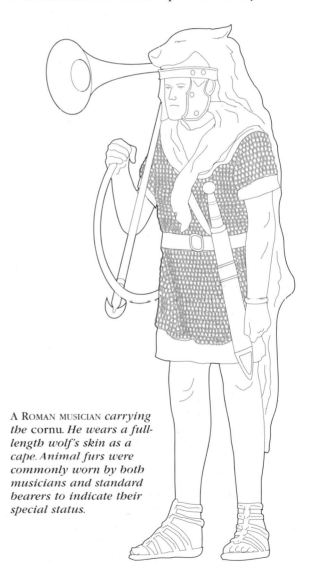

A ROMAN MUSICIAN *carrying the* cornu. *He wears a full-length wolf's skin as a cape. Animal furs were commonly worn by both musicians and standard bearers to indicate their special status.*

problems involved in controlling two large armies were solved before this battle: they had to be solved for the battle to have occurred in the first place. By the time of the New Kingdom, Egypt had an established, and better documented history of military activity in lands far distant from the Nile, and proven ways of projecting force abroad. Rameses himself could read and benefit from the experiences of Egypt's many former general-pharaohs, including the inscription modern scholars read today detailing Thutmose III's great battle at Meggido in 1458 BC, some two centuries before.

The understanding that peasants had to be levied, trained and fed for great projects went back

in Egypt to the the Old Kingdom's massive construction projects. Rameses set forth with a great army for the purpose of chastising the troublesome Hittite Empire, the particular foe being the King of Kadesh, Mutwallis, whose ancestors had opposed Thutmose himself. King fought king on the chessboard of battle; both sides enjoyed a unified supreme command structure, but the simple limitations on the abilities of a single man to control nonetheless required compensatory measures.

The Egyptian solution, which is the one Rameses recorded on his own inscription of the battle, was fairly effective. Rameses divided his army of approximately 20,000 men into 4 divisions

ROMAN LEGIONARIES *using their* gladii *to good effect during one of Trajan's campaigns against the Dacians in modern-day Romania. The standard-bearer (*signifer*) *carries a manipular standard, which carried portraits of the emperor and empress, and awards for bravery. The standard-bearers did not hang back from the mêlée but fought in the front line with the legionaries.*

A ROMAN LEGION crosses the Danube led by the Second Pannonian cavalry. This illustration demonstrates the large number of standards carried into battle by a legion. Note the image of the emperor, and the legion's eagle, at the front of the column.

of equal size under trusted subordinates, men with positions and possessions back in Egypt and hence a stake in the victory. Rameses hit upon a useful combination of divine patronage and unit identity by christening each of his divisions after a divine patron, those being Amon, Ra, Ptah and Sutekh, while at the same time keeping his own person, bodyguard and immediate subordinates outside of that structure in a separate, mobile unit.

During the march, these four divisions moved at some distance apart, a tactical trade-off between access to such roads as there were, time for assorted water sources and reservoirs to refill or be replenished, and the considerable – and in this case realized – risk of the army's pieces encountering the enemy while still separated, and being fought in detail.

Organization and wealth allowed Rameses both to acquire mercenaries to support his native

levies and to make a very quick march from Egypt to the north of Syria, where the battle took place. The Hittites managed, at what the Egyptian account notes as considerable expense and disruption, to produce a matching army of their own by the time the Egyptian forces approached the walled city of Kadesh.

Always involved in any exercise of command and control is the flow of information to and from the commander. Mutwallis cannily fed some 'disinformation' into Rameses' control machine, with two spies planted in the path of Rameses' army. These two informed the Pharaoh that the Hittite army was still some distance off, prompting him to make another tactical gamble and take his foremost division, that of Ra, and his own command and bodyguard to Kadesh with the hope of seizing the city before the Hittites arrived. Rameses and his bodyguard encamped to the

THE ASSYRIAN KING *Tiglath-Pileser III (744–727 BC) in his chariot, with a parasol for protection from the sun. Although there are only two horses shown, it is likely that three would have pulled the chariot, as three pairs of reins are depicted.*

north of the city, while the division of Amon rendezvoused with them the following morning.

The Hittite army, probably smaller than the Egyptian army, accordingly had two great advantages. Rameses was unaware of their actual position, and they themselves were unified, in a position to annihilate the division of Ra and perhaps win the war by capturing or killing Rameses himself. For all the advantage the king as commander gave the ancient armies, struggles in which the king was cause could, like the chess game, be lost with the neutralization of one man.

With visual reconnaissance being apparently the only sort Rameses felt the need to employ, the Hittite army's simple strategy of using Kadesh itself as cover worked quite well against the Egyptians. As divisions of Amon and Ra approached from the south and west of the city, the Hittites moved to the east, poised to move across the Egyptian line of march. Mutwallis

himself made a very sound command decision to hold his army outside of the city. The difficulties of controlling an army in an urban environment are to this day most grave, and in those days, using his complete force for a tactical offensive would have been impossible for Mutwallis, as walls and streets would have muted audible and visual signals and disrupted his unit formations.

The Hittites struck the second of Rameses' divisions, that of Ra, as it approached their new positions, and did great execution by hitting it in the flank. The Egyptians, surprised and panicked, fled for safety to the encamped division of Amon and threw that formation into disorder and confusion as well, just as the victorious Hittites attacked again from the south, directly across the Egyptian's escape route. Disaster loomed.

At that point of the battle, Rameses and the Hittites each faced differing problems of command and control. The panic and disorder of half of his army left Rameses physically unable to transmit countering orders to his own forces, and no message could be sent that would dramatically hurry the impending arrival of the divisions of Ptah and Sutekh to the battlefield, where they were desperately needed. Mutwallis, for that matter, found his own ability to command his forces disintegrating as his own men stopped to plunder the enemy camp – including the tents of the Pharaoh – as the disorganized Egyptian forces gave ground. Moreover, a failure of both reconnaissance and intelligence gathering meant that Mutwallis himself remained unaware that the other half of the Egyptian army was marching directly into his rear, while a formation of mercenaries hired by Rameses was moving in from the Mediterranean coast and about to take him squarely in his eastern flank.

Rameses and his army would live or die upon his ability to regain control of his forces, and the Pharaoh took the only, and therefore best, means of doing it, by very visibly leading his own bodyguard into a headlong counter-attack upon the advancing Hittites. Instantly, every Egyptian on the field knew where his commander was and where his own duty lay, and a general movement against the Hittites allowed the division of Ptah to strike the Hittites in the rear just as the mercenaries pitched into the Hittites from the flank. Mutwallis withdrew in some confusion. It is worth noting that in even the most autocratic of armies, retreat is a decision made democratically, when the majority of soldiers 'vote with their feet' and force even the officer corps to retire. Moving into Kadesh, the Hittites were sheltered against any further Egyptian surprises.

Rameses' reverses prompted him to withdraw his remaining forces from the vicinity of Kadesh, while the Hittites had seen enough of Egypt's military resources to agree to a lasting peace in the battle's aftermath. Both sides had shown good and bad exercises of central command, both sides had had their failures of communication, and the result was a tactical win for the Egyptians, a strategic victory for the Hittites and, in the light of the treaty, an international 'draw'.

Plataea: The Problem of Subordination

A full millennium later, an army such as one Mutwallis and Rameses might have led, faced an opposing force of wildly different origins and composition in a battle of annihilation. Both Egypt and the whole of the Hittite empire had fallen to the genius and numbers of Cyrus the Great of Persia and his heirs. The Persian empire of the fifth century BC extended as far to the east as the Indus

A RELIEF IN THE BRITISH MUSEUM, *London, depicting the reign of Ashurnasirpal II. Here the king (drawing his bow in the royal chariot) participates in the fighting during an unknown siege.*

Plataea

479 BC

The Greek council of war voted to withdraw from the Asopus, closer to Plataea. The retreat began at night, but the Spartan Amompharetus refused to withdraw his own small command in the face of the enemy. Pausanias, the Greek commander, was forced to countermarch in mid-redeployment. Mardonius, the Persian commander, noticed the disorder in the Greek line and launched an all-out attack. A slower Athenian withdrawal allowed those forces to take the charging Persians partly in the flank, and a grim struggle began. The élite Persian unit of a 1000 picked troops, 'The Immortals', surrounding Mardonius in the centre, were attacked by Spartan heavy infantry. Mardonius was killed in the savage fighting, prompting a crisis in Persian command, with his subordinate Artabazus holding his own forces out of a battle he considered lost. With the battle clearly now in the Greeks' favour, Artabazus assumed command of the entire Persian army and retreated swiftly back into the Persian Empire.

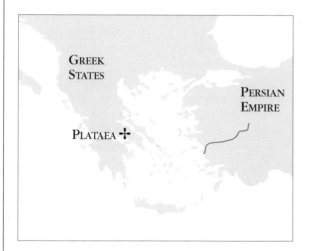

The battle at Plataea saw the ultimate defeat of the invading Persian army and their Greek allies after the loss of the Persian fleet at Salamis the previous year..

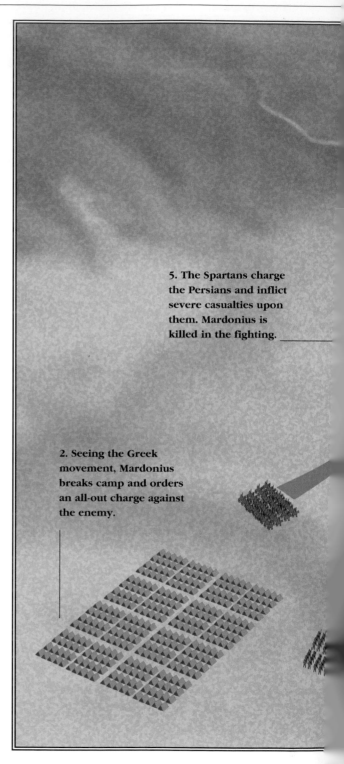

5. The Spartans charge the Persians and inflict severe casualties upon them. Mardonius is killed in the fighting.

2. Seeing the Greek movement, Mardonius breaks camp and orders an all-out charge against the enemy.

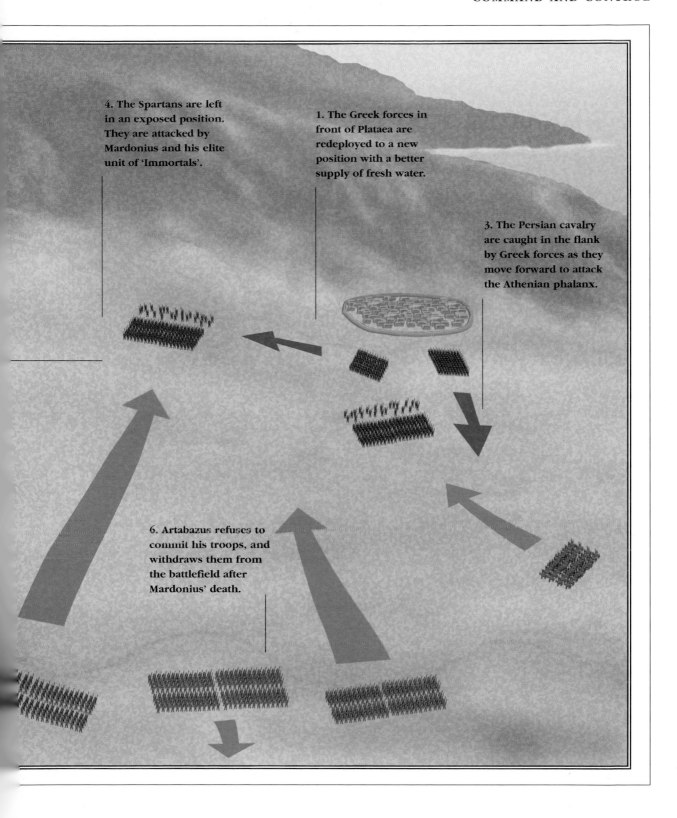

4. The Spartans are left in an exposed position. They are attacked by Mardonius and his elite unit of 'Immortals'.

1. The Greek forces in front of Plataea are redeployed to a new position with a better supply of fresh water.

3. The Persian cavalry are caught in the flank by Greek forces as they move forward to attack the Athenian phalanx.

6. Artabazus refuses to commit his troops, and withdraws them from the battlefield after Mardonius' death.

AN ASSYRIAN KING and his personal escort are greeted by one of his commanders. Kings and generals were expected to lead their men in the front line, and if they perished in the battle, as at Plataea, it usually meant the end of the campaign.

River, as far to the west as modern Libya, and as far to the north as the Danube. The Greek conquests in Asia Minor had proved troublesome; a tendency to prefer home rule and so revolt against Persian domination had received support from the as yet-unconquered cities of Greece. For an expansionist empire, the solution was a simple one. Darius' effort to chastise the Athenian Greeks had met horrible misfortune at the battle of Marathon in 490 BC, and his son Xerxes' solution was the classic one of mustering overwhelming force against the problem.

To the southernmost Greeks, the Persian onslaught was the most dire threat imaginable to their assorted ways of life, however diametrically opposed the democracies, tyrannies and Sparta's slave-dominating society might have been in their theories and practice of government. A common language and a common religious and mythical background for once drove the Greeks into a unity that, however shaky, managed to repel, and, at great cost, maul the vast Persian forces at Thermopylae, and stand off and then defeat the Persians' subject Phoenician–Greek navy at Artemisium and Salamis. Xerxes' organizational ability had formed and launched the expedition against the Greek states, but his strategic and tactical skills left much to be desired, and the Greeks had in those cases taken advantage.

Quality of Leadership

What the Greeks lacked in unity of command, they to some extent compensated for in the quality of their leadership. At Thermopylae, the Spartan king Leonidas had set an example of courage and dedication that endures to the present day, when he sacrificed himself and his command to buy the Greeks below the pass additional time for their preparations to meet the Persians. In Themistocles, Athens produced a master of strategy, tactical expertise, and even psychological warfare, who successfully neutralized Xerxes' ability to command his forces in Greece with a shrewd letter to the Persian king, which pointed out the dangers to his lines of communication and the possibility of Xerxes himself being trapped in a hostile Greece. Again, king equalling cause, Xerxes' corresponding flight back to Persia is perhaps understandable.

The result of Xerxes' departure, however, was to leave two quarrelling subordinates facing the divided and quarrelling Greek commanders when the time came for the final, decisive battle of the invasion at the central Greek village of Plataea in 479. Herodotus' magnificent *Histories* preserves the account.

Mardonius as senior commander was a respected and capable man, trusted by the army and necessarily under some suspicion from Xerxes. As a check to the potential for disloyal ambitions in his absence, Xerxes attached Artabazus as second in command. Artabazus was a special favourite of Xerxes. Disagreements in the command were profound and took on an increasingly personal and political edge, with Mardonius' possibly superior command ability conflicting with Artabazus' prudence and desire to prevent Mardonius from posing a threat to Xerxes' supreme authority. The final result of their rivalry would manifest itself in the ultimate course of the battle.

Themistocles himself suffered from the suspicions of the other Greeks that the interests of his native Athens were paramount to him, as indeed they were. With many of the northern Greeks under Persian control or influence, the Greeks of the Peloponnese and the west were willing to abandon the north and Athens itself, which had already been ruthlessly levelled to the ground by Xerxes in retaliation for the Persian defeat at Marathon and Athenian activities in Asia Minor. Themistocles had only been able to convince the united Greeks to fight and win at Salamis by revealing their plans to withdraw to Xerxes, who blocked the escape route. The Spartan regent, Pausanias, shared the traditional Spartan desire to preserve Sparta at all costs, but proved susceptible to Themistocles' persuasion, particularly when it was clear that the remaining Persian army would have to be fought, and that any sort of good ground might be as suitable as any other.

The ground selected, then, by Mardonius and Pausanias was on either side of the Asopus river. Mardonius, taking advantage of the slow decisions of the Greeks' divided commanders, had chosen a battle where his great numbers of Persian infantry could be supported by superior Persian cavalry on either flank. Pausanias noted the Persian advantages, and sought for means to counter them, starting out by placing the Athenian infantry on his left, directly opposite the main Persian infantry. Here he relied on history for his decision, the Athenians having done bloody execution on the Persians' best 10 years previously at Marathon. He also declined battle, leaving his forces on a high ridge - as the Athenians had occupied at that same battle - where the downhill run would add impetus to the charge of their heavy infantry.

'When the general leads his men out to battle, he should present a cheerful appearance, avoiding any gloomy look. Soldiers usually estimate their prospects by the appearance of [their] general' – EMPEROR MAURICE

The Battle Commences

Mardonius desired battle and success as much as Artabazus feared both, and sought to bring the Greek forces to him by attacking their rickety lines of supply with roving Persian cavalry. These actions were compromised when his own trusted and capable subordinate, Masistius, died in a Greek ambush. Both sides tinkered with their lines of battle, Mardonius shifting the Persians away from the Athenians, Pausanias shifting them back as both the commanders of both armies argued alternately for battle or retreat. Groups tend to agree upon the safest course of action; it is a truism that councils of war never vote to fight, but in this case each commander was able to force his view and course of action upon his army. Finally, Mardonius dispatched cavalry to foul and block the central spring from which the Greek army had been taking its water, and managed to block a sizable Greek supply train in a pass on Mount Cithaeron. Accordingly, the Greek council of war voted to withdraw from the Asopus, closer to Plataea, where a watered tract offered a solution to one problem, while troops were to be sent to solve the other. The actual retreat began at night, and here Pausanias faced his own greatest crisis of command when the Spartan Amompharetus refused to withdraw his own small command in the face of the enemy. Pausanias was faced with

Gaugamela

331 BC

Darius had chosen a wide and level battlefield near Arbela, even having the terrain levelled to assist his scythed chariots. Alexander sent his élite cavalry and phalanx at an oblique angle into the much longer Persian line, directly for Darius' position. Alexander's archers and javelin throwers killed Darius' charioteers, while his elephants proved useless and more of a danger to their own side. The moment of danger for Alexander came when the onrushing Persian cavalry got past the Thessalians and hypaspists on the flank and drove for the Macedonian rear. The Persians drove through the reserve line and moved miles to the rear to plunder the Macedonian camp. Distance and Alexander's pressure upon him cost Darius control at the vital moment. Darius had no way of either summoning his victorious, loot-obsessed cavalry to his rescue or ordering it to take Alexander's line in the rear. As a result, Darius' nerve failed once again, and he abandoned his army in wild flight.

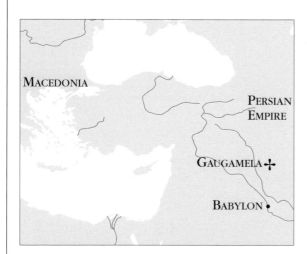

The battle was fought in the heart of the Persian empire. Soon afterwards Darius was executed by one of his own generals for his cowardice, but the empire was soon conquered by Alexander.

3. The Persian left tries to outflank the Macedonians, but they cannot get past the light troops and cavalry.

4. Alexander and the Companions break through a weak spot in the Persian line and swing leftwards.

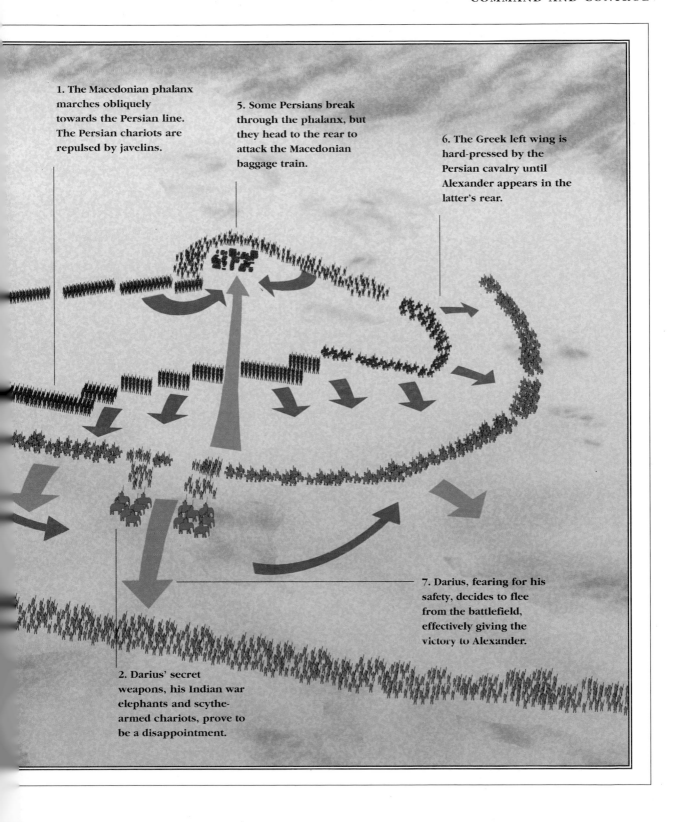

1. The Macedonian phalanx marches obliquely towards the Persian line. The Persian chariots are repulsed by javelins.

5. Some Persians break through the phalanx, but they head to the rear to attack the Macedonian baggage train.

6. The Greek left wing is hard-pressed by the Persian cavalry until Alexander appears in the latter's rear.

7. Darius, fearing for his safety, decides to flee from the battlefield, effectively giving the victory to Alexander.

2. Darius' secret weapons, his Indian war elephants and scythe-armed chariots, prove to be a disappointment.

the Hobson's choice of letting that portion of his command be annihilated or countermarching in mid-redeployment.

For his part, Mardonius noticed the changes and disorder in the Greek line and sought to exploit both by an all-out attack at once. A slower Athenian withdrawal allowed those forces to take the charging Persians partly in the flank, and a grim struggle began in which Persian courage and numbers ground into Greek armour and determination. The élite unit of the Persian army, a band of 1000 picked troops called 'The Immortals', surrounded Mardonius in the centre of the Persian line. These men engaged in close combat with Spartan heavy infantry, who had Leonidas' death to avenge. With Mardonius' death came a crisis in Persian command, with Artabazus himself holding his own forces out of a battle he considered lost – lost indeed, perhaps by his own action. With the battle clearly in the Greeks' favour, Artabazus assumed command of the entire Persian army and retreated swiftly back into the Persian Empire. On both sides, insubordination and disorder had played their part, but for the Greeks, the victory proved decisive and final.

Aegospotami: Politics and Incompetence

Persian revenge for the empire's earlier defeat came by indirect means. Athens and Sparta faced each other in the long and gruelling series of campaigns known today as the Peloponnesian War, in which Athenian naval imperialism faced Sparta's own superlative army and land allies. In one of the great vindications of sea power, the Athenians' fleet and overseas sources of supply had served to counter Spartan superiority in land combat, leaving Athenian territory and allies devastated while the city itself survived attack, plague, military disaster in Sicily and siege thanks to resupply from the grain fields of the regions around the distant Black Sea.

Sparta, accordingly, had to find some means of severing the Athenian jugular, and needed a fleet to do it. Plutarch's biographies of Lysander and Alcibiades record the means and the eventual success. The Persians, after a careful and undoubtedly satisfactory diplomatic courtship and humiliation of both sides, finally agreed to underwrite the construction of a Spartan-controlled navy, an inevitable decision given a series of Athenian attacks upon the Persian empire itself in the early part of the fourth century. The new Spartan squadron under the first Spartan admiral, Callicratidas, managed to destroy a rickety Athenian squadron off Eretria in the year 411 BC, but found disaster against a rebuilt Athenian fleet at Arginusae in 406, when Callicratidas drowned.

In the light of that débâcle, both sides underwent a major shift in command, which makes the result at Aegospotami most pertinent to the subject of command and control in the ancient world. Sparta replaced its fallen admiral with the brilliant, opportunistic and unscrupulous Lysander. Six of Athens' finest surviving admirals were in command of the Athenian fleet at Arginusae; all six were executed by the sovereign vote of the Athenian assembly for their failure to rescue the survivors of 27 vessels crippled during the action. In effect, Athenian rage at that failure resulted in the suicidal decapitation of the vital Athenian navy, and the disastrous result of that exercise of civilian control over the military was not long in coming.

Lysander's competence and diplomatic abilities succeeded in increasing Persia's financial support, which manifested itself in a rebuilt and dangerous Peloponnesian fleet. The Athenian traitor and exile Alcibiades took advantage of the disaster to assume a brief and victorious command of the Athenian fleet, but his own and quite justified suspicious political nature resulted in his flight into exile before he, too, could be executed by a vengeful and suspicious Athenian electorate. The three admirals sent out to replace Alcibiades were Tydeus, Menander and Adimantus, who provided history with one of its clearest examples of the disastrous effects of blatant incompetence.

Unwilling to engage the Athenian fleet after the disaster at Arginusae and reverses in other skirmishes, Lysander chose to shadow it as it moved to a new anchorage near the vital bottleneck in the Athenian supply route created by the Hellespont. The site was excellently chosen for the supply and comfort of the Athenian crews, large numbers of whom were voters, of whose wrath the admirals could admittedly be excused for fearing. As a defensive position, however, it was so staggeringly ill-chosen that Alcibiades himself came down from a secure place of exile to warn his successors of their peril, with the Spartan fleet based and defended at Lampsacus on the opposite shore. His warnings fell upon deaf ears, and the three Athenian admirals settled into a comfortable and disastrously predictable routine of putting to sea in the morning, offering the outnumbered Spartan fleet battle, returning to their anchorage, and sending the men ashore for a leisurely lunch.

Lysander was not one to overlook so elaborate an opportunity. As the Athenian crews debarked, the Spartan fleet put to sea and fell upon the entire assembly of over 200 ships, the attack timed by an optical signal – the flash of a burnished shield – from a single Spartan reconnaissance vessel. Spartan ships swept down on the Athenian anchorage and towed off the unmanned vessels. Slaughter followed. Spartan marines landed, surrounded and then butchered the 3000 captured Athenian crews and officers. Having let their men scatter ashore, the Athenian admirals had no way of manning their ships quickly or of mounting any kind of defence. One alert Athenian commander, Conon, and eight ships escaped the disaster. The Athenian democracy found a swelling number of refugees forced within their city by the advancing and augmented Spartan fleet, with the climax of the campaign and the war coming when Lysander methodically starved the city and the Athenian democracy into submission and surrender to the authority and occupation of Sparta. An empire and an authoritarian state combined their resources and their relative tenacity into a victory over the tumultuous and ultimately self-destructive Athenian democracy.

Gaugamela: Genius Overcoming all Obstacles
Gaugamela, as the greatest victory of antiquity's undisputedly greatest military genius, deserves

> *'... the general should be manly in his attitudes, naturally suited for command, profound in his thinking, sound in his judgment, in good physical condition [and] hardworking'* – ANON

study from all angles, but is particularly interesting from the perspective of the problems of command and control. Indeed, the battle seems almost to have been carefully constructed so that the very difficulties Alexander faced in controlling his own army in the face of the Persians ended up augmenting Alexander's plan, instead of hindering it. Arrian's excellent *Anabasis* of Alexander's battles is the preferred source here. During his campaigns from 336 to 323, Alexander was blessed in his principal opponent, Darius III, who let him complete his father's dream of conquering the Persian empire and territories in the east. Darius was a good leader and a sub-par general, whose ability to bring huge numbers of Persia's military assets into the field did not match his skill in using them. Moreover, as it had been since Kadesh, the king was still the cause; if Darius could be captured, Persian organized resistance to the invasion could (and did, in the end) collapse. As a result, in every battle with Alexander, Darius stripped his country's reserves of manpower, then lost them when he fled the battlefield as soon as Alexander's own advance posed a credible threat to his person. That had not been the case when the Persians themselves had tried a 'decapitation strike' on Alexander at the Granicus. Alexander's bodyguard had prevented the Persian cavalry's effort to dispatch him, while Alexander kept control of his own anxieties and his army and won battle after battle.

Darius' forces consisted of the Immortals, the élite division of the Persian Army, which had fought well at Plataea, and a sizeable force of Greek mercenaries, who continued in Persian service despite the gruesome treatment Alexander had meted out to the Greeks who had penetrated the Macedonian phalanx at Issus. Darius' confidence in facing Alexander again came largely from two secret weapons he had procured while Alexander had been busy campaigning in Egypt. From his Indian subjects, Darius had secured a number of war elephants, and one of the most terrifying weapons from the traditions of Eastern warfare re-appeared in chariots equipped with scythe blades upon their wheels and traces, weapons designed to inflict dire casualties upon Alexander's infantry. In addition, there were the nobility of the Persian Empire, the cavalry divisions under Bessus and Mazaeus. Exploiting the fact that he was himself the objective of Alexander's campaign, Darius was able to control Alexander's movements. He chose a wide and level battlefield near the city of Arbela, going so far as to have the terrain levelled to assist the action of his chariots.

Alexander, with a genius' pragmatism, camped 6.4km (4 miles) from Darius' army, just far enough to prevent a surprise attack, and reconnoitred Darius' prepared battlefield for traps. The leader's very confidence itself became a command asset, for Alexander chose to leave his troops comfortably encamped, rather than, as their

ALEXANDER *leads his Companion cavalry across the Granicus, seizing the initiative from the Persians. Like most successful military commanders, Alexander was no stranger to luck.*

Persian counterparts, in arms and watchful throughout the night. The commanding general himself managed a good night's sleep, having to be roused for action the following day.

As had been so disastrously the case at Plataea, there was another crisis of command. Alexander's father's adjutant and most competent general Parmenio approached him with his own plan for the battle: the very night attack that the Persians were dreading. Contrary to Parmenio's usual reputation for prudence, such a suggestion was, in fact, bold and consequently risky. Alexander's dismissive rejection, that he would not 'steal a victory', was the final word against such action, but Parmenio's very anxiety about the battle became yet another liability turned asset in Alexander's master plan.

It was a tendency of all shoulders with shields to move to the right in the course of an advance, as each man sought to cover the exposed portion of his body with the shield of his comrade next in the line. The great Theban military genius Epaminondas had learned to exploit that tendency with an obliquely directed and focused attack on an advancing enemy line as it stretched and thinned in response. Philip himself had spent time in Thebes, and the tactic became an integral and vital part of Macedonian success in the decades following. Alexander's plan made full use of it when he formed his lines on what was to be the morning of the battle.

Both Alexander's élite cavalry and the awe inspiring Macedonian phalanx would move at the oblique angle into the much longer Persian line, impact – as usual – being set directly for Darius' visible position in the centre of his line, and the Macedonian line moving at an angle as it advanced. Alexander knew that Darius' cavalry, chariots and elephants would attempt to flank him and get behind his forces, so he dispatched crack light infantry called 'hypaspists' and his Thessalian allied cavalry to both ends of his line. Both arms were broken into small units, which could move aside in the face of elephants and chariots, showering javelins on those and the cavalry as they would inevitably be driven back by the Persian thrusts. The retreat of these smaller units became an asset to Alexander's grand plan, for

behind his front line, under the worried Parmenio, Alexander placed a reserve phalanx, as difficult to attack as the front line. In effect, as his smaller army waded into the massed Persian forces, Alexander's formation would become a forerunner of the renowned British 'square' of the nineteenth century, a formation that became the stronger as it was driven into itself.

Alexander's Success

For the most part, the plan worked. Alexander's archers and javelin throwers killed the charioteers of the scythed chariots. Darius had not, in fact, employed these in the attack for which they were most suited, which was to increase the slaughter of a disorganized and retreating enemy. As often happened with elephants and warfare, the elephants felt no stake in the battle sufficient to wade into the bristling spears and arrows of the enemy army, and proved useless and uncontrollable, more of a danger to their own side. Meanwhile Alexander's pike-equipped cavalry and infantry bore inexorably down, at the oblique angle, upon Darius' visible standard.

The moment of danger came when the onrushing Persian cavalry got past the Thessalians and hypaspists on the flank and drove for the Macedonian rear. Parmenio found himself the victim of a thinned, but advancing, line as the Persians drove through his reserve line and moved miles to the rear to plunder the Macedonian camp. Distance and Alexander's pressure upon him cost Darius the control of the most dangerous part of his army at that moment. Darius had no way of either summoning his victorious cavalry to his rescue or ordering it to take Alexander's line in the rear as a desire to win – as opposed to a desire to loot – should have prompted.

Darius' nerve failed once again, and he abandoned his army and camp in wild flight, this one to be ended some time later when a disgusted Bessus executed his monarch and attempted in vain to lead further resistance himself. Loss of communication kept the Persians fighting and their losses rising even after their king's flight. Parmenio himself, under pressure and out of contact with Alexander's line, had abandoned the original idea of a box and sent frantically to

Alexander for assistance. Alexander returned to find that his Thessalian cavalry had counterattacked, Parmenio had reversed the direction of the reserve advance and destroyed the Persians to the rear, and that Darius had, yet again, escaped him. There would be a reckoning with Parmenio for his premature panic and dissension with Alexander's plans and tactics but, although it was not clear at the time, Alexander was for the rest of his life the virtual master of the entire Greek and Persian worlds.

Chios: A Coalition Command

The legend has it that the dying Alexander was asked who was his heir, and answered, 'The strongest'. The wars among his generals, later called the Successors (*Diadochoi*), resulted in three powerful military states clustered around Greece and other fragments of the empire on and within the Mediterranean. None of these 'Hellenistic' states ever entirely shook off the ghost of the vanished empire; all, at times, sought by various means to put their monarchs at the head of that reunited empire. Looking back over the ruins of Greek history was the Roman soldier-scholar Polybius, who left the bulk of the following account.

As haunted as anyone by that ghost of empire, and more capable and vicious than most, was Philip V of Macedonia, no descendant of Alexander or Philip, but in possession of some of their holdings and desiring more. King being cause, Philip's efforts as a commander would follow his own will and whim.

In the way stood the two other great Successor kingdoms, Antiochid Syria and Ptolemaic Egypt, and a collection of smaller states that looked to be easier prey than either of the two larger rival powers. Particularly troublesome was the island democracy of Rhodes, with the most superlative navy in the ancient world, and the fortress-city of Pergamon, whose rulers had no intention of yielding their sceptres to anyone else while their powerful walls held. Philip's threat drove Rhodes and King Attalus of Pergamon into alliance, while in the years before 201 BC the king of Macedon built a strong navy, to which he added by seizing Egyptian war vessels before that degenerate

power could react. Philip captured several islands among the Cyclades and moved his army and navy down the coast of Asia Minor, poised to menace and destroy separately both in turn.

The Rhodians and Attalus had not been idly trembling before Philip's advance. Philip's *bête noire* in the campaign and the nemesis of his long-laid designs against Rhodes would prove to be the Rhodian admiral Theophiliscus. This man's ability and skill would face Philip's craft and superior resources, for the Rhodian had correctly anticipated Philip's plans and taken every possible step to undo them.

Philip sought to divide the forces of Rhodes and Pergamon with a siege of the island of Chios, from which he would be well situated to prevent Attalus and the Rhodians from aiding each other. Attalus had quite correctly realized that Philip intended an eventual stroke against him and was feverishly steeling his fortress-city for the onslaught. Theophiliscus, however, equally correctly understood that Pergamon could resist any attack Philip could mount. He convinced Attalus to abandon his preparations and join his fleet with Rhodes' while he was still able to do so.

Philip had been digging away beneath the Chians' walls when the news came of the allied fleet's arrival. From the first moment, Theophiliscus had seized the initiative from the Macedonian king, who suddenly found himself trapped on an island with a hostile fleet across his supply lines. Polybius portrays Philip as indecisive at first, before deciding to abandon his siege and make for Samos, possibly with the intention of outfitting still more Egyptian warships.

The allies were not disposed to let him go. Macedonian resources, which by that time featured a strong naval tradition, included some of the heaviest and most dangerous vessels in the ancient world, 53 of the heaviest class, an unknown number of medium vessels, and 150 of the lightest vessels that could carry rams.

Philip deployed this imposing force slowly enough for most of the allies to convert their own picket formation into a line of battle and move to engage. The battle was fought in the strait between Chios and the Erythraean promontory of the Asian coast. Initially, Philip's line was parallel to the coast of Chios, preparatory to swinging south. As the allies bore down rapidly from the north, Philip was forced to reverse his line, which he drew up in the middle of the strait, facing north-east with his right on the Asian side, arranged in front of the strait's two small islands. The king being the supreme commander, there was no resistance among Philip's officers to his commands.

Our source gives the allies' complete strength as 65 heavy warships, 9 medium cruisers and 3 other medium craft. At first, Attalus showed more confidence in the strength of his navy than his Macedonian opponent, for he took his own lavishly appointed flagship directly into the line, while Philip preferred to wait in the van with his own squadron of lighter ships. A flagship (*nauarchis*) was as visible as any standard in telling crews and officers where a commander thought it necessary to be. Theophiliscus' Rhodians seem to have been more deliberate than the Pergamene contingent in committing to the action. They crossed the strait at speed to prevent Philip's escape around the northern end of Chios. Some ships were slow to launch from where they had been drying their waterlogged hulls on the Asian shore, while those on station waited for some time in front of Philip's advancing left. Theophiliscus appears to have been on his guard lest Philip's light vessels spill out into the Aegean while the larger ships engaged, but committed his own forces once it was clear that the smaller ships were remaining in the line.

Philip seems to have been chary of exposing the flanks of his larger warships, which he finally placed on the right of his line, protected by the shore and each other. For his own part, Attalus successfully frustrated any effort by these monsters to get away from him by closing with his own heavy vessels. From the casualty reports, his own vessels consisted mostly of 'fours' and 'fives'

> *'When people are entering upon a war they do things the wrong way round. Action comes first, and it is only when they have already suffered that they begin to think'* – THUCYDIDES

(the number of rowers per bank of oars), probably built on the proven models of his Roman allies. Such vessels would not have been as suitable for manoeuvre as, apparently, were those favoured by the Rhodians, but were large enough to carry marines and other weaponry to match Philip's, and sufficiently massive to block his advance.

The worst came first for Philip when his flagship perished along with his admiral immediately after Attalus himself accounted for one of Philip's 'eights'. In the confusion of the opening prow-to-prow rush of the Pergamene and Macedonian squadrons, an Attalid cruiser had turned her broadside to the Macedonian flagship. What might be thought to have been the perfect ramming attack proved fatal to the Macedonian ship. The lighter vessel stood high enough out of the water to trap her destroyer's bow under the overhang of her topmost oarbenches. Philip's flagship was literally trapped like a dog with a bone in its throat while two of Attalus' vessels rammed and sank her in her turn with her admiral and complement.

Brother saved brother as the mêlée on Philip's right intensified. The bow of another of Philip's large ships, and consequently its ram, was riding high out of the water when Attalus' admiral Deinocrates hit her bow on and wedged his own ship's beak into the enemy's bow timbers. The Macedonian ship's death grip was shaken loose by a heavy Pergamene vessel commanded by Deinocrates' brother, Dionysodorus. The Pergamene vessel rammed the monster apparently again in its bow timbers, for Deinocrates' ship was shaken loose and the Macedonian ship herself stayed afloat while she was boarded and captured by Pergamene marines and towed behind the line, apparently abandoned by her oarsmen during the battle on deck. Family ties were as strong as any in the battles of the ancient world in compelling cooperation and assistance, in the absence of any central, directed command

Chios

201 BC

Philip was besieging Chios.when the Pergamenes
and Rhodians arrived. Philip lost his flagship in the
opening clash of the Pergamene and Macedonian
squadrons, but the Rhodians waited until the
struggle with the Pergamenes began to draw
Macedonian ships from the left side of the line
before attacking with their faster ships. As Philip's
ships tried to withdraw, they lost their formation
and several heavy vessels were damaged. When
Philip's lead ships turned to assist their own rear, the
Rhodians committed the balance of their fleet.
Although the Macedonian marines forced the
Rhodians to avoid close contact, their heavier
vessels nonetheless closed and engaged with the
main Macedonian battle line. Philip's own escort
captured Attalus' flagship after forcing him to beach
near Erythrai. Philip then rallied his scattered vessels
while the allied vessels made for harbour on the
mainland and Chios itself. Philip claimed the victory,
but his losses were severe.

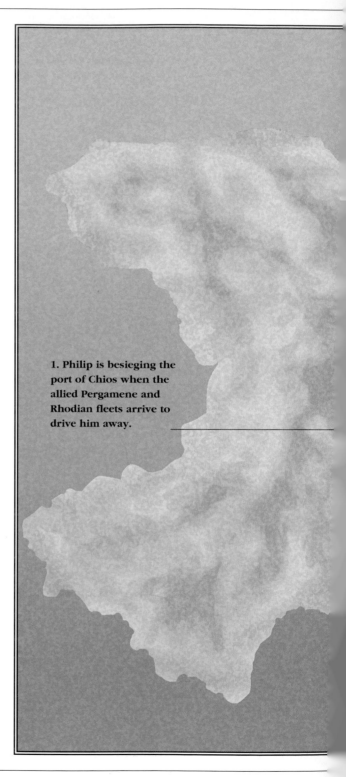

**1. Philip is besieging the
port of Chios when the
allied Pergamene and
Rhodian fleets arrive to
drive him away.**

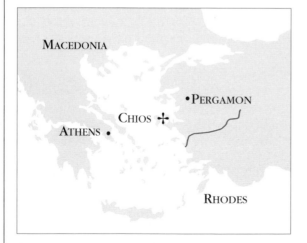

MACEDONIA

•PERGAMON

CHIOS ✛

ATHENS •

RHODES

*Chios sat between Pergamon and Rhodes, and
Philip knew that if he could capture it he would
be able to defeat the allies in turn. His strategic
loss at Chios gave the allies a breathing space.*

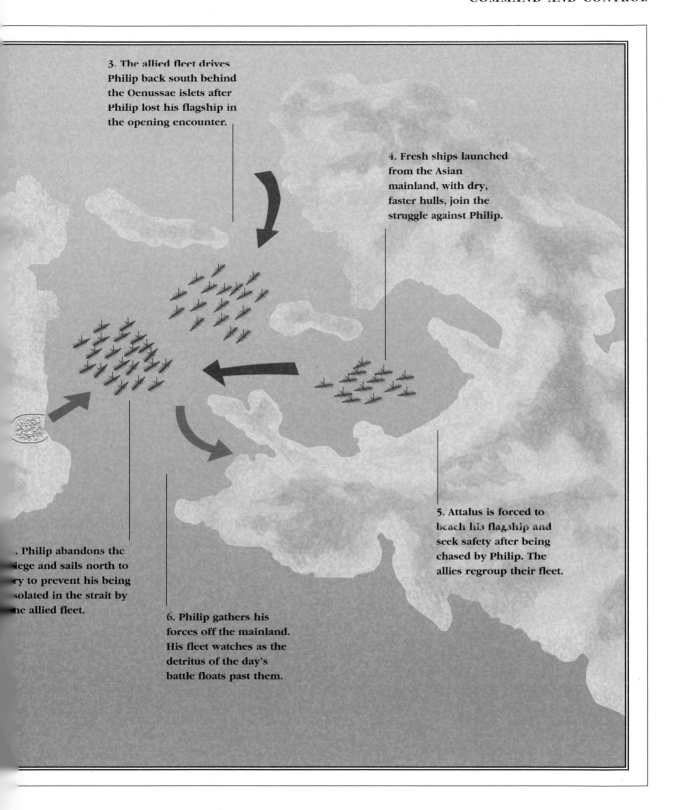

3. The allied fleet drives Philip back south behind the Oenussae islets after Philip lost his flagship in the opening encounter.

4. Fresh ships launched from the Asian mainland, with dry, faster hulls, join the struggle against Philip.

5. Attalus is forced to beach his flagship and seek safety after being chased by Philip. The allies regroup their fleet.

. Philip abandons the iege and sails north to ry to prevent his being solated in the strait by he allied fleet.

6. Philip gathers his forces off the mainland. His fleet watches as the detritus of the day's battle floats past them.

If one assumes that Philip had divided his numbers of heavier ships into two groups, with the heaviest vessels facing Attalus on the right, that would place around 27 heavy warships opposite the Pergamene ruler, less than the fleet of 35 ships known from earlier accounts to be in the Pergamene fleet. That would explain our source's statement that Attalus had the advantage in numbers of such vessels, and the relatively even nature of the battle, with Philip's larger vessels balanced by the quantity of the enemy as Attalus slowly forced the Macedonians behind the islets where their king waited.

The Rhodians waited with most of their ships close to shore until the ongoing struggle with Attalus began to draw Macedonian ships from the left side of the line facing them.

Theophiliscus immediately engaged. His faster ships had apparently stayed on the beach until the last possible moment, and the reason for the tactic became clear as the dryer hulls of the Rhodian vessels made their speed advantage decisive. As Philip's ships tried to withdraw around the Oenussae islets, they lost their line abreast formation and were at their most vulnerable to Rhodian ships launching from the Erythraean promontory. Several of Philip's heavier vessels were rammed in their unprotected sterns, while others had their oarbanks shattered by the beaks and well-trained crews of the Rhodian galleys. The speed of a decision is as important at times as the decision itself.

The Battle Continues

When Philip's lead ships turned again to assist their own rear, Theophiliscus committed the balance of his fleet, including those vessels that had just been launched and his personal tactical command of three older, heavier vessels that the Rhodians had received some time previously from a friendly power. As the two squadrons clashed, the Rhodians found that Philip V had apparently read his history. Their favoured tactic was the old Athenian dash between the ships of an enemy's line to their rear. Just as the Rhodians were used to employing their smaller, faster ships to penetrate an enemy's formation in order to get at the vulnerable sterns and oars, Philip unleashed his numerous small craft with precisely the same intention against the Rhodians themselves. The smaller vessels protected the flanks of Philip's larger ships, once formation had been re-established, and were able to interfere with the Rhodians' movements as the battle was joined in the 4.8-km (3-mile) passage between the northern-most of the Oenussae and the mainland. Attalus and the Macedonian left were already well within the strait.

Philip had succeeded in frustrating an easy Rhodian victory, but his success was markedly limited. Our source refers to a particular tactic that seems to be partially responsible for the very large numbers of light vessels listed among Philip's casualties. If the Rhodians were forced to meet an enemy ship bows on, they would transfer their crews forward to drop the bows and the rams of their vessels beneath the water-line. The enemy's ram accordingly struck timbers that would be raised once normal trim had been restored, while the Rhodians' own ram could penetrate bow or 'cheek' timbers beneath the protection of the foe's ram's bronze casing and, incidentally, the water-line.

Philip's greatest advantage lay in his Macedonian marines, who were undoubtedly equipped with some form of missile weapon as they did their best to keep the Rhodians from closing. They were successful, once the *lemboi* (ships) had been dispersed, to the extent of forcing the Rhodians back to their previous tactics of ramming in the stern, oars or flank as opportunity offered, avoiding close contact. Theophiliscus and his *quinqueremes*, however, closed and engaged with the main Macedonian battle line.

> '*After gaining a victory, the general who pursues the enemy with a scattered and disorganized army gives away his victory to the foe*' –
> EMPEROR MAURICE

Nicostratus' Rhodian galley had shown her age when she left her ram in the hull of an enemy vessel, which sank with all hands. The Rhodian ship herself was also filling with water, disabled and quickly surrounded by the enemy's vessels. Failure to relieve a distressed subordinate weakens overall resolve and morale, as Pausanias had known at Plataea, and Alexander at Gaugamela. Autolycus, the navigation officer, whose fault the accident possibly was, redeemed himself by resisting with the last of the Rhodian marines. The deck soldiers were dead and Autolycus had drowned, wounded in his armour, by the time Theophiliscus' squadron was able to punch its way through to the stricken warship, saving her escaping oarsmen and surviving officers even as they forced two rammed enemy vessels' marines to take to the water. Light and heavier ships immediately surrounded the admiral's galley, but Theophiliscus' three wounds, received before Philostratus' galley could break the flagship free, would eventually kill him. With most of his own marines dead, Theophiliscus continued to press the Macedonian left.

The Macedonians left's reverse to engage their Rhodian attackers had created a gap in Philip's line of battle, which Attalus moved very quickly to exploit. He had apparently got through the initial position of the enemy line and was now far into the strait, chasing after the ships of Philip's right, which were making for the Asian shore in accordance with Philip's earlier orders. Philip here enjoyed his greatest success of the battle. Attalus' flagship and the two lighter vesses of his escort were racing to the rescue of another Pergamene vessel. As Attalus chased the faster enemy fleeing toward the Asian shore, he passed the islands where Philip and his personal flotilla were waiting. The Macedonian king took his own royal escort of four medium cruisers, three light cruisers, and the available small craft, and successfully intercepted Attalus before he could return to the rest of his fleet.

King being cause, Attalus was himself an objective, one for which Philip had tried before and would try again. Attalus, however, had the presence of mind to beach his ships on the shore near the town of Erythrai, to which he fled while

THE FIGURE ABOVE *is a Roman auxiliary standard-bearer from 1st–2nd century AD. Top, from left to right, are two manipular standards with bravery awards attached, and a* vexillarum.

Philip's crews looted the royal galley. Philip was able to take Attalus' flagship in tow but, aside from an undoubtedly bad fright, Attalus had made good his escape.

Philip was cheered enough to rally his scattered vessels and to promulgate with the towed flagship the idea that Attalus was dead. At the sight, Attalus' admiral Dionysodorus maintained presence of mind enough to signal the Pergamene vessels to regroup and make for an agreed-upon harbour on the mainland. The Macedonian left was only too happy to disengage from the Rhodians, and ran back down the strait under the pretext of rushing to the other ships' aid before it, too, made for the mainland, leaving the Rhodians free to salvage pragmatically those remaining Macedonian vessels fit for towing back to Chios while they sank the rest with their rams.

Philip managed one last tactical error after the actual day's combat had ceased. Apparently, the final stage of the fighting on his right had taken place off the Argennan promontory on the Asian shore, in the lee of which he now anchored. The idea was to claim the victory – as he did – by continuing to occupy the area of combat, in addition to the indisputable fact that he had captured Attalus' flagship. However, prevailing winds and currents carried the day's grisly harvest down among his ships; the corpses and other detritus from the fighting brought the message home to the king, and his crews, that Chios had been his costliest battle. Philip had lost his own flagship, 5 other heavy vessels sunk or captured, along with 25 of his lighter ships and their crews, 10 other heavy vessels, and 3 of his own cruisers against Attalus. The Rhodians demonstrated their virtuosity by destroying 40 of Philip's light ships and capturing 7 with their crews. They also sank 10 of Philip's heavier vessels and chose to salvage 2 of Philip's medium units. Attalus had lost the hapless cruiser, Dionysodorus' and one other medium vessel sunk, and again, his flagship and the two escorts captured. In human terms, 3000 Macedonian marines and 6000 sailors died in the strait, while our source, Polybius, admits to 70 Pergamene and 60 Rhodian casualties. A total of 2000 Macedonians and 700 Egyptian conscripts survived to become the allies' prisoners.

The dictates of military chivalry were all very well, and Philip had obeyed the old rules, even to the extent of recovering recognizably Macedonian bodies from among the drifting wreckage. The reality of his defeat Philip himself admitted on the next day when, by joint decision, the Rhodians and Pergamenes put off from Chios and again drew up in line of battle opposite. Philip refused the challenge and remained by the Asian shore while the allied fleets at least initially lay in front of him, preventing his retreat. The allies themselves each had their own reasons for not pressing the battle home. Attalus, besides his bad fright of the day before, now had Philip's army on the Asian coast near his capital city, with nothing in between Philip and Pergamon but the city's walls. Individual considerations began to assert themselves, and the Rhodians were in the process of losing their admiral, and with him, his strategic vision for Philip's defeat.

After appointing his successor, and writing his report to his government, Theophiliscus died. His greatest monument was not as immediately enduring as those voted to him on Rhodes. He had convinced Attalus to join forces at the onset of Philip's attack, but for a crucial period, Pergamene–Rhodian cooperation lay in the Rhodian admiral's grave. Attalus correctly reasoned that Philip would continue his personal vendetta against him, and took his fleet and the soldiers on board back to his fortress-city, leaving the Rhodian fleet alone to mourn their dead and move in between Philip's surviving navy and their home island. Eventually, the threat Philip continued to pose to them both prompted Attalus and the Rhodians to invite the Romans eastward, and in the years to come a different people would possess the whole of Alexander's empire.

The Trebia: a Clash of Command Cultures
To the west, two differing products of a differing international situation were engaged, like eaglets in the nest, in a struggle to see which of the two would survive. In the wake of Alexander's comparatively well-documented successes, commanders in succeeding ages acquired an appreciation of what a skilled general could accomplish by the careful use of his military

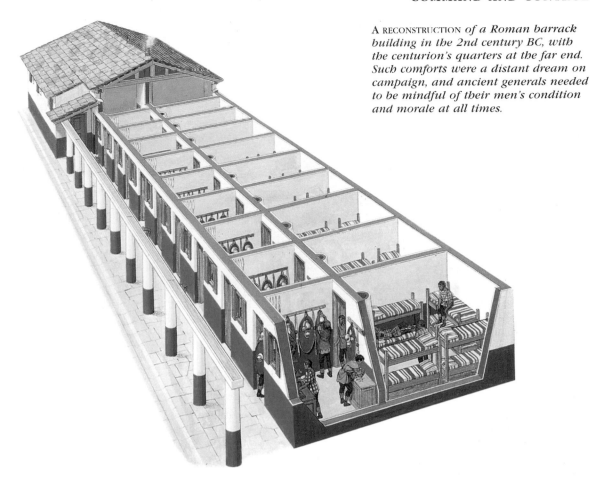

A RECONSTRUCTION *of a Roman barrack building in the 2nd century BC, with the centurion's quarters at the far end. Such comforts were a distant dream on campaign, and ancient generals needed to be mindful of their men's condition and morale at all times.*

assets. Nationalism was also becoming a force to be reckoned with in the military picture. Philip II's creation of a national army, paid by the king and loyal to the king, had allowed his son and heir to defeat the subject armies of the Persian empire and the smaller, divided armies with which the Greek city-states had sought to prevent his hegemony. Professional armies were a parallel development. The general-kings who fought over Alexander's empire used the captured treasuries they inherited to finance their campaigns using armies composed of professional soldiers who had literally spent decades in the field. One of the most successful of these had been Pyrrhus, King of Epirus (a smaller nation next to Macedonia), who had briefly conquered that country and sought conquests in the west.

Pyrrhus' celebrated encounters with the national army of the Roman republic between 200 and 275 BC are celebrated for his skill in battle and the Romans' grim determination to win, which, in the end, prevailed. Pyrrhus left a written memoir of his achievements against the Romans (a major source for Plutarch's biography of him), and one of his most avid readers – and consequently the beneficiary of that general's experience – was a descendant of the ancient Phoenicians by the name of Hannibal Barca.

Hannibal's hatred of Rome and Romans was hereditary and legendary, but it was never blind. Rome had defeated Punic Carthage with great difficulty in the first Punic War of 264–241 BC, but what made a second struggle as inevitable as the Treaty of Versailles in 1918 was the Romans' opportunistic seizure of Sardinia and Corsica while Carthage was in the throes of a revolt by its own army of mercenaries. A Roman declaration of war against Carthage in 238 secured not only the two islands, but also an indemnity of 1700 talents of silver and the undying hatred of the Barcid family for Rome.

Nowhere is the 'Grandpa's knee' school of military education for commanders more apparent in antiquity than in the wars of Carthage and Rome. Hamilcar Barca was the general who suppressed the revolting mercenaries, only to see the Romans ruthlessly exploit his nation's weakness. Carthage sought new revenues and new opportunities in Spain, and sent to secure them was Hamilcar, who took his eldest son for an education in the field. After Hamilcar's death by drowning in a river crossing, Hannibal succeeded his father in command and began a long military career with marked successes against the fierce inhabitants of Spain. Roman efforts to circumscribe his operations, obviously directed in the end against them, prompted Hannibal to move his mostly mercenary army from Spain to Italy through the Alpine passes in the dead of winter. Willpower and planning made possible a tremendously difficult and effective piece of military celerity.

To expose the younger child of a military family, the Romans sent as consul in 218 the patriarch of a famous military family, Publius Cornelius Scipio. The elder Scipio had already decided to attack Hannibal's base of supply in Spain, but Hannibal's speed in arriving in Italy forced him to send an officer he trusted, his brother Gnaeus, ahead with limited forces to Spain while he himself returned and sought to bring Hannibal and his army to battle near the crossing of the Po river valley.

Hannibal's Threat

Hannibal's deft handling of his army, on top of the incredible feat of transporting elephants over wide rivers and tall mountains in winter, made him by far the most terrible opponent Rome ever had or would encounter. Publius Scipio met with Hannibal's superbly trained and deftly-handled cavalry and light infantry at the crossings of the Ticinus River, which Scipio could not prevent, and

found himself severely wounded and forced to retreat backwards into the defended city of Placentia. There, a second consular army, a force originally destined to invade Punic Africa under his colleague Sempronius Longus, reached him, proving how decisively and effectively Hannibal's rapid movement had wrested the initiative from the Romans.

As they had in the disaster at Aegospotami, politics soon played a devastating role in a vital tactical decision. A minor success in a skirmish with the Carthaginian advance guard convinced Sempronius that a decisive victory, and the political fruits thereof, were his for the taking. Taking sole command, he moved to the Trebia river with the combined consular armies of some 40,000 men in December of 218 BC.

Hannibal enjoyed Napoleon's prerequisites of a successful commander: incredible good luck and a stupid enemy. Rome's traditional Gallic enemies had flocked to Hannibal's standard as their liberator, but these undisciplined reinforcements would not linger long in the Carthaginian camp without the prospect of action. Hannibal had good and capable subordinates as long as he had younger brothers. Taking one such, Mago, with him, Hannibal scouted the course of the Roman advance and found a declivity where Mago and 2000 infantry and cavalry could be concealed until an opportune moment.

Perhaps the bitterness of a Roman survivor influences Livy's enduring account of the suffering of the Roman Army as it walked shivering into Hannibal's intricate trap. At dawn, Hannibal's Numidian cavalry appeared in front of Sempronius' fortified camp and invited the Romans to battle with a shower of javelins and other missiles. Sempronius at once sent his own cavalry and light infantry to exhaust their bodies and missile weapons in a vain response, despite a worsening winter storm and his men's lack of food or fire. The Trebia itself was bitterly cold, and came up to the chests of the Roman infantry as they grimly forded it and advanced toward the cheerful fires of the Carthaginian camp, where Hannibal's well-fed and well-warmed troops awaited them. An well-fed and well-warmed troops awaited them. An officer can, if he chooses, ignore the condition of his men, but their physical and mental condition exerts tremendous influence upon the strength and nature of their fighting.

Hannibal's plan of battle involved using his soldiers as a virtual meat grinder, with light infantry (the *Baliares*) in the front of his line and showering the lumbering Romans with javelins from a safe distance. These fell back before the close and effective Roman legions, four of Roman citizens in the centre, four of Rome's Italian subject allies on the wings. Having read his accounts of Alexander and Pyrrhus' battle, Hannibal kept his elephants behind his line of battle where they could serve as missile platforms in some safety, while his light infantry made a well-organized withdrawal behind the long line of Hannibal's 20,000 Spanish infantry and an unknown number of Gallic allies.

'When two work side-by-side, one or the other spots the opening first if a kill's at hand. When one looks out for himself, alert but alone, his reach is shorter – his sly moves miss the mark' – HOMER

There is something to be said for following a military tradition when that is a good and sound military tradition, and Rome's legionary tactics, centuries in the evolving, continued to serve the Roman army well. The Roman legionary's own throwing javelin, the *pilum*, made a strong response to Hannibal's bombardment as the legion drew near to the very centre of the Carthaginian line. The Roman cavalry, however, discovered the reason that Hannibal had gone to such great lengths to transport his elephants into Italy. The Italian horses could not abide the sight and smell of the huge, strange animals, and they bolted. The elephants and Hannibal's superior cavalry began to crush in the Roman flanks.

Sempronius' marked limitations as a commander could offer him no better solution for the worsening tactical situation than to continue his advance directly into Hannibal's centre – a tendency in Roman commanders Hannibal would exploit with horrific results in the subsequent battle of Cannae. Hannibal turned his elephants against the Roman light infantry, who drove the animals off with their pikes, and sprung Mago's ambush by some means or other that succeeded, despite the continuing deterioration of the weather. Sempronius, out of touch with the whole of his army and the true and dire nature of the situation, thought he had the victory when a fourth of his army burst through the Carthaginian centre, but those 10,000 men proved to be the sole survivors of a truly disastrous defeat as the rest of Hannibal's forces methodically slaughtered the remaining two-thirds of the Roman army. The survivors escaped through the storm to Placentia in small groups.

Family connections would determine much of the rest of course of the fighting. Publius Cornelius Scipio would eventually join his brother in Spain and operate in Hannibal's rear, defeating and being defeated by Hannibal's younger brother Hamilcar until both men's defeat and death in 211 BC. Hasdrubal, another brother, would die, caught by a fresh Roman army while attempting to join his brother in Italy at the Metaurus river in 207. Seeing his brother's head left in the line of his advance by a Roman cavalryman, Hannibal is reported to have despaired, finally, of victory. The son of Publius Scipio, meanwhile, had enjoyed great success with his father and uncle's remaining forces in Spain, and would meet and defeat Hannibal himself in Africa at Zama in 203 BC, winning the legendary name of 'Africanus' for the feat. Years after the battle, the two supposedly met off the battlefield in the Greek city of Ephesus. Plutarch's account has Hannibal and Scipio Africanus walking along and discussing the great leaders of their own history. Hannibal ranked Alexander first, Pyrrhus second, and himself third. 'And if you had beaten me?' asked Scipio. 'I would have ranked myself first,' said Hannibal.

Trebia

218 BC

At dawn, Hannibal's Numidian cavalry appeared in front of the Roman camp and invited them to battle with a shower of javelins and other missiles. Hannibal's light infantry, in the front of his line, showered the Romans with javelins, falling back in front of the legions behind the long line of Hannibal's Spanish infantry and Gallic allies. The Roman legionaries' pila made a strong response to Hannibal's bombardment as the legion drew near to the Carthaginian line. However, the Roman cavalry's horses could not abide the elephants, and they bolted. The elephants and Hannibal's superior cavalry began to crush in the Roman flanks, but Sempronius continued his advance directly into Hannibal's centre. Hannibal turned his elephants against the Roman light infantry, who drove the animals off with their pikes, and sprung Mago's ambush. Ten thousand Romans broke through the Carthaginian centre, but these proved to be the sole survivors; the rest of the Romans were slaughtered.

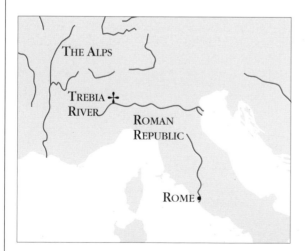

After his epic crossing of the Alps, Hannibal encountered Sempronius, the Roman consul, on the Trebia. The Roman defeat left the way open for Hannibal to march on Rome.

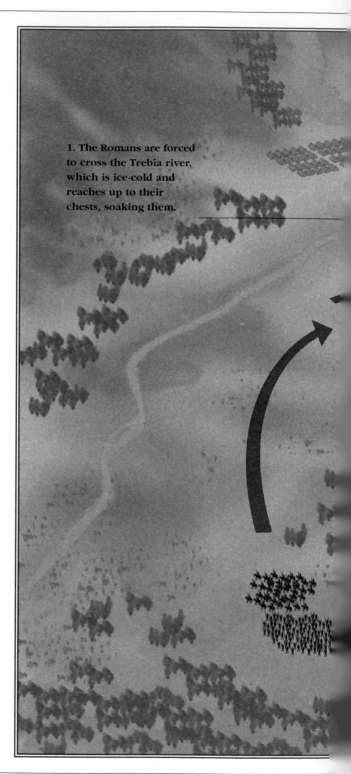

1. The Romans are forced to cross the Trebia river, which is ice-cold and reaches up to their chests, soaking them.

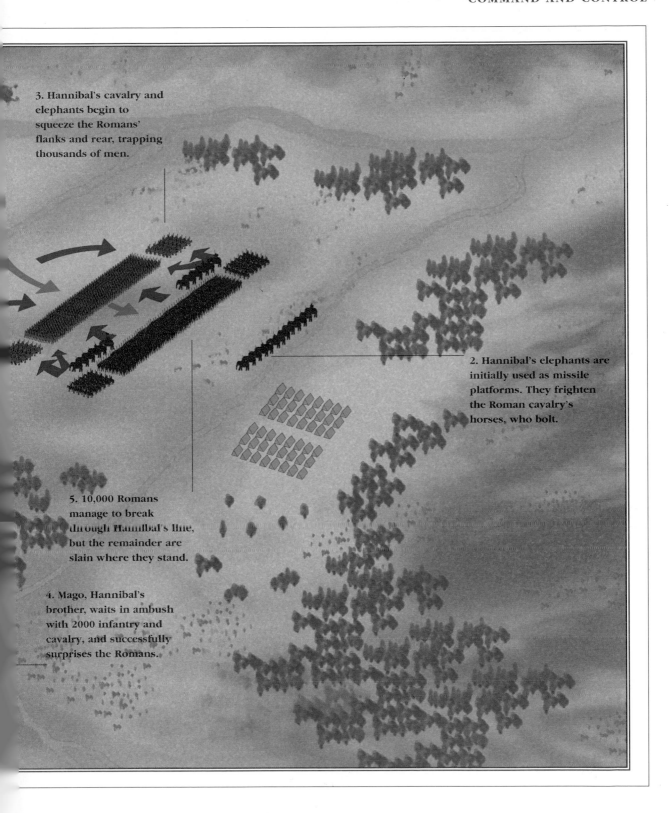

3. Hannibal's cavalry and elephants begin to squeeze the Romans' flanks and rear, trapping thousands of men.

2. Hannibal's elephants are initially used as missile platforms. They frighten the Roman cavalry's horses, who bolt.

5. 10,000 Romans manage to break through Hannibal's line, but the remainder are slain where they stand.

4. Mago, Hannibal's brother, waits in ambush with 2000 infantry and cavalry, and successfully surprises the Romans.

Actium: Divided Commanders

The course of the epic battle of Actium in 31 BC found its directions from the outcome of two major problems of command and control. The defeated Antony and Cleopatra, like Attalus and the Rhodians at Chios, had differing concepts of the war, differing objectives and, at the end, differing tactical plans that resulted in neither of the two being implemented well. Octavian, the victor, faced the obstacle of his own limited military ability, and overcame it with a successful selection and use of a powerful subordinate. Marcus Vipsanius Agrippa's outstanding ability as a ship builder, organizer and admiral handed the victory and the Roman empire to Octavian (who became known as Augustus as emperor), and his imperial heirs.

Rome's traditional distaste for the difficulty and expense of maintaining a strong central fleet had left the combined ships of the old republic in the hands of Pompey the Great's last surviving son, Sextus. After Julius Caesar's death in 44 BC, Sextus employed his naval resources in his own bid to dominate the empire, interdicting Rome's vital grain shipments and raiding the coasts of Sicily and Italy. Octavian, Julius Caesar's adopted heir, had attempted to contest with Sextus at sea, with dire and humiliating results. Lacking military talent himself, the future emperor did the next best thing and hired it, obtaining at the same time tremendous and life-long loyalty from the man he selected to be his commander.

Agrippa's genius manifested itself quickly in the solution he found to constructing and training a powerful navy – in the face of an actively hostile one poised to prevent exactly such a threat to Sextus' domination of the sea. Due to the lack of truly secure harbours along the western coast of Italy, the area most endangered by Sextus' fleet in Sicily, Agrippa built a new harbour and trained his fleet in safety.

'[Scipio Africanus] refrained from exposing his person without sufficient reason ... conduct characteristic not of a commander who relies on luck, but of one gifted with intelligence' – POLYBIUS

The ships built and based at Portus Julius were of good size and mounted powerful weaponry of Agrippa's own invention. As oarsmen he had 20,000 freed slaves, all Octavian could obtain, who learned the basics of rowing and seamanship in the shallow waters of the Lucrine Lake. Agrippa gave his rowers and marines special training by forcing them to sail out into rough weather, so that they would not be taken by surprise by the high waves. In two sharp, brutal battles, Sextus' fleet met disaster and final destruction at Naulochus and Mylae, off Sicily, in 36 BC. In the space of three years, Octavian had gone from having no navy to one supreme in the western Mediterranean.

Mark Antony's scheme to establish himself as Julius Caesar's true heir took form as Antony tried to carry out Caesar's unrealized dreams of conquest in the East. For that, he needed soldiers, not ships, and just after Octavian had lost his first fleet to Sextus and the storm in 36 BC, Antony offered Octavian 300 vessels in exchange for some of his Italian legions. He had then moved to avenge a disastrous Roman defeat in Parthia, but his campaign there was considerably less successful than Octavian's and Agrippa's war against Sextus, possibly because Antony had no lieutenant as capable as Agrippa. Soon the queen of Hellenistic Egypt was replacing Italy and Rome as the source of Antony's support and the fuel for his ambitions. As Antony planned a series of operations against Armenia and Parthia, it became Cleopatra's role to build and maintain a fleet capable of keeping Octavian's now-formidable force from extending its influence eastwards.

In return for Cleopatra's support, in 34 BC, Antony handed over control of Cyprus, most of Syria, Libya and Southern Asia Minor to Cleopatra and her children, the entire eastern coast of the Mediterranean, with the exception of part of Syria, and Herod's Judea. In Italy this sparked the belief that Mark Antony had begun giving away Rome's sempire to the Queen of Egypt. Octavian's propaganda helped to spread this rumour, and the stage was set for the last two of Julius Caesar's would-be heirs to settle the matter once and for all.

Clash of East and West

Antony remained in the East and began mobilizing his forces. According to Plutarch, Antony and Cleopatra's combined fleet numbered 800 vessels, including support ships, which Antony gathered at Ephesus in eastern Asia Minor. As many as 200 of these vessels were Cleopatra's, the rest being Antony's earlier fleet and ships contributed or constructed by the client kings who held their allegiance to Antony. Plutarch said that 500 of these vessels were large warships; Cleopatra's large flagship was named the *Antonia*. These were very large ships, in the tradition of eastern Mediterranean naval design.

The Romans of the late Republic had a tradition of fighting their civil wars in Greece. Antony had had some notion of launching an amphibious invasion of Italy, but he abandoned this plan because of rumours that Octavian and Agrippa's fleet was already in Greece. As it had at Kadesh, bad intelligence influenced the commander's decision, due to the mistaken report that a reconnaissance force Octavian had sent to the Greek coast was his main fleet. After getting as far as the island of Samos, Anthony sailed back with his fleet and army to Patrae, in the Peloponnese, and wintered there, waiting for the new campaigning season in 32 BC.

Octavian and Agrippa began moving forces to Greece in early spring. Antony paused to rebuild the crews of his fleet, since he had lost many sailors to disease over the winter. Agrippa, however, began the first of a series of swift amphibious assaults on the Greek coast, taking and keeping the initiative. He stormed and captured Methone, and from there his ships began intercepting Antony's supply vessels, while also periodically landing elsewhere on the coast. Antony began to be disturbed by these tactics, which prevented him taking the initiative and limited the options available to him. Agrippa's tactics kept Antony's fleet busy patrolling the coast while Octavian successfully crossed the

Adriatic from Brundisium, bringing his 80,000 soldiers and supplies. Octavian landed his soldiers and brought his war fleet fairly close to Antony's base at Actium, to a place called Corcyra. The harbour itself was called 'the ladle', possibly because of the river running into it. Cleopatra, who had sailed her fleet to Antony's base at Actium, said there was nothing to fear about Octavian sitting in a ladle, but the joke had a certain hollow ring. Octavian and Agrippa should never have been allowed across the Adriatic without a fight. Both sides fortified their positions and waited for the other to make a move.

On Antony's part, this was a mistake. Agrippa, with easy access to the open sea, did not allow his fleet to sit idly by when there were tactical opportunities elsewhere. Agrippa took the fleet and captured a squadron and garrison Antony had stationed at Leucas. He then moved south to Patrae and defeated the ships Antony had left there. He next took Corinth. Agrippa returned to Actium just in time to destroy a flotilla of Antony's ships which had chanced an attack under cover of fog against the blockade of ships Agrippa had left to prevent Antony's escape. Antony found his fortress rapidly turning into a trap, his situation made worse by disease and hunger, as malaria and the loss of his supply ships began to take their toll on his crews and army.

Considering the naval situation, it seems that Antony was waiting for the whole of his army to join him at Actium and, when the army was completely assembled, he would attack Octavian on land. His army was slightly larger than Octavian's. Moreover, he was a far more experienced general on land than either Octavian or Agrippa, seeking to take advantage in that area of what he hoped was a command superiority. Once Octavian's army had been defeated, Agrippa's fleet would be left to watch as Antony marched on Italy. Agrippa's successful severing of his supply line, and Octavian's fortified camp – which meant that Octavian could and did decline battle – trapped him in a situation where he could either lose his fleet, lose most of his army, or stay where he was and gradually lose both as the malaria – and, by this time, camp dysentery – took their toll.

Agrippa's presence outside his harbour meant that Antony had no chance of re-establishing his overseas connection with the grain in Egypt, and the supply route by land was not proving adequate for the task of sustaining 100,000 soldiers and 70,000 oarsmen. The longer Antony hesitated, the worse his situation became. His men began deserting to Octavian, and the client kings also started abandoning him. His best admiral, Domitius Ahenobarbus, defected to Agrippa's fleet in a rowing-boat, already dying of camp fever. Antony finally came to a decision.

The choice, upon which Antony and Cleopatra would have agreed, was to break out with the fleet and all the soldiers it could carry, hoping that the remaining legions could march north through Macedonia to friendly areas in the East. The result of this choice was the naval battle of Actium.

That decision, with the benefit of hindsight, has been criticized from 31 BC down to the present. As events later proved, it was a wrong decision. Whether there was a right decision is open to question. If Antony had tried to march to Italy, Octavian would have had plenty of opportunities to select battle conditions where a land version of Actium could have occurred. There was also the possibility of Antony finding himself without an army: in fact, his legions eventually did go over to Octavian, after Antony's defeat. A naval battle had the advantage of forcing Antony's troops into a fight for survival, and, even if only partially successful, the war could be continued if Antony and Cleopatra's resources were both available for future use.

Antony's fleet consisted of powerful heavy ships, which Agrippa had never fought in a large-scale battle. If the army marched away, the ships would either have to be burned or handed over to Agrippa, which would have meant that Antony's army would either have had to march back to Egypt overland or else move on to a hostile Italy, which Octavian, commanding the sea, could reach before them. It is likely that Cleopatra would not have supported Antony further if his bungling left her without her expensive fleet, vital for Egypt's long-term future.

A VIEW OF A ROMAN CAMP *on campaign. The large tent on the left with the standard outside is the centurion's, while the legionaries sleep in the smaller tents. The centurion's tent was always positioned to be easily found by his men.*

TO THE VICTOR *the spoils: a Roman cavalry commander is decorated for his bravery. Rewards for successful commanders were great, but the cost of failure was even higher.*

Antony had already lost considerable numbers of his oarsmen to disease before he made his choice. As a result, he was forced to send out press-gangs to fill the oarbanks of fighting ships with anybody capable of pulling an oar. Despite his efforts, the oarbanks of his ships were undermanned. Some of the fleet was in very poor condition. Only 60 of the heavy Egyptian war vessels were found suitable for the breakout. The rest were burned. Cleopatra's treasure was loaded onto her squadron of merchant vessels under cover of darkness, probably more to deceive Octavian, watching from the heights, than Antony's people, as Plutarch maintained. The money was more portable – and perhaps more valuable – than the men, and it would not do to give Octavian such an obvious target. Unusually, sails were shipped on all vessels.

As Plutarch correctly pointed out, this was not the usual procedure for a battle fleet. In combat, masts and sails prevented effective use of the upper deck for either rowers or marines, besides making the vessel more likely to capsize. The sails alone prove that Antony was not planning to fight a decisive naval battle. The sails could have been tactically helpful to Antony's fleet; as noted earlier, his were large, heavy ships, slow and not manoeuvrable, and very hard to stop once they got going. With sails, Antony's fleet, in close formation, could potentially crash right through Agrippa's blockaders. They could then take troops and treasure to Egypt where the war could continue.

After four days of storm, on 2 September 31 BC, Antony and Cleopatra's fleet moved out of the Gulf of Ambracia and formed in line of battle. Exactly how many ships remained of the 500 Antony had had at the start of the war is uncertain. He had lost some to Agrippa at Methone, Leucas and Patrae. Others were still in Egypt and others had been burned. The accepted modern number is 230 heavy warships. This figure cannot include Cleopatra's transport fleet, those ships which had not been burned, since Plutarch agrees with

Octavian's account that his fleet captured 300 ships after the battle. Other ships also successfully escaped from the encounter.

Agrippa and Octavian expected the breakout, especially after witnessing the burning of the Egyptian ships. Octavian, basing his plan upon his own naval experience, suggested that Antony and Cleopatra be allowed to escape, after which he and Agrippa could give chase. Agrippa had more faith in the ability of his ships to stop Antony and Cleopatra's monsters, if they could be denied a chance to build up speed under sail, and prevailed upon his nervous employer to fight.

Antony's ships spread out in a battle-line perpendicular to the nearer shore, in front of Cleopatra's treasure ships and the *Antonia*. Antony embarked some 20,000 legionaries and 2000 slingers in his ships, stationed on the decks and towers. This amount surely was all they could hold: when the ancient historians call Antony's ships 'undermanned', they are referring to the lack of rowers. The line of battle formed, they waited close to the shore, both to prevent Agrippa's ships from getting behind them and to give themselves as much room as possible to build up speed when the afternoon breeze filled their sails.

Agrippa's ships did not close at once. Once before, Antony had deployed his fleet in battle formation, only to withdraw back into the harbour, and Agrippa did not wish to risk the fire from Antony's fortified towers on the shore. Antony was waiting for the afternoon breeze, which comes briskly out of the gulf in the direction of the Adriatic. With that, and the power of his oars, he could either sail past Agrippa's fleet or through it; it wouldn't matter once his large ships built up momentum. At sea, he could choose his course. By the time Agrippa's ships could be rigged for sailing, Antony's fleet would be well on its way to Egypt, or Italy, although it is unlikely that Cleopatra would have followed Antony to the latter.

> *'In choosing their centurions the Romans look not so much for the ... fire-eating type ... but those who will stand their ground even when worsted or hard-pressed, and will die in defence of their posts'* – POLYBIUS

Instead Antony got some bad luck. At around noon, a stiff breeze began blowing into the bay. The gale caused disorder among Antony's ships which, standing near the shore and with their sails unfurled, were obliged to row against the wind to no purpose, their tight formation being thrown into disorder. Since his oarsmen were wearing themselves out while still in danger of being run aground, Antony began moving his vessels away from the threatening shore. With the breeze behind him, Agrippa at first backwatered to lessen what impact Antony's ships might have had under oars, and then began trying to turn the flanks of Antony's line. A fierce engagement began on either side of the two fleets. Undoubtedly, Agrippa knew what Antony was waiting for, and by the time the seaward breeze came up, Antony's formation had been shattered, his ships grappled and the battle lost.

The fight between the two lines was still going on when the breeze Antony had been waiting for finally appeared. It was at this time that the crews of Cleopatra's squadron made their escape, reverting to the original plan. Raising their sails, which they had lowered during the earlier wind, Cleopatra and her command sailed through a gap in the centre of the battle at high speed. Antony had deliberately concentrated his heavy forces at the ends, both to prevent Agrippa from getting behind his line and also to weaken Agrippa's centre. The tactic seems to have worked. Cleopatra successfully reached the open sea. As she was vital to the war effort, Antony made his famous decision to follow her. His own flagship was held immobile by Agrippa's ships, so he transferred his flag to a lighter vessel and successfully disengaged.

The rest of Antony's ships began attempting to follow Antony and Cleopatra's original idea of a breakout, rather than a battle. Crews threw their towers overboard and raised their sails again, trying to break out of their line and escape through the gap. The result was disastrous. In the original tight formation planned by Antony, Agrippa's fleet would not have been able to stop the escape. Once Antony's ships left the line, however, Agrippa's vessels began destroying their oars with rams. Eventually the numbers of Agrippa's fleet overwhelmed the men of Antony's who, left without a leader, eventually surrendered the 300 surviving ships to Agrippa and Octavian. Most could not believe that Antony had successfully escaped. They had suffered 5000 casualties, severe but not overwhelming losses. Antony's commanders accepted defeat when they realized that there could be no other outcome.

The survivors of Antony and Cleopatra's fleet, around 60 ships, reached Alexandria. Antony travelled the entire way sitting in the bow of the *Antonia*, holding his head in his hands. The breakout had saved about one-fifth of the fleet, and Antony must have anticipated the desertion of the legions he had left behind to Octavian, which occurred a week after the defeat. When Octavian arrived in Alexandria some months later, the surviving navy surrendered to him after a brief fight, as did the last of Antony's army. Antony and Cleopatra met their ends by suicide, after Cleopatra's plan to escape beyond the Roman world to the Red Sea perished with the ships she had managed to drag there, which were burned by the Arabs of Petra. Cleopatra could not, as Antony and Agrippa knew, hold Egypt with the resources of the entire Roman Empire turned against her.

Antony and Cleopatra, lovers and allies, had agreed, disagreed and lost. Agrippa would go on to honours and esteem until his death in 12 BC, and Octavian, who had known when to hire the ability that he himself lacked, would reign as Emperor Augustus of the Roman world until his own death in AD 14.

The Milvian Bridge

The emperor Diocletian had come to the conclusion that the Roman Empire was too large, under the pressures that would eventually destroy it, to be governed by one man. In AD 293, he divided it into a 'tetrarchy' of four districts, with two greater and lesser emperors to govern and protect them. It had been centuries since Actium and the struggles for sole rulership of the Empire, but Diocletian's administrative insight overlooked the clear historical point that the rulers of pieces of the Roman Empire would fight among themselves to be sole overlord of all of it.

Rome and Italy were much less vital to the Empire than they had been in the days of Hannibal, or Augustus, but the ancient seat of power still had the mystique of possession to make it of great moral value to its imperial possessor. In the year 306, this was Maxentius, the son of one of Diocletian's original four emperors. The other rulers of the Roman world moved to evict him from the capital city, but it had been heavily fortified in 271 by the Emperor Aurelian, and when Galerius invaded Italy in 307, Maxentius and his supporting troops remained behind their defences and let Galerius' attack grind to a slow halt. Prudence allowed Galerius to make a safe retreat from a desperate situation, but Maxentius, whose military experience, like Octavian's, was limited, had a strategic precedent to follow when he faced his next challenge in 312. Most of what we know of this struggle comes from the religious history of Eusebius.

Maxentius' third challenger was Constantine, who appears from the event to have read his history. There are ways to secure one's rear areas that do not involve parcelling out an army. Constantine's method of securing his holdings in Gaul and Britain was by good government. He remitted taxes, treated the people well and had protected them from external threats before making his move to rule the empire. The other provinces, noting Constantine's good government of a portion of the Empire, were less motivated to oppose his rule of the whole. Maxentius foolishly provided him with a counterpoint, moreover, by seeking military glory in the brutal suppression of a small revolt in Africa, followed by a wholescale looting of the province by the emperor and his supporters. The Roman Senate by now provided only a mantle of legitimacy for a military emperor, but Maxentius forfeited even that by the persecution of suspect senators and unpredictable exactions of revenue. Money is vital in warfare, but it can cost more to gain than the benefits it may provide once obtained.

Milvian Bridge

312 AD

The wide stone bridge over the Tiber, the Pons Milvius, had been cut in order to delay Constantine's attack and hinder his supply lines during the expected siege of Rome. Maxentius, however, decided to offer battle on the far side of the Tiber at a place called Saxa Rubra, and he constructed a wooden pontoon bridge in order to form his line of battle. Their commander's sudden change of strategy could not have been lost on Maxentius' soldiers. On 28 October Constantine's battle-hardened veterans, inspired by their commander's vision of a cross in the sun, smashed into Maxentius' garrison troops, and the result was a panicked flight by the defenders either over the stone Pons Milvius or the wooden pontoon structure. Either way brought final catastrophe, for the wooden bridge collapsed under the weight of the fugitives, and Maxentius himself drowned in the Tiber, weighted down by his armour. His head alone returned to Rome the following day, when Constantine exhibited it in triumph.

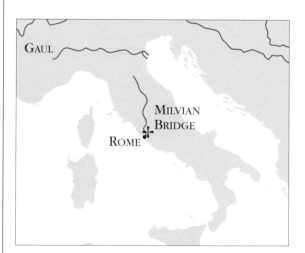

The Milvian Bridge was on the outskirts of Rome, and was one of the crossing points for the Tiber. Properly defended, it could have been a significant barrier for Constantine.

2. Deciding to cross the river and fight Constantine at Saxa Rubra, Maxentius builds a pontoon bridge.

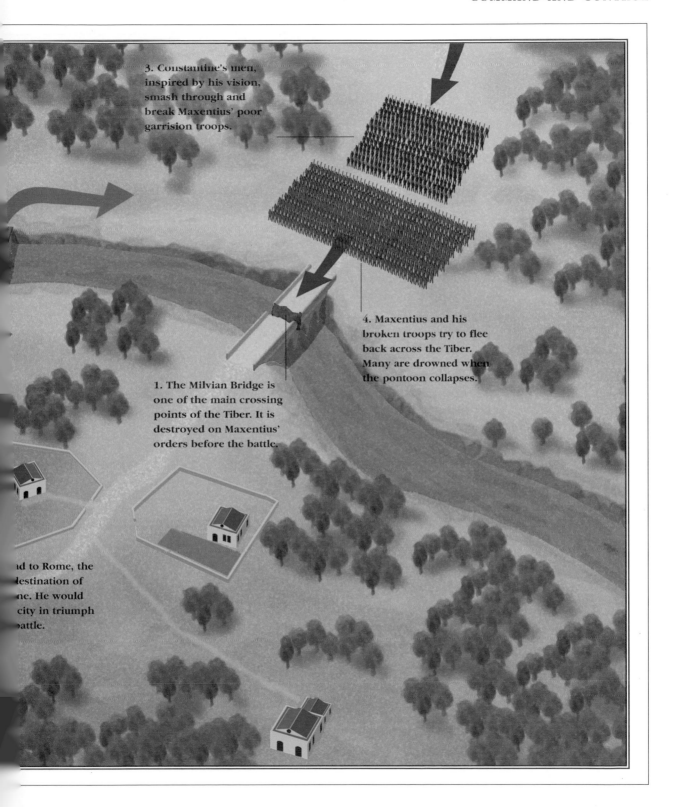

3. Constantine's men, inspired by his vision, smash through and break Maxentius' poor garrision troops.

4. Maxentius and his broken troops try to flee back across the Tiber. Many are drowned when the pontoon collapses.

1. The Milvian Bridge is one of the main crossing points of the Tiber. It is destroyed on Maxentius' orders before the battle.

...d to Rome, the ...destination of ...ne. He would ...city in triumph ...battle.

Constantine emulated Julius Caesar by using Gaul to support his advance on Rome. He also copied Rome's most famous enemy in the speed of his attack south. Hannibal had demonstrated that an army could cross the Alps swiftly and remain effective. Constantine moved his loyal troops from Gaul over the later imperial roads through the passes and was in Italy before Maxentius could react. Remembering the 'quickness' (*celeritas*) that had given Rome to Julius Caesar, Constantine moved swiftly towards the capital, with an army barely one-fourth of the size Maxentius had at his own disposal. Constantine defeated a force of heavy cavalry at Turin, near the passes, and destroyed his rival's northern army at Verona.

Pressures began to mount on Maxentius. When his shattered army had tried to retreat into Turin, that city had closed its gates against it and gone over to Constantine. Maxentius had placed his faith on a new weapon on the battlefield, heavy armoured cavalry, which the Persians had employed with great success against conventional Roman armies such as Constantine's. Constantine, however, demonstrated Alexander's flexibility, by dividing his forces in the face of the cavalry's charges, letting them pass between his smaller units, and striking at them as they rode through his formations. Maxentius' best and loyal general, Rufus Pompeianus, had been the garrison commander at Verona. Constantine again defeated Pompeianus' heavy calvary at Brescia. Maxentius' army formed a longer line of battle at Verona, poised to envelop Constantine's small force. So good was the training of Constantine's soldiers, however, that they went from a line two ranks deep into a single, broader line just before engaging Maxentius' men, and prevailed, killing Pompeianus in a battle that lasted until nightfall. Maxentius' secret weapon and his best general had proved useless against the latest claimant for the title of emperor.

Faced with those reverses, Maxentius, for his part, at first followed the strategy that had worked against Galerius. He had large granaries and warehouses in Rome; these were filled in preparation of a long siege, in which Constantine's troops would face many opportunities for discouragement or defection. Maxentius had bought the loyalty of the Praetorian Guard in Rome itself, and these men, elite soldiers all, would keep the city obedient while they remained loyal. There was also the possibility that another challenger would attack Constantine's own bases of support, or come to Maxentius' relief in an image-building alliance and 'rescue' of eternal Rome. Those hopes were, however, faint, and more than one emperor had perished when the Praetorians decided to change their allegiance to a challenger who looked more likely to win. All this might explain why Maxentius now made the fatal and otherwise inexplicable decision he did.

Constantine himself needed a way to unite and inspire his troops, unable as he was to claim a 'legitimate succession' to the position of emperor under Diocletian's system. He found the Christian God, or God found him, in a vision of a cross across the sun, a phenomenon that can naturally occur under proper atmospheric conditions. Having seen the amazing sight, Constantine later told a biographer of a dream in which the God of the long-persecuted Christians had shown him the Greek letter *chi* crossed with a *rho*, and commanded, 'In this sign, conquer' (*In hoc signo, vincere*). If for no other reason than their remarkable persistence in the face of extensive and lengthy persecution, the Christians were a moral force in the empire. Constantine's soldiers accepted their general's vision and painted the emblem upon their shields. Constantine's army had victory and vision on their side, and quickly moved south along the old Via Flaminia of Punic War fame.

What cost Maxentius was a fatal attack of vacillation. King being cause again, that meant ultimate defeat. The general account is that the wide stone bridge over the Tiber, the Pons Milvius, had been cut in order to delay Constantine's attack and hinder his supply lines during the expected siege of Rome. That destruction would have made sense if Maxentius had chosen to stay where he was. Maxentius, however, decided to offer battle on the far side of the Tiber at a place called Saxa Rubra, and for that he had to construct a wooden pontoon bridge in order to form his line of battle. Their commander's nervousness and sudden reversal of strategy could not have been lost on Maxentius' soldiers.

On 28 October 312, Constantine's battle-hardened and undeniably inspired soldiers smashed into Maxentius' garrison troops, and the result was a panicked flight by the defenders either over the stone Pons Milvius or the wooden pontoon structure. Either way brought final catastrophe, for the bridge collapsed under the weight of the fugitives, and Maxentius drowned in his armour. His head alone returned to Rome the following day, when Constantine exhibited it on a lancehead in testimony to his victory and decisive superiority of command.

Conclusion

Emphasis on the means by which commanders were successful is useful, but the ultimate focus of any analysis of generalship should be on results. Organized warfare itself is a process begun with an end in view; as Clausewitz put it, the continuation of policy by other means. Praise or criticism of a commander can best be phrased in terms of that person's success at achieving the goal for which he exercised that command.

At Kadesh, Rameses did inflict a great deal of damage on the Hittite army, at a considerable, and inadvertent, risk of losing his crown and life due to his own credulity in the story planted by the two captured spies. At a considerable cost in time and treasure, and the blood of both armies, Rameses did secure a peace treaty and security on his northern frontier, not to mention a *stele* of his own to rival the enduring military glory of Thutmose III and the other military pharaohs. In his own view – and no one else's mattered – the battle was a success, whatever else shows up under the glaring spotlight of modern analysis.

Xerxes had performed prodigious feats of organization and supply in moving the immense army he sent to Greece. His desire was the subjugation of the democratic Hellenes and an end to the revolts their interference and example prompted within his empire. There was the defeat of his father's invasion at Marathon to avenge. Athens had been burned, but there would be more interference in Asia Minor, at a great cost to the Persians who succeeded Xerxes, and indeed his own defeats at Salamis and Plataea were not what Xerxes had intended to purchase with his troops, time and treasure. The gold that paid for the Spartan fleet at Aegopotami did more to harm Athens in the long run, and if the Greeks had bought their freedom with their blood during the invasion, they sold it to the Persians in the course of their own internal warfare.

Alexander wanted it all, and had the genius and the means to get it. He asked no more of his army than he himself was willing to give, but his army eventually lost its own willingness to march ever onward for more conquests, and Alexander's empire left him when a body wracked by wounds and disease could no longer support the powerful mind that had prevailed so brilliantly at Gaugamela. Philip was less brilliant, and his opponents considerably wiser than Darius, and Chios secured that ruler no more than an anchorage amidst the corpses of his own sailors. Rhodes and Pergamon stayed free of Philip, but not, forever, free in the growing empire of Rome.

Hannibal's hatred for Rome and his military genius expressed itself in three of the most severe disasters ever suffered by the Romans, but secured him only his own defeat in the end, at Zama, at the hands of a man he'd schooled by his own example. Antony and Octavian fought for sole mastery, and Agrippa's hired expertise proved superior to Antony's native talent, for Octavian's greatest gain. Constantine had learned from the past, and profited; Maxentius faltered under pressure and perished. The means to an end are as varied as the ends themselves, but successful command and control of an armed force are proven by the commander's success in attaining those very ends for which the fighting took place.

> '...through the peculiar virtues of their constitution and their ability to keep their heads, [the Romans] ... within a few years had made themselves masters of the whole world' – POLYBIUS

CHAPTER 4

SIEGE WARFARE

Dans les vieux temps
Les Princesses étaient fidèles,
Et les sieges duraient dix ans.

(In the ancient past
When princesses were faithful
And sieges ten years did last.)
Bonnard, *Ephître à Zéphyrine*
(Letter to Zéphyrine)

The words of eighteenth-century French poet Chevalier De Bonnard refer, of course, to the most famous siege of all time, the ten-year struggle before the walls of Troy between the Trojans and the Greeks – as told by Homer in the *Iliad*. From the time that mankind began to settle in cities, the siege as a form of warfare was born. One of the primary purposes of the early development of cities was defence, as illustrated by the large amount of early settlements upon naturally defensible terrain, such as hilltops, and the appearance of walled cities very shortly after the first major urban centres were founded in the

LEGIONARIES CONSTRUCT DEFENSIVE WORKS. *The Roman army were unparalleled in the ancient world as builders of small fortresses. They were also highly skilled at building defensive walls. This illustration represents what the Roman army would have looked like in front of the walls of Masada.*

Near East, in the fifth millennium BC. Furthermore, the quotation from Bonnard also illustrates how, early on, these places were nearly impossible to capture. Whether the a war between the Mycenaean Greeks and the Trojans actually happened does not matter; the *Iliad*, written c. 750 BC, still serves to demonstrate how, until the eighth century in the Near East and until the fifth century in Greece, armies had no way of taking a fortified urban centre other than by sitting outside the walls and trying to starve it into submission. Thus Greece developed into a patchwork of independent walled *poleis* ('city-states'), as the armies had the ability to defeat each other in open battle, but had no reliable way of taking cities. States could win disputes and, at times, territory from their neighbours, but lacked the capability to fully take them over, because they could not breach their walls. Greece remained in this divided state until the mid-fourth century BC, when it was unified by Philip II of Macedonia. It is no coincidence that he was the first in Greece to master siege warfare.

The difficulties of taking cities mean it is scarcely surprising that, to protect themselves from hostile forces and to preserve themselves and their way of life, humans congregated in cities from early times. As these proved so easily defendable, any imperialist state that sought a firm and a lasting grip on an empire had to discover a way of reducing the advantage possessed by these urban fortresses. The first state to develop technology to smash down walls was also the world's first major empire. In the twelfth century BC, Assyrians emerged as the dominant power in the Near East. Their supremacy was also reinforced by the invention of machines designed to breach walls and give them access to cities. Now those opposed to them could no longer hide behind their protective walls. Their siege towers and battering rams allowed them to retain power until the seventh century BC. Their siege technology passed from the Near East into the western Mediterranean by means of the Phoenicians. In this sense, siege technology actually bypassed mainland Greece and was first pioneered in Europe by the Greeks of Sicily, who adopted it from the Phoenician colony of Carthage, which mainted a military presence on the western half of the island. Dionysios I, tyrant of Syracuse (405–367 BC), assembled engineers from all over the Greek world and used their expertise to develop the first siege artillery. The rams and towers first used by the Assyrians were now aided by strong double-armed catapults. Dionysios used this new technology to gain dominance over all of Sicily and to become the most powerful Greek of his day.

Philip II of Macedonia (359–336 BC) realized the importance of siege technology and passed this on to his son Alexander, who used it to breach the walls of cities from Greece to India. Adopted by his successors who fought over his legacy, Greek siege technology reached its height in the struggles of the third century. Defenders no longer held a great advantage over attackers in a siege, the balance having at last been redressed. As a result, from this point onwards, Greek defensive fortifications began to improve dramatically. Now, both offensive and defensive siege technology developed in tandem, with improvements in engines resulting in an improvement in defences, and vice versa.

Roman Inheritance

This is the legacy that Rome inherited. At first, the Romans, like the Greeks, could only lay siege to a fortified city by camping outside and starving the place into submission. But gradually, throughout the third century, as they came into greater contact with the Greeks of southern Italy and Sicily, they began to adopt Greek siege technology. Although the Romans were never as inventive as the Greeks in terms of new machines, they did significantly improve existing models. In this way, they developed the most awesome siege train of the ancient world, and at the height of Roman power in the first two centuries AD, there was no city or fortress that could resist them. After this point, Roman siege technology went into decline, with machines becoming simpler in design and somewhat less effective. Nevertheless, they continued to excel in defensive architecture, and it was this that was greatly responsible for keeping various foreign invaders at bay for a significant time. This technology would disappear in the sixth century AD, only to be rediscovered in the thirteenth century, when it had a great influence upon the development of the late medieval castle.

The purpose of this chapter is to illustrate the origin and development of siege warfare techniques, from both an offensive and defensive standpoint. It describes their inception in the eighth century BC Near East, to the fall of the Roman Empire in the west in the fifth century AD. The first section explores the origins of siege warfare and centres on the siege of Lachish in 701 BC. The Assyrian technology used in this siege gradually took hold in the Mediterranean, and from the Near East we shall go on to examine the art of the siege in classical and then Hellenistic Greece, using the sieges of Syracuse (416–413 BC) and Rhodes (305–304 BC) as our examples, respectively. In the second century, the Romans assumed the mantle of the strongest military power in the Mediterranean, and they took siege warfare to its height in the ancient world. The final triumph of Julius Caesar in Gaul at the siege of Alesia in 52 BC was the height of Roman blockading technology, while the victory at the siege of Masada (AD 73–74) was one of the greatest feats of Roman military logistics and engineering. The latter also returns the chapter to the Near East, which is also the setting for our examination of the siege in late antiquity. Here, we centre on the defeat of the Romans by the Sasanid Persians at the Siege of Dura Europos in AD 256–257. Even before this point, however, siege technology was gradually being lost, at least in the Mediterranean, as there were fewer and fewer skilled artisans to construct the complex engines necessary, and the middle of the first millennium AD would see further decline. The skills of the ancients at conducting siege warfare would not be equalled until the thirteenth century, and shortly afterwards the advent of gunpowder weapons would alter every aspect of warfare. The ancient siege therefore stands out as

one of the peaks of the application of science, technology, engineering and logistics in the history of warfare.

The Origins of Siege Warfare
The world's first walled settlement was the small city of Jericho, situated just over 10km (6 miles) off the north coast of the Dead Sea in the ancient region of Canaan in modern Israel. The walls at the site have been dated to the early seventh millennium BC. Modern scholars have hypothesized that there are two major reasons that lie behind the construction of walls around settlements. Primarily, walls were developed as a defence from missile weapons – which were largely, at this point in history, the bow and arrow. The second reason is the development of sedentary agriculture.

'With battle and slaughter I stormed the city and captured it; 3000 of their warriors I put to the sword; their spoil and their possessions, their cattle and their sheep I carried off.'
— ASSURNASIRPAL II

The two are intrinsically linked, since protection against missile weapons was possible only once humans had settled and began to farm in a fixed place, thus giving them the opportunity to construct permanent defensive works.

Jericho was fortified very early in comparison to most walled settlements. Its first set of walls were constructed in early Neolithic times, using stone tools. The 2500 inhabitants of Jericho appear to have been displaced c. 6800 BC, when another Stone-Age people occupied the town. It is doubtful that a people who were stationary enough to construct fortifications would simply have abandoned the site, and therefore it appears improbable that this was a case where a new people merely took possession of a vacant town. Therefore, though no evidence exists for a battle, this may represent the world's first siege, for it is unlikely that the settlement could have been taken over wholesale without a struggle. In turn, these people were forced out in 4500 BC, and the new inhabitants remained until the city itself was finally destroyed c. 1325 BC. It is doubtful that this was the result of the famous siege of Jericho by the Israelite King Joshua, as described in the Bible (*Joshua* 6, 1–25). Biblical scholars have cast doubt on the historical authenticity of the siege, as well as on many of the military aspects of the *Book of Joshua* in general. Furthermore, the violent conquest of Canaan by the Israelites did not occur until at least two centuries after the destruction of c. 1325 BC, by which time the city had been abandoned.

Nevertheless, the account of the destruction of Jericho by the Israelites in the *Book of Joshua* represents our oldest written account of a siege. Regardless of its veracity, it reveals several aspects of Bronze Age siege warfare in the Near East. The siege is probably more well-known by the old Christian song that it inspired; the chorus goes 'Joshua fought the Battle of Jericho; And the walls came tumbling down.'

In fact, the walls did not, come tumbling down, at least not until the city was destroyed from within. We know that, at the time, the Israelites – or anyone else for that matter – did not possess siege technology. The *Book of Joshua* describes the Israelite Army marching around the city, which probably means that they surrounded the walls, or perhaps patrolled their perimeter, to prevent resupply and thus starve the garrison into surrender. In the end, the city was taken only by ruse, as Joshua sent two of his men into the city, and these hid in the house of a harlot. The account does not say what function these men performed; however, it is likely that they liaised with some locals who betrayed the city and opened the gates, otherwise it is difficult to understand why they warranted a mention. Afterwards, the city was utterly destroyed and all of the inhabitants were put to the sword.

Regardless of its authenticity, the biblical account of the siege of Jericho describes nothing

that is too far-fetched and can be accepted as a solid rendering of a Near Eastern Late Bronze Age siege. The fact that *Yahweh* (God) must intervene to destroy the walls of the city serves only to reinforce the fact that the Israelites did not have any siege weapons. Having no way to breach the walls, the Israelites attempted to starve the place into submission. In addition to this, or perhaps when this tactic failed, they sent spies into the city and subverted it from the inside. There was simply no other way of gaining access to a fortified city other than by blockade and surrender, assault, mining and deceit. It seems, therefore, that this account can be taken as typical for any siege prior to the ninth century BC and the development of engines. Until this point, defensive technology ruled the day.

Although Jericho was walled by the seventh millennium BC, it remained relatively small in size. The first great fortified cities appeared in

AN ASSYRIAN SIEGE *from a relief from the palace of Ashurnasipal II (883-859 BC). On the left, sappers work on the wall. In the middle, a mine is being dug under the walls. The other side of the city is being assaulted by a covered battering-ram with a tower on top. The defenders have dislodged the ram with chains but the attackers are attempting to free the ram's beam with books while archers give covering fire.*

Mesopotamia around 3000 BC. Ur in modern Iraq is one of the best and earliest examples. The city was famous in its day for its great fortifications, which were in places more than 30m (100ft) thick at their base. The city's engineers grasped the importance of planned fortifications, and over time the walls were strengthened with balconies, curtain walls and towers. The latter were positioned no further apart than the maximum range of a bow (at that time about 30m/100ft), so that all points of attack could be brought under fire. In other cities in Mesopotamia, designers built walls with several right angles, thus creating a zigzag pattern in order to maximize angles of fire.

A similar fortification process was taking place in Egypt at this time. From the first decades of the Old Kingdom (c. 2159 BC) comes some of our earliest pictorial evidence of siege warfare. A relief from Dishashe in central Egypt depicts a siege in which the attacking forces are utilizing ladders and are attempting to pry open gates with crowbar-like tools. Another Egyptian relief, from Saqqara in the north and dating to the twenty-third century BC, features a mobile-ladder. This was the first mechanism designed specifically for siege warfare. It would have been difficult for a defender to displace, and its wheels meant that it could be brought quickly to bear on any point of the wall. The relief also shows the besiegers using axes and picks to chip away at the enemy fortifications. Although this is our first evidence of an attempt to gain access to a fortress by actually bringing down a wall, it should be emphasized that these walls would have been built of mud-brick. The ability to bring down a stone wall was still centuries away.

Siege warfare remained largely unchanged until the eighteenth century BC brought with it an increase in fortification across the Near East. Previously, sieges could only be conducted by

ASHURNASIPAL II HIMSELF is depicted here in another panel from his palace, shooting his bow at a city he is besieging. The ram with its tower for archers is destroying the enemy's wall with ease.

blockade or assault, so it would appear that the greater emphasis on fortification came about as a result of the development of the first siege engines. In Mesopotamia, which was politically fragmented at this time, there was an effort to reduce the advantage enjoyed by defenders behind walls. And this advantage was overwhelming; Egyptian sources speak of the frustration felt when the Pharaoh's army defeated an enemy on the battlefield, only for the latter to shut themselves up inside their walls. Unless the Egyptians were willing to sit outside the city for the duration, there was little they could do, particularly if the city was well-fortified; often they had to be content with devastating the surrounding countryside as they retired. Now Mesopotamian warlords sought to follow up their victories on the battlefield by breaking down enemy walls and seizing their city.

First Siege Engines

Our first recorded use of engines comes from the siege of Nurrugum Shamshi-Adad (1813–1761 BC), a warlord who had conquered much of Assyria in north-eastern Mesopotamia.

Contemporary accounts of the siege have him utilizing rams and towers. Although it is not known whether he invented these machines, or was merely applying the technology of others, his efforts and those of his contemporaries were effective. Both archaeological and historical remains indicate that many cities throughout the Near East fell to their attackers in the eighteenth century BC.

Nevertheless, siege engines were still in their infancy, and the principal way of capturing an enemy city at this time was by circumvallation and the construction of siege mounds. At the commencement of a siege, the attackers often threw up works that surrounded the city so that defenders might not escape. By the late nineteenth century BC, these had become quite sophisticated, and included moats, earthen walls, wooden palisades and towers. The besiegers would then begin construction of the mound; this was a large earthen ramp that gradually moved forward until it reached and equalled the height of the enemy wall. A tower might then clear the battlements of defenders, and an infantry assault could take place, with the soldiers using the mound to take themselves over the wall.

Siege works, towers and mounds all required the skill of experts for their construction, and thus engineers make their appearance on the battlefield for the first time in history. Warfare amongst the great Near Eastern powers was no longer a pursuit to be left to kings and conscripts: it was now a science, and the ability to build effective siege works was now a necessary part of every general's arsenal. These engineers, however, did not only ply their trade for the attackers; as previously mentioned, the success of the new offensive techniques in siege warfare brought with them improvements in fortification. In the late eighteenth century BC, more and more cities began to be surrounded by moats; double - and sometimes even triple - walls featuring more towers made their appearance; cities now featured citadels on high ground and with walls of their own; earthen or stone slopes were placed in front of fortifications to deter ladders, sappers and towers from approaching the walls; entrances were now heavily fortified and sometimes raised off the ground, being accessible by ramp only, while the gates covering these entrances became more sophisticated, using a series of overlapping walls or double doors with a crossbeam. Finally, in order to combat the wooden siege engines, defenders exploited a new innovation - incendiary arrows.

The new siege techniques were first put to great use by the Hurrian people. In the sixteenth and fifteenth centuries BC, they emerged to form a confederacy that united states from northern Mesopotamia and Syria. Although they were never sufficiently organized to found a great empire, they were the first rulers in the world whose power was based upon their ability to knock down or successfully assault the walls of their enemies. Their skill and technology was inherited by the Hittites, a people from Anatolia who built an empire that incorporated much of Asia Minor, Palestine, Syria and northern Mesopotamia. Skilled on the battlefield and blessed by a series of fine generals, they also had the skill, organization, logistics and persistence to carry out long sieges and emerge victorious. No longer was it enough for a defeated army to simply retreat into their city and hide behind their walls.

Methods for breaking down walls were now more refined, but by the sixteenth century BC, the balance was again tipped firmly in favour of the defenders. Sieges were still largely based on blockade and assault. While it remains true that certain well-organized powers could be very successful at sieges, this was usually true only when the attackers had the numbers and logistical capabilities to sit outside a city until it surrendered. Small cities did doubtless fall victim to engines and direct assault, but even these could be long and drawn-out affairs. Technology was playing an increasingly important part, but still the advantage lay with those behind the walls, for successful sieges required tremendous efforts on the part of the attackers. This would not change until a power emerged that could carry out sieges on a large scale, with the ability to take heavily fortified cities not by blockade, but by direct assault with complex works and multiple engines. In the twelfth century BC, a power of this sort emerged and founded the first empire based on the siege. These were the Assyrians.

Assyrian Siege Warfare

The Assyrians are known to history as a people of brute force, with a strong military organization, who were reponsible for several advancements in military technology. Yet most of all, they are remembered for their utter savagery. They created the world's first great army, and the world's first great empire. This was held together by two factors: their superior abilities in siege warfare, and their reliance on sheer, unadulterated terror. It was Assyrian policy always to demand that examples be made from those who resisted them; this included deportations of entire peoples and horrific physical punishments. One inscription from a temple in the city of Nimrod records the fate of the leaders of the city of Suru on the Euphrates River, who rebelled from and were reconquered by King Ashurbanipal (668–626 BC). 'I buil[t] a pillar at the city gate, and I flayed all the chief men who had revolted, and I covered the pillar with their skins: some I walled-up inside the pillar, some I impaled upon the pillar on stakes.' Such punishments were not uncommon. Furthermore, inscriptions recording these vicious acts of retribution were displayed throughout the empire to serve as a warning. Yet this officially sanctioned cruelty seem to have had the opposite effect: though the Assyrians and their army were respected and feared, they were most of all hated, and the subjects of their empire were in an almost constant state of rebellion. Throughout much of Assyria's history, this had the positive effect of giving the army a core of highly experienced troops and placing it in a state of perpetual combat readiness. However, the constant warfare eventually depleted Assyria of much of its manpower; shortly after the empire had reached its zenith in the mid-seventh century BC, it began to crumble. As a result of the great loathing the peoples of the empire felt towards the Assyrians, the first cracks to appear were quickly exploited, and the end was brutally swift. By the last quarter of the seventh century BC, nearly every part of the empire was in a state of rebellion; these were not just struggles of freedom but wars of revenge. In 612 BC a coalition of rebels seized the empire's capital at Nineveh, and burnt it to the ground. According to the Bible (*Nahum* 3, 7), the sentiment that echoed across the Near East as one of the world's most brutal empires came to a brutal end was this: 'Nineveh is laid to waste. Who will mourn her?'

> *'I buil[t] a pillar at the city gate, and I flayed all the chief men who had revolted, and I covered the pillar with their skins: some I walled-up inside the pillar, some I impaled upon the pillar on stakes'* – ASHURBANIPAL

More than anything else, the Assyrian army excelled at siege warfare, and was probably the first force to carry a separate corps of engineers. Precisely when the Assyrians adopted siege engines is unknown. However, by the eighth century BC, they had become masters of the art of the siege, as evidenced by the increasing prominence of sieges on various laudatory reliefs and inscriptions throughout the Empire. Assault was their principal tactic against the heavily fortified cities of the Near East. They developed a great variety of methods for breaching enemy walls: sappers were employed to undermine walls or to light fires underneath wooden gates, and ramps were thrown up to allow men to go over the ramparts or to attempt a breach on the upper section of wall, where it was the least thick. Mobile ladders allowed attackers to cross moats and quickly assault any point in defences. These operations were covered by masses of archers, who were the core of the infantry. But the pride of the Assyrian siege train were their engines. These were multistoried wooden towers with four wheels and a turret on top and one, or at times two, battering rams at the base. They were covered in hides and canvases to protect against incendiary arrows and also featured numerous eyelets through which archers could shoot to clear the enemy battlements. Forward motion was provided by soldiers pushing at the tower's back, or by animals pulling ropes that were wrapped around stakes in front of the tower, and then were looped around the engine's rear. The crew consisted of various archers; those who operated the rams; men who used large shovel-like devices with water to fight fires; and soldiers who operated poles with hooks on the end and who would attempt to catch any chains lowered by the defenders in order to dislodge the rams. Due to the fact that Assyrian reliefs are not in scale, it is impossible to know the exact dimensions of these towers, though modern estimates have varied between 8m (26ft) and 10m (32ft).

The towers were brought close to the wall and the ram, perhaps stretching across a moat, would go to work while the archers cleared the battlements. Occasionally the tower would feature a drawbridge that would deposit infantry on top of the enemy wall, though this approach does not appear to have been used heavily. The engine was at its deadliest when combined with a siege ramp; after throwing up an earthen mound to about halfway up the enemy wall, the Assyrians would then cover this in stone slabs, giving the tower a smooth surface on which to operate. The ram was then brought to bear on the middle and upper sections of the wall, which tended to be weaker. The Assyrians appear to be the first people to have combined siege towers with siege ramps, a tactic that would have great influence upon the Romans centuries later.

As stated earlier, the first technique employed by the Assyrians at any siege was assault. They did have the capability to take a city by blockade, and were at times successful with this tactic, but they tended not to attempt this; for whatever reason, they shied away from long sieges. Only when assaults failed did they resort to a blockade, but would they just as often abandon the campaign altogether and make another attempt the following year.

The Siege of Lachish

Still, most Assyrian sieges were successful, and one of the best documented sieges was that of Lachish in 701 BC. This was part of a campaign to conquer Judea by King Sennacherib (704–681 BC), who was probably seeking a major victory to legitimize his young reign. He had the events of the siege recorded on a relief and placed in his palace and thus we are well placed to reconstruct the events. The siege began with ovations from the Assyrians to the besieged. The latter were told that if they surrendered, they would be treated with leniency; however, if they resisted, the entire force of the Assyrian army would be brought down on them, and they would be punished in the traditional,

brutal Assyrian manner. When the defenders refused to surrender, the siege began. The city was first surrounded to prevent escape, and then archers were brought forward. Under the cover of giant shields, they cleared the battlements while the engineers began construction of a siege ramp and a tower. When the former was completed, it was paved with flat stone slabs to make the way smooth for the tower. The Assyrians then staged a two-pronged assault; the tower was wheeled up the ramp and the ram was brought to bear against the mid-section of the enemy wall. Archers in the tower cleared the battlements while bowmen on the ground pushed up close to the wall to cover an infantry assault with scaling ladders. The fighting appears to have been intense, and the assault probably took several days, yet eventually the Assyrians took the city. Archaeology has revealed that the place was looted and hundreds of men, women and children were put to the sword. The relief of the siege shows prisoners begging for mercy at the feet of Sennacherib. Others less fortunate, perhaps the city's leaders, have been impaled upon stakes.

While the siege of Lachish was successful, the siege of Jerusalem was not, as the Assyrian army there was devastated by a plague. This, combined with a heavy defeat by the Egyptians shortly afterwards, forced their withdrawal. Nevertheless,

AN EARLY ASSYRIAN BATTERING RAM *from the reign of King Sargon II. Later rams had towers built on top of them for archers to give covering fire. The beam was tipped with a sharp metal point to make it more effective. The rear of the ram was open.*

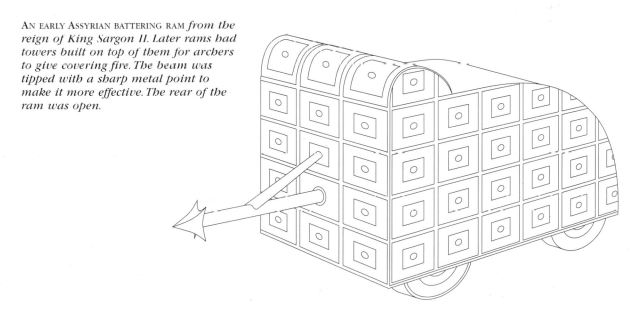

THE SIEGE OF LACHISH (701 BC); *this relief from the palace of Sennacherib is now in the British Musuem. This part shows Assyrian archers, with their accompanying shield-bearers shooting at the walls of Lachish while a combination battering-ram and tower assaults the walls from a siege ramp. Underneath, men attempt to undermine the wall's foundations. The inhabitants paid a horrible price for their resistance; as seen here, several prisoners were impaled upon stakes.*

Sennacherib and his engineers returned in 684 BC and this time were victorious, as Judea was incorporated into the Empire. By these methods of siege and horror, technology and terror, the Assyrians became the unrivalled masters of the Near East for five centuries. By the time of their fall, their expertise in siege technology had spread throughout the region. It was then brought westwards by the Phoenicians in the seventh century BC; their colony at Carthage would go on to establish a sea empire of its own in the western Mediterranean, and this eventually brought them into armed conflict with the Greeks who had settled in eastern Sicily. It was here, in the fifth century BC, that the Greeks first encountered engines designed specifically for the siege. And although they were slow to adopt them, once they did, they would create a revolution in siege technology and bring the art to new heights.

Early Greek Siege Warfare

The period between the fall of Assyria in 612 BC and the rise of Dionysios I of Syracuse in 405 BC saw very little development in engineering and siege technology. The expertise of the Assyrians was largely lost during this period. Though it was adopted by the Persians, the new great Near Eastern power, they failed to realize its full potential, and used engines only sparingly, making no significant improvements upon existing designs. As for the Greeks, they did not have most of this technology available to them. Throughout the first half of this period at least, Greek science had not progressed far enough to make the construction of these large engines feasible. The Carthaginians, the new force in the western Mediterranean, did have this technology available to them because of their Phoenician inheritance. However, the art of the siege largely fell into disuse because their empire was sea-based, and because the cities they encountered in Africa, Sardinia and Spain were not heavily fortified. This changed only once they began to make serious incursions into Greek territory on Sicily in the sixth and fifth centuries BC, for here they were forced to contended with walled fortresses. Still, it would be left to Syracuse, their main opponents in Sicily, on the south-east of the island, to create a renaissance in offensive siege technology. During the late fifth century BC, they began to adopt and greatly improve upon Punic engines. Within a century, they had eclipsed anything that had come before, and had returned engineering to the forefront of warfare.

Until this Greek revolution came about, it was defensive technology that ruled the day. Fortification had reached a pinnacle and offensive technology either could not keep pace or was simply unavailable. The walled fortress governed the way wars were fought in the sixth and fifth centuries BC. In the Mediterranean, conflicts were often short and inconsequential, where an army, if defeated on the battlefield, would simply retire behind its walls. The victors, being unable to take the city, tended to devastate the surrounding territory before retiring. Major wars, on the other hand, could often last for decades, as the protection of the walls meant that one side could never deal the *coup de grâce*. As a result, in this period of constant warfare, territorial gains were largely insignificant, and much of the Mediterranean remained a patchwork of independent city-states.

Fortification also failed to register any significant advancements within this period, but this is largely due to the fact that, in the absence of offensive technology, defences did not have to improve. The brick walls of the Archaic period (eighth to sixth centuries BC) had, by the fifth century, given way to stone structures that featured ramparts and crenellations. These small but sturdy walls were now expanded to encompass entire cities, which had outgrown their old fortifications. In the centre there was a walled citadel, often situated on a hill – called by the Greeks an *acropolis* (literally 'high city'). These sets of fortifications were enough to keep all but the most resolute attackers at bay for over two centuries.

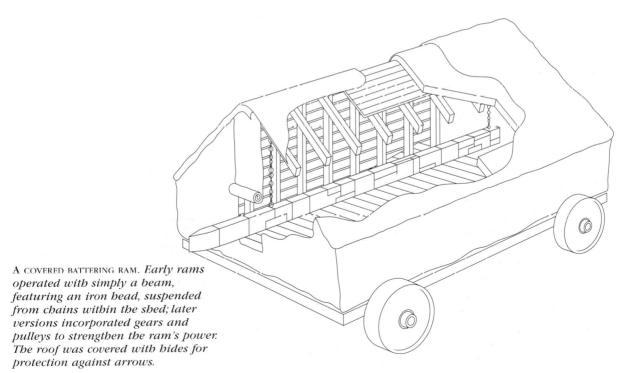

A COVERED BATTERING RAM. *Early rams operated with simply a beam, featuring an iron head, suspended from chains within the shed; later versions incorporated gears and pulleys to strengthen the ram's power. The roof was covered with hides for protection against arrows.*

Lachish

701 BC

In an attempt to conquer Judea, King Sennacherib of Assyria (704-681 BC) laid siege to both Lachish and Jerusalem. At Lachish, the city was first surrounded to prevent escape. Next, archers were brought forward; under the cover of giant shields, they cleared the battlements. The king then used the tried-and-tested Assyrian method of building an earthen ramp close to the enemy wall, covering it with flat stone and wheeling forward a machine that combined a siege-tower with a battering ram. The Assyrians then staged a two-pronged assault. The tower was wheeled up the ramp and the ram was brought to bear against the mid-section of the enemy wall. Archers in the tower cleared the battlements while bowmen on the ground pushed up close to the wall to cover an infantry assault with scaling ladders. The fighting appears to have been intense, and the assault probably took several days, yet eventually the Assyrians entered the city. Although Lachish fell, Jerusalem did not, and Sennacherib was eventually driven out of Judea.

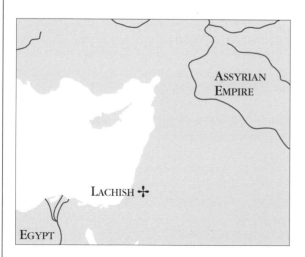

The siege of Lachish is one of the earliest recorded sieges, and was part of a campaign by Sennacherib to conquer the rich province of Judea from the Egyptians.

3. At the same time, Sennacherib's men assault the city with scaling ladders, the archers giving support.

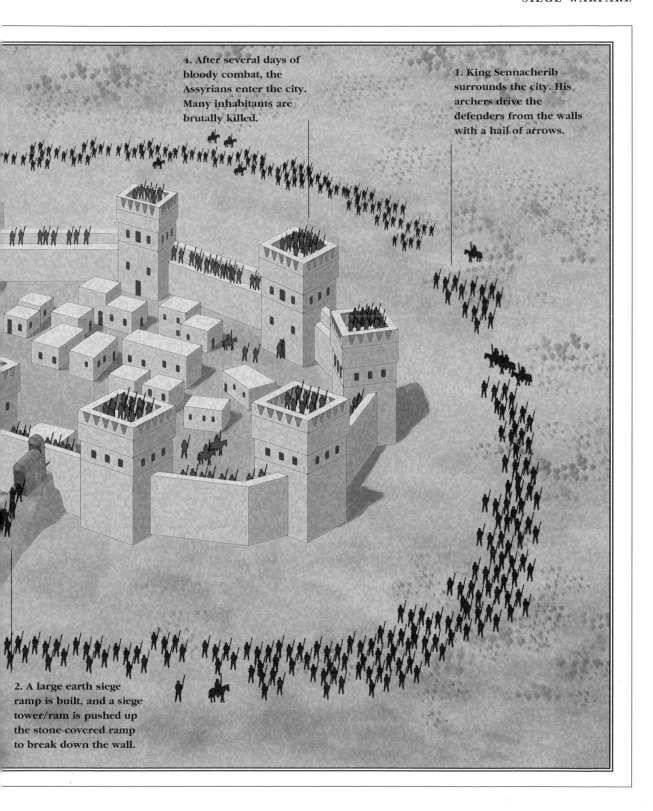

4. After several days of bloody combat, the Assyrians enter the city. Many inhabitants are brutally killed.

1. King Sennacherib surrounds the city. His archers drive the defenders from the walls with a hail of arrows.

2. A large earth siege ramp is built, and a siege tower/ram is pushed up the stone-covered ramp to break down the wall.

The two Peloponnesian Wars (460–445 and 431–404 BC) saw Greece polarized between two opposing camps: Athens and its empire, and Sparta and the Peloponnesian League. The latter, although able to defeat Athens on land, was unable to take the city because of its walls and because the might of the Athenian navy maintained the city's supply lines. Only when the Spartans matched the Athenians at sea were they able to emerge victorious, as they were then able to surround and cut off the supply lines to Athens. These wars are typical of the lack of siege technology during this period; an enemy without the ability to breach walls, meant that fortified cities remained impervious to everything, save starvation.

Exceptions tended to occur only when a city was taken by ruse, surprise or betrayal. The Spartan siege of Plataea, 429–427 BC, is the only Greek example from this period where technology played a major role. The Spartans and their Theban allies first threw up siege works around the city; these contained ramparts, ditches and wooden walls that faced both inward and outward, to prevent escape and relief. They then constructed a siege mound made from timber and rubble, and assaulted the walls. To counter this, the Plataeans first raised the height of their existing wall, and then built a second wall behind this. The Spartans then brought forward battering rams, but these were destroyed by dislodging the beams with nooses or smashing the heads with large beams. When an attempt to set the city alight by lobbing in flaming brushwood failed, the Spartans abandoned their assault and bolstered their fortifications surrounding the city. Over the next two years, most of the defenders were able to sneak away, but the handful that remained were eventually starved into submission. The Spartans sold all the women into slavery, executed the men, and burnt Plataea to the ground.

The Siege of Syracuse

More characteristic of a siege for this period is that which occurred at Syracuse in Sicily between 416 and 413 BC. Recorded by the historian Thucydides (VI. 30–VII. 87), it is one of the most famous military engagements of all time, both because it was the turning point of the Second Peloponnesian

War and because of the crushing and complete nature of the defeat inflicted upon the Athenians. Seeking to break the deadlock in the war against Sparta, the Athenians seized upon the idea of intervening in Sicilian affairs and conquering Syracuse, thus depriving the Spartans of a vital source of supply and forcing them to sue for peace on terms advantageous to Athens. This would also be a major blow to Corinth, who was both Athens' enemy and major trading rival. The democratic Athenian assembly voted to send an expedition against Syracuse, but in typical fashion it feared putting complete power in the hands of one man, and therefore placed three generals in charge.

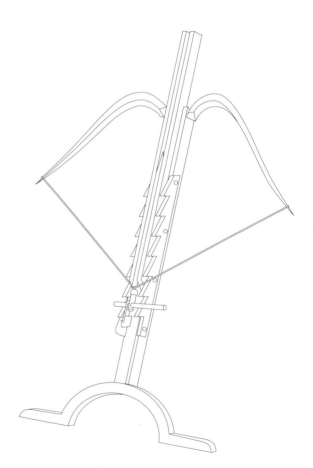

THE *GASTRAPHETES* OR 'BELLY-BOW', *the very first piece of artillery in the Greek world, developed by Dionysios I, (405–367 BC). It operated by means of tension, using wooden arms bent backwards to shoot bolts, similar to a modern crossbow.*

Ironically, the first, Nikias, was the chief opponent of the expedition, and had spoken out against it vehemently. Yet he was also an able general, who had earned the assembly's trust. He may also have been the victim of political intrigue, as his imperialist opponents may have hoped to rid themselves of a rival who was the leader of the peace party at Athens. Lamachos, the second commander, was also an experienced, but only moderately successful, general. The final partner was Alkibiades, one of the main proponents of the expedition, and one of the most ambitious characters in Athenian history. Friend of Socrates and an unyielding advocate of Athenian expansion, Alkibiades swore allegiance to no one and switched sides twice during the war, most notably while en route to Syracuse in 415 BC. Accused of religious sacrilege by his political enemies, he fled to Sparta, where he became a military advisor. The intrigues and cunning use of propaganda and oratory of this historical figure make for an exciting read, though they eventually led to his downfall and murder in 404 BC.

Upon arrival in Sicily, minus Alkibiades, the Athenians managed to defeat the Syracuse force sent to oppose them, leaving the route to the city open. However, Nikias failed to follow up this victory and exercised caution, thus allowing the Syracusans to regroup and to prepare the city's defences. This would not be the last time that his prudence would prevent the Athenians from exploiting their enemy while they were at their most vulnerable. After waiting some months, the Athenians marched on Syracuse and immediately seized the Epipolai Plateau that lies north of the city. Here they constructed two forts, the Labdalon and the Round Fort; and from the latter they began to build siege works consisting of walls and ditches, designed to hem the city in from the landward side. The Syracusans attempted to stop this construction, first with a cavalry attack, and

> *'[O]f all the Greek events which have been recorded, this was for the victors the most magnificent....For the defeated ...met with utter destruction[;] all perished, and few...came back home'* – THUCYDIDES

then with two sets of counterworks, designed to prevent the Athenians from completing the encirclement. However, the besiegers were able to thwart all of these efforts, and by 414 BC, the city looked doomed.

Filled with confidence, Nikias now committed a tremendous blunder. Convinced that Syracuse would surrender, he simply ceased the construction of the works, and thus the city was never fully surrounded. Why he made this decision is uncertain, but in the meantime, Syracuse had appealed to Sparta for aid, and Alkibiades advised the Spartans to send out Gylippos, one of their generals. Gylippos landed in Sicily and managed to raise 3000 reinforcements before proceeding to Syracuse. He marched towards the city in battle order, expecting a fight, but the Athenians, in another miscalculation that would prove costly, allowed him to enter unopposed.

After taking command of the Syracusan forces, Gylippos determined that the only way to break the siege was to take the fight to the Athenians, who must have seemed extraordinarily lax to this professional Spartan soldier. He immediately sallied out and captured the Labdalon fort in a lightning raid. Under constant skirmishing, he then constructed a wall that ran from the fort back to the city, thus blocking any Athenian attempts to complete their siege works and encircle Syracuse. The Athenian fleet in the city's Great Harbour was then attacked, an action in which the Syracusans were defeated. Gylippos was, however, successful with a land assault and he managed to capture the enemy supply depots. The logistical situation only worsened for the Athenians, for the Syracusans then defeated a supply fleet sent from Athens.

In early 413 BC, the Syracusans sent out a call to all of Sicily, and reinforcements arrived from all over the island. The fighting by land and sea now became frequent and savage. Often this took the

Syracuse
415–413 BC

The siege was an attempt by the Athenians to capture Syracuse and thus cut-off their enemy, Sparta, from a major source of grain. In 415 BC, the Athenians began constructing a series of walls and forts designed to hem in the city. Over the next year, two attempts by the defenders to build counter-walls met with failure. In 414 BC, the Spartans sent their general Gylippos to take command of the garrison. He immediately went on the offensive, capturing a major enemy fort and building a successful counter-wall, thus preventing the Athenians from completing their siege works. By 413 BC, the Athenian army began to suffer greatly from disease, and the Syracusan navy managed to trap the enemy fleet in the Great Harbour. The Athenians, realizing that the expedition was now a failure, abandoned the fleet and attempted to escape overland. Harassed by cavalry and running out of water, the Athenians surrendered. Many of the 7000 prisoners died after being imprisoned in the stone quarries of Syracuse, and few ever returned to Athens.

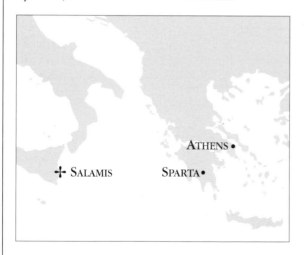

+ SALAMIS

ATHENS •

SPARTA •

Seeking to break the deadlock in the war against Sparta, the Athenians decided to attack Syracuse, hoping to deprive the Spartans of a vital source of supply and force them to sue for peace.

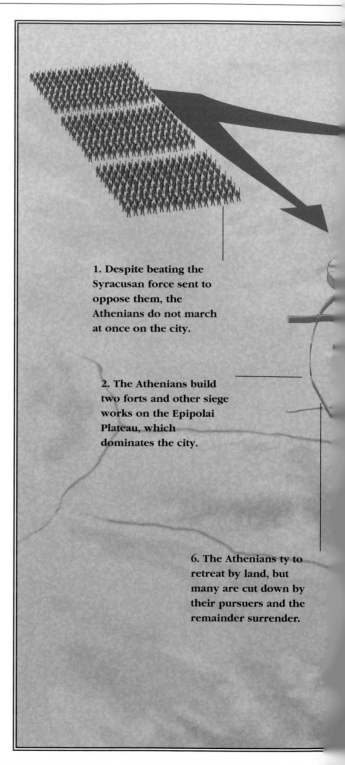

1. Despite beating the Syracusan force sent to oppose them, the Athenians do not march at once on the city.

2. The Athenians build two forts and other siege works on the Epipolai Plateau, which dominates the city.

6. The Athenians try to retreat by land, but many are cut down by their pursuers and the remainder surrender.

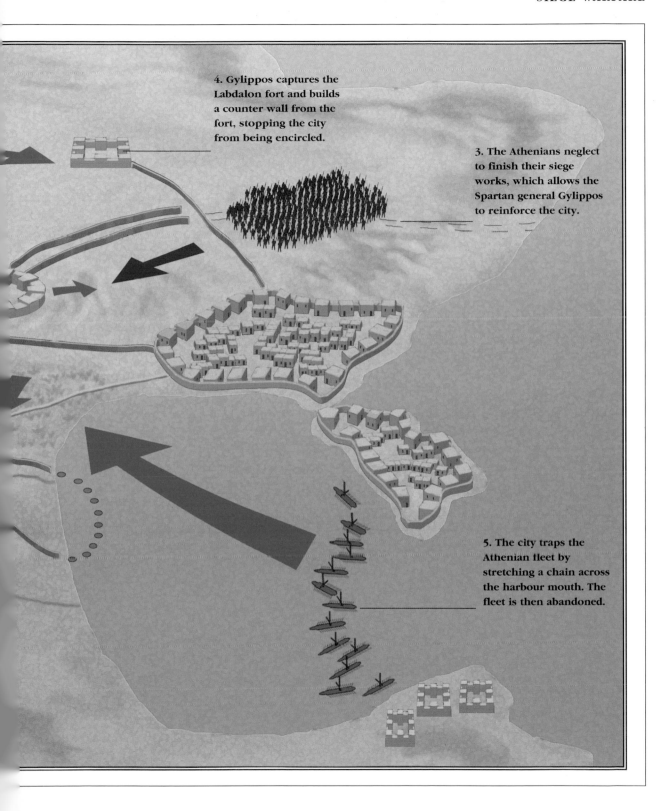

4. Gylippos captures the Labdalon fort and builds a counter wall from the fort, stopping the city from being encircled.

3. The Athenians neglect to finish their siege works, which allows the Spartan general Gylippos to reinforce the city.

5. The city traps the Athenian fleet by stretching a chain across the harbour mouth. The fleet is then abandoned.

form of skirmishing, but several major battles were also fought. These engagements were largely indecisive on land, save for one notable Syracusan victory. Still, every fight, regardless of the outcome, meant more casualties, which the Athenians could ill afford. The arrival of 5000 reinforcements from Athens did little to stem the tide and only put more pressure on the food supply. The situation was also desperate at sea, where the Syracusans scored two major victories in the Great Harbour. They now stretched a chain across the harbour's entrance. The Athenians, knowing the end was near, desperately tried to break out, only to lose half of their remaining fleet in the effort. With this, the trap was finally closed on the Athenians and the besiegers had now become the besieged.

The Athenians abandoned their fleet and retreated overland from Syracuse. Pursued by cavalry and missile troops, many were cut down in the flight. Finding the route north impassable, they vainly turned south and then west. Realizing that escape was now impossible, they surrendered. Of the 50,000 who were sent out from Athens over the past 2 years, only 7000 remained. The Athenian generals were executed, while the rest were imprisoned in the stone quarries of Syracuse, where most died in horrible conditions. Those few who survived were eventually released and returned to Athens, along with the tiny amount who had made good their escape before the main body surrendered. So ended the darkest chapter in Athenian military history.

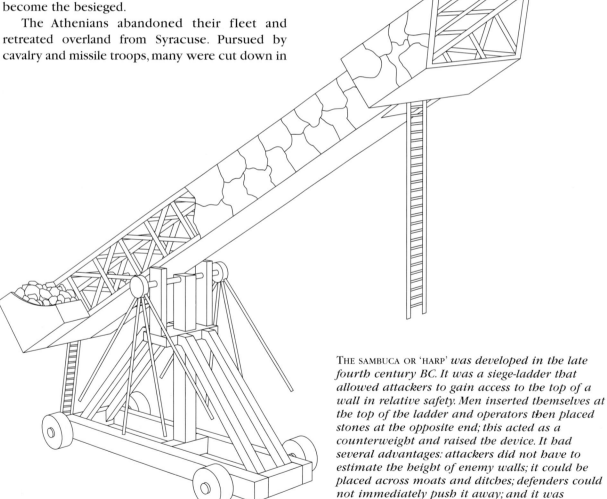

THE SAMBUCA OR 'HARP' *was developed in the late fourth century BC. It was a siege-ladder that allowed attackers to gain access to the top of a wall in relative safety. Men inserted themselves at the top of the ladder and operators then placed stones at the opposite end; this acted as a counterweight and raised the device. It had several advantages: attackers did not have to estimate the height of enemy walls; it could be placed across moats and ditches; defenders could not immediately push it away; and it was covered in hides to protect against fire.*

While relatively unimportant to the history of siege warfare, the Athenian siege of Syracuse is nevertheless important because it is typical of a siege for the fifth century BC. It never occurred to the Athenians to attempt to breach the Syracusan walls; the technology was simply not available to them. They therefore had no choice but to invest the city and hope to starve it into submission. And if they had completed their works, they would probably have been victorious. The siege is also important for changing the course of the history of the Mediterranean: it broke the power of Athens and signalled the end for its Empire. Without the victory at Syracuse, Sparta may not have been able to emerge victorious from the Peloponnesian War and Athens would have remained a major power well into the fourth century, perhaps even preventing the Macedonian ascendancy over Greece. The extent of the defeat suffered by the Athenians cannot be overstated; it was a catastrophe. They lost a significant proportion of their manpower, and most of the losses were men of prime military age. In fact, it is safe to say that with this humiliation, Athens ceased to be a major force in the Mediterranean. Never again would it achieve the power it had enjoyed prior to 415 BC. Thucydides says of the defeat:

'[I]t seems to me, of all the Greek events which have been recorded, this was for the victors the most magnificent, and for the vanquished the most disastrous. For the defeated, thoroughly beaten in every respect…met with utter destruction, army and navy – all perished, and few out of many came back home (VII. 87. 5-6).'

The Height of Greek Siege Technology

Unlike other periods in the history of siege warfare, the age of the Greeks did not develop the technology gradually. In fact, innovation came about at the behest of one man: Dionysios I, tyrant of Syracuse (405-367 BC), perhaps the most innovative non-Macedonian general ever produced by the ancient Greek world. By the time of his ascension to power in the late fifth century, Carthage and Syracuse had been fighting on and off for well over a century. Neither side had ever been able to inflict a decisive defeat on the other, but Carthage, having greater resources in manpower, often held the upper hand, and Syracuse was periodically forced to endure Punic sieges. Dionysios was determined to break this cycle and it was his lifelong ambition to drive the non-Greek barbarians from Sicily.

The tyrant knew that in order to achieve this, an extraordinary effort was required; Syracuse had defeated Carthage on the battlefield before, but its opponents had always been able to retire to their fortified cities. As these were mostly maritime centres, the contemporary Greek siege method of blockade was useless – Carthage was the leading sea power in the western Mediterranean, and therefore could always keep supply lines open. After signing a peace with Carthage on disadvantageous terms in 405 BC, Dionysios realized that in order to fully defeat Carthage, he had to find a way of taking their fortresses by assault.

To this end, between 399 and 397 BC, he planned a new war with Carthage. His preparation was scrupulous: he hired mercenaries and drilled them along with a new Syracusan force; he formed new alliances across Sicily; and he built a new fleet. In addition, he was responsible for two innovations that would change European warfare forever: he refortified Syracuse and he constructed a siege train.

Dionysios' purpose when refortifying the city was to mimic the advantage that the Carthaginians had always enjoyed by making Syracuse into a formidable fortress to which he could retire if the campaign went wrong. In doing so, he created the greatest set of fortifications the Greek world had ever seen. The great Athenian siege of 415-413 BC had illustrated quite clearly that the key to Syracuse lay with commanding the heights of the Epipolai Plateau; he therefore began his defences by constructing a wall around the Epipolai, a fortification that was nearly 27km (16.7 miles) in length. This featured towers at regular intervals and six fortified gates. One of these, known as the Epipolai Gate and sited at the westernmost part of the walls, was guarded by the most brilliant of these defences, the Euryalos fort. The exact design of Dionyios' Euryalos is unknown, as the structure went through a few substantial renovations, the last of which was conducted by the great engineer and mathematician Archimedes (287–211 BC). In its final form, it represented the epitome of Hellenistic defensive architecture, the likes of which would not be seen again until the castles of medieval Europe. A testament to the strength of the Euryalos fort is that it never fell to an attacker, and was wholly avoided by the Romans in their siege of 213–211 BC. Syracuse went from being a fortified city to a fortress in its own right. As a result, the entire Epipolai Plateau, as well as the Euryalos fort, would have to fall before the city itself would come into danger.

Now that Dionysios had safeguarded his rear, he turned to the offensive. Issuing a call all over the Mediterranean for skilled craftsmen to descend upon Syracuse, he intended to construct the first siege train in the Greek world. By promising them high wages and substantial rewards, Dionysios assembled a team of the finest engineers the ancient world had ever seen. Greeks came from Sicily and Italy as well as mainland Greece; even Carthaginians, the enemies of the Syracusans, answered the call and they too were welcomed. Research, experiments and tests were now conducted all over the city as the craftsmen from vastly different scientific backgrounds combined their knowledge, producing remarkable results.

Out of this synthesis of almost worldwide learning came the first catapults, the *gastraphetes* (literally 'belly-bow') and *oxybeles*. The former was a handheld weapon and is the precursor of the crossbow, while the latter was a larger standing weapon. It also fired bolts and, like the *gastraphetes*, operated on the principle of torsion, whereby wooden arms were bent and drawn backwards for power. The influence of the *oxybeles* in particular was wide-ranging, as it is the ancestor of all the most successful Greek and Roman artillery pieces of the future.

> '*At the storming of a city the first man to scale the wall is awarded a crown of gold....the men who receive these trophies enjoy great prestige in the army and soon afterwards in their homes.*' – POLYBIUS

Dionysios would use these new weapons with devastating effect, as he brought the Carthaginians on Sicily to their knees, and destroyed their capital. Although in the end he was unsuccessful in his quest to drive them fully from the island, his influence was felt long after his death in 367 BC; Syracuse was now the Greek centre for siege technology, as many of the craftsmen who answered Dionysios' call settled within the city. They would go on to further develop their machines and make great strides in artillery technology.

This was the environment that gave birth to Archimedes. This man, while undoubtedly a genius, was not some sort of maverick scientist, but a product of his time and of his environment – a place filled with like-minded scholars who understood his machines, and craftsmen who had the ability to build them. Archimedes represents the culmination of Greek science, and no other ancient had such an understanding and innovative approach to siege warfare. He was able to flourish in Syracuse, for its engineers understood and had the ability to construct his fantastic machines. His designs built upon established traditions in ballistics at Syracuse. In offensive siege technology, he used the invention of torsion to assemble gigantic double-armed stone-throwers, his largest having the ability to shoot balls of 80kg (176lb), a weight heavier than anything that had previously been achieved. His most important contributions to military science, however, lay in defensive technology; he greatly strengthened the Euryalos Fort and improved the defences of Syracuse as a whole. His true genius lay not in his ability to construct huge and fearsome machines but in positioning these artillery to concentrate their fire to maximum effect. He was a master at constructing defensive works that operated hand-in-hand with a large and varied amount of artillery. The machines were expertly placed by himself in order to concentrate masses of fire on specific trouble spots, thus giving the defenders of Syracuse the maximum advantage. He also developed other countersiege machines, including a pulley system with a pivoting head that swung out over a wall to drop boulders onto enemy ships; others had arms that stretched over the wall to drop heavy beams onto attacking huts and rams. More fantastical devices are also attributed to him, including the iron hand that lifted ships out of the water and the geared winch that could lift 100 tonnes with hardly any effort from the operator. (These last two are, of course, devices described by men who could not understand many of Archimedes' machines, and who therefore allowed their imaginations to get the better of them.) After his death, Archimedes took on a godlike status in the ancient world, which means that the figure standing before us today belongs more to myth than to reality. Yet he remains one of the greatest minds that the ancient world ever produced, and on an individual level, his contribution to siege warfare is unmatched. No work on the subject is complete without him.

Archimedes built upon the ideas of his predecessors, those engineers and scientists at Syracuse who gathered together to push forward siege technology. Dionysios' call for scientific innovation was renewed by King Philip II of Macedonia (359–336 BC), conqueror of Greece and father of Alexander the Great. He envisioned a great invasion of the Persian Empire (which was eventually accomplished by his son after his assassination). Philip realized that his plan meant he would first have to contend with the heavily fortified cities of the Anatolian coast, and later the great fortresses inside the Empire. A siege train was therefore necessary: without the ability to take walled cities with celerity, he risked becoming bogged down in blockades, where he could, after a time, be surrounded by superior Persian forces. Accordingly, Philip called engineers from across the Mediterranean to come together in his court at Pella.

This meeting of minds produced new developments in offensive siege techniques, specifically in the realm of artillery. The engineers in Macedonia developed torsion to replace tension as the force propelling catapults. While tension used wooden arms bent backwards like a horizontal bow, torsion used tightly twisted vertical ropes with solid wooden arms placed horizontally in them for greater power and range. Torsion was an innovation that led to the improvement of the *oxybeles* for use against personnel, and that also gave birth to the *lithobolos* ('stone-thrower'), the first artillery piece capable of demolishing walls. This machine came in many different sizes, the largest of which could hurl stones of 4.5kg (10lb) approximately 450m (1674ft). And their accuracy allowed fire to be trained on a small section of wall. If Dionysios invented siege artillery, then Philip perfected it; the former's tension machines started a revolution in military technology that culminated with the torsion engines of the latter. So monumental was this achievement that, although later improvements would be made, the use of torsion would be a feature in all subsequent artillery pieces for over 800 years. Indeed, the design of these machines remained relatively unchanged until the third century AD. The power of the fortified city in Europe was broken.

Alexander used this new technology with devastating effect against the cities of Anatolia, and in particular at the Siege of Tyre in modern Lebanon in 332 BC. After his death nine years later, his generals, known as the Successors, carved his empire up amongst themselves, and kept up a near-constant state of war with one another until they were eventually all absorbed by Rome. The centres of their power were the many fortified cities that dotted the eastern Mediterranean and the Near East. Many of these were much older and more technologically advanced than their counterparts in the west – Carthage, Syracuse and a few other western Greek cities being exceptions – and were heavily fortified with large walls and sophisticated defences. Therefore, it is no coincidence that siege warfare for the Greeks reached its height in this age, from the late-fourth to the second century. Siege warfare advanced more in these 200 years than at any other time in the ancient world. Improvements were made in range and accuracy, and machines became immense. The largest recorded was 6m (17ft) tall and could launch stones weighing 82kg (180lb). The ropes for twisting, once made of horsehair, were now made from sinew for greater strength and durability. The casings for the ropes also grew stronger; earlier machines tended to break at the head after a short while, due to the violent forward motion of the arms, and the head was therefore now encased in iron plates, giving the machines longer lives. A machine also was invented to plait the ropes, twisting them much tighter and thus giving artillery more spring, and hence power. Outside the realm of artillery, another development from the Hellenistic world was the *sambuca*, a large, covered, mobile ladder that afforded protection to the men inside and allowed them the element of surprise, as the machine could be moved quickly. Rams also became more sophisticated; most were now sheltered in large, wooden huts; earlier models tended to be suspended on a chain, while the fourth century saw the increasing use of gears to move the beam

back and forth with fewer men and with greater force. In response to these developments, defences became stronger; walls were made thicker and higher, and ramparts and towers were now made large enough to hold a substantial amount of artillery. Finally, the era gave birth to the first technical treatises on siege warfare, as Aineias Taktikos (The Tactician) composed a treatise called *Poliorketika* (Siegecraft) c. 350 BC; Ktesibios of Alexandria wrote a lost work c. 270 BC on the construction of artillery; Biton's *Construction of War-Machines and Artillery* appeared c. 240 BC; while Philon of Byzantion published his *Belopoeika* (On Making Missiles) c. 200 BC.

Of the many sieges that took place in the Hellenistic world, none are more illustrative about the application of this new technology than the siege of Rhodes (305–304 BC). This was conducted by Demetrios, who was the son of Antigonos I Monophthalmos ('The One Eyed'), one of

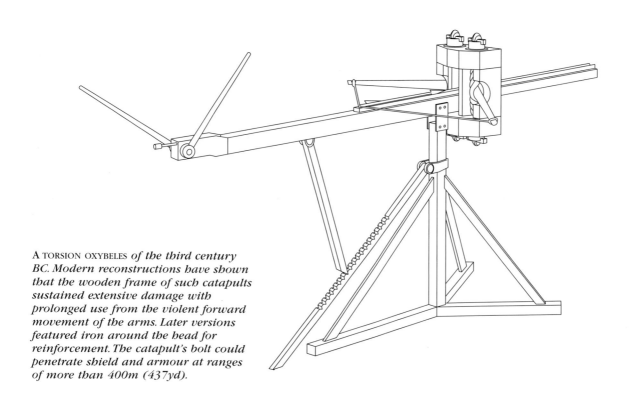

A TORSION OXYBELES *of the third century BC. Modern reconstructions have shown that the wooden frame of such catapults sustained extensive damage with prolonged use from the violent forward movement of the arms. Later versions featured iron around the head for reinforcement. The catapult's bolt could penetrate shield and armour at ranges of more than 400m (437yd).*

Alexander's generals, and afterwards a Successor king. In 305 BC, the father and son were at war with Ptolemy I of Egypt, another of Alexander's Successors. Seeking to strike a major blow in the conflict, Demetrios attacked Rhodes, a Ptolemaic ally and the wealthiest trading state in the eastern Mediterranean. Demetrios, although only 31 years old, was already an accomplished general who had claimed victories on both land and sea. Yet he was best known for his ability to take fortified cities using a large siege train and some massive engines. For this, his contemporaries called him *Poliorketes*, or the 'Besieger'. He now brought the full weight of his reputation down upon Rhodes.

Demetrios first attempted to take the city from the seaward side. He lashed four pairs of cargo vessels together and placed two penthouses and two towers on top of them. He used these to begin a night assault on the harbour under the cover of artillery. The fighting lasted well into the daytime, and Demetrios appeared to have the advantage until the Rhodians managed to destroy one of the towers by fire, thus forcing a withdrawal. Another attack was foiled when the ships holding two more of the towers were sunk by the Rhodian navy. Demetrios abandoned his seaborne efforts, now being forced to assault the city on the landward side. This actually suited him well, for it was his normal tactic, but at Rhodes he was left with little choice. His failure at the harbour had eliminated the possibility that the city could be blockaded and starved into submission, and from this point onwards Rhodes was constantly being resupplied and reinforced by Ptolemy.

Demetrios the Besieger now constructed and attacked with the engine for which he is most famous – the gigantic *helepolis* or 'city-taker'. This was a tower 43m (141ft) high with a base of 430m^2 (4628 sq ft) and was operated by a team of 200 men who turned a capstan that operated 8 wheels. Covered with iron plates to protect against fire, and featuring a large variety of stone-throwers and bolt-shooters, it must have been a terrifying sight to the defenders of Rhodes as it approached the walls of their city. This colossal tower was supported on either side by wooden passages covered in hides. These led to huts where men operated either massive 54m (177ft) rams

that operated on rollers on the huts' floors, or 25m (82ft) long wooden beams with sharpened points, which were used as drill-like mechanisms to knock holes in the enemy walls. The passages also led to penthouses, from where other men filled in the intervening moat and were then able to attempt to sap the walls.

When the attack came, the fighting was intense. The *helepolis* cleared the battlements, while the rams did extensive damage. Eventually a large tower and a stretch of wall were brought down, only for Demetrios to discover that the Rhodians had built an inner wall. The defenders also managed to countermine the walls and fight off all of the sappers. Finally, a timely sortie forced the attackers back. After such heavy fighting, both sides took a respite; Demetrios repaired his engines while the Rhodians constructed a new moat and a third wall behind the destroyed outer wall and the temporary second wall. When he was ready, Demetrios launched a second assault; fighting was again desperate, but he pierced the second wall and at times it looked as though he would overrun a major tower and break into the city. But the resolute defenders held out, though suffering heavy casualties, and he again withdrew.

By now, it was 304 BC and the siege had lasted 15 months. Demetrios decided to put all of his efforts into a combined night attack by land and sea, and floating engines sailed into the harbour once again. His machines managed to pierce the third wall and 1500 hoplites broke into the city. Fighting lasted throughout the night and raged at the harbour, landward walls and even on several streets. However, Rhodians and the Ptolemaic mercenaries serving with them at last managed to force the attacking infantry out of the city and a general retreat ensued. Both sides were exhausted, and Demetrios in particular did not have the strength to mount another assault. Even if he could bring down another stretch of wall, his efforts to take the city could again easily be thwarted by Ptolemy, who was constantly pouring more defenders into Rhodes. He therefore made a truce with the Rhodians and negotiated a peaceful withdrawal for his forces and an end of hostilities between his dynasty and the city. In the end, his mammoth effort came to nothing – though even in

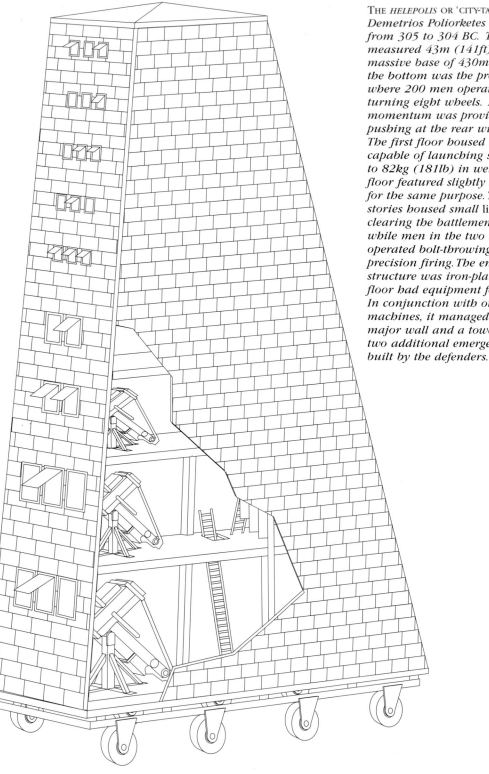

THE *HELEPOLIS* OR 'CITY-TAKER' *used by Demetrios Poliorketes against Rhodes from 305 to 304 BC. The* helepolis *measured 43m (141ft) in height, with a massive base of 430m² (4628 sq ft). On the bottom was the propulsion system, where 200 men operated a capstan turning eight wheels. Additional momentum was provided by men pushing at the rear with large beams. The first floor housed large* lithoboloi, *capable of launching stones perhaps up to 82kg (181lb) in weight. The second floor featured slightly smaller* lithoboloi *for the same purpose. The following stories housed small* lithoboloi *for clearing the battlements of defenders, while men in the two top floors operated bolt-throwing* oxybeleis *for precision firing. The entire outer structure was iron-plated and each floor had equipment for fighting fires. In conjunction with other smaller machines, it managed to bring down a major wall and a tower at Rhodes, plus two additional emergency curtain walls built by the defenders.*

defeat he increased his reputation as a master of siege warfare. He would go on to win some notable successes and even became the king of Macedonia (294–287 BC), but his growing power caused the other Successors to ally against him, and he ended his life as a prisoner-of-war in 283 BC. For their part, the Rhodians destroyed the engines and machines that he had been forced to leave behind, as he had no way of transporting them off the island. They sold all of these for scrap, the iron from the plates of the *helepolis* in particular bringing in a hefty profit. With the money, they erected an enormous bronze statue of the sun-god Helios, known as the Colossus of Rhodes and one of the Seven Wonders of the Ancient World.

The siege of Rhodes represents the high-water mark of Hellenistic siege technology, and never again would such massive engines be used. The Successors continued to fight amongst themselves and several more epic sieges were contested, but their disunity eventually led to their downfall. In the end, it is not the Greeks that show us the true measure of the influence of the Hellenistic scientists and engineers who had advanced weaponry so far, and of the generals like Demetrios who understood how to apply the new technology. Rather, it is the sleeping giant

who lay to the west – Rome. At first ignorant of anything beyond blockade and infantry assault, the Romans gradually learned and improved upon Greek siege tactics, eventually turning this technology against its inventors and conquering the entire Mediterranean.

Early Roman Sieges

In terms of technology, the Romans actually contributed very little to siegecraft. Their early sieges were not sophisticated affairs, as the cities of central and northern Italy to which they were opposed usually did not have very complex defences, and therefore could be taken by infantry assault. All of this changed once they encountered the Greek cities of southern Italy and Sicily in the third century BC. Here, for the first time, they experienced strong Hellenistic defences, which were bolstered by artillery and too large to be taken without the aid of machines.

These did not daunt the Romans, however. Instead it made them strong, for two of the greatest attributes possessed by the Roman Army were imitation and fortification. More than any other army, they borrowed from the ancient world. Nearly every aspect of the Roman military, from their equipment to their tactics, had at some point been copied – and then perfected. The same was true of Hellenistic siegecraft: within less than three decades after their first encounter with a fortified Greek city, the Romans had adopted Greek siege techniques and were using

THE ROMAN WORKS AT ALESIA *showing the inner and outer walls, ditches, moat and rows of other defences used to contain Vercingetorix in Alesia during Caesar's siege of the town in 52 BC.*

Greek artillery and engines. Although they would go on to improve on these, they never altered the basic designs.

It has been said that the Roman Empire was won as much by the spade as it was by the sword, as the Romans were the great fortifiers of the ancient world. Every night, regardless of their position in friendly or hostile territory, the legions constructed fortified camps. This gave them a base of operations from which to direct a campaign, as well as a supply depot and a place to which they could retreat if necessary. The far-reaching conquests of the Romans were made logistically possible by these bastions along supply lines, and some of these camps developed into permanent forts that attracted traders and would later see life as medieval towns and modern cities. One of the greatest examples of these is Manchester, where remains of the permanent Roman fortifications can still be seen.

This technology lent itself well to siege warfare, and the Romans excelled at the art of blockade. The excellent use of blockade by the Romans was underpinned by three factors. Firstly, thanks to the same construction methods as those used when erecting their nightly forts, the legions had the ability to surround completely a besieged city with camps, pickets and ditches. While other armies were content with a blockade that cut off the main gates and roads and then patrolled the perimeter, the Romans made sure to bar all methods of escape with an unbroken line of works. If it looked as though the siege might be disrupted by a relief army, the Romans would construct a second set of works facing outward and maintain their army within the fully protected area between the two sets of fortifications, as at the siege of Alesia in 52 BC.

The second key to Roman success was the fact that they had the logistical capabilities, the manpower resources and the determination to undertake sieges of great length. The Romans were logistical experts and, by the late third century BC, had mastered the techniques necessary for long-distance supply, allowing them to supply an army besieging a city for an unlimited time. This also meant that they could rotate troops at the front. Furthermore, most other military powers from the

ancient world did not have the manpower to attempt lengthy sieges, as they risked being surrounded by superior forces that their enemy could build up over time. The Romans, utilizing manpower resources from all over Italy, could field several armies at once, and therefore protect their forces conducting a siege. It was rare that one of their sieges was threatened with disruption from the outside, forcing them to use works that faced outwards as well as inwards. This, combined with Roman determination and ambition, gave them the power to conduct a siege for as long as it took – up to 10 years. (They sat in front of Lilybaion on Sicily from 250 to 241 BC.)

The final factor involved with Roman success at siege warfare was control of the sea. The fame of their legions has overshadowed the fact that the Romans were actually a great naval power from the mid-third century BC onwards. Their control of the Mediterranean and skilled use of ships let them supply their troops over great distances, giving them the ability to blockade ports and thus completely shut off besieged cities from resupply. The siege works that surrounded a city on land would have been useless without the ability to also block off sea-lanes if the besieged city had a harbour. Control of the sea allowed the Romans to surround cities completely and cut off all methods of resupply and escape. These three factors – landward fortification techniques, logistical resources, and control of the sea – combined with the adoption of Greek artillery and engines for assault made the Roman army a veritable juggernaut in terms of siege warfare.

Perhaps the greatest illustration of Roman blockading technology and their ability and determination to press on until victorious is the Julius Caesar's siege of Alesia in Gaul in 52 BC. Over a period of six years, Caesar (100–44 BC) had conquered nearly all of Gaul, and in the process had won several battles, bridged the Rhine (55 BC), twice invaded Britain (55 and 54 BC), and succeeded in creating the most experienced and battle-hardened army in the Roman world. Its soldiers were all fiercely loyal to their commander, for his ability to lead them to victory seemed to know no bounds. The Gauls, for their part, did resist, and outnumbered the Romans by a large margin, but they were too divided and disorganized to mount any concerted resistance, and Caesar defeated them, one by one. Only in 52 BC did they rally together under the leadership of Vercingetorix, the chieftain of the Arverni of southern Gaul (modern Auvergne); he led the Gauls in a full-scale rebellion that threatened to undo all of Caesar's conquests and expel the Romans from Gaul. The war against Vercingetorix consisted of three sieges. At Avaricum in central Gaul, Caesar used Greek assault techniques, constructing a large siege ramp upon which he pushed two towers up close to the enemy wall. These were supported by a wide range of artillery at the ramp's base. After some intense fighting, Caesar made a successful attack upon the battlements during a downpour, and the fortress fell. The survivors fled 160km (99 miles) south to Gergovia. Here, Caesar built siege works outside the town, but was forced to divide his forces to deal with a revolt elsewhere in Gaul. The legionaries in front of Gergovia maintained their position, but were unable to win an advantage. When Caesar returned, an attempt on a fortified plateau went wrong and the Romans suffered heavy losses. Seeing that Gergovia would not fall to assault, and afraid of having to split his forces in two again, he abandoned the siege.

This reverse caused Caesar's oldest Gallic allies to defect to Vercingetorix's cause. Nearly all of Gaul was now in revolt and all of Caesar's conquests of the previous six years were under threat. After a small battle with the Romans, Vercingetorix retired to the fortified town of Alesia, hoping to repeat the success of Gergovia. Alesia was situated on a plateau near the Brenne River in central Gaul. Seeing the height and fortifications of the town, however, Caesar would not risk an assault and opted for a blockade. Because this meant spreading out his army thinly around the town in order to fully surround it, he

> *'[We must attack] the walls and bodies of the enemy, which they will yield to bravery, to the sword, to despair....this very day must decide for us either a complete victory or... death'* – MARK ANTONY

constructed one of the greatest set of siege works for which we have record. It was an intricate web of forts, towers and pickets that would eventually completely seal off Alesia and stretch for a total of 28km (17.4 miles).

The Romans began by erecting 7 camps and 23 forts around Alesia; they then dug a trench to the west of the plateau in order to protect the workers behind, who dug two other trenches that surrounded the town. These were both 5m (16.4ft) wide, and the inner one was filled with water. The earth from these trenches was then used to construct a rampart, upon which they placed a wooden palisade with towers every 25m (82ft). In front of these works were placed rows of traps, all having names that indicate the black humour with which soldiers often look at their profession. There were five rows of sharpened stakes woven together so that they could not be uprooted, which were called *cippi* ('tombstones'); then several rows of V-shaped pits that concealed fire-hardened stakes, referred to as *lilia* (lilies); and in front of these were 30cm (11in) stakes embedded diagonally in the ground with iron barbs protruding from the top, known as *stimuli* ('stingers'). During the construction of these works, the Gallic cavalry, useless to the defenders, attempted to break out of the encirclement, and were successful on the second attempt after sustaining heavy losses. Fearing that these men would raise a relief army, Caesar now constructed a similar set of siege works facing outwards, with forts and 200m (656ft) of space – to facilitate large troop movements to trouble spots – in between the two sets of works.

To preserve food, Vercingetorix either allowed or forced the women and children of Alesia to leave, but Caesar would not take them in, both because he wanted to tax the enemy food supply and to keep from burdening his own. These women and children were forced to camp in the

Alesia

52 BC

The entire Roman conquest of Gaul hinged on the success of the siege of Alesia. Seeing the town's fortifications, however, Caesar decided to blockade it, encircling the fortress with a series of palisades, towers, trenches and booby traps. The Gallic cavalry broke out of the encirclement, and fearing a relief army, Caesar now constructed a similar set of defences facing out, with forts between the two sets of works. The women and children of Alesia, forced out of the town to save food, had to camp in the open between the lines. The first sorties from Alesia failed, as did the first attempts of a massive relief army that arrived to break the siege. Finally, the relief army and the defenders coordinated their attack. Fighting was savage, and the Romans teetered on the brink of collapse, but Caesar's timely use of his German cavalry, combined with the discipline of the legions, eventually won the day. The garrison surrendered, and most of the survivors were either executed or sold into slavery.

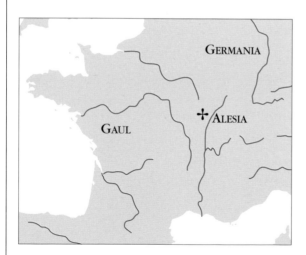

The town of Alesia is now called Alise-Ste.-Reine, on Mount Auxois, near the source of the Seine river. It was in Central Gaul, a province that Caesar himself had added to Rome's empire.

5. A large relief army of about 240,000 men arrives, and makes three serious attempts to lift the siege of the town.

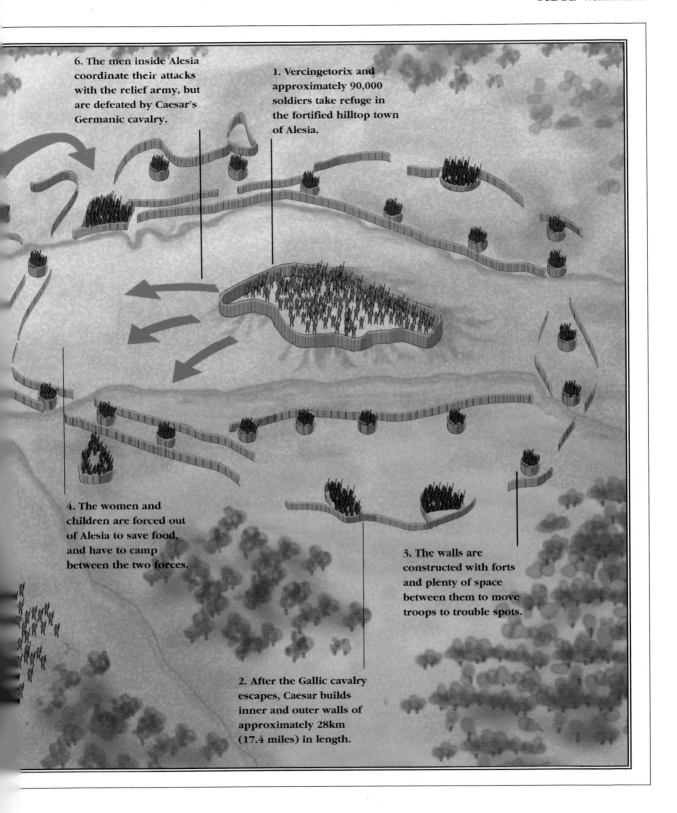

6. The men inside Alesia coordinate their attacks with the relief army, but are defeated by Caesar's Germanic cavalry.

1. Vercingetorix and approximately 90,000 soldiers take refuge in the fortified hilltop town of Alesia.

4. The women and children are forced out of Alesia to save food, and have to camp between the two forces.

3. The walls are constructed with forts and plenty of space between them to move troops to trouble spots.

2. After the Gallic cavalry escapes, Caesar builds inner and outer walls of approximately 28km (17.4 miles) in length.

open between the lines. Caesar's foresight in building the outer works proved fruitful for, in the third month of the siege, a massive Gallic relief army did arrive. It staged an attack that was combined with a sortie by the forces in Alesia. The issue lay in the balance for some time before Caesar unleashed the German cavalry, which he had hidden beyond the siege works. They drove off the relief army with heavy losses, while the Romans forced Vercingetorix back into Alesia. Two nights later, the Gauls again sortied; although Caesar comments that casualties on both sides were at times caused by friendly fire, the attack was again repulsed. Finally, the Gauls sought one supreme push, and at high noon on the following day, they attacked from both within and without. Fighting was intense, and in several places the Romans were on the verge of collapse, but each time Caesar's skilful redeployment of reserve troops to trouble spots held the lines. In one particular action, he personally led a contingent to a hard-pressed area, and the sight of his uplifted scarlet cloak as he charged forth on horseback rallied the troops and caused a counter-attack. At last he threw in his German cavalry, who again drove back the relief army,

ROMAN LEGIONARIES *and auxiliaries construct defensive works, in a scene from Trajan's column in Rome. The troops shown here represent what soldiers would have looked like at Masada in AD 73–74.*

giving him more men with which to repulse the Gallic sortie.

The relief army now dispersed. Vercingetorix, seeing that the situation was hopeless, surrendered. The conquests of Caesar in Gaul were restored and the enemy's back was broken. After some mopping-up operations in 51 BC, Gaul would remain a province of the Roman Empire for more than five centuries. What happened to Caesar afterwards needs little retelling; he crossed the Rubicon River into Italy to begin a civil war against Pompey that he eventually won. After subduing the rest of the Roman world, he made himself dictator for life before being assassinated on the Ides of March, 44 BC. Vercingetorix was imprisoned in Rome for six years so that he could eventually be paraded at Caesar's triumphal procession before being ritualistically strangled. What is unknown, however, is the suffering and loss of life that was inflicted upon Gaul in the seven-year Roman conquest. Caesar's writings rarely speak of losses and enslavements in specific terms, and give us little impression of the genocide he inflicted upon the Gauls, the relative scale of which compares with the mass loss of life that accompanied the Mongol campaigns in the Middle East and the European conquest of the Americas.

Nevertheless, there is no finer illustration of Roman blockading technology than the siege of Alesia. Wherever possible, the Romans combined these techniques with the use of Greek artillery and engines to undertake a siege by both blockade and assault. The thoroughness of their siegecraft and their determination to see sieges through to their conclusion, regardless of the length of time involved, made the Roman war machine a near-unstoppable force.

Roman Sieges by Assault

As mentioned previously, the Romans did not significantly alter Greek artillery designs until the late Empire, although modifications and improvements were made. The *ballista* was a new version of the stone-throwing *lithobolos* that featured improved accuracy and range by using a reconstructed head and tighter springs. The *scorpio* was the Roman version of the bolt-shooting *oxybeles*; it was reduced in size so that it

was lighter and more mobile, yet at the same time it could fire larger bolts, and its metal reinforced head and concavely curved arms gave it greater power. It was a popular machine with precise accuracy and enough power to kill two enemies with one shot. These second- and first-century BC modifications by the Romans led to the innovation of the *cheiroballistra* in the first century AD. Although maintaining Greek designs and principles, this was revolutionary in its construction. The head was now almost entirely made of metal, with the spring encased in bronze cylinders, protecting them from the elements and from enemy fire. The wooden arms of older machines were now replaced with metal versions for increased power, and the accuracy of the *cheiroballistra* is demonstrated by the addition of a sight-arch on the head.

The Romans applied these machines to both attack and defence – with devastating force. These innovations in the field of military science, combined with their efficient use of blockading, goes a great way towards explaining the success of their military and the survival of their empire for a millennium in the west, and for two millennia in the east. The combined use of blockade, assault and Roman determination which meant that no fortress was unassailable is perhaps nowhere better demonstrated than at the Siege of Masada in Israel from AD 73 to 74.

Masada was the final action in the Jewish Revolt of AD 66–74; it was seized by a quick raid early on in the revolt, and its small Roman garrison was massacred. The revolt itself was a vicious and bloody conflict for both sides, as the Jews sought to free themselves from Roman rule. It was effectively crushed with the fall of Jerusalem in 70, but several pockets of resistance remained for the next four years. By November of 73, only the 1000-strong garrison of Masada remained. This was a small but nonetheless imposing fortress situated on top of a plateau 457m (1499ft) high, whose walls straddled jagged cliffs and featured only two gates. All paths of ascent were treacherous and completely exposed to defensive fire. The defenders were well-equipped with artillery, and there were large storehouses and cisterns dug into the rock,

Masada

AD 73-74

Masada was the last outpost of the Jewish Revolt. Situated on a plateau 457m (1499ft) high, it was nearly impregnable. The fortress was well supplied and watered, but the region around it is barren and desolate, so the besiegers' food and water had to be transported a considerable distance. The Romans at first tried to starve the 1000-strong Jewish garrison into surrender, building eight camps around the hill and linking them with a wall and towers. However, they then built a wooden and earthen siege ramp leading up to the western wall, and placed a metal-plated tower at the top. Siege artillery then cleared the defenders from the ramparts while a ram went to work. Although this breached the wall, the defenders had thrown-up an emergency rampart behind the original. Fighting at this point was savage, but at last the Romans gained the upper hand. As they prepared for the final assault, the Jews chose suicide over surrender, and only two women and five children, all in hiding, survived.

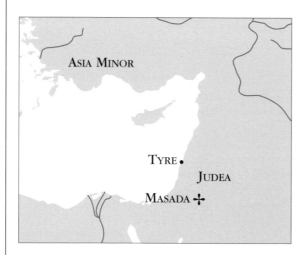

Masada was originally fortified by King Herod of Judea, of Biblical fame. Its small Roman garrison had been overpowered at the beginning of the revolt, but it stood alone by the end of AD 73.

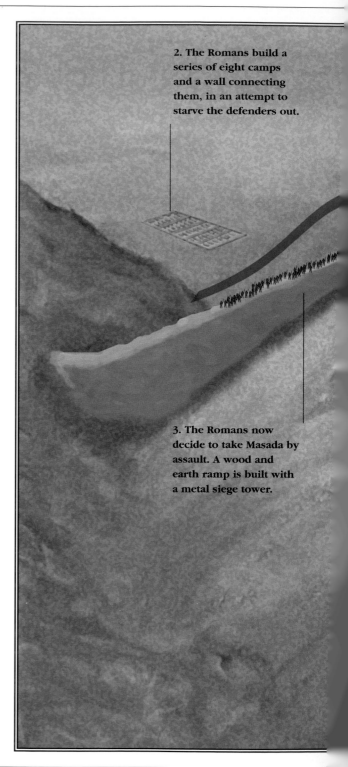

2. The Romans build a series of eight camps and a wall connecting them, in an attempt to starve the defenders out.

3. The Romans now decide to take Masada by assault. A wood and earth ramp is built with a metal siege tower.

4. While Roman artillery keeps the defenders' heads down, the ram destroys part of the western wall.

1. This fortress had been captured by the Jews in AD 66. Its location and fortifications made it seem impregnable.

5. The defenders build an inner wall, but that too is breached. In despair, all but a handful commit suicide.

THE *BALLISTA*. *In the third century BC, the Romans began adopting Greek siege warfare technology; although they kept the basic designs, by the first century BC they had made several improvements to the older Greek models. The* ballista *was a new version of the stone-throwing* lithobolos. *The frame and base were now sturdier, the holes through which the rope was inserted and the washers by which it was secured went from being square in earlier models, to an oval shape. This allowed more rope to be used in the springs and these were also twisted tighter. The springs were now exclusively made of sinew, much stronger than the old horse-hair versions. All of this gave the machine much greater range and accuracy.*

meaning that the garrison could hold out for years if necessary. Built by the Jewish King Herod (40–4 BC) between 36 and 30 BC, the heights of Masada look unassailable even to the modern observer, but the Romans would not be deterred.

The Romans first attempted to starve the Jews into submission through a blockade. They built eight camps and then joined these together by a wall with intervening towers 75–90m (246–295ft) apart. The area around Masada, arid and desolate, was devoid of timber, so the Romans were forced to use stone for these constructions. This gave the camps and walls a more permanent nature and has left impressions on the landscape to the present day, giving us vital archaeological clues about Roman military buildings. When these works were completed, they formed an unbroken line of 3.5km (2.1 miles) across some precipitous territory – another feat of Roman engineering.

Even completely surrounded, however, the Jews in Masada would not capitulate; they were still well provisioned and in a highly defensible position. The Romans determined therefore to undertake the momentous task of assault. The only incline that sloped enough to facilitate an attack was a chalk ridge on the west side of the fortress, known as the White Spur. Here the Romans began construction of an *agger*, or siege ramp. They were forced to import timber, which they placed in cross sections, filling in the gaps with rubble. All the while, this work was under attack from those inside Masada, and fire was returned from Roman bolt-shooters and heavy- and light- stone-throwers in an artillery duel that lasted several months. When it was finished, the agger was 617m (2024ft) long and reached a height of 206m (676ft) at a steep incline. It was a massive siege ramp, even by Roman standards. At its base was placed a tower that was

30m (98ft) high and iron-plated against fire. It featured a large battering ram on the ground floor and *ballistae* and *scorpiones* on the upper stories.

In April of 74, all was at last ready. Under heavy fire, the Romans pushed the tower up the agger to the base of the enemy wall, where the ram went to work, with the tower's artillery keeping the battlements clear. It was not long before the wall was breached, but the Romans found that the Jews had erected a temporary rampart of earth and timber. Against this, the Romans launched an attack with incendiary missiles, and managed to set it alight. A westerly wind nearly set the Roman tower on fire as well, as its iron plates were not designed to resist such masses of flame, but a timely change in wind direction set the rampart completely ablaze and a major breach had opened by nightfall on 14 April.

The next morning, the Romans assaulted the wall with their infantry. Upon bursting into the fortress, found that the inhabitants had committed mass suicide. In a speech made during the night, the leader of the defenders, Eleazar, had exhorted his people to take their own lives rather than surrender to the Romans. The legionaries who took the fortress found two women and five children in hiding; they had managed to escape the slaughter and related their tale of the garrison and its suicide to the Romans.

Though neither a large siege nor one of great significance for the Romans, Masada is nevertheless important as an example of Roman military technology and logistics at their best. Not only did they have to import timber from a great distance to the siege, but the barren nature of the land around Masada also meant that food

THE *CHEIROBALLISTRA*, *which first appeared in the first century AD. This bolt-shooting weapon had a sturdier frame, but the greatest innovation was that its head was now constructed almost completely from metal. The springs were encased in bronze cylinders to protect them against weather and enemy fire, which gave the machine a longer life. The cylinders allowed for increased twist in the springs and this, combined with the innovation of metal arms, further increased the power of the* cheiroballistra. *It was a supremely accurate piece of artillery, and was aimed by the use of a sight-arch in between the two springs.*

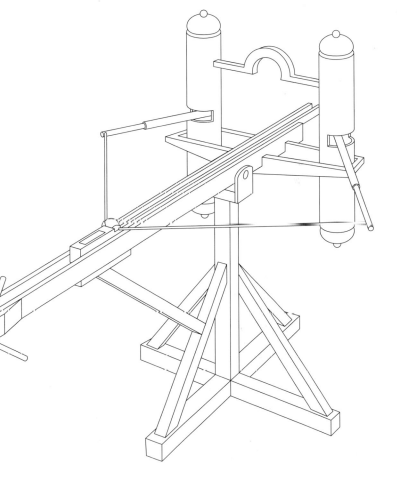

and water had to be brought in constantly. Although these logistics were the supporting cast to the main event at Masada, the siege would not have been possible without them, and it was a triumph of not just the legions, but also of the Roman commissariat.

The feat accomplished at Masada cannot be overstated: this was the high-water mark of Roman siegecraft. After painstakingly constructing a blockade that completely surrounded the fortress with stone walls, they constructed one of their largest ever siege ramps up a sharp ascent. When this was completed, they cleared the battlements with artillery of every size and assaulted with

ferocity. By the first century AD, the Roman siege techniques were the culmination and combination of all that had come before them. Their ability in engineering, science and technology, combined with the traditional diligence and tenacity of the Roman army – who accomplished all of this under the blazing sun, wearing plate armour – made the legions of Rome the greatest besiegers in the ancient world.

Perhaps the greatest influence of those events at Masada is the archaeological legacy that they have bequeathed to us. Excavations at the site have taught us a great deal about Roman camps and siege techniques, and the Jewish fortifications and structures inside. Scrolls, clothes, money, mosaics and *ballistae* ammunition have also been found. However, the greatest remnant of the siege is the only surviving Roman *agger* in existence, which can still be seen on the western slope of the plateau. The dry climate around the site has

A TYPICAL LEGIONARY CAMP. *Between AD 73 and 74, the Romans constructed eight of these camps, connected by a wall with intervening towers, around the fortress of Masada. Several Roman camps around the empire eventually developed into permanent settlements in their own right.*

IMPERIAL ROMAN GATEHOUSES. *By the second century AD, defensive works took on a much more permanent nature, with cut stone preferred to earth or wood. Above is a gatehouse from modern Germany, while right is a fort from Hadrian's Wall.*

even preserved some of the wood of the original frame. This ramp, over 1900 years old, is a most lasting and fitting testament to the Roman ability in siege warfare.

The Siege of Dura Europos

The Romans not only excelled at offensive siege warfare but were also skilled in the art of fortification. Urban defences remained largely unchanged, as the Romans did not improve upon earlier Greek designs, but they did make several advances in military architecture, utilizing finely cut stone, baked brick and concrete. Many of their legionary fortresses became permanent structures and attracted traders and settlers outside of the walls, eventually becoming medieval towns. They also constructed great walls across long expanses in some of the world's first man-made borders. Hadrian's Wall in northern England and Scotland is the greatest and most

famous example of this. At these forts and walls, the Romans were also particularly adroit with the building of fortified gates. Previously, ancient techniques had used overlapping and circuitous walls, but Roman gates now featured multiple levels, with eyelets and windows for artillery and heavy portcullises, wooden doors and drawbridges. These would be of influence to the later medieval gatehouses in some of Europe's greatest castles.

These fortifications served the Roman Empire well when it began its decline in the third century. The defences managed to keep invading tribes at bay for nearly two centuries before the empire in the west finally crumbled. During this period, Roman abilities in siegecraft also diminished, largely because internal problems within the empire led to a decline in the number of skilled artificers and engineers who could build and maintain siege equipment, and also pass on their knowledge to the next generation. Roman blockading techniques were now not as efficient, and technology became simpler and less effective. This meant a decrease in the number of double-armed torsion catapults in use and the rise of single-armed devices such as the *onager* or 'wild ass' (its name deriving from the machine's recoil, similar to the kick of an ass). This catapult was easier to construct and could throw stones of a similar weight to the largest double-armed *ballistae*, but it was not nearly as accurate. The days of double-armed torsion technology were, in western Europe at least, rapidly coming to an end, and the practice would disappear in the middle of the first millennium AD.

Although the Romans lost some of their skill in sieges, some of their enemies, particularly those in the Near East, learned much from previous Roman techniques. By the third century, the Sasanid Persians had distinguished themselves by the skilled use of offensive siege techniques, almost all of which they had learned from the Romans. At Dura Europos in modern Syria in AD 256 and 257, the Persians illustrated to the Romans that they now knew well the latter's siege techniques, and that the students were now the masters.

Almost nothing is known about the siege of Dura Europos, and most of the events must be pieced together from archaeological evidence.

Dura Europos was a small city on the Euphrates River that was founded in c. 300 BC by Alexander the Great's general and one of the Successor kings, Seleukos I. It was protected by cliffs in several places and the sophisticated Macedonian walls made it a highly defendable position. Seleukos named it after Europos, his birthplace in Macedonia. To the locals, however, it was known simply as Dura, or 'the Fort', and the two names eventually became one. It was an important way station on the road between Seleukos' two capitals, Antioch and Seleukia. The Parthian seizure of lands east of the Euphrates, including Seleukia in the mid-fourth century, saw the importance of Dura Europos decline, although it still remained a vibrant trading centre. It was

THE *ONAGER* OR 'WILD ASS'. *Large single-arm catapults first appeared in the second century BC, but become popular only in the third century AD as skill levels declined. It could launch stones of 80kg (176lb) from its basket made of hemp; it was mounted on an earthen or brick base in an effort to control its great recoil. It was operated by a crew of 8.*

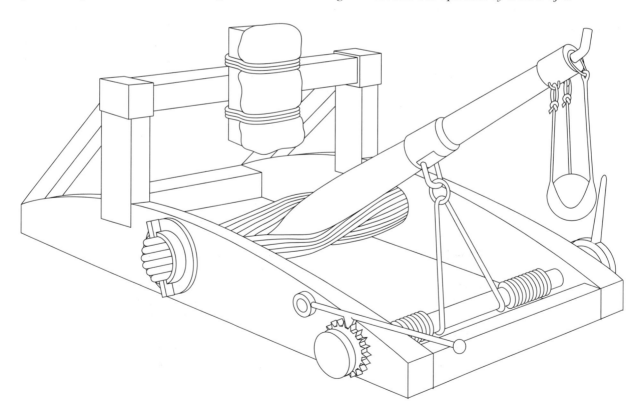

taken by Parthia c. 100 BC and, from this point forward, would serve as a border town, first guarding the western frontier of the Parthian Empire and then, after its capture by Rome in AD 165, as an outpost on the Roman western frontier.

Because of its position, Dura Europos was always going to be the target of attack when powers on either side of the border came to blows. In AD 256, the new power in the Near East, the Sasanid Persians, invaded Roman territory under the leadership of their emperor Shapur, and Dura was, of course, one of the first places to come under attack.

The siege of Dura Europos warrants only a couple of brief mentions in the literature of the period. Whether Shapur first tried blockade or assault is unknown, but at some point he began the construction of a mine with the purpose of weakening the foundations of one of the towers in the northeastern part of the city and causing a breach. When all was ready, the Sasanids fired the mine, but the tower did not fall, only buckling in the middle. A countermine from the city then intercepted the Sasanid mine and a battle appears to have taken place underground. The mine collapsed and buried 18 soldiers underneath the tower. This has come to be known as Tower 19 by modern archaeologists, and it is one of the most significant finds for our knowledge of the Sasanid and late Roman armies. The men, perhaps already dead when the mine caved in, were buried with full armour and weapons; this has contributed greatly to our knowledge of the Sasanid and late Roman eastern armies. Found on or amongst the skeletons were remnants of swords, a spear or javelin, axes, coats of mail, helmets, shield bosses, coinage (which dates the siege), and large pieces of a rectangular Roman shield (our finest example of such a piece of Roman equipment).

Various explanations and reconstructions have been put forward about what happened in the mine and the countermine, and about why the countermine was at some point sealed off at both ends. Such postulations are, however, mere speculation, and rather than mislead readers by recounting a narrative for which there is no evidence, it seems better to relate the few facts we have and then to suggest hypotheses based on the available data.

New Offensive

In late 256 or early 257, the Sasanid Persians began a new offensive on the opposite side of the city. They dug two more mines; one appears to have had the same purpose as the original mine that failed at Tower 19. The new mine went underneath Tower 14, and this time it was successfully fired. The Romans, however, seem to have forecast the enemy's intentions and buttressed the tower with earth and mud brick; this saved part of the structure, but archaeological evidence clearly shows that the burning did significant damage to the defences. The second mine appears to have had the purpose of introducing soldiers into the city: there is no other way to account for its size – 3m (10ft) wide and nearly 1.75m (5.7ft) high – and the fact that it snaked its way deep into the city. Our knowledge of ancient and medieval siege mines makes it clear they were difficult and time-consuming to construct and therefore would only be made spacious if they were meant to act as tunnels for masses of infantry. A skeleton at the mine's end underneath the city either speaks of a battle or an accident; it is not known whether the mine was finished and soldiers used it to invade the city, or whether it was abandoned because of a collapse.

Along with the two mines underneath the southwest wall, the Persians also attacked that area by constructing an earthen siege ramp near Tower 15. The second mine went partially underneath this ramp, which might lead to the conclusion that they were constructed in tandem, the mound of earth muffling the sound of the digging. Support for this hypothesis is the fact that this is the only mine of the three that provoked no reaction from the defenders, meaning that it was probably undetected. The ramp was certainly a major factor in the siege; in front of the ramp the Romans raised the height of their battlements by constructing a mud brick wall on top of them. The ramp was successfully completed, however, although the fact that it did not possess a levelled thoroughfare suggests that it could not have sustained a tower, and was probably used simply for an infantry assault.

Dura Europos

AD 256-257

The Sasanid Persians laid siege to the Roman outpost at Dura Europos, and began construction of a mine to cause a breach in the walls. The mine was fired so as bring down the tower, but this was unsuccessful, as the structure only sagged. The mine was then intercepted by a Roman countermine, and it appears that a battle took place underground. At some point, the mine caved in. The Sasanids then began construction of two new mines; one was successfully fired and brought down a significant portion of a tower, while another went under the city walls and allowed the attackers access to the city. This was combined with an assault from a Persian siege ramp that led up to the wall nearby. The combination of the breach in the wall caused by the collapsed tower, the assault from the mine under the walls, and the assault via the siege ramp appears to have been successful. Dura Europos was then sacked by the Sasanids, and shortly afterwards abandoned.

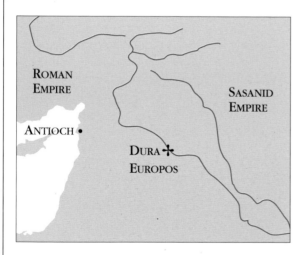

Dura Europos was a small city on the Euphrates River founded in c. 300 BC by a Successor king, Seleukos I. It was protected by cliffs in several places and was a highly defensible position.

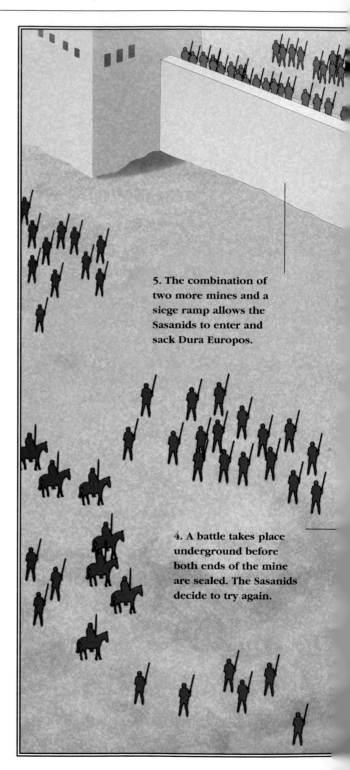

5. The combination of two more mines and a siege ramp allows the Sasanids to enter and sack Dura Europos.

4. A battle takes place underground before both ends of the mine are sealed. The Sasanids decide to try again.

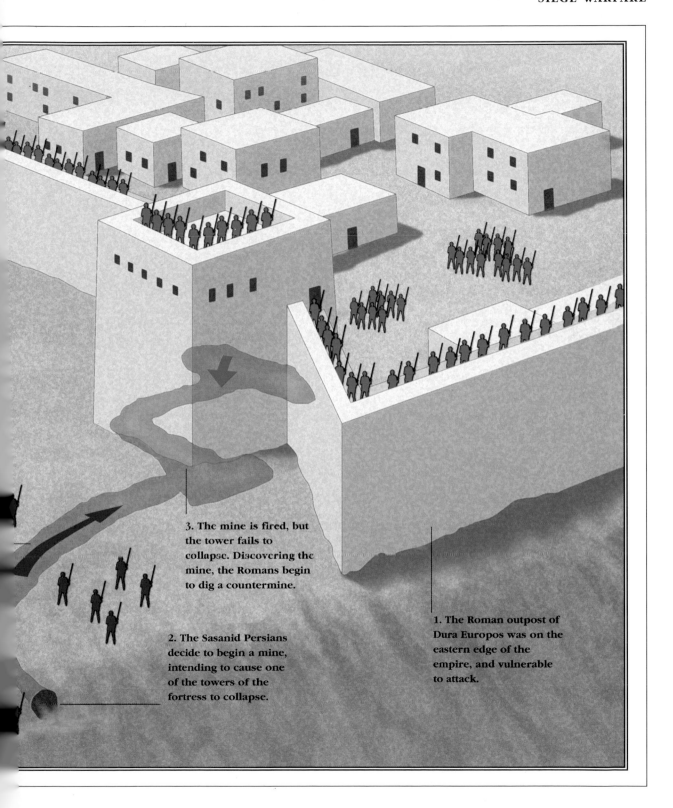

3. The mine is fired, but the tower fails to collapse. Discovering the mine, the Romans begin to dig a countermine.

2. The Sasanid Persians decide to begin a mine, intending to cause one of the towers of the fortress to collapse.

1. The Roman outpost of Dura Europos was on the eastern edge of the empire, and vulnerable to attack.

The combination of the firing of the first mine and damage caused to Tower 14, the second mine underneath the city, and the siege mound appear to have carried the day, as there is no other evidence of action at other parts of the city. Although we will never know for certain the circumstances behind the city's fall, the fact remains that Dura Europos, after a long fight until the siege's end (probably in 257), was captured by Shapur. The city was sacked and disappears from the historical record; archaeology tells us that shortly after the siege, it was abandoned. Shapur would go on to lead a successful campaign against the Romans, winning much territory and even capturing the emperor Valerian in 261. Afterwards, however, he was beaten back by the independent Roman kingdom of Palmyra, so that by AD 266 all of his conquests were lost.

The siege at Dura Europos is of more note for the wealth of knowledge it has given us than for its significance to Roman history. It was neither a decisive nor relatively important engagement, but merely the first small action in a large ten-year war. But to modern archaeologists, it is a treasure trove; it has added substantially to our knowledge of Sasanid and late Roman arms and armour, and siege and countersiege techniques. It also illustrates that the Persians now had the ability to capture fortified cities, and provides us with our only examples of ancient siege mines. These mines alone make it of immeasurable value to the student of ancient siege warfare, giving us an understanding of digging and support methods, and also providing us with a clearer picture of just how mines were used during siege operations, and how they could be combined with other forms of attack.

Conclusion

In this chapter, I have related a history of siege warfare from its earliest documented use until the end of antiquity in the western Mediterranean. This has been described both through analysis of historical developments and scientific innovations, and through examples of important sieges in the history and archaeology of siege warfare. The sieges included were chosen by a combination of how well they are evidenced, their historical importance, their importance to modern archaeology, and most of all for their power to illustrate the siege techniques in use in any given period. Lachish is a well-sourced siege because of the relief of Sennacherib in the British Museum, while at the same time it is our greatest example of Assyrian siege technology at work. Syracuse is indicative of the fact that much siege technology had not yet reached the Greek world in the fifth century BC, and even blockading was still in its infancy and little understood. More importantly, Syracuse is perhaps the most famous siege in the ancient world, thanks to the writings of Thucydides. More than any other siege in this chapter, it changed world history, preventing Athens from expanding into the western Mediterranean and signalling the beginning of the end for its empire. Without the Syracusan victory in this siege, the destinies of Carthage, Macedonia and perhaps even Rome would have been substantially altered.

Rhodes gives us our best example of just how far Greek siege warfare had progressed in a century, and is a tribute to the Greek engineering and science that constructed the *helepolis* and made use of torsion weapons. The siege was an epic struggle of machines against fortifications, and never again would engines so large be used to assault a city. Alesia is one of several good examples of the meticulous nature of Roman blockading techniques, but more than other sieges it is well-sourced through the writings of Caesar and was decisive in undermining Gallic resolve. Masada was relatively unimportant to the

> *'There is sound sense in the ancient practice of sounding trumpet blasts ... and raising a battle cry from all throats [which serves] both to terrify the enemy and to heighten the ardour of one's own men'* - CAESAR

history of the Romans, though it has always been symbolic for the people of Israel. The Jewish Revolt of which it was a part was largely over, and with no one to come to their aid, the fall of Masada was a *fait accompli*. It is a fine example of the combined use of blockade and assault, and remains as a testament to Roman determination. The only surviving example of a Roman siege mound also gives the siege great value to modern scholars. By comparison, Dura Europos seems the poor cousin to the previous five sieges described within this chapter, as we know next to nothing about it. We are ignorant of fierce battles, heroic struggles and epic last stands, but over time the stones of Dura have spoken loudly, and have unearthed treasures that make this site unique for the entire ancient world. Its mines in particular give it immense value to the archaeologist and ancient historian. Dura Europos also represents how, at the dawn of the Middle Ages, the peoples of the east were the new masters of siege warfare, having learned from the methods of the Romans before them. Siege warfare had come full circle: it was the peoples of the Near East who turned it into a science in the eighth century BC; it was improved by the Greeks, and then perfected by the Romans. By the third century AD, it had returned to the easterners. And mastery of the art would remain in their hands until the rediscovery and reimportation of Greek and Roman fortification and siege techniques to Europe by the crusaders of the Middle Ages.

The Influence of Ancient Siege Warfare

In the east under the Byzantines, the attack and defence of walled cities continued much as before. The Byzantines of the fifth century were not as skilled as their predecessors had been 300 years earlier, but military science and engineering was still used to a degree that was lost in the west. The Germanic tribes that conquered the west had very little siege technology, and the art went into serious decline. Some technology, specifically double-armed torsion, was lost forever, though simpler and less powerful double-armed tension artillery did have a renaissance. Only when the crusaders ventured to the Holy Land in the eleventh century was some technology reimported. Gradually, the medieval Europeans of the west began to use mobile towers, more sophisticated rams and single-armed torsion catapults. These never matched the skill of the ancients. That said, the twelfth century saw the invention of the trebuchet, a machine that hurled stones forward by means of a counterweight. Though lacking the accuracy of ancient machines, it surpassed them in destructive force.

The true legacy of ancient siege warfare in medieval Europe was in the realm of fortification. Many of the defences that characterized the medieval period were introduced in late antiquity. The rise of the Sasanids in the east, Germanic invasions from the north, and chronic civil war led to a strengthening of fortifications across the Roman Empire from the third century onwards. Some cities, particularly in the west, became walled for the first time, while others reinforced their defences and often concentrated in as small an area as possible, in order to maximize the number of defenders. Thus cities had sometimes become physically smaller by the dawn of the Middle Ages. Smaller settlements were now established, outside the safety of fortified hilltops. As Imperial authority declined, people of the countryside tended increasingly to look to local aristocrats for protection. The latter fortified their villas and these eventually evolved into the medieval castle. To bolster these defences, late antiquity also saw the greater use of moats, drawbridges, portcullises and fortified gates – all features that would remain common in medieval defences.

Defensive architecture in western Europe would greatly improve once the crusaders imported Arab, and reimported Roman, fortification techniques from the east. This brought about the introduction of gatehouses and the use of double- and triple-walls. It is fitting that the place of most influence upon the western Europeans was a Greek city built and fortified by the Romans: Constantinople. Its defences, crowned by monumental triple walls constructed by Emperor Theodosius II in the fifth century, were copied in urban centres across medieval Europe, and remained unmatched and unbroken for a thousand years.

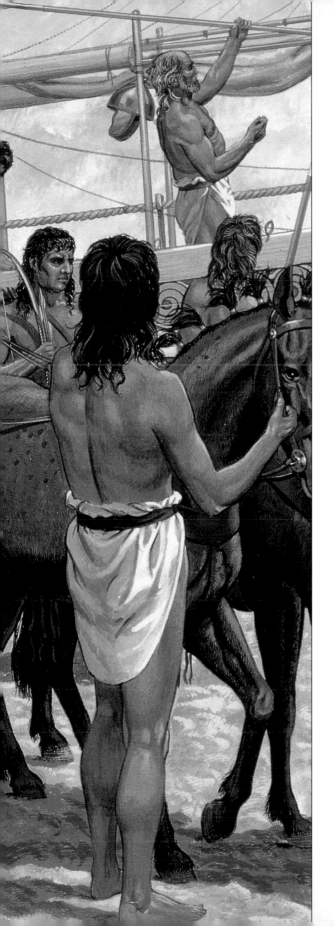

CHAPTER 5

NAVAL WARFARE

Control of the sea was much desired in the ancient world, for whoever had it could reinforce or resupply their troops at will, and move quickly to their objective.

Naval warfare in the ancient Mediterranean world was a necessary corollary of warfare on land. Thanks to the relative ease of travel by sea, amphibious operations were common from an early age. The earliest attested was around 2450 BC, when the Egyptians used ships to transport troops to Palestine. In the most famous war of antiquity, the Trojan War, the abduction of Helen led to the launching of 'a thousand ships' to win her back. Over time, ships developed to the point where engagements of ship against ship were possible, and eventually naval warfare grew to a massive scale. War at sea was, in many ways, different from war on land in the ancient world: there was a much higher dependence

MYCENAEAN WARRIORS *pull their ships ashore and prepare for battle in the fifteenth century BC. As seafaring became more common and shipbuilding skills became more advanced, ships began to be built for combat. They were unstable platforms balanced by the oars of their rowers.*

on technology (most notably the ships themselves) and a level of training and cooperation was necessary that rivalled the training of the finest Roman legion. At the same time, however, war at sea was much more uncertain. Fragile ships, dependent in battle on human muscles, were very subject to the vagaries of weather. For even limited safety from storms, the naval fighting season was restricted to between April and November. Beyond all this, the coordination of tactics between hundreds of individual vessels taxed the skill, intelligence and often diplomacy of even the greatest commander. Despite the enormous challenges involved, naval warfare was often denounced as 'unheroic' by aristocrats; the Greek philosopher Plato even claimed that the great Greek naval victory at Salamis made the Greeks worse as a people. Certainly there was little room for individual prowess in naval warfare; worse yet, the oarsmen were recruited from among the poorer citizens, those who could not afford heavy infantry equipment. It was the development of Athens' fleet that made her the most radical democracy of the ancient world.

Legend makes King Minos of Crete the first ruler to create a navy, in the Bronze Age of around 2000 BC. He is supposed to have used it above all to patrol the sea against pirates, and also to have conquered and colonized the Aegean islands, creating a thalassocracy ('rule of/by the sea'). The Greek historian Thucydides' report of Crete's great navy may be pure myth, although a fresco excavated at Thera in the early 1970s does indeed show Cretan ships – long, narrow and propelled by oars – that seem to have been intended for war. The first clearly attested use of ships for war was by the Egyptians, at first to transport troops to war in Palestine. By the late Bronze Age, Egyptian ships were also capable of engaging in combat with other ships, as in 1190 BC when Pharaoh Rameses III defeated a large-scale attack by the mysterious and formidable fighters known to history as the 'Sea Peoples'. A well-preserved wall relief at Medinet Habu commemorates this victory, and illustrates well early naval fighting techniques. Rameses' fleet (we have no way of knowing the size of the opposing forces) clearly surprised the invading fleet as it lay at anchor in the mouth of the Nile; on the relief the Sea Peoples' ships do not have oars ready, and their sails are brailed up. The Egyptian ships advanced under oar and, as the range closed, marines on deck hurled arrows and javelins at the enemy. Once side by side, Egyptian deck crews armed with swords and shields boarded some ships. They also threw grapnels up into the rigging of the enemy vessels, and apparently succeeded in overturning some of the ships by then backing water, which suggests how lightweight, unstable and top-heavy these ancient galleys were.

Egyptian Limitations

Although Rameses III won a great victory against the Sea Peoples, his navy was really not suited to

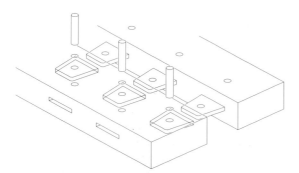

FIXING PLANKS TOGETHER *to make the hull was a difficult task. Slots were cut in the side of the plank in which a piece of wood would be inserted. A wooden rod would hold the piece in place.*

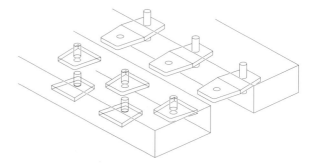

THE NEXT PLANK *was then added, with its own slots and holes already drilled. This system was surprisingly waterproof, and only a minimal amount of caulking was needed.*

Mediterranean conditions. Egyptian sea ships were essentially oversized boats of the sort that had been used on the Nile River for hundreds of years. They had no keel and only a few light ribs. Instead, the planks were pinned to each other, not to an internal skeleton. This made a ship unlikely to stand up to even a moderate Mediterranean storm. The Egyptian ships were also not strong enough to carry a ram, which would later become the most important weapon of a Mediterranean warship. As a result, the ships depicted at Medinet Habu were essentially fighting platforms for marines. The rowers, protected from missiles with sidescreens, were only there to bring the ship close enough to the enemy to fight (Egyptian warships also had sails, but no ancient ship under sail was able to manoeuvre close enough for short-range weapons, so sails were never used in battle), and then to join in the hand-to-hand fighting themselves if necessary.

By the time Rameses III won his victory over the Sea Peoples, though, the peoples of the eastern Mediterranean had developed a true warship suitable for the open sea. As early as the fourteenth century BC, piracy by individuals and whole states had become common as a form of warfare or gain. Fleets of pirates blockaded ports and preyed on commerce, besides raiding lands near the sea for slaves and other goods. The Phoenician cities of Beirut, Tyre and Sidon, all prosperous ports with a strong city government able to invest considerable sums in warfare, responded by building their own fleets. These consisted of oared fighting ships, manned by 20–100 rowers. The basic characteristics of these ships can be seen from a wreck excavated off Ulu Burun in 1982. This ship, either Mycenaean or Phoenician, was thoroughly seaworthy. Unlike northern ships, the planking did not overlap. Instead, the planks of the shell were joined with mortise-and-tenon joints – like cabinetry – with a dowel inserted into each joint. Then a complete

framework was inserted into the shell, making a ship much more seaworthy than those depicted on the Medinet Habu relief. Hulls built in this way needed little caulking to waterproof them, although it was customary throughout the ancient period for shipbuilders to smear the seams or the whole hull with pitch or a pitch-and-wax mixture. Many ships of all sizes also had a sheathing of thin lead plates below the water-line.

They were built for speed, from a lightweight material (preferably fir) and with no room to spare, they were more like racing shells than modern naval craft. The only storage space was under the rowers' benches. These ships had both a square sail and oars. The mast could be unstepped and lowered into a crutch aft when it was not in use; when the rowers were not needed, they had no place to sit except at their benches. These characteristics were standard in the warships used throughout the ancient world. It is because of this crowding and lack of storage area, not because of inability to navigate, that ancient warships almost always hugged the land, beaching at night and sometimes even for a noon meal. A ship going into action rarely carried more than a day's supply of food and water. Indeed, captains who anticipated battle normally left the mast and sails on shore: the space was simply too cramped for the deck crew otherwise, besides there was a substantial fire hazard posed by the rigging and sails if the enemy threw fire pots (containers of burning pitch).

For centuries the *pentecontor*, the 'fifty-man' ship with a single bank of oars, was the standard Mediterranean warship. This vessel was very long and slender, expensive to build, hard to manoeuvre and not very seaworthy, especially when using the great technological innovation of ninth-century naval warfare, the ram. The ram, a heavy beam sheathed in bronze and attached to the keel under the water-line, first appears in art in about 850 BC.

> *'As for those who had assembled before them on the sea...They were dragged, overturned and laid low upon the beach; slain and made heaps from stern to bow of their galleys'* – RAMESES III

Battle of Salamis

480 BC

Xerxes had his Egyptian squadron block the Megara channel, while two squadrons blocked either side of Psyttáleia and one patrolled the southern coast. The Corinthian squadron of 50 *triremes* simulated flight, hoisting their sails and running north. The Athenian and Peloponnesian squadrons followed suit. The entire Persian fleet was sent into the strait to attack, believing they were pursuing a demoralized foe. But there were too many Persian vessels to manoeuvre in the constricted space, and the channels on either side of Psyttáleia were so full of ships that no organized withdrawal was possible. The Persians were then attacked, first by the Greek right wing which had been lurking in a side passage, and then by the main fleet. Xerxes' sailors fought hard, but the Phoenician squadron finally broke and fled, leaving a gap for the Athenian *triremes* to break through the line and allowing them to attack another Persian squadron in the flank and rear. The battle ended in a Persian rout. The Greeks lost 40 ships, while 200 Persian vessels were destroyed and many others captured.

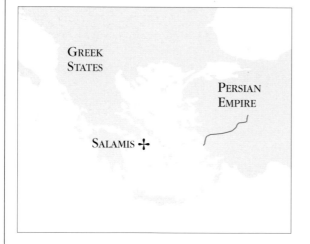

The Persian empire had been expanding westwards for some time, and the Greek states were an obvious, rich target. If they had lost at Salamis, the states would have been overrun.

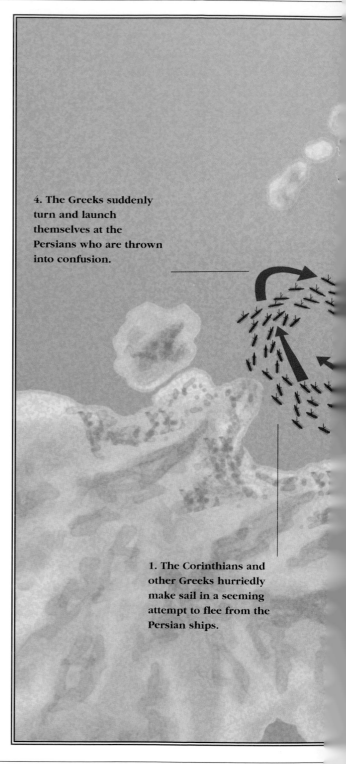

4. The Greeks suddenly turn and launch themselves at the Persians who are thrown into confusion.

1. The Corinthians and other Greeks hurriedly make sail in a seeming attempt to flee from the Persian ships.

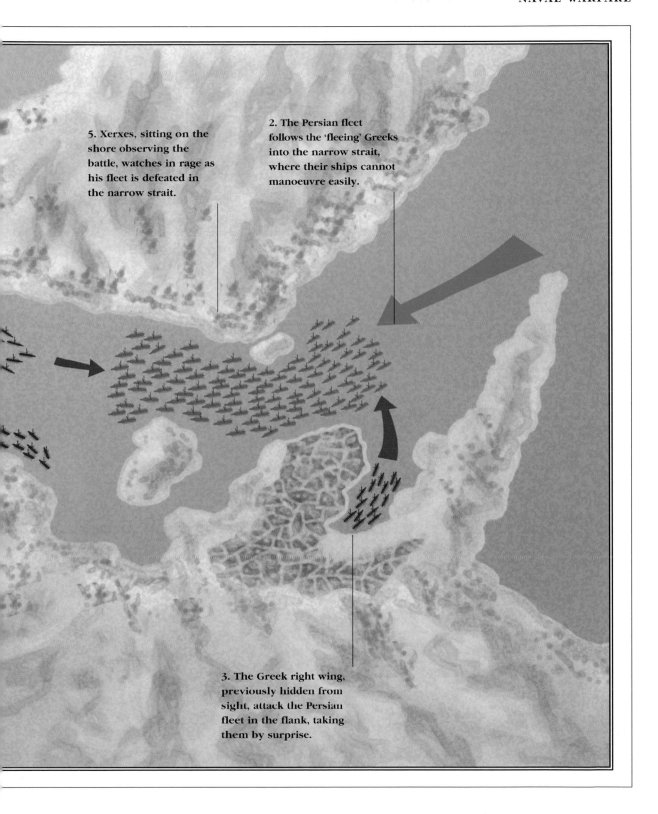

5. Xerxes, sitting on the shore observing the battle, watches in rage as his fleet is defeated in the narrow strait.

2. The Persian fleet follows the 'fleeing' Greeks into the narrow strait, where their ships cannot manoeuvre easily.

3. The Greek right wing, previously hidden from sight, attack the Persian fleet in the flank, taking them by surprise.

It seems to have been a Greek invention. With the addition of the ram, the ship itself became an instrument of war, rather than just transport or a platform for warriors. A well-trained crew could rapidly bring their ship about to ram the relatively unprotected stern or side of an enemy vessel, then back water to let water in, swamping the enemy craft: unballasted lightweight fighting ships were actually too buoyant to sink. A clever crew could even hope to shear off the enemy's oars with their vessel, passing close beside the opposing ship and pulling in their own oars at the last second. Their victims would be left unable to manoeuvre.

Rams in Battle

The first recorded battle won by ships using rams was in 535 BC, but they must have seen service well before that time. In this battle, the Phocaeans (inhabitants of a Greek city-state who had resettled in Italy) met a combined Carthaginian–Etruscan fleet twice the size of their own off the coast of Sardinia. The Phocaeans won the day, thanks to a very high level of training that enabled the whole fleet to penetrate through the enemy line, then swivel and ram the sterns of enemy ships. This manoeuvre – the *diekplous* or 'breakthrough' – is one of the two main naval manoeuvres made possible with the ram. The other, the *periplous* ('sailing around'), was easier, running ships around the enemy's flank to take his line from the rear.

Use of a ram puts a premium on speed sufficient to penetrate an enemy hull while

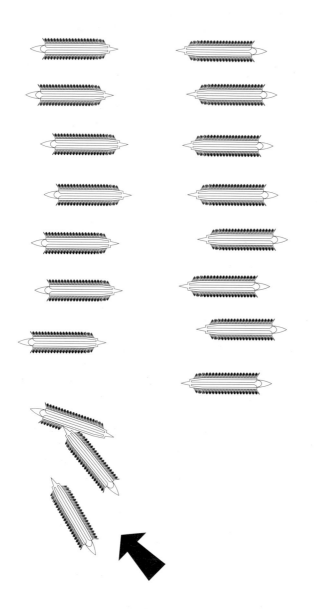

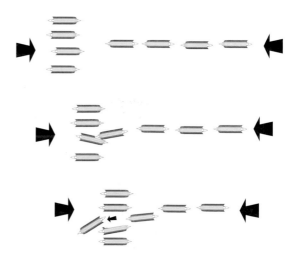

THE *PERIPLOUS* (*above*) *was a classic manoeuvre involving one fleet outflanking the other and the excess ships ramming the enemy ships in the flank. Simple and effective, it could decide the outcome of a battle very quickly.*

THE *DIEKPLOUS was used by a more mobile fleet to break up the enemy and defeat him on a ship-by-ship basis, using their superior manoeuvring skills. The fleet on the left charge at their opponent's line, disrupting them and leaving them open to ramming.*

avoiding the enemy's own rams. But how to increase speed? The only source of power available during battles was human muscles. An ambitious ruler could not simply increase muscle power by increasing the length of his ships to contain more oarsmen. The *pentecontor* was already disproportionately long and correspondingly unseaworthy. So already in the eighth century BC, there was experimentation with adding a second level of oars, creating a *bireme*, a two-level vessel in which two oars could operate in the same length of ship. The oldest picture of a *bireme* is an Assyrian relief from Sennacherib's palace in Nineveh, dating to 701 BC. The new ships were at least one-third shorter and more compact and sturdier than single-banked galleys, while having the same amount of muscle power available to move them in the water. From the *bireme* it was a short step to the *trireme*, a three-banked ship rowed with one man to an oar, seated in three ranks: in the hull, at the deck level and on an outrigger that projected from the gunwales over the water. The *trireme*, with 170 rowers propelling it at speeds of up to 10 knots for short periods, became the dominant battle ship of the ancient world. The *Olympias*, a very impressive replica *trireme* built in 1987, has demonstrated the great manoeuvrability and power of these vessels. The replica is seaworthy under both sail and oar, and can travel for hours at 4 knots, with half the crew rowing at a time. It can execute a 180-degree turn in one minute, with a turning arc no wider than two and a half ship lengths. Clearly this was a ship to be feared.

Little use was made of this innovative technology for a long time, however. The problem was cost. It is very expensive to build and outfit a *trireme*; even more expensive was paying the wages of the rowers. The oarsmen required months of intensive training to be able to work as a team. Contrary to popular fiction, these rowers were almost never slaves, both because the oarsmen might be required to fight and because it was simply too expensive to buy and maintain slaves for occasional naval use. Instead the crews of warships were recruited from among the poorer citizens, who were unable to afford the heavy equipment required for infantry fighting or the time away from their regular work, unless they received wages. Between the cost of the ships and the cost of the rowers, only a developed state with strong economic organization could maintain a fleet. In the Mediterranean, political structures which had sufficiently developed to support a navy did not exist anywhere except Egypt and Syria before about 500 BC.

Then came the Persians, rising to military dominance in the Near East with alarming speed in the mid-sixth century. Persia began as a land power, but had to create a Mediterranean fleet to invade Egypt: an invading army could only use the desert coast road if it could be supplied by sea, with a fleet to protect transports from the large Egyptian fleet. The new Persian fleet, consisting of state-of-the-art *triremes*, relied mainly on the Phoenician cities that had been conquered by the Persians to supply expertise and oarsmen, the Persians themselves usually supplying the marines. This new Persian fleet had its first real test in 494 BC when the Persians defeated the fleet of Ionian rebels who had tried to declare their independence. This battle, near Lade, was the first time in Mediterranean history when a sea battle was a decisive turning point. By 490 BC, the Persian king Darius I had a fleet of 600 ships to transport and supply his troops for the landing at Marathon, many more vessels than the fleets of all the Greek city-states combined.

Despite their defeat at Marathon, it was clear to the Greeks that the Persians would return. The Greeks had little hope of stopping them without a fleet. When Darius's son Xerxes renewed the attack in 480 BC, that a Greek allied fleet was able

'His majesty [Thutmose I] sailed down-river, with all countries in his grasp, that wretched Nubian Troglodyte being hanged head downward at the [prow] of the [barge] of his majesty' – AHMOSE

229

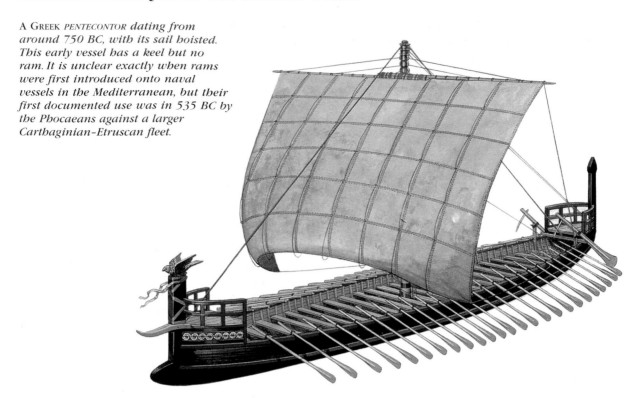

A GREEK PENTECONTOR dating from around 750 BC, with its sail hoisted. This early vessel has a keel but no ram. It is unclear exactly when rams were first introduced onto naval vessels in the Mediterranean, but their first documented use was in 535 BC by the Phocaeans against a larger Carthaginian-Etruscan fleet.

to confront him was due to the vision of the Athenian statesman Themistocles. Themistocles had a long-term goal: to quadruple the number of *triremes* in Athenian service to 200 ships or more. He worked on public opinion, arranging the political ruin of aristocratic rivals who put their faith in hoplite infantry. Themistocles must have been a magnificent orator, well able to play on the fears of his fellow citizens. And he was assisted by luck. In 484/3 BC a very rich silver vein was discovered at the state-owned Laurion silver mine. The profits from the first year of exploitation amounted to 100 *talents* – about 2.45 tonnes (2.5 tons) of pure silver. The conservatives wanted a public distribution of this new wealth, 10 *drachmas* to each adult citizen. Themistocles and his supporters, however, convinced the assembly to commit the profits to building Athens a fleet of *triremes*. In all, about 200 *triremes* were produced in a massive building campaign. The ships were put to sea so swiftly that the wood cannot have been properly seasoned; indeed, the sources

report that the new ships were heavy and slow when they were pressed into action. But they were needed in a hurry, and were Athens' best hope of survival. Indeed, as the Delphic oracle proclaimed when the Persian invading force had already entered northern Greece in 480: 'the wooden wall only shall not fail, but help you and your children ...' It was yet another mark of Themistocles' genius that he managed to convince the Athenians that what the oracle was referring to was the fleet. Certainly the mobilization of the new fleet used all available manpower, including the dregs of the city, foreign residents and perhaps even conscripted slaves. The Athenians thus provided a majority of the fleet of 300–400 *triremes* that the Greek allied states put to sea to stop the Persian invasion. The Athenians wanted Themistocles to command the allied fleet, but in face of violent opposition by the Peloponnesians, waived their claim. Themistocles, however, is generally regarded as the mastermind behind the Greek victory.

Xerxes had made careful plans for a massive land and sea invasion of Greece, including the digging of a canal through the Athos peninsula, so his fleet could avoid the dangerous storms in that region. A massive fleet was assembled. There were 600–800 Persian *triremes* at the first naval battle of the campaign, at Artemisium, and at least 600 more ships were used to construct two bridges over the Dardanelles for the passage of the Persian Army, not to count the ships used for a first bridge, which was destroyed by a storm. As the squadrons of the fleet arrived in Greece, the ships were beached and dried. Thus the Greeks were not only outnumbered and uncertain when the attack would come, but had ships that were heavier and slower than those of the Persians. However, the Persian ships were top-heavy, since each vessel included 30 additional Persian marines besides the normal crew of each ship. These large numbers must have proved a serious inconvenience; *triremes* normally carried 10 marines and 3 or 4 archers. *Triremes* were so lightly constructed that even the movement of a single person on deck could affect the rowing. Marines were trained to throw javelins sitting or even lying on deck, to minimize any such movement.

After a first battle against the Persians at Artemisium, which ended in a draw (thanks largely to heavy Persian losses in two storms), the allied Greek fleet withdrew south to the isle of Salamis off the coast of Attica to help with the now necessary evacuation of Athens. The fleet that assembled at Salamis was larger than at Artemisium, with more cities represented: probably about 310 ships in all. Nearly two-thirds of them were Athenian. Most of the cities involved wanted to withdraw the fleet to the Isthmus, and some city squadrons fled when they saw Athens burning in the distance, victim of the Persian land army. In the end, the Athenian commanders had to threaten to withdraw completely before the Peloponnesians would agree to stay at Salamis and fight. The allied fleet stationed itself between the island of Salamis and the mainland, a passage about 1.6km (1 mile) wide and a little over 4.8km (3 miles) long. The Persian fleet still outnumbered the allies by at least two to one, especially as the Persians had been reinforced by defecting Greeks from central Greece, and Persian troops controlled most of the shoreline. The Greeks' only chance of success against a fleet that at the smallest estimate had over 700 *triremes* was to entice the Persians into narrow waters where the Persians could deploy only part of their fleet at a time.

According to the historian Herodotus, Themistocles sent a message to Xerxes, declaring his willingness to defect to Persia and warning that the Greek fleet was getting ready to make a

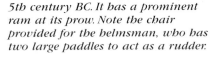

A Greek Bireme *dating from the 4th to 5th century BC. It has a prominent ram at its prow. Note the chair provided for the helmsman, who has two large paddles to act as a rudder.*

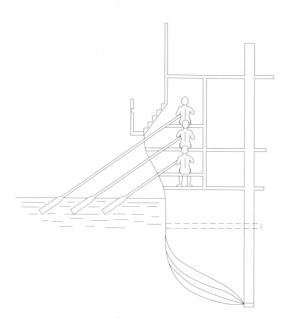

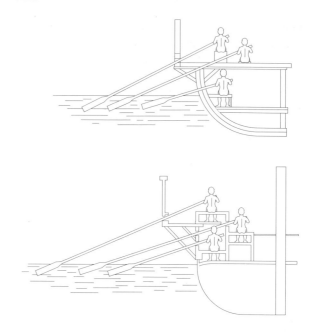

ROWERS IN A *TRIREME* *sat vertically, with progressively longer oars. This method had the disadvantage of making a ship very tall to accomodate the rowers, increasing its instability at sea.*

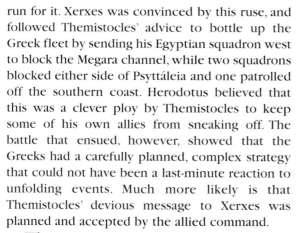

ALTERNATIVE SEATING ARRANGEMENTS *staggering the rowers resulted in much lower, wider and therefore more stable, ships. In the top example, the bottom rower is partially below the waterline.*

run for it. Xerxes was convinced by this ruse, and followed Themistocles' advice to bottle up the Greek fleet by sending his Egyptian squadron west to block the Megara channel, while two squadrons blocked either side of Psyttáleia and one patrolled off the southern coast. Herodotus believed that this was a clever ploy by Themistocles to keep some of his own allies from sneaking off. The battle that ensued, however, showed that the Greeks had a carefully planned, complex strategy that could not have been a last-minute reaction to unfolding events. Much more likely is that Themistocles' devious message to Xerxes was planned and accepted by the allied command.

What came next was a simulated flight by the Corinthian squadron of 50 *triremes*. They hoisted their sails – normally these would have been left on land before a battle – and ran north. This ploy was apparently so effective that even some Greeks misunderstood it as real flight. The Athenian and Peloponnesian squadrons followed the Corinthians and took up a new line, redeploying to three in line abreast (a difficult manoeuvre). Xerxes, who had established his high command on

a hill nearby (known as 'Xerxes' throne'), could see the Greeks fleeing in seeming disorder, apparently about to run into the trap of his own blockading squadrons. So the entire Persian fleet was sent into the strait to attack, believing they were pursuing a demoralized foe. But there were too many of them to manoeuvre in the constricted space. The Persian vessels jammed up the channels on either side of Psyttáleia so that no organized withdrawal was possible. Once they were well into the strait they were attacked, first by the Greek right wing which had been lurking in a side passage, and then by the main fleet.

Two elements caused additional disorder for Xerxes' fleet at Salamis. First, the Phoenician admiral Ariabignes who was in charge of the largest squadron was killed at the beginning of the battle. There was no clear second-in-command appointed to assume control, so no coordinated response to the Greeks' unexpected tactics was possible. Second, the allied fleet at Salamis had knowledge of local weather conditions. They attacked at exactly the right time, when a rising swell made many of the Persians' more top-heavy ships pitch, disrupting their rowing stroke and even turning their vessels sideways so they presented their broadsides to the Greeks in an invitation to ram.

Against these handicaps, Xerxes' sailors fought their best, but the Phoenician squadron finally broke and fled, leaving a gap for the Athenian *triremes* to break through the line and allowing them to attack another Persian squadron on the flank and rear. The battle ended in a Persian rout. The Greek allies lost 40 ships, while 200 Persian vessels were destroyed and many others captured. Persian losses were especially heavy since few Persians, the bulk of the marines in Xerxes' fleet, could swim, while most Greeks in the water managed to get ashore on Salamis.

Disaster for Persia

After Salamis, the Persian fleet could no longer fight. Many of Xerxes' surviving ships were disabled, and morale was very low, especially since the angry Xerxes had some Phoenician captains executed immediately after the battle. The king took the marines from the ships and put them into army units, and then on the night 21/22 September, the remnants of the fleet sailed for the Hellespont to guard the route of the Persian army's retreat. For the victory at Salamis meant that the invasion of Greece had been effectively stopped. The land army depended heavily on the sea for provisions, and it was too dangerous to use transport ships without the navy to protect them. The loss of the fleet also meant that the Persians could not outflank the Greek forces defending the Isthmus of Corinth. In the following year, the allied Greek navy defeated what remained of the Persian fleet off Mycale on the south-east coast of Asia Minor. The Persians were never again a great sea power. Furthermore, Athens had suddenly risen to prominence as Greece's great naval force.

In the fifth century the Greek states continued to develop extensive navies, Sparta offering serious competition to the Athenian navy by the later stages of the Peloponnesian war (431–404 BC). Athens, however, continued to lead the way in manoeuvring capability. It was only when the Athenians committed serious strategic blunders that their fleets could be overwhelmed. Thus, in the Sicilian expedition of 415, two Athenian fleets – more than 200 ships in all – were trapped in the harbour of Syracuse, where their superior skill could not be put to good use. In addition, the Syracusans reinforced their own *triremes* with extra timbers

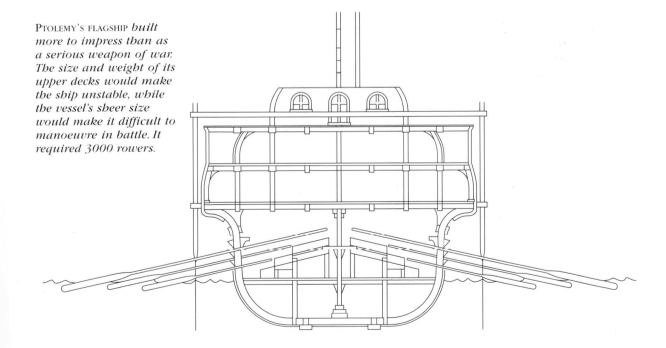

PTOLEMY'S FLAGSHIP *built more to impress than as a serious weapon of war. The size and weight of its upper decks would make the ship unstable, while the vessel's sheer size would make it difficult to manoeuvre in battle. It required 3000 rowers.*

on the bows and catheads. In the narrow waters where the Athenians had to attack prow to prow, the lighter Athenian ships were at a severe disadvantage. In the end, not a single one of those ships escaped that military débâcle. The other great Athenian naval defeat of the Peloponnesian war, the battle of Aegospotomi, shows even more clearly the limitations of *trireme* fighting. In September 405, the entire Athenian navy of 180 vessels (built from scratch after Syracuse) was sent to the Dardanelles to protect the grain fleet. The entire force was drawn up on a bare beach; after all, *triremes* could carry hardly any supplies and could not cruise for any length of time. Since no settlement was near, the crews had to walk 3.2km (2 miles) to buy food at a market. While the ships were mostly abandoned, the Spartan king Lysander swooped in, seizing 171 ships. Only nine escaped to tell Athens of the disaster. Without a fleet to protect her, Athens soon fell to a Spartan siege.

The navy did not play an important role in the conquests of Alexander the Great, although he equipped a fleet to explore the Indian Ocean and, at the time of his death, was beginning to build another for a planned invasion of North Africa. On the Mediterranean, Alexander – who could not trust the fleet of his unwilling ally Athens – dealt with Persian sea threats by marching down the eastern coast of the sea and taking all the Persian ports, an enterprise that required two major battles and the long siege of Tyre. Nonetheless, it was necessary to protect his communication lines to Greece. The generals who carved up Alexander's empire after his death, however, soon turned to the sea, especially in a series of wars between the Antigonids of Syria and the Ptolemies of Egypt.

These Hellenistic successor states soon began what was effectively a naval arms race. They commissioned ships that were bigger and bigger, especially after the introduction of small shipboard catapults in the fourth century, which required a heavier ship to sustain their weight. The addition of longer-range missiles, along with ever-increasing numbers of marines, soon undermined the importance of the ram. Instead, what became popular among prestige-seeking Hellenistic kings were *polyremes*, ships that increased the rowing power of a *trireme* by adding more oarsmen per oar. The greatest extreme reached was a '40', a ship with 40 rowers in each bay of the ship, with

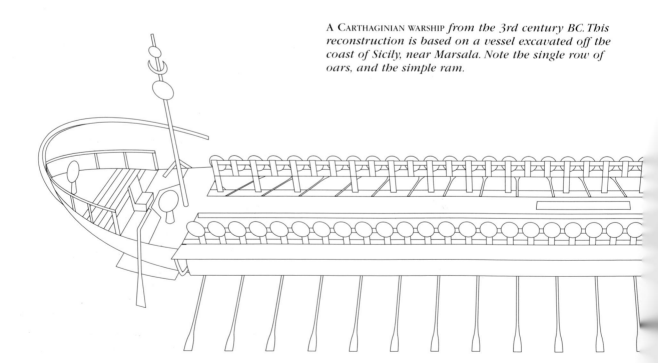

A CARTHAGINIAN WARSHIP *from the 3rd century BC. This reconstruction is based on a vessel excavated off the coast of Sicily, near Marsala. Note the single row of oars, and the simple ram.*

probably up to 5 men per oar, the oars in up to 3 ranks. This was a monster ship more than 122m (400ft) long that was probably never used in battle, but showed off the power of Ptolemy IV of Egypt (221–203) very impressively.

The most effective of these 'big ships' were *quinqueremes*, or 'fives', commonly used by Carthage, the rising power of the western Mediterranean. Carthage, which formed a great mercantile empire based on North Africa, was the unquestioned master of the western Mediterranean. The city's double harbour held more than 200 warships, probably usually manned by citizens, unlike the mercenaries the Carthaginians usually employed for infantry fighting. It was a formidable force, as the Romans soon discovered in the First Punic War (264–241).

The Threat from Carthage

The First Punic War was the longest continuous war in Greco-Roman history, and naval encounters played a central role, including the battle of Ecnomus (256) which probably involved more people than any other sea battle in history. This is the more surprising because at the start of the war Rome had no fleet to speak of. In the late fourth century the Roman senate had dabbled with the idea, equipping two small squadrons to try to deal with pirates on the Tyrrhenian Sea. Their failure was so ignominious that the Romans scrapped the idea, instead requisitioning ships from their subject allies, the Greeks of southern

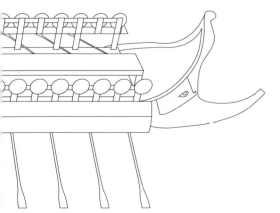

Italy, to guard the sea-lanes. When the war with Carthage began, the Roman legions had to be ferried over to the fighting in Sicily by allies. In fact, the Romans failed to cross the Straits of Messina by day, because a Carthaginian squadron was patrolling the area. The Carthaginian force took a number of ships, but returned the ships and prisoners to the Roman commander, perhaps trying to convince Rome that it was useless to attack Carthage with its strong fleet. The Carthaginian emissary is supposed to have boasted that they would not even allow the Romans to bathe their hands in the sea.

Finally the Roman Army crossed to Sicily by night, and gradually won to a dominant position against the Carthaginian Army in Sicily. But it was impossible to win a complete victory without a fleet. Not only were the Carthaginian-held cities of western Sicily able to re-provision by sea, but by 261, the Carthaginian fleet was trying to distract Roman energies by raiding in Italy.

So in early spring of 260 the Roman senate voted to build a fleet of 100 *quinqueremes* and 20 *triremes*, to be ready in time for the summer campaign. The ships were produced in 60 days in an impressive display of Roman organization. The model for the *quinqueremes* was a Carthaginian ship that had run aground four years before; probably not because the southern Italian Greeks had no *quinqueremes*, but because the Roman policy-makers preferred the Carthaginian design. The Roman authorities raised crews for the *triremes* from their Greek allies, but Rome itself supplied 30,000 men to row the *quinqueremes*, 300 to a ship, from among its Italian subject allies and the poorer citizens of Rome. While the ships were still being built, the oarsmen were taught to row in mock-ups on the land. And, knowing that they could not compete with the Carthaginians in training or seamanship, the Romans resolved to make their ships into massive boarding platforms from which their legionaries could fight a land-style war on sea. To that end, a naval engineer – it could have been Archimedes of Syracuse – invented a secret and novel weapon, the *corvus*.

The *corvus* ('crow') was a boarding platform, mounted in the bows of the Roman ships. It was 11m (36ft) long and 1.2m (4ft) wide and could be

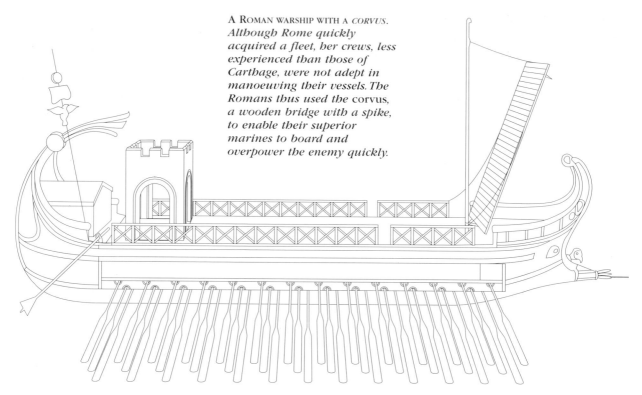

A ROMAN WARSHIP WITH A *CORVUS*. *Although Rome quickly acquired a fleet, her crews, less experienced than those of Carthage, were not adept in manoeuving their vessels. The Romans thus used the* corvus, *a wooden bridge with a spike, to enable their superior marines to board and overpower the enemy quickly.*

swivelled and dropped onto an enemy's deck; a large metal spike on the bottom would grapple and fix the opposing vessel, allowing Roman marines to board the enemy. To take advantage of this new tactic, when anticipating battle the Roman ships took aboard up to 80 extra men from the legions in addition to their regular complement of 40 marines.

The Romans got a chance to try out their secret weapon at Mylae, the first significant sea battle of the war, fought in September of 260. The Carthaginian and Roman fleets were well-matched, with about 130 ships each. The Carthaginians were so confident of victory that, instead of forming proper battle-lines, they attacked the Roman ships individually. Some Roman ships were rammed. But then the Carthaginians found themselves grappled with the *corvi*, and Roman marines swarming to board them in superior numbers. In the first attack, the Romans took 31 ships, including the Carthaginian flagship; their commander Hannibal (not the more famous land commander of the Second Punic War) had to escape in a rowing-boat, which no doubt

increased the Carthaginian disorganization. The Carthaginians then attempted to encircle the Roman ships. Despite their more unwieldy ships and lack of training, the Roman crews were able to turn their vessels around, to the point where the *corvi* in their bows could again be dropped to grapple the enemy. Finally the Carthaginians, who appear to have been caught completely by surprise by the *corvi*, disengaged and retreated, having lost 31 vessels captured and 13–14 destroyed. The Roman commander, the consul Caius Duilius, was granted Rome's first naval triumph, decorating the speaker's platform in the forum with the prows (*rostrata*) of the captured ships, thus giving the 'rostrum' its name.

The victory at Mylae might be attributed to the surprise of a new weapon and poor Carthaginian leadership (soon afterwards, Hannibal allowed his fleet to be trapped in a Sardinian port, and was arrested and crucified by his own officers). The battle of Ecnomus in 256, however, showed that the new Roman fleet was a force to be reckoned with. In that year the Roman senate decided to carry the war to North Africa. They ordered the construction of more ships, mostly warships rather than transports, bringing the Roman fleet up to 330 *quinqueremes*. This would have brought the number of men in the Roman fleet up to nearly 140,000, including their reinforced marine contingents. The fleet set out in the summer of 256, commanded by both Roman consuls, and the Carthaginians put together 350 ships to oppose it. When it became clear off the coast of Sicily that they would be attacked, the Romans divided into four squadrons, a dense formation with the first and second squadrons forming a wedge, the third squadron in line towing horse transports, and a fourth squadron behind. The Carthaginian plan, as the historian Polybius reports, was to draw the first two Roman squadrons away from the others, so they could be attacked in a pincer movement by the two wings of the Carthaginian fleet. But it is hard to organize a large fleet action without modern communications systems. Either there was a misunderstanding, or the Carthaginian captains were unable to implement their plan when the Romans adopted the wedge formation. So the Carthaginian right wing rushed to attack the fourth Roman squadron at the rear of the fleet, while the left attacked the third squadron, whose ships cast off the transports they were towing and engaged. What developed were three separate battles, the first two Roman squadrons soon winning an advantage over the Carthaginian centre. As at Mylae, the Carthaginians had no answer to the *corvus*, and without room to manoeuvre around the Roman ships, superior Carthaginian training counted for little. When the Carthaginian centre broke and fled, the first and second Roman squadrons turned back to aid the rest of their fleet in a fine display of discipline and communication. A total of 24 Roman ships were destroyed in the battle but Carthage lost nearly 100 ships destroyed or captured. After resting and repairing in Sicily, the Roman fleet was able to continue with the invasion of North Africa, which proved to be a costly failure.

Roman Confidence

The Roman sailors must have been feeling very confident by the time they were sent in 255 to rescue the remnants of the army from Africa. Off Cape Hermaeum they met a Carthaginian fleet which, with about 200 Carthaginian ships, was much smaller than that of the Romans, and had hurriedly assembled crews. The Carthaginian commander chose a weak position, with his ships' backs to the shore and no room to manoeuvre. Again, the Romans won an overwhelming victory, capturing 114 Carthaginian ships and destroying 16 more. It was five years before Carthage could assemble another fleet. The Carthaginians were only saved from final defeat because the Roman navy encountered a much more formidable enemy: the weather. The Roman fleet, 364 ships strong, was caught in a severe storm off Camarina (south-east Sicily). Only 80 ships survived the disaster and probably more than 100,000 men were drowned. This was a devastating blow to Rome; one modern historian has estimated that no less than 15 per cent of Italy's able-bodied men went down in the storm.

In 254 BC Rome built and outfitted another fleet of 220 ships, a massive undertaking that took only three months; that fleet was also lost in a storm. It was probably at this point that the Romans decided to abandon the *corvus*. Effective as it had proved in battle, this heavy boarding apparatus apparently made the Roman ships top-heavy and less seaworthy; hence their heavy losses in storms. Without the *corvus*, the poorer quality of the Romans' ships and training became obvious at the battle of Drepana in 249, Rome's only serious sea defeat. The Roman consul Publius Claudius Pulcher, with about 123 ships under his command, mounted a surprise attack on the main Carthaginian naval base at Drepana. He put to sea at night so the Carthaginians would not have warning of his approach. But the Romans could not keep close formation in the dark, especially since 10,000 of their rowers were a new, inexperienced draft. The Carthaginians saw the Roman fleet coming and put to sea to confront the enemy before they could be blockaded in harbour. Superior training then showed. The Carthaginian fleet took line further out to sea than the Romans. The Roman ships, trying to form into battle-line, were in great confusion, many fouling each other. A ramming battle then developed. The Roman

Battle of Mylae

260 BC

Mylae was the first significant sea battle of the war between Rome and Carthage. The Carthaginian and Roman fleets were well-matched, but the Carthaginians were so confident of victory that they did not form proper battle-lines. Some Roman ships were rammed, but the Carthaginians then found themselves grappled with the *corvi*, and Roman marines swarming to board them in superior numbers. In the first attack, the Romans took 31 ships, including the Carthaginian flagship; their commander had to escape in a rowing-boat, increasing the Carthaginian disorganization. The Carthaginians then attempted to encircle the Romans. Despite their more unwieldy ships and lack of training, the Roman crews were able to turn their vessels around, dropping the *corvi* in their bows again to grapple the enemy. Finally the Carthaginians, caught completely by surprise by the *corvi*, disengaged and retreated, having lost 31 vessels captured and 13–14 destroyed.

Mylae was off the coast of Sicily, at this stage a pawn in the power struggle between Carthage and Rome. Without Sicily's grain, Rome would have gone hungry.

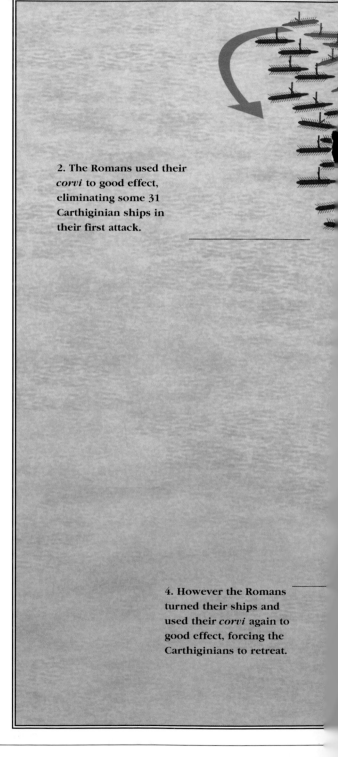

2. The Romans used their *corvi* **to good effect, eliminating some 31 Carthiginian ships in their first attack.**

4. However the Romans turned their ships and used their *corvi* **again to good effect, forcing the Carthiginians to retreat.**

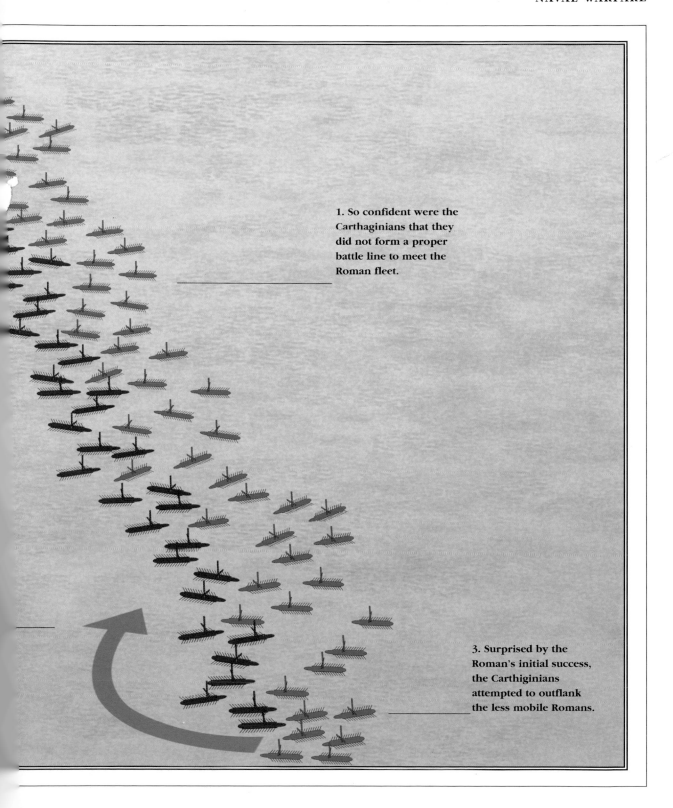

1. So confident were the Carthaginians that they did not form a proper battle line to meet the Roman fleet.

3. Surprised by the Roman's initial success, the Carthiginians attempted to outflank the less mobile Romans.

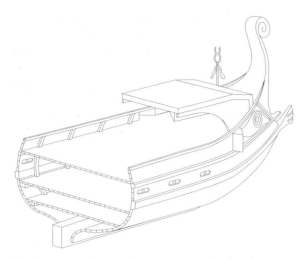

THE FOREDECK *of a Carthaginian* pentecontor, *showing the thick keel and frame giving the vessel enough strength to survive ramming an enemy vessel. The rower's deck was immediately below the top deck, although their benches are not shown.*

ships did not have the room or the skill to manoeuvre and avoid the Carthaginian rams, and no longer had *corvi* to engage in their typical boarding attack. Only 30 of the Roman ships, including Claudius Pulcher's flagship, managed to escape. Soon afterwards, Claudius Pulcher was put on trial in Rome for treason, the only Roman commander in the war to suffer such an embarrassment. Not only had he lost a fleet by employing unsound tactics, he had done so by angering the gods, drowning the sacred chickens carried in the flagship who could predict the outcome of the battle by the way they ate. When they proved uninterested in eating at all, he is supposed to have thrown them into the sea, proclaiming 'then let them drink'. The gods' anger became even clearer within a few days when the other half of the Roman fleet was lost in a gale, again at Camarina. The Romans were so discouraged that for a time they gave up fighting at sea. As Polybius points out, the Romans were used to dealing with enemies by brute force. This would not work against the elements.

Finally, late in 243 BC, the Romans built yet another fleet, collecting private contributions to pay for 200 more seaworthy ships (also copied from a captured Carthaginian original). This new fleet, commanded by Consul Lutatius Catulus, was intensively drilled throughout the summer of 242, while the Carthaginians were scrambling to find the manpower for their own ships. On 10 March 241, the two fleets met near the Aegates Islands. Now the tables were turned. Rome had the better ships and crews, and also outnumbered the Carthaginians by 200 to 170 ships. The Romans destroyed 50 Carthaginian ships and captured 70 more, effectively ending the war. Rome had lost about 600 warships and 1000 transports – four times as many to bad weather as to enemy action – but now controlled the Mediterranean.

Control of the Mediterranean

The Romans used their fleet to good advantage in the conquest of Macedon in 168, then let it fall into decay. Instead, the senate relied on Greek subject states of the eastern Mediterranean for naval matters. Unfortunately for security in the Mediterranean, the decision to abandon the Roman fleet coincided with a Roman decision in 167 BC to curb the independence of Rhodes, an island city-state in the eastern Mediterranean. For over a century Rhodes had been a great mercantile centre, and trade was so important to her economy that she had equipped a major fleet to combat Mediterranean pirates. The Rhodians had played a widely-recognized role as the official

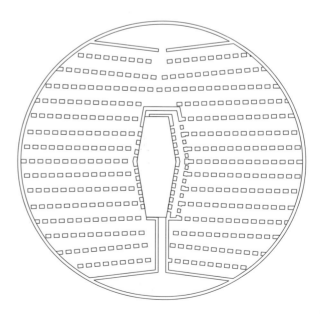

policemen of the eastern Mediterranean; after Rhodes was devastated by an earthquake in 226 BC, all the Hellenistic kings had contributed timber to help them restore their ships; one ruler even gave 10 fully equipped *quinqueremes* to the city. But Roman policy undermined the Rhodian economy, and Rhodes no longer had money for an anti-pirate fleet.

Piracy was a plague. It was not simply a matter of individual ships preying on sea traffic. Instead, whole fleets of pirates were common again by the first century BC, raiding the coasts and often lending support to land forces in war. With the decline of Rhodes, the problem grew to mammoth proportions. Worst were the Cilician pirates, whose bases were on the rugged southern coast of Asia Minor. They eventually attracted so many fighters and ships that they organized themselves on naval lines with flotillas and whole fleets under the command of admirals. They also added warships, even *triremes*, to the smaller, swift ships – *liburnians*, which had two banks of oars, and *hemiolas* – that were handiest for piracy. It has been estimated that by the early first century BC, there were more than 1000 pirate ships operating all over the Mediterranean and the Black Sea. The pirates became bolder all the time. By the 70s BC, they were raiding Italy, carrying off noble Roman women for ransom.

One pirate squadron even carried off two high Roman officials, along with their staffs. Another squadron attacked Rome's own port of Ostia, and sacked other cities. Cilician pirates also aided Rome's inveterate enemy Mithridates VI of Pontus (120–63) and, according to one later account, even made a treaty with Spartacus, the leader of the slave rebellion that shook Italy in the 70s. Although that deal, if it ever really existed, was betrayed by the pirates, clearly they were an enemy force which gravely affected the Roman Republic and its growing overseas empire. The last straw was when pirates started interfering with the grain fleet of Rome itself.

Finally, early in the year 67 BC, the Roman tribune Aulus Gabinius proposed a comprehensive campaign to sweep pirates from the sea. The senate opposed such an action almost unanimously, fearing the power that such a special command would give to a single individual in Rome's unstable political environment, especially since they knew that the likely candidate was the ambitious Gnaeus Pompeius Magnus, or Pompey the Great. Pompey was well on the way to achieving political dominance over Rome through his reputation as a military hero, and the threat of force from the soldiers who had served under him. He needed a spectacular role as 'saviour of Rome', and that is precisely what Gabinius

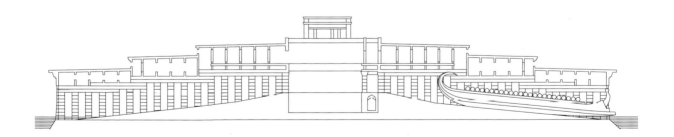

A TOP AND SIDE VIEW *of the building on the island of the military harbour at Carthage in the 3rd century BC. At the centre of the island was the admiral's headquarters, raised sufficiently to allow him to observe what was happening out at sea. Around this*

central core were ship sheds, which allowed the vessels to be pulled out of the water for repair. Other ship sheds lined the horseshoe-shaped shore opposite this island, providing enough space in total to berth approximately 200 galleys.

Pompey's Sea Campaign
67 BC

Pompey, ordered to clear the seas of pirates, had full authority over the entire Mediterranean and Black Seas, and all land within 80km (50 miles) of the sea. He raised 500 ships, 120,000 soldiers and 5000 cavalry. He then divided this force into 13 commands. The only area left (deliberately) unguarded was Cilicia. Pompey took a squadron of 60 ships and drove the pirates from Sicily, into the arms of another squadron. Then he swept down to North Africa, and completed the triangle by linking up with another legate off the coast of Sardinia, thus securing the three main grain-producing areas that served Rome. Pompey then swept across the Mediterranean from Spain to the east, defeating or driving pirates before him. The remnants duly gathered in Cilicia, where Pompey had planned a full assault by both land and sea. A few pirate strongholds were destroyed, and there was a final sea battle in the bay of Coracesium, but thanks to Pompey's clemency, most pirates surrendered easily.

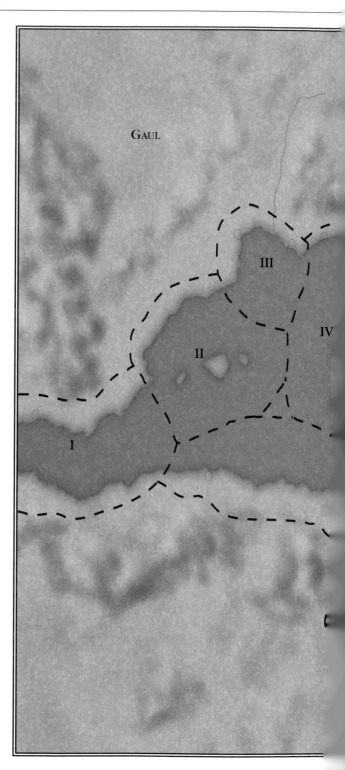

THE MEDITERRANEAN

The Mediterranean was a Roman 'lake' by the time that Pompey launched his campaign against the pirates, and his success ensured that no challenge to Rome's navy would emerge again.

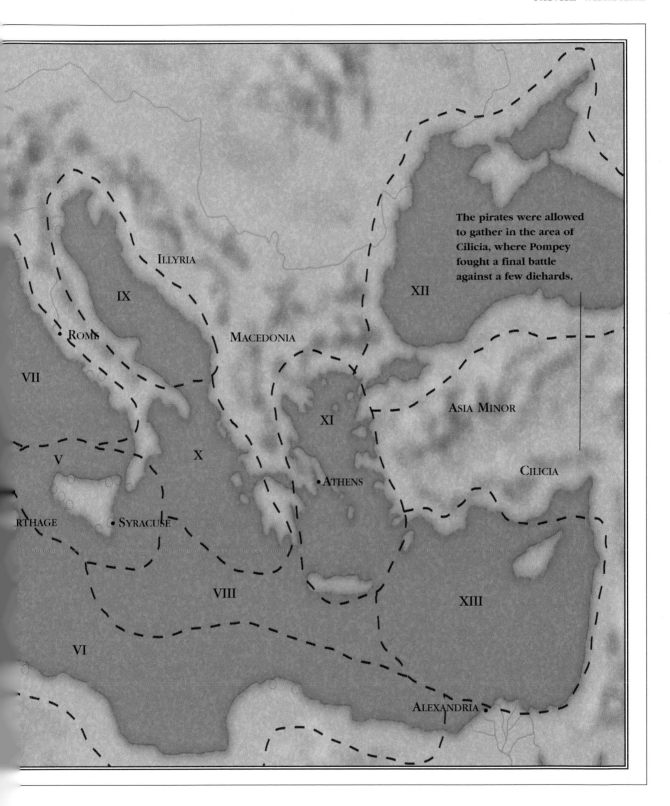

ILLYRIA

IX

MACEDONIA

• ROME

XII

VII

ASIA MINOR

XI

CILICIA

V

X

• ATHENS

RTHAGE

• SYRACUSE

VIII

XIII

VI

ALEXANDRIA •

The pirates were allowed to gather in the area of Cilicia, where Pompey fought a final battle against a few diehards.

arranged for him. The tribune bypassed the senate by presenting his anti-pirate proposal directly to the Roman popular assembly. The *lex Gabinia* (Gabinius' law), when passed, gave massive power to the person appointed: Pompey. He was granted a three-year appointment to clear the seas of pirates, with power to raise troops in all Roman provinces. He was allowed up to 25 legates working under him, and had full authority over the entire Mediterranean and Black Seas, as well as all land within 80km (50 miles) of the sea, along with a large budget to outfit a huge army and fleet.

Pompey had clearly begun planning well before passage of the *lex Gabinia*, and was able to jump immediately into action. According to Plutarch, Pompey raised 500 ships (from subject allies), 120,000 soldiers and 5000 cavalry. He then divided this force between himself and 15 legates, political appointees rather than his trusted military allies; obviously Pompey was using his naval command to increase his political capital. Pompey then divided the Mediterranean and Black Seas into 13 commands (keeping 2 legates serving directly under him), assigning a legate to each area with orders to patrol his own command by both sea and land, attack strong points, and prevent pirates from entering or leaving his sector. The only area left unguarded was Cilicia. This was left as a gathering point for escaping pirates, so they could all be dealt with in a full-scale assault. Pompey himself started operations early in the spring, before the time considered safe for shipping. He took a squadron of 60 ships and drove the pirates from Sicily, into the arms of another squadron led by one of his legates. Then Pompey swept down to North Africa, and completed the triangle by linking up with another legate off the coast of Sardinia, driving or fighting pirates as they went. Thus he secured the three main grain-producing areas that served Rome, the justification for the campaign in the first place. It is clear that he wanted to look good in Italy.

With the grain supply secure and all legates in place, Pompey himself swept across the Mediterranean from Spain to the east with part of the fleet, defeating or driving pirates before him. The remnants duly gathered in Cilicia, where Pompey had planned a full assault by both land and sea. He equipped his land forces with an elaborate siege train, which in the event was not needed. A few pirate strongholds were destroyed, and there was a final sea battle in the bay of Coracesium. But even that was not a hard fight. The pirates had nothing to fight for, since word had already spread of Pompey's clemency; instead of executing captured pirates, he offered them land in exchange for their ships. Pompey, for political reasons, needed quick victories. Most pirates had been driven to the profession by need and, hearing of Pompey's generous treatment, surrendered without a fight.

Roman Dominance

This campaign was proof, if proof was needed, that Rome was the only superpower of the Mediterranean world, the only state with the enormous resources and far-reaching control necessary for such an ambitious plan. The only enemy that could compete with Romans, then and for centuries to come, was other Romans. Pompey's campaign against the pirates, as much a political as a naval coup, carried the Roman world yet another step towards civil war.

Civil war called for fresh naval build-up, as rivals for control of Rome carried their warfare to every corner of the Mediterranean world. Pompey's fleet became the core of a new navy, although its creator fell to his rival Julius Caesar in the first civil war. But Pompey the Great's son, Sextus Pompey, gained control of the Roman fleet – about 200 ships – after Julius Caesar died in 44 BC. Caesar's heir, the young Octavian (the future Augustus Caesar), had to create a navy to oppose the younger Pompey. By 38 BC Octavian had pulled together a fleet of 370 ships, commanded by his close friend, the naval genius Marcus Vipsanius Agrippa. Since Agrippa's crews were not well enough trained to fight by ramming the enemy, Agrippa invented a new weapon, a catapult with grapnel and line, to seize enemy ships and draw them close for boarding. Agrippa handily defeated Pompey in September of 36 off Naulochus (north-eastern Sicily) in a battle that included over 600 ships.

The expertise gained in that war was soon needed for the Mediterranean-wide war that marked the final demise of the Roman Republic. At first Octavian collaborated with Julius Caesar's former second-in-command, Mark Antony. Relations deteriorated, however, and by 32 BC Octavian, claiming leadership of the Roman world, was at open war with Antony, or more precisely Rome was at war with Egypt, ruled by Queen Cleopatra VII, Antony's wife and ally. By late in the year 32, Antony had mustered an army and fleet in central Greece, ready to invade Italy, while Octavian had done the same in Italy to attack Antony. Octavian had an army of 80,000, while Antony had mustered 100,000, but with fewer trained Roman legionaries. Antony had also 500 warships (200 were Cleopatra's) and 300 merchantmen for the invasion, while Octavian had a comparable force. Antony, drawing on the eastern Mediterranean, had larger ships of Hellenistic design, ranging from 'sixes' up to a 'ten', which he used as flagship.

'Once more may I remind you [the Athenian navy] *that you have beaten most of the enemy's fleet already; and, once defeated, men do not meet the same dangers with their old spirit'* – PHORMIO

Most of Antony and Cleopatra's fleet wintered in a harbour just inside the promontory of Actium, with further detachments up and down the coast of Greece. There they were caught by surprise. Agrippa, commanding Octavian's fleet, attacked at the very beginning of the sailing season, crossing far south of the usual route to Greece. He defeated Antony's garrison at Methone, then sailed north and attacked Antony's other outposts. During the diversion, Octavian ferried his entire army from Brundisium (Brindisi) to Greece. The speed apparently unsettled Antony's forces which were already divided because of Antony's liaison with Cleopatra, differences of opinion about objectives, and intensive propaganda spread by Octavian, including reports of omens which all foretold defeat for Antony and Cleopatra. Desertion was a common problem for Antony even before Octavian's forces arrived. In addition, Antony's rowing crews were decimated by disease. As a result, Antony could put at most 300 ships into action, while Agrippa's fleet had more than 400. Since Antony had built towers on either side of the narrow entrance to the Gulf of Ambricia, where his fleet was harboured, it was impossible for the enemy to enter. Agrippa offered battle in open water but Antony's commander refused. So Octavian's fleet was offered no choice but to blockade Antony's fleet in their harbour. Octavian established his headquarters on a hill about 8km (5 miles) north of the entrance to the gulf and built a mole to provide some protection for his ships. It was clear that this was going to be an endurance contest.

Antony's position was stronger by land, but he needed to avoid battle for two to three weeks, time to gather his legions that were disbursed in western Greece. He could see clearly that he could only extricate his fleet by means of a land battle. His plans started successfully, but in late April when his army was ready and offered battle, Octavian refused. Agrippa went on to win a series of victories along the coast, putting himself in a position to intercept Antony's supply ships. All the while, Antony's troops and oarsmen were concentrated in an unhealthy area, and disease – probably malaria or dysentery – ravaged his camp. By midsummer, Antony had to send press gangs inland to find replacement rowers. He tried repeatedly to end the blockade by forcing a land battle, but more and more of his officers defected to Octavian, lowering morale still further. By the end of August, Antony was very short of provisions. He was left essentially with two choices: to abandon the fleet and fall back with the army to eastern Greece, or to fight his way out by sea, leaving the army to its fate.

Antony's decision to break past Octavian's fleet led to the battle of Actium, the closing battle of the Roman Republic. Antony's plan was not secret; all his movements were in full view of the enemy, and in case Octavian had missed anything, an old

Battle of Actium

31 BC

Antony's fleet was divided into four squadrons, with their sails on board, ready for flight. Agrippa took up a position out to sea, hoping to lure Antony out to open water. Antony, however, tried to provoke a fight close to the shore, where his fleet could not be encircled, leading to a standoff. By noon a breeze arose that could take Antony's ships out of range of Agrippa's fleet, whose sails were ashore. So Antony moved out to sea to catch the rising wind. Antony's left wing advanced first, and the fleets engaged. Agrippa, commanding his left wing, started to extend his line to outflank Antony, who was on the right. Antony's right wing had to move north to counter this attempt, and became detached from its centre. In the confusion, Cleopatra's rear squadron was able to flee through the centre of Octavian's line with part of Anthony's right wing. His flagship was too hard-pressed to disengage, but Anthony transferred to another ship and escaped. Two hours later, the rest of Antony's fleet started to surrender.

Actium was between Octavian's powerbase in Rome and Antony and Cleopatra's in Egypt. The battle was to be Antony's last throw in his challenge to Octavian's rule.

3. The left wing was the first to enter battle. Some two hours after Antony's flight, the rest of the fleet began to surrender

2. Antony's camp was ridden with disease and sickness, which inspired the general to attempt to break out.

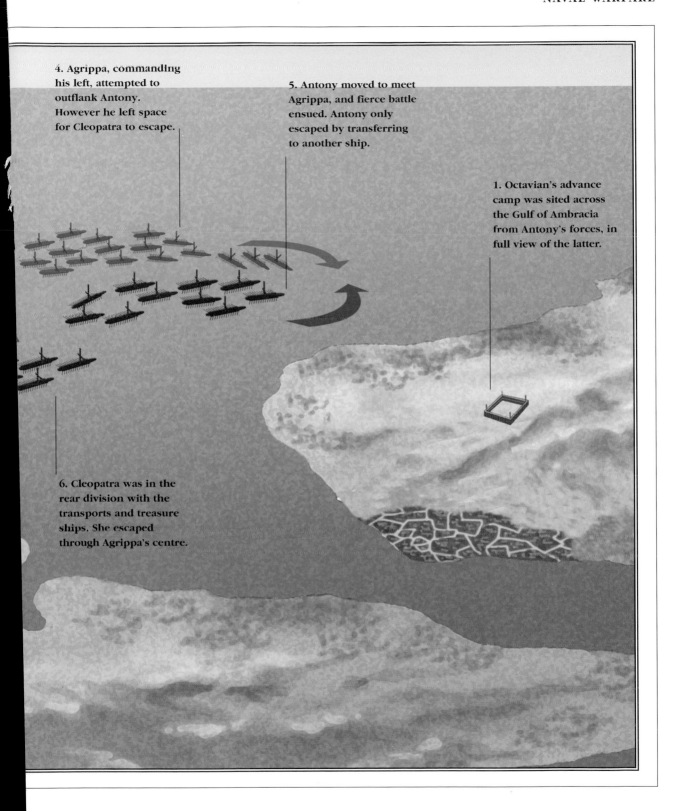

4. Agrippa, commanding his left, attempted to outflank Antony. However he left space for Cleopatra to escape.

5. Antony moved to meet Agrippa, and fierce battle ensued. Antony only escaped by transferring to another ship.

1. Octavian's advance camp was sited across the Gulf of Ambracia from Antony's forces, in full view of the latter.

6. Cleopatra was in the rear division with the transports and treasure ships. She escaped through Agrippa's centre.

friend of Antony's defected and took full details of the war councils with him. Antony burned his spare ships, including almost all the transports, and was left with a fleet of about 230 ships against about 400 under Agrippa's command (Octavian wisely left naval matters to Agrippa). His plans were ready by 29 August, but he was delayed for several days by storms. Finally, on 2 September, he made his way out of the gulf.

The Battle Begins

Antony's fleet was divided into four squadrons. Cleopatra's squadron included the remaining merchant ships, along with the treasure chest and valuables, and it stayed to the rear, apparently never meant for the fighting. The bulk of the 20,000 legionaries and 2000 archers who were embarked on Antony's ships were divided among the other three squadrons. What was intended? Later historians, from the victorious side, blamed Cleopatra for the defeat of Antony's fleet, reporting

that while the engagement still hung in the balance her squadron of 60 ships turned tail and fled, the besotted Antony following after her. Octavian, a brilliant propagandist, enjoyed laying blame on the exotic queen of Egypt. The truth of the matter is that Antony's fleet could not have hoped to have won the day, outnumbered so heavily, with crews that were sickly, underfed, discouraged and under-trained. Antony knew this. He ordered that the ships' sails be kept on board. This was unheard-of in combat; he could only have intended flight from the beginning.

Meanwhile, Agrippa embarked about 40,000 fighting men, and took up a position about 1.6km (1 mile) out to sea, hoping to lure Antony's larger ships to open water, where each could be attacked by two of his own vessels. Antony for his part tried to provoke a fight close to the shore where his fleet could not be encircled, leading to yet another standoff. But the winds at Actium are predicable in good weather. By noon a firm breeze rises from

A ROMAN *QUINQUEREME powers through the sea propelled by five oarsmen on the banks of oars on three levels. It is equipped with a* corvus *at its prow, ready to entrap any enemy ship which survives a ramming. Marines stand on the deck.*

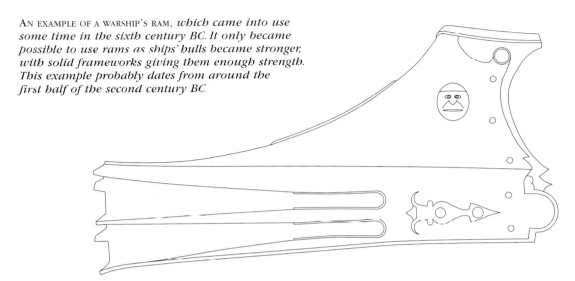

AN EXAMPLE OF A WARSHIP'S RAM, *which came into use some time in the sixth century BC. It only became possible to use rams as ships' hulls became stronger, with solid frameworks giving them enough strength. This example probably dates from around the first half of the second century BC.*

the south-west, a breeze that could take Antony's sailed ships out of range of Agrippa's fleet, whose gear was back in camp. So in the afternoon Antony tried to get as far to sea as possible, where he could catch the rising wind. The historian Plutarch has left the best account. Antony's left wing advanced first, and the fleets engaged. Meanwhile Agrippa, commanding his own left wing, started to extend his line to outflank Antony, who was on the right. Antony's right wing had to move north to counter this attempt, and in the process became detached from its centre. In the confusion that resulted, Cleopatra's squadron was able to flee through the centre of Octavian's line, which had apparently been Antony's plan all along. Antony also managed to save part of the right wing. His flagship was too hard-pressed to disengage, but he himself transferred to another ship and was thus able to escape, at precisely the time of the afternoon when the wind was strong enough and veered enough for his ships to use their sails. About two hours later, at around 16.00 hours, the rest of Antony's fleet started to surrender.

Partial Victory

Thus Actium was only a partial victory for Octavian, and it was his later propaganda endeavours that made it into the great triumph that ended the civil wars. Both Antony and Cleopatra had escaped to fight another day, and about a third of their ships had also survived. After

the sea battle, Antony's army began to withdraw. When Octavian's army caught up, Antony's troops refused to fight. Instead, in a week of intensive bargaining, they negotiated a surrender, winning equal treatment with the victorious army. The next year both Antony and Cleopatra committed suicide in Egypt, and Rome learned to live under a new master.

Rome, or to be specific the Roman emperor, was now truly the master of the Mediterranean. Actium marked the end of classical naval warfare in which massed fleets, consisting of multi-level warships, fought battles in which ramming was decisive. There was no enemy that could challenge Rome. After Actium, Augustus Caesar created a standing navy, a pre-emptive strike against anyone who might try to usurp his power. This imperial fleet was maintained in the Mediterranean for over two centuries, preventing the rise of any rival, ferrying armies, carrying officials and dispatches, and suppressing pirates as necessary. Without large-scale enemies, the fleet gradually came to rely on *triremes* and the *liburnian*, rather than larger ships. Only one significant sea battle was fought in the entire course of the Roman Empire, in AD 323, when the western emperor Constantine defeated his eastern rival Licinius. In this battle, Licinius's 200 *triremes* were roundly defeated by 80 of Constantine's lighter craft. After that, the *trireme* vanishes from the historic record. Truly the age of the ancient navy was at an end.

SELECT BIBLIOGRAPHY

Adcock, Frank E., *The Greek and Macedonian Art of War*. Berkeley, University of California Press, 1957.

Anderson, J.K., *Military Theory and Practice in the Age of Xenophon*, Berkeley, University of California Press.

Caesar, Julius. *Commentaries*. (Ed. and trans. John Warrington), London: 1953.

Carter, John M., *The Battle of Actium*, London, Hamish Hamilton, 1970.

Casson, Lionel, *The Ancient Mariners: Seafarers and Sea Fighters of the Mediterranean in Ancient Times*, 2nd ed., Princeton, Princeton University Press, 1991.

Connolly, P., *Greece and Rome at War*, London, Macdonald Phoebus, 1981; American ed. Englewood Cliffs, Prentice-Hall Incorporated, 1981.

De Souza, Philip, *Piracy in the Graeco-Roman World*, Cambridge, Cambridge University Press, 1999.

Diodorus Siculus, *Bibliotheca Historica*. (trans. C. H. Oldfather), Loeb Series. 12 vols. Cambridge, Mass.: 1933-1957.

Ducrey, Pierre, *Warfare in Ancient Greece*, (trans. Janet Lloyd), New York, Schocken Books, 1986.

Ellis, John. *Cavalry: The History of Mounted Warfare*. New York: G. P. Putnam's Sons, 1978.

Ferrill, Arther, *The Origins of War: from the Stone Age to Alexander the Great*, New York, Thames and Hudson, 1985.

Fuller, J.F.C., *Julius Caesar*. New Brunswick: 1965.

Fuller, J.F.C., *The Generalship of Alexander the Great*, Wordsworth Military Library, Cambridge, Wordsworth Editions Ltd., 1998.

Gardiner, Robert, ed., *The Age of the Galley*, London, Conway Maritime Press, 1995.

Garlan, Yvon, *War in the Ancient World*, (trans. Janet Lloyd), London, Chatto & Windus, 1975.

Gibbon, Edward, *The Decline and Fall of the Roman Empire*, two vols., Everyman's Library Series, New York, Knopf, 1993.

Gilliver, C. M., *The Roman Art of War*, Stroud, Gloucestershire, Tempus, 1999.

Goldsworthy, Adrian, *Roman Warfare*, London, Cassell, 2000.

Goldsworthy, Adrian, *The Punic Wars*, London, Cassell, 2000.

Grayson, A.K., 'Assyrian Civilisation' in J. Boardman *et al.* (eds), *Cambridge Ancient History 2* 3.2., Cambridge, Cambridge University Press, 1991, p.194-228.

Green, Peter, *The Year of Salamis 480-479 BC*, London, Weidenfeld and Nicolson, 1970.

Green, Peter, *The Greco-Persian Wars*, Berkeley, University of California Press, 1996.

Gurval, Robert A., *Actium and Augustus*, Ann Arbor, University of Michigan Press, 1995.

Hackett, J. (ed.), *Warfare in the Ancient World*, London, Sidgwick and Jackson, 1989.

Hanson, Victor Davis, ed., *Hoplites: the Classical Greek Battle Experience*, London, Routledge, 1991.

Hanson, Victor Davis, *The Wars of the Ancient Greeks*, London, Cassell, 1999.

Hopkins, C., 'The Siege of Dura' in *Classical Journal*, 42, 1947, p.251-259.

Humble, Richard, *Warfare in the Ancient World*, London, Cassell, 1980.

Hyland, Ann. *Equus: The Horse in the Roman World*, London and New Haven, Yale University Press, 1990.

Keegan, John, *A History of Warfare*, London, Hutchinson, 1993.

Kern, P.B., *Ancient Siege Warfare*, London, Souvenir, 1999.

Lazenby, J. F., *The First Punic War*, Stanford, Stanford University Press, 1996.

Leach, John, *Pompey the Great*, London, Croom Helm, 1978.

Livy. *History of Rome*. (trans. B. O. Foster, E. T. Sage, and A. C. Schlesinger), Loeb Series. 14 vols. Cambridge, Mass.: 1919-1957.

Marsden, E.W., *Greek and Roman Artillery*, Oxford, Clarendon Press, 1971.

May, Elmer C., Gerald P. Stadler, and John F. Votaw, *Ancient and Medieval Warfare*, The West Point Military History series, Wayne, N.J., Avery Pub. Group, 1984.

McCartney, Eugene S., *Warfare by Land and Sea*, New York, Cooper Square Publishers, 1963.

Morrison, J.S., J.F. Coates and N.B. Rankov, *The Athenian Trireme*, 2nd ed., Cambridge, Cambridge University Press, 2000.

Plutarchus. *Lives of Themistocles, etc.* New York: 1937.

Polybius. *Histories*. (trans. W. R. Paton), Loeb Series. Cambridge, Mass.: 1922-1927.

Pritchett, W.K., *Ancient Greek Military Practices,* Part I, University of California Publications, Classical Studies, vol. 7, Berkeley, University of California Press, 1971.

Pritchett, W.K., *The Greek State at War,* Part II, Berkeley, The University of California Press, 1974.

Pritchett, W.K., *The Greek State at War*, Part V, Chapter 1, 'Stone Throwers and Slingers in Ancient Greek Warfare', Berkeley & Los Angeles, University of California Press, 1991, pp.1-67.

Richmond, I.A., 'The Roman Siege-works at Masàda, Israel', *Journal of Roman Studies*, 1962, p.142-155.

Rodgers, William Ledyard, *Greek and Roman Naval Warfare*, Annapolis, US Naval Institute, 1964.

Rostovtzeff, M.I., *The Excavations at Dura Europos*, Preliminary Report of the Sixth Season of Work, October 1932 to March 1933, New Haven, Yale University Press, 1936.

Sage, Michael M., *Warfare in Ancient Greece*: a Sourcebook, London, Routledge, 1996.

Shipley, G., *The Greek World after Alexander, 323-30 BC*, London, Routledge.

Starr, Chester G., *The Influence of Sea Power on Ancient History*, New York, Oxford University Press, 1989

Sun Tzu. *The Art of War*. (trans. Samuel B. Griffith), New York, 1963.

Thucydides. *History of the Peloponnesian War*. London, 1954.

Warry, John G, *Warfare in the Classical World: An Illustrated Encyclopedia of Weapons, Warriors, and Warfare in the Ancient Civilisations of Greece and Rome*, Norman, University of Oklahoma Press, 1995.

Vegetius. '*The Military Institutions of the Romans*.' In T. R. Phillips (ed.). Roots of Strategy. Harrisburg: 1940.

Xenophon. *Anabasis*. (trans. W. Miller, et al.), Loeb Series. Cambridge, Mass.: 1914-1925.

Xenophon *Cyropaedia*. (trans. W. Miller, et al.), Loeb Series. Cambridge, Mass.: 1914-1925.

Yadin, Y., *The Art of Warfare in Biblical Lands*, London, McGraw Hill, 1963.

Yadin, Y., Masada, *Herod's Fortress and the Zealot's Last Stand*, London, Weidenfeld and Nicolson, 1966.

GLOSSARY

ACCENSI That division (or *vexillum*) of a Roman company consisting of the least reliable men in terms of age and experience.

ACIES A battle line.

ACROPOLIS Literally 'high city'. The acropolis contained the city's important buildings and treasury, and was a refuge for its citizenry.

AGGER A rampart or earthwork, such as a siege ramp.

ALA First used under the Republic for units of Italian allies, roughly equivalent in size to a Roman legion. Later used for the cavalry units of the Imperial *auxilia*.

ALA MILLIARIA A wing of 24 turmae.

ALA QUINGENARIA A wing of 16 turmae.

AMUN An Egyptian god.

ANABASIS A march inland from the sea.

ANCILE A Roman shield shaped like a figure-of-eight.

ANGON A Frankish spear.

ANKUSH (HARPE, CUSTIS) A rod with a hook projecting from the shaft a little way down from its point to help the mahout (qv) control his elephant.

ANTEPILANI The front-line soldiers in the Roman army.

AQUILA An eagle. The standard of a Roman legion.

AQUILIFER Literally 'eagle-bearer'. A Roman standard-bearer.

ASPIS A flattish bronze bowl shield 60cm (24in) across, carried by all phalangites.

AUXILIA Auxiliary troops in the Roman army, recruited from overseas non-citizens.

BALLISTA A Roman two-armed, torsion catapult capable of firing bolts or stones with accuracy.

BARRITUS The German war-cry.

BIREME A two-level vessel in which two oars could operate in the same length of ship.

CAETRA Small round bucklers carried by the Spanish.

CALIGA (pl. CALIGAE) Heavy sandal of a Roman soldier.

CANTABRIAN RIDE A manoeuvre of the Roman cavalry in which men rode in turn towards a target, wheeling to the right at short range and then riding parallel, keeping their shields towards the enemy. The object was to maintain a continual barrage of missiles at a single point in the enemy line, weakening the enemy before charging home, sword in hand.

CAPITE CENSI The lowest class of Roman citizen who owned no property but were introduced into the Roman army by Marius.

CATAPHRACT Close order, heavily armoured cavalrymen whose main tactic was the shock charge. Often the horses were also protected by armour.

CATAPULT Spring-operated artillery weapon developed by the Greeks and later used by the Romans.

CENTURION An important grade of officers in the Roman army for most of its history, centurions originally commanded a century of 60–80 men.

CENTURY The basic sub-unit of the Roman army, the century was commanded by a centurion and usually consisted of 60 (later 80) men.

CHAMFRONS Protection for a horse's head.

CHEIROBALLISTA A version of the scorpion (qv) with metal frame and casings for improved strength.

CHILIARCH A unit of approximately 1000 men consisting of four speiriai and commanded by a chiliarch.

CIPPI Rows of sharpened stakes which were part of Caesar's siege works at Alesia, 52 BC.

CLIBANARII *see* cataphract. Literally 'oven men'. Heavily armoured cavalrymen, often mounted on armoured horses.

COHORS EQUITATA A mixed infantry/cavalry formation providing a mobile patrolling and striking force when garrisoning frontier fortifications.

COHORT The basic tactical unit of the army by the end of the second century BC. It usually consisted of 480 men in six centuries, but there were also larger units of 800 in five or ten centuries.

COMES Officers of the later Roman army, ranking below the *magistri militum*.

CONSUL The year's two consuls were the senior elected magistrates of the Roman Republic, and held command in important campaigns. Sometimes the Senate extended their power after their year of office, in which case they were known as proconsuls.

CORVUS A 'raven'. Naval grappling hook.

CRINETS Protection for a horse's neck.

CUNEUS A formation intended to break through an enemy line by concentrating a charge at a single point. It may have been triangular in shape or alternatively a deep, narrow-fronted column.

DATHABAM A subdivision consisting of ten men, commanded by a dathapatis.

DECURIONES Each Roman *turma* (squadron) was commanded by three *decuriones* (officers).

DIADOCHUS (pl. DIADOCHOI) Literally a 'successor'. Used to describe the successor kings of Alexander the Great's empire.

DIEKPLUS (DIEKPLOUS) A Greek naval manoeuvre of breaking through the enemy line.

DRACO A Roman standard in the shape of a dragon's head, producing a moaning sound when travelling at speed – for example when charging into battle.

DROMEDARII Roman dromedary cavalry.

DUX Officers of the later Roman army.

ELEPHANTARCHOS Greek court official, head of the elephant corps.

ENOMOTIA (pl. ENOMOTIAI) Unit of the Spartan army, usually a platoon of 36 men. Literally, a group "sworn in".

ENOMOTIARCH Commander of an *enomotia*.

EQUITES Roman cavalrymen.

EXPLORATORES Scouts or reconnaissance troops in the Roman army.

EXTRAORDINARII The *extraordinarii* were a group of backup cavalry and light infantry, often consisting of non-citizens.

FALCATA A scythe-shaped, curved sword.

FALX *see* rhomphaia.

FRAMEA A German spear or javelin.

GAESUM A long Gallic javelin.

GASTRAPHETES Literally 'belly-release'. A Greek crossbow, supported against the user's waist.

GERRON A wicker shield, used by the Persians.

GLADIUS A sword. Conventionally used to describe the *gladius hispaniensis*, the short Spanish sword which was the standard Roman close-quarter weapon until well into the third century AD. It was primarily intended for thrusting.

GORYTUS A combined quiver and bow-case, typical of the Scythians.

HAMIPPOI Greek infantry 'runners' to co-operate with cavalry. Similar to Egyptian *peherers*.

HASTA A spear.

HASTATUS (HASTATI) The first line of heavy infantry in the Republican legion, recruited from younger men.

HAZARABAM A subdivision consisting of one thousand men.

HEILOTES (HEILOS) A helot, or Spartan serf.

HELEPOLIS Literally 'city-taker'. A giant assault-tower on wheels, used at the Siege of Rhodes.

HEMIOLA Light craft originally from Rhodes.

HETAIROI Literally 'Companions'. The élite cavalry of Macedonia.

HIPPARCHIA (pl. HIPPARCHIAI) Senior cavalry commander in Greek or Macedonian army.

HIPPEIS Greek 'knights'. Either cavalrymen or men of cavalier status.

HIPPIKA GYMNASIA. Mounted tournament display with highly decorated sports equipment and complex manoeuvres.

HOPLITES (pl. HOPLITAI) Hoplite. The Greek heavy foot soldier of the classical period.

HOPLON The large round shield of a hoplite.

HYPASPISTAI (s. HYPASPISTES) Hypaspists or shield-bearers. Also a special infantry corps in the Macedonian army.

ILE A body of men. A cavalry unit in Greek and Macedonian armies.

KARDAKA Young Persian noblemen who faced Alexander at the battle of Issos.

KHOPESH One-handed bronze chopper with a highly curved edge but no point.

KONTOS A pike-shaft or pike.

KOPIS A cleaver or slashing sword.

KSHATRYA. The Indian warrior caste, from which Porus drew his formidable infantry.

KYKLOS Literally a 'ring' or 'circle'. A Greek defensive tactical naval formation.

LANCEA Light spear or javelin.

LEGATUS (LEGATI) A Roman subordinate officer who held delegated power rather than exercising it in his own right. Legates were chosen by a magistrate rather than elected.

LEGATUS AUGUSTI PRO PRAETORE This title was given to the governors of the military provinces under the Principate, who commanded as representatives of the emperor (first to third century AD).

LEGATUS LEGIONIS The title given to legionary commanders under the Principate (first to third century AD).

LEGION (LEGIO) Originally a term meaning levy, the legions became the main unit of the Roman army for much of its history. Under the Republic and Principate they were large, predominantly infantry, formations of around 4–5000 men, but by late antiquity most seem to have dwindled to a strength of about 1000.

LEGIONES COMITATENSES Troops of the line consisting of 1000 men.

LIBURNA (pl. LIBURNAE) Light, fast galley, named after a nation in Illyria.

LILIA Literally 'lilies'. Fire-hardened stakes concealed in pits at the siege of Alesia, 52 BC.

LIMITANEI Garrison units made up of heavy and medium elements,

LITHOBOLOS Stone-throwing catapult, *see* oxybeles.

LOCHOS Greek army unit of varying strength.

LORICA A corselet or breastplate of armour.

LORICA HAMATA Ring-mail armour. Probably copied by the Romans from the Gauls.

LORICA SQUAMATA Scale armour. Less flexible and offered poorer protection than mail.

LORICA SEGMENTATA The name invented by modern scholars to describe the banded armour often associated with the Romans. It offered good protection and its design helped to spread its weight more evenly than mail, but was complex to manufacture and prone to damage, which may explain its later abandonment.

MACHAIRA Large knife, curved sword, sabre, or scimitar.

MAHOUTS Elephant riders or 'drivers'.

MANIPLE (MANIPULUS) The basic tactical unit of the Republican legion, the maniple consisted of two centuries. It was commanded by the centurion of the right hand (senior) century if he was present.

MARYANNU A chariot warrior in the Near East. A valued professional, strong, athletic and skilful.

MORA Literally a 'division'. A unit of the Spartan army. Six *morai* constituted a Spartan phalanx.

NAKHTU-AA Egyptian 'shock troops'.

NAUARCHIS A flagship.

NE'ARIN Egyptian 'youths', an elite unit.

NUMERI The *numeri* developed out of the provincial Roman militia. Some were bodies of infantry, others of cavalry, and they varied in strength from 90 to 300.

ONAGER Literally 'a wild ass'. A one-armed torsion catapult designed to throw stones.

OPTIONES Junior officers who were file closers. There were three in each *turma* (qv).

OTHISMOS The 'shoving' match during phalanx versus phalanx encounters.

OURAGOS Second in command of a Greek *enomotia*.

OXYBELES A catapult shooting arrow or bolts.

PARMA A light round shield.

PEDJET An Egyptian battalion.

PEHERER An Egyptian runner: light-armed man fighting in support of a chariot.

PELTASTAI (s. PELTASTES) Light-armed troops or skirmishers, so named from their use of the *pelte* (qv).

PELTE (PELTA) A crescent-shaped wicker shield covered with goat or sheepskin and carried by a central handgrip.

PENTECONTEROS (PENTECONTOROS) A pentecontor or 50-oared galley.

PENTECOSTER. An officer in the Spartan army commanding 50 men.

PENTECOSTYS Small unit of the Spartan army, nominally 50 strong.

PERIPLUS (PERIPLOUS) Literally 'circumnavigation'. A Greek tactical naval manoeuvre.

PEYTRALS Protection for a horse's chest.

PEZETAIROI Literally 'Foot Companions'. The Macedonian phalanx.

PHALANX A Greek or Macedonian battle formation or the heavy infantry which adopted such a formation.

PILOS A metal helmet shaped like a felt cap.

PILUM The heavy javelin which was the standard equipment of the Roman legionary for much of Rome's history.

PLUMBATA (pl. PLUMBATAE) A Roman lead-weighted dart.

POLEMARCH Commander of a Greek mora.

POLIS A concept developed by Aristotle: a self-sufficient state united by a sense of community, with a set of laws that bound all citizens equally.

POLYREMES Ships where the rowing power was increased by adding more oarsmen per oar. The tallest of these (5 rowers) was difficult to manoeuvre and probably never used in battle. See Ptolemy's flagship as an example.

PREFECT (PRAEFECTUS) A Roman equestrian commander of an auxiliary cohort or *ala*.

PRINCEPS (PRINCIPES) The second line of heavy infantry in the Republican legion, recruited from men in the 'prime of life'.

PRODROMOI Greek scouts or reconnaissance troops.

PTAH An Egyptian god.

PTERYGES That part of the cuirass skirt which was split into 'wings' for ease of movement, as worn by hoplites.

PUGIO A Roman dagger.

PYKNOSIS Intermediate order formation where men and ranks were separated by 1m (3ft).

QUINCUNX The chequerboard formation used by the Republican legion in which the three lines were deployed with wide intervals between the maniples, the gaps being covered by the maniples of the next line.

QUINQUEREMIS A quinquereme or war galley operated by five ranks of rowers on each side.

RE An Egyptian god.

RHOMPHAIA or Falx. A one- or two-handled scythe originating from the Balkans, with a curved iron blade of 39cm (15in).

RORARII A division (or *vexillum*) of a Roman company consisting of men younger and less experienced than the *triarii*.

SAMBUCA Mechanical scaling ladder (named after a musical instrument).

SARCINA (pl. SARCINAE) A Roman soldier's pack.

SARISSA Long pike, as used in the Macedonian army.

SATABA A subdivision consisting of one hundred men.

SATRAPY Province of the Persian empire, governed by a satrap.

SAUNION A javelin.

SCORPIO Literally 'scorpion'. Lighter, more mobile Roman version of the *oxybeles*. It could fire large bolts and its reinforced head and concave arms gave it great power.

SCUTARII (SCUTATI) Troops armed with the SCUTUM (qv). Usually on foot, but sometimes mounted.

SCUTUM A shield, particularly the heavy, legionary shield. This was semi-cylindrical and usually either oval or rectangular. It was held by a single, transverse handgrip behind the central boss.

SCYTALE A Spartan system of encoding orders.

SOCII Literally 'allies'. Particularly, Italian allies who fought in the Roman army.

SOLIFERRUM Iron javelin carried by the Spanish.

SPARA A rectangle of cloth interweaved with osiers, extending from shoulder to ankle.

SPARABARA Pavise bearers.

SPATHA The Roman long sword used by the cavalry of the early empire and eventually adopted by most of the later army. It was well balanced for both cutting and thrusting.

SPEIRA The basic Macedonian Phalangite unit which consisted of 256 men. Four *speiriai* made up a *chiliarchy* (1024 men).

SPICULUM Literally a 'spike'. A javelin or arrow.

STIMULI Literally 'goads' or 'stings'. Pointed stakes or pegs planted as a defence by the Romans against enemy attack. Used at Alesia, 52 BC.

STRATEGAI A 4000-man unit commanded by a *strategos*.

SUTEKH An Egyptian god. A division of Pharaoh's army.

SYNASPISMOS Greek close order formation (with locked shields) where men and ranks were separated by 30cm (1ft): the position used to meet an attack.

TAKA (TAKAE) A large leather shield.

TAKABARA Bearers of *takae* (qv) and thrusting spears.

TALENTS Greek currency where 100 talents equated to 24.5 tonnes (2.5 tons) of pure silver.

TAXIARCH Commander of a *taxis* (qv).

TAXIS (TAXEIS) A 'company' of around 120–130 men. Ten taxeis (regiments) constituted the Athenian army, together representing the ten tribes of Athens.

TERRETS Metal rings on the draught pole through which control lines were passed to link up with donkey nose rings.

TESTUDO The famous tortoise formation in which Roman legionaries overlapped their long shields to provide protection to the front, sides and overhead. It was most commonly used to approach enemy fortifications and allow the legionaries to undermine them.

THORAKIA Wooden towers big enough for two to four fighting men, installed on elephants in Macedonia. They were protected by shields hung from their sides.

TRIARII The third and senior line of heavy infantry in the Republican legion, recruited from veteran soldiers.

TRIREME A three-level vessel in which three oars could operate in the same length of ship: in the hull, at deck level and on an outrigger that projected from the gunwales.

TURMA (TURMAE) The basic sub-unit of the Roman cavalry for much of its history, a *turma* consisted of around thirty men. Until the third century AD it was commanded by a decurion.

VELES (VELITES) The light infantry of the Republican legion, recruited from the poor or those too young to fight as heavy infantry. It is unclear whether they were identical to or superseded the *rorarii* (qv).

VERICULUM A light spear used in Imperial Roman armies.

VERUTUM A Roman javelin or dart.

VEXILLATIONES A detachment of the Roman army.

VEXILLUM A third of a Roman company. The three sections or *vexilla* comprised sixty soldiers, two centurions and one *vexillarius* (standard bearer).

ZEIRA A cloak worn by Arabs and Thracians.

PICTURE CREDITS

All illustrations Amber Books Ltd except:

AKG London/ Peter Connolly: 6–7, 38–39, 50–51, 54, 70–71, 78–79, 110, 111, 118, 119, 134–135, 142, 143, 154, 163, 170, 171, 178–179, 203, 208, 214, 215, 222, 223, 230.